NUMBER EIGHT
Eastern European Studies
Stjepan G. Meštrović, Series Editor

The War in Chechnya

The War in Chechnya

Stasys Knezys and Romanas Sedlickas

Texas A&M University Press
College Station

Library of Congress Cataloging-in-Publication Data

Knezys, Stasys.
    The war in Chechnya / Stasys Knezys and Romanas Sedlickas.
        p. cm. — (Eastern European studies ; no. 8)
    Includes index.
    ISBN 0-89096-856-X
        1. Chechnia (Russia)—History—Civil War, 1994–1996.
I. Sedlickas, Romanas.   II. Title.   III. Series: Eastern European
studies (College Station, Tex.) ; no. 8.
DK511.C37K597   1999
947.5'2—dc21   98-53500
                                                                        CIP

Contents

List of Figures   ix

Series Editor's Statement   xi

The National Anthem of Chechnya   xv

Introduction   3

Part 1. A Nation That Could Not Be Forced to Its Knees

Chapter 1.   Chechnya's Road to Independence   9

Chapter 2.   Preparations to Defend Chechnya's Independence   33

Part 2. The First Period of the War in Chechnya

Chapter 3.   The First Stage of the War   43

Chapter 4.   Preparations for Military Operations in Chechnya   53

Chapter 5.   The Operation to Blockade Grozni   71

Chapter 6.   The Assault of Grozni and Its Defense   90

Chapter 7.   Preparations for Military Operations in the Other Regions of Chechnya   113

Chapter 8.   Warfare in the Flatlands   127

Chapter 9.   Warfare in the Mountains   148

Chapter 10.   The Tragedy of Budionovsk   158

Chapter 11.   Results of the First Period of the War   179

Part 3. The Second Period of the War in Chechnya

Chapter 12.   Negotiations for Peace   193

Chapter 13.   The "Election" Campaign   217

Part 4. The Third Period of the War in Chechnya

Chapter 14.   The Second Terrorist Operation   235
Chapter 15.   The "Peace Protocols"   252
Chapter 16.   War during Negotiations   267
Chapter 17.   The End of the War in Chechnya   286
Chapter 18.   Dudajev as a Symbol of the Fight for Freedom   305
Chapter 19.   Closing Words   324

Notes   335
Index   349

Figures

FIGURE

Combined Federal Forces Command Structure   *page* 331

MAPS

Chechnya and surrounding regions   *page* 10

Republic of Ichkeria   19

Chechnya   20

Divided Chechnya, November, 1994   23

Invasion by Russians, December, 1994   72

Russian plan of assault against Grozni   91

New Year's assault on Grozni   97

Rescue operation to save rifle brigade   100

Situation in Grozni after assault   110

Regions controlled by various forces   115

Chechen forces, February, 1995   128

Western Chechnya, February, 1995   130

April campaign in Western Chechnya   137

Samashk   138

Joint federal forces mountain operation   155

Route of Chechen terrorists crossing into Russia   160

Hospital rescue   167

Baasjev group's return to Chechnya   172

Gudermes   229

Dagestan and Chechnya   238

Escape of Salman Radujev's group   244
Bamut stronghold   274
Operations around Bamut   276
Assault on Bamut   278
Battles of the "Zero Option" campaign   289
Battles in the center of Grozni   290

Series Editor's Statement

This book breaks new conceptual ground: It is *not* an ideological or polemical statement about the rights and wrongs of this nasty war, though such issues do come up as marginal. It does not toy with chic ideas in contemporary war analyses such as postmodern war or cyber war, the idea that future wars will be fought remotely and electronically, making the soldier obsolete.[1] What is amazing, and new, about the story told in this book is the painstakingly documented analysis of how and why Russia, with one of the world's largest armies, failed so miserably to subdue the Chechens, and how the Chechens fought among themselves (something hardly noticed in the media coverage) but still managed to fight off the Russian Goliath. In other words, it tells a dramatic story that should be of great interest in the post–Cold War world which has already witnessed a similar case of a huge Yugoslav army failing to subdue weaker opponents in Slovenia, Croatia, Bosnia, and now, perhaps, Kosovo. This is a lesson in military history as well as sociology. Because the United States is still on a course of developing technologically superior weapons against future enemies—even though that strategy failed miserably in Vietnam—U.S. analysts and planners might benefit from reading this very detailed account of how a seemingly small, helpless and hapless David can slay Goliath.

The authors of this book depict the strengths and weaknesses of both the Russians and Chechens in excruciatingly minute detail. While other books on the war in Chechnya tend to be either the compiled observations of *Western* journalists[2] or broad, sweeping political generalizations by *Western* analysts,[3] this one is unique. Like Norman Cigar's book, *Genocide in Bosnia,*[4] which relied on Yugoslav, not just Western newspaper accounts for substantiation, this book on Chechnya relies on Russian, Chechen, and Lithuanian sources. Such an approach makes an immediate difference in the reading and feel of a book. The reader senses passions, motives, and styles that are often overlooked by Western journalists who are often ethnocentric in their dealings with non-Western cultures. For example, in *Balkan Ghosts,*[5] Robert Kaplan cannot seem to refer enough times to the Yugoslavs as dirty, drunken, and smelly. Similarly, in *Blood and Vengeance,* New York Times correspondent Chuck Sudetic confesses to an egregiously arrogant attitude toward the people he wrote about:

> There is a method to presenting the reality of war in *Times* style, a restrictive method but a perfectly valid one just the same. It focuses mainly on institutions and political leaders and their duties and decisions, while leaving the common folk to exemplify trends, to serve as types: a fallen soldier, a screaming mother, a dead baby—literal symbols. . . . This method is described by various terms: detachment, disinterestedness, dispassion, distancing, and others with negative prefixes engineered to obliterate any relationship between observer and observed. . . . I once walked though a town littered with the purple-and-yellow bodies of men and women and a few children, some shot to death, some with their heads torn off, and I felt nothing.[6]

In contrast to these and many other recent war books, the authors of the present book on Chechnya manage to be objective at the same time that they engage the reader's emotions. It is clear that the emotions of the authors are deeply engaged in this war for liberation in Chechnya. And perhaps that is how war books should be written if readers are to break through their ingrained prejudices and learn something new.

Most of the authors and sources in this book are Lithuanian. What is it about Lithuania that compares but also contrasts with the situation in Chechnya? This is an important question that should serve as the point of departure for a discussion, and should not be given a pat answer. Lithuania is a small country that used to be part of the Soviet Empire. It has a large Russian "minority" population that is clearly unhappy with Lithuania's independence. If Russia, which dominated the Soviet Empire every bit as much as Serbia dominated the Yugoslav Empire, were to attack Lithuania in order to "persuade" her to return to the former fold, what would the Lithuanians do? Would they respond as the Chechens did, with what is often called terrorism? Would they respond as the Bosnians did, meekly turning to the West and relying on the West's principles derived from the Enlightenment (justice, self-determination, liberty, and so on) to save them from the Russians? These are important questions, given that one of the conclusions reached by the authors is that terrorism will become a feature of future wars of separation and independence.

The West's failure to save Bosnia from Belgrade-sponsored genocide has many parallels with the West's failure to save Chechnya from Moscow-sponsored slaughter. Of course, the technical difference between the two situations is that Bosnia was an internationally recognized country, and Chechnya was not. But beyond this technicality, the situations are parallel: two, giant, predominantly Christian nations slaughtering Muslims in two small, weak nations that begged the West to save them from their cruel fate. Surely future secessionists have concluded, perhaps rightly, that for all its grandiose talk about principles, the West does not really favor or help secessionists. The alleged terrorists in Kosovo today have apparently drawn just this conclusion and are vowing to fight Serbia to the death for their independence.

Slovenia is not a country that evokes images of terrorism, but Slovenia saved itself from the Serbian juggernaut primarily by using "terrorist" tactics in its mountainous terrain. Unlike Slovenia, but foreshadowing Bosnia, Croatia threw itself on the mercy of the West, and took heavy losses in its war for independence. Given these recent examples, what would Lithuania do? What will happen in Tibet? Even Quebec? I leave these as open questions.

A minor but distinctive and perhaps important aspect of this book is the analysis of in-fighting among the Chechens based on "mountain" versus "flat-lands" clans that is in line with a long line of anthropologically based research (including my own *Habits of the Balkan Heart*).[7] One wonders whether the anthropological conclusion of such research will eventually prove true: as remote, mountain-dwelling people in Chechnya, Kosovo, Bosnia, Cambodia, Tibet, and elsewhere gain more access to a cosmopolitan world and its values through better roads, the Internet, and other technology, they will become less nationalistic and more content to become a part of what is often referred to as the global village. But an alternative conclusion is also likely: Increasing numbers of people who feel threatened by and remote from globalization will respond with violence to what they perceive as attacks on their sovereignties.

One thing is certain: The many analysts who had predicted that nationalism would eventually disappear in the present century were simply wrong. Nationalism has emerged as the strongest social force in the contemporary world. Contemporary culture is fragmenting, Balkanizing, and undergoing fission. Bosnia and Chechnya foreshadowed the current violence in Kosovo, which in turn suggests many similar hot spots around the globe. Terrorism may well turn out to be the primary method of attempting to secede because terrorism has always been and will always be the method of the powerless who are possessed by powerful passions. Their opponents are the modernist and/or postmodernist powers who rely on rational planning, huge bureaucracies, and technology in waging wars—but who often lack passion, or even a clear vision of what they are fighting for. Robert McNamara and others sought the perfect, scientific, rational, electronic, computerized, and technologically superior war in Vietnam, and planners have been pursuing this utopia ever since. But this policy failed in Vietnam, and in its most recent manifestation, as NATO—the world's mightiest, most expensive, and technologically most superior military alliance in history—failed again. NATO was simply impotent against Serbian aggression. Technological superiority cannot respond to the fundamental questions: Why were American soldiers dying in Vietnam? Why were Russian soldiers dying in Afghanistan, and then Chechnya? And most recently, Why *should* Western soldiers die in Bosnia or Kosovo?

—Stjepan G. Meštrović
Series Editor

The National Anthem of Chechnya

Death or Freedom

We came onto this earth when the wolf cubs began to whine under the
    she-wolf's feet.
Our names were picked for us at day-break while the lion roared.
Our gentle mothers nurtured us in our eagle nests.
And our fathers taught us to tame the oxen of the forests.

Our mothers dedicated us to our Nation and our Homeland.
And we shall all rise up to the last one if our nation needs us.
We grew up free as the eagles, princes of the mountains.
There is no threshold from which we shall shy away.

Sooner shall cliffs of granite begin to melt like molten lead than any one
    of us shall lose in battle the honor of our noble nature.
Sooner shall the earth begin to crack in silence from the heat than we shall
    lie under the earth, having lost our honor.

Never to bow our heads to anyone, we give our sacred pledge.
To die or to live in freedom is our fate.
Our sisters heal our brothers' bloody wounds with their songs.
Our loving women see us off on our campaigns.

If we shall be forced to starve from famine, we shall gnaw the roots of trees.
If we shall be deprived of water, we shall drink the dew from the grass.
We came onto this earth when the wolf cubs began to whine under the
    she-wolf's feet.
We pledge our lives to God, our Nation and our Homeland.

Translated by Romanas Sedlickas

The War in Chechnya

Introduction

When war broke out in Chechnya, the region immediately grabbed the attention of journalists, politicians, and others all around the world. Without doubt, the Russian incursion into Chechnya was also of great interest to military specialists.

The war in Chechnya arose out of a great multiplicity of conflicting political, economic, legal, and military situations. These were not chance happenings but had ripened over decades and even centuries. The factors giving rise to the war were many and were so intertwined that it is difficult to separate out which were the most significant. Only the most primary purposes of the war are readily discernable: for Russia, this was an effort to preserve its "territorial integrity"; for the Chechens, it was the fight for national independence.

As with any war, the war in Chechnya can be evaluated in various ways. The conclusions drawn by military experts and specialists from the large, militarily more powerful countries are likely to be starkly different from those originating from small, less secure countries. For small countries, especially those in Eastern Europe, the analysis of the war in Chechnya is of crucial importance. The Chechen experience in defending its home territories is of great interest to them, if only as an example of a very small country's successful resistance of one of the most powerful armies on earth. At the very beginning of its war against Russia, the Chechen government's Armed Forces had been yet in a building stage and were comparable in structure, numbers, and maturity to the military defense establishments of the Baltic States of Lithuania, Latvia, and Estonia. The Chechen forces exceeded them perhaps only in the numbers of weapons and combat equipment they had available.

Various theories can be constructed as to the organization of a small country's defenses and the possible variations, strategy, and tactics to be used in the event of an armed attack by a foreign power. But it is also very useful to take into consideration what is actually shown by recent reality. Completely unexpectedly, a small country having less than a million inhabitants showed itself able to resist a much more powerful state, a state whose armed forces numbered more than the total population of Chechnya. There are few comparable examples of this in recent history. The only notable example in Europe since the Soviet Union became a superpower was perhaps Finland in 1940.

In preparing this book, use was made of information published in the open press and in various analytical descriptions of events. During the course of writing this book, we evaluated material from almost two thousand published sources: books, brochures, journals, daily and weekly newspapers, and a multiplicity of video and film materials. We trust that the submitted facts and figures as to the development of combat actions, the primary events, and the situation in Chechnya in general are sufficiently comprehensive. We also took into account that the press reported a great deal of often conflicting information about the war and the events related to Chechnya. In an attempt to set out a comprehensive picture of the combat actions, their character and peculiarities, as objectively as possible, such information was systematized and generalized. Much attention was also given to the analysis of preparations for combat actions. In this book, the Chechen war is considered for the most part from a military viewpoint. Other aspects are included only to the extent that they had an effect on the course of the war.

It should be noted that in evaluating the war activity in Chechnya, the opinions of Russian and other countries' politicians, analysts, and military experts quite often differ as to when Russia's war against Chechnya actually began. Mentioned most often is the date of December 11, 1994, when Russian Federal Army columns physically began to move toward Chechnya's capital, Grozni. Facts, however, confirm otherwise: the war was begun much earlier, and from that moment, war activity continued on almost without interruption.

The Kremlin had sought at the beginning to make use of the internal splits among the various political groups in Chechnya and had supported the pro-Moscow opposition against Chechen president Dzhochar Dudajev. When it became apparent that its ends could not be achieved solely by political means, Russian Security Services then attempted to escalate the conflict into an internal war, with Russian troops and equipment secretly participating on the opposition's side. Only when even these efforts met defeat did Moscow resolve to mount an undeclared war openly, using its own forces against the "rebels" in Chechnya. This was all done under the banner of "reestablishing constitutional order and disarming illegal armed formations," purposes announced as the primary goals of the military operation by Russian president Boris Yeltsin in his November 30, 1994, decree.

Note should also be taken of the fact that until the middle of June, 1995, the Kremlin had not taken any political steps to stop the war other than issuance of ultimatums and threatening pronouncements. Attempts to regulate the "crisis" in Chechnya by peaceful means had been studiously avoided. When such means were mentioned, it was done only superficially and in passing. Only the military terrorist operation conducted in the city of Budionovsk in the Russian district of Stavropol by the famous Chechen field commander Colonel Shamil Basajev and his "diversion" group forced the Russian government to stop further war actions and to enter into negotiations with the Chechen government. But even then, war activity was suspended only temporarily and was later renewed with even greater force.

Based on the intensity of war activity, the course of the war in Chechnya can be divided into three distinct periods:

The first period, which lasted from the end of October, 1994, until June 18, 1995, marked Russia's attempt to liquidate the "threat to its territorial integrity" and to preserve its federation by military force alone. During this eight-month period, four stages of war activity are discernable. The first stage began the end of October, 1994, and lasted until November 26, 1994. During this time, attempts were made with the pro-Russian opposition to overthrow Chechnya's president Dzhochar Dudajev and to nullify Chechnya's Declaration of Independence. This stage ended when the opposition's armed formations, augmented by Russian troops and combat equipment, were soundly defeated during the first battle for Grozni. The second stage lasted from October 27 until December 10, 1994. It consisted of the preparations of the Russian Armed Forces to mount an incursion into Chechnya and included the continuation of air strikes against the most important military objectives in Chechnya. The third stage, from December 11, 1994, until January 19, 1995, began with the incursion of the Russian Federal Forces into Chechnya and ended with the takeover of the presidential palace. The fourth stage lasted from January 20 until June 18, 1995, when the Combined Russian Federal Forces officially announced that they were suspending further war activity in Chechnya because of the agreement extracted by Shamil Basajev at Budionovsk.

During the second period, from June 19 to the middle of October, 1995, peace negotiations took place in the background of continuous armed provocations, skirmishes, and small-scale engagements. These negotiations were broken off after the attempt on the life of the Commander of the Combined Federal Forces Group, General Anatoli Romanov.

During the third period, from the middle of October, 1995, until August 31, 1996, characteristic partisan warfare elements appeared. Although there were no clearly noticeable stages in this period, episodic operations, conducted successfully as usual by the concentrated Chechen formations, are clearly distinguishable.

During the course of this war, a new military tactic was also put into use. Once the Russian Federal Army mounted its incursion into Chechen territory, few could have had any lingering doubts that sooner or later the boot of the Russian soldier would crush Chechnya and its resistance would be suppressed. But the course of this war was changed by a series of Chechen military terrorist operations involving the taking of hostages. The usual theoretical schematic of the relationship of "politics and war" was changed to a triangle of "politics, war, and terrorism." Thus, unavoidably, a new question was forced to the surface: Is military terrorism, in fact, a new tactical element, ensuring the success of a small country's resistance to a powerful army?

The war in Chechnya has also raised a number of other questions, and perhaps readers will notice an absence of answers to some of them. The primary purpose of this book, however, is to set out sufficiently comprehensive, objective, and unbiased information as to the course of the military operation in Chechnya and the strategies of both sides, their tactics, and the character of their combat actions. It should be noted that much concerning the events in Chechnya is still unknown and that the cloak of secrecy has not as yet been completely withdrawn. Although additional investigation and deeper analysis is needed, we trust that this book will be a valuable information source despite the still unanswered questions.

Part 1

A Nation That Could Not Be Forced to Its Knees

CHAPTER I

Chechnya's Road to Independence

The Chechen Republic of Ichkerija is a small country in the Northern Caucasus. The name "Ichkerija" is a geographical term referring to two of the mountain regions of Chechnya, Shatoja and Vedeno, located in its southern part. On the north, the republic is bordered by Russia's Stavropol province, on the north and east by Dagestan, on the south by Georgia, and on the west by Ingushia. It is quite difficult to find this country on a map, nestled as it is along the great Caucasus mountain range. One has to look for it along the southern frontiers of the Russian Federation, near Georgia.

The territory of present-day Chechnya covers about 7,000 square kilometers, and in 1989, about 1 to 1.2 million people lived within it. Among the Autonomous Republics of the Russian Federation, Chechnya was one of only three in which the indigenous nationality continued to make up a marked majority of the local population. But even in 1994, almost 30 percent of Chechnya's inhabitants were Russians.

The first time that the Chechens are mentioned as a distinct people is in seventh-century Armenian writings. Very little information is available about the Chechens prior to that time, as they had lived in a very closed society. Their indigenous territory, however, has been inhabited since the stone age.

The Chechen people had earlier called themselves the Nochchi. The name "Chechens" was given them by the Russians in the early part of the eighteenth century because the nearest village to the Russian fortress at Grozni in which the Nochchi lived was Chechen Aula. The Russians did not control the terri-

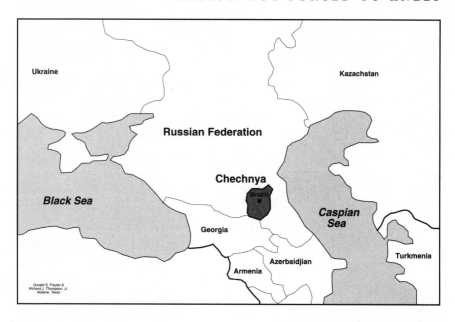

Donald S. Frazier &
Richard J. Thompson, Jr.
Abilene, Texas

tory past this village or further on into the mountains. Thus for a long time Chechen Aula delineated the frontier between Russian-controlled territory and the lands of the "Chechens."

Ethnographically, the Chechens are a branch of the Vainach nation, which is descended from the Benos people, the other branch being the Ingushians. The term "Vainach," introduced by the Russian scholar N. Jakovlev in the 1930s, translates as "our nation." The term "Ingushians" is derived from the geographic designation "Angushta." Chechens, however, still call themselves Nochchi, and the Ingushians call themselves Galgalians. The Chechens and the Ingushians are ethnically quite closely related, and their languages are similar. Some of the Chechen dialects are in fact more distant from each other than the main Chechen and Ingushian languages.

The Chechens have traditionally divided themselves into teips, or clans. The teip is a distinctive and independent ethnic unit in which individual Chechens are united by both family ties and territorial origins. There are some 165 to 170 teips in present-day Chechnya, 100 of which inhabit territories in the mountain districts of the country. The Chechens have thus survived more as mountain people than as flatlanders.

The social structure of the teip is not complex, its basis being the patriarchal family, locally called the nakji. The nakji is an extended rather than a nuclear family and includes not only the immediate parents, children, grandchildren, and grandparents but also all those related to it by some degree of kinship. A Chechen normally carries the name of one of his near forefathers (grandfather or great-grandfather) who is either still alive or has died not all that long ago. By taking on the name of such a recent forefather, the family clan preserves the memory not of a distant and obscure ancestor but of a concrete individual whose actions, personality, and often exploits are well known.

Such nakji, however, are also related as kin to other patriarchical families. A number of such nakji form a much larger social unit called a gar. Their common bond again is that they are all descendants of a common ancestor or founder.

Ultimately, related gars living in a common territory then come together to form a teip. In a teip, the growing tenuousness of the extended family relationship is supplemented by the factor of a common place of origin and regional ties. Territorial origins and proximity of residence (in the same village, valley, or region) unavoidably add a sense of a common fate, foster common attitudes and values, and instill a somewhat unified view toward the world outside the region. Not the least practical benefit of this sense of relationship is that it provides mutual security and protection from the dangers of a hostile outside environment. On a societal level, it also serves to foster the acceptance of the other members of the teip as social equals.

All these elements intertwine to form a strong common bond among the teip members and give the teips strong social cohesiveness. For the contemporary Chechen, the teip to a large extent is the group that determines his identity. Such extended family structure is governed at each level by its respective elders, who make most of the important decisions for it. Religion (Islam) and the traditions passed on from generation to generation set the rules.

On a larger scale, Chechen society is first and foremost a conglomeration of teips. The relationships of the teips among themselves and with the outside world determine the dynamics of life of Chechnya. The ancient tradition of blood vengeance or blood feud has survived among the teips, although in the last decades it has become more of a formalism.

The teips are not alike. They differ not only in their size—the numbers of people who consider themselves members of a teip—but also by their ethnic purity. Some of the teips are considered "pure-blooded," others "adulterated," or mixed with the blood of other peoples. For example, the Benoja, Centoroja, and Kurchaloja are held to be pure-blooded Chechen teips, while the Gunoja (having blood ties with the Terek Cossacks), the Charachoja (intermixed with the Cherkassians), and the Dzumsoja (interrelated with the Georgians) are considered adulterated teips. The pure teips live mostly in the mountains, while the adulterated teips make their homes in the flatlands. The people of the mountains have always distinguished themselves from those inhabiting the flatlands by the fierceness of their desire to gain back their national independence. For this reason, they have also suffered the most from their tsarist and then Soviet oppressors.[1]

The religion of the Chechens is Islam. It arrived in Chechnya at about the end of the eighth century and began to be accepted widely by the end of the ninth century. By that time, Georgia and Armenia already had long traditions of Christianity. But when the Slavs of Kieven Rus also converted to Christianity during the tenth century, the Chechens and the other mountain peoples such as the Ingushians, Avars, and Ossetians became part of an Islamic enclave in a region where political and military power was gradually beginning to pass into the hands of Christians.

The first contacts between the "Nochchi" and the Russians took place at the end of the sixteenth century. Tsarism had already established itself in Russia, and one of its most distinctive features was its aspiration to establish Russia as an empire. This had tragic results for the Chechen people.

The Russian empire was begun by the unification of the neighboring Slavic principalities under the rule of the tsar, achieved by force. Blood had always flowed until the will of the tsar was established and his domains were extended. In the Russian language, the word "tsar" must be understood as "ruler" and "tsarism" as "domination."

Once tsarism established itself in Russia, the tsars began to expand their territories by conquering other nations. Russia thus sent its armies in all directions, warring to the east, west, north, and south. At that time, the conquest of new territories by force was still called by its real name, and great pride was taken in such annexations. Now Russia's official historians attempt to explain those annexations of neighboring territories by force as purely "voluntary" unions. According to them, such nations "voluntarily sought to gain the tsar's support" and "to find refuge" in his empire from attacks by aggressive neighbors. The nations of the Northern Caucasus could not avoid such "conquest." The tragedy of the Chechen people began with these first contacts.

Russia began its attempt to conquer the Caucasus nations in 1663. Although resistance was fierce, Russia slowly was able to establish its power and completed its conquest of Chechnya by the beginning of the eighteenth century. Chechnya's first steps along its long and arduous road to independence and freedom began from that moment. For more than three centuries, the Chechens never once laid down their arms, and armed resistance to the aggressors was never discontinued.

The Chechen people rose up innumerable times against their Russian overlords. Each time the insurrections were put down, the Chechens reverted to protracted partisan warfare. Some Chechens even carried on the battle alone.

Such lone freedom fighters were known as Abrekians. Chechen armed resistance effectively ceased only during the 1944–56 period when, in fact, there were no more Chechens left within their indigenous territories to carry on the battle, as almost all still able to do battle with weapons in hand had been deported. The only new change in the Soviet efforts to suppress the Chechens was that the Soviets attempted to disguise Chechen national resistance by covering it with the cloak of criminality.

The Northern Caucasus region has always been for Russia the focus of special attention, principally because the region's resistance to its rule has always been fierce. But even among the nations of the Caucasus, the most resolute have always been the Chechens, a nation that Russia could not force to its knees. Thus, not without basis, the Chechen national anthem proudly proclaims: "We grew up free as the eagles, princes of the mountains. There are no thresholds from which we shall shy away."

The nations of the Caucasus mountains are not large in numbers, and thus their fight for independence has often forced them to unite. The resistance of the Adygians, Cherkassians, Chechens, and Dagestanians became especially persistent after the Chechen Sheik Mansur appeared on the Northern Caucasus political arena in 1785 and began to lead a combined insurrection. Sheik Mansur ruled the Chechen nation for almost eleven years, from 1780 to 1791. When he was finally captured and his fellow insurrectionists were cruelly massacred, the first stage of the Chechen fight for independence drew to a close.

But complete victory against these fierce mountain people had not been achieved. After a number of renewed insurrections, the Russian army in 1817 began to assault them in a planned fashion. Led by General Jermolov, the Russian forces began to move slowly forward, building permanent fortifications and establishing Cossack communities along the peripheries of their newly captured territories.

In 1818, the fortress of Grozni was established. Erected in four months by five thousand soldiers, it was built in the bend of a river and surrounded by earthworks and six bastions. Its strategic purpose was to cut off the Chechens' passage from the mountains along the Chankala gorge into the flatlands.[2]

It was not within the spirit of these freedom-loving mountain people to adapt easily to slavery. Thus, the second stage of resistance reached its climax when, two years after the death of Imam Gazi Muchamed, his friend and compatriot, Imam Shamil, an Avar, stepped up as leader of the insurrectionist forces. While fighting alongside Imam Gazi Muchamed, Imam Shamil himself had also been almost killed. But after pulling a Russian bayonet from his own body, he succeeded in escaping the Russian encirclement. Imam Shamil soon created an imamate, a country that united the Dagestanian and Chechen nations and a part of the western Caucasus mountain people. This imamate succeeded in resisting Russia for almost thirty years. But on September 25, 1859, it also was finally defeated.

By 1858, the Russian Army had already gained many years of experience in fighting the Chechen people. That year, it finally succeeded in completing the encirclement of Vedeno Aula and Imam Shamil's mountain fortress. Imam Shamil was forced to retreat with the remnants of his trusted naibu (local chieftains) guard to Guniba Aula, where he was finally forced to accept the surrender offer of Count Aleksander Baratynski, the commander of the Russian Army in the Northern Caucasus. As he and his guard exited the aula, the Russian soldiers greeted Imam Shamil and his retinue with a loud "hurrah" in honor of his courage and talents as a military leader.[3]

It thus took the Russian Army more than half a century to reconquer the comparatively small territory of Chechnya. History has a way of repeating itself, and present-day Chechen fighters contend that they will also fight Russia for fifty years if need be, or at least as long as even one Chechen is left alive and is able to lift a weapon. There will always be sufficient fighters to carry on the fight, they argue, as every Chechen woman will go into the mountains to give birth and will raise sons there until they too will be able to hold weapons in their hands. And the Chechen elders will pass onto them the fighting spirit. In the Chechen tradition, young people from the time they are small are trained to be brave. The elders inspire them, saying: "Do not fear the enemy because he may not have a weapon. Even if he does have a weapon, it may not be cocked. But even if it is cocked, it may not fire, and even if it is fired, it may not hit its target. But even if the bullet strikes you, the wound may be only superficial. And even if you die, you will then gain Allah's eternal grace."

Armed insurrection against the Russians did not cease after Imam Shamil was suppressed. As insurrections were constantly erupting, tsarist Russia decided on a "final solution" for the problem of the Caucasus mountain people. In 1865, it deported 700,000 Chechens and Ingushians from their home territories. Thus dispersed, the Chechens were not able to resist as fiercely. Their every subsequent attempt at resistance was met with cruel suppression.

Chechnya's importance to Russia grew even more when the wave of industrialization surged through its territories. Chechen lands, was discovered, were soaked in oil; oil could literally be scooped up in buckets. The first oil well on Chechen territory was drilled in 1893. By 1914, Chechen oil made up 14 percent of all the black gold produced by Russia. Chechen territory also provided Russia with a convenient route for transport lines to its other southern regions. During the last decade of the nineteenth century, the Vladikaukaz railroad line was built across Chechnya.

In 1917, with the onset of the Russian Revolution, the long awaited glimmer of freedom reappeared. The imamate of Dagestan and Chechnya was once again quickly proclaimed, and by 1918, the Mountain Republic was established. This republic, however, was not to last very long. The Bolshevik regime led by Lenin proved to be no better than the tsarist government. By 1920, Russia had again forcibly occupied Chechnya, and in 1921, Chechnya was attached to the Mountain Autonomous Region of the new Soviet Union. In 1922, Chechnya itself became an autonomous part of Soviet Russia. In 1934, Chechnya and Ingushia were joined into one autonomous district, which in 1936 was renamed the Chechen-Ingushian Autonomous Republic.

During this revolutionary period, the mountain people of Chechnya and neighboring Dagestan revolted twice more. The first revolt began in September, 1920, and lasted until May, 1921. The second revolt, in 1932, lasted only two weeks, but the Chechens fought fiercely during that short time. Even women, weapons in hand, went on the attack against the Red Army units that were sent to put down the insurrection.

In 1944, Chechnya suffered its most severe blow. Hitler's armies neared this Northern Caucasus region, and the Chechens, using the opportunity, revolted. Soon, however, they were once again suppressed by the Red Army. Taking revenge against the mountain people for a revolt during wartime, Stalin deported more than 60 percent of all the inhabitants of the territory of Chechnya, including almost the whole Chechen nation. They began to return to their home territories only in 1956–57, after Khrushchev declared a general amnesty following Stalin's death.

The New Stage of the Battle for Independence

The most recent stage of the fight for Chechen independence began on October 27, 1991, when retired Soviet Air Force general major Dzhochar Dudajev, elected president of Chechnya from a slate of three candidates, proclaimed on November 1 the independence of Chechnya. The time for such action seemed right, as the Soviet Union was itself writhing in separatist agony. Favorable conditions for the proclamation of Chechnya's independence had been ripening for quite some time. By 1990, it was becoming clear that the collapse of the Soviet Union was imminent. Lithuania, Latvia, and Estonia had already declared their independence. In Russia itself, Boris Yeltsin was stubbornly attempting to disassociate the Russian Federation from any subordination to the Soviet Union's government. For Yeltsin, support from the Russian Federation's Autonomous Republics had suddenly become very important. There was nothing very surprising in this new turn of events. If one takes a quick look at a map of the Russian Federation, one can easily understand the reasons for Yeltsin's concern: the Russian Federation's cloth is itself woven out of mostly autonomous republics of which only several can be considered in all fairness to be ethnically "Russian." These are all located in the European part of the Russian Federation. Ethnic Russia is at best a circular territory centered on Moscow whose radius is only several hundred kilometers. Immense Russian Federation territories stretch to the east of Moscow, but lands attributable to ethnic, traditional, and historic Russia extend only up to the Volga River. Past it lie only the autonomous republics peopled by other nationalities.

Autonomous republics have always been only symbolic in nature. The tsars on their part, and then Lenin and Stalin under the pretext of furthering "Marxist internationalism," had made diligent efforts to ensure that the indigenous nationalities of the conquered regions would become minorities in their own lands, lorded over by ethnic Russians. This legacy was inherited by Yeltsin when he became president of the Russian Federation.

Under the new circumstances, however, Yeltsin suddenly had to come up with a new unifying concept and a name by which all the Russian Federation's inhabitants could be referred to as a united people. He had to think hard. But as Yeltsin had been brought up in the spirit of communism and had climbed the career ladder only by faithfully serving the Party, he did not have to think very long. He simply dug down into the soviet lexicon and "borrowed" an old concept from his predecessor thrice removed, Leonid Brezhnev. Brezhnev's ideologists had suggested that he refer to the citizens of the Soviet Union as "soviets," thus freeing the names of its citizens from any nationalistic connotations. And so in the quest to appropriately rename an old inheritance, Yeltsin reversed the concept. Thus all the territories of the Russian Federation suddenly became "Russian" territories. If one is a citizen of Russia, the term suggested, then he or she is a Russian.

Yeltsin did not have to take any special measures to gain the support of the autonomous republics for his breakaway policies. Talk of greater autonomy, national rebirth, and even independence was being heard more often and louder as time went on in the autonomous republics of the Russian Federation. Thus, in attempting to strengthen his own hold on power and his support within the autonomous republics, Yeltsin began to make use of the prevailing undercurrents, even throwing out the slogan: "Take as much of independence as you can handle."

It would have been even more surprising had the Chechens not begun to make their own move, particularly as the majority of Chechnya's inhabitants were clearly disposed against the Russian-imposed Communist "particrat" government of their own autonomous republic. This government of lackeys had long thrived on corruption and was controlled by certain clans. Even the most influential posts in its hierarchy could be bought almost openly if the right price was paid. Having fully lost, or to be more exact, never having gained the confidence or loyalty of the people, there could have been few doubts that, given the right opportunity, the party nomenclatura, or ruling class, would eventually be swept from power.

On the other hand, the new Russian Federation government could not have had much liking for the ever strengthening separatist forces in Chechnya that were unequivocally proclaiming complete Chechen independence and separation from the Russian Federation. Jaragi Mamodajev and the well-known Chechen writer Zelimchan Jandarbijev had become the leaders of this separatist movement, and the concept of an Islamic nation state propagated by them held a strong attraction for a large number of Chechens. The Chechens only lacked unity and a unifying national movement such as the Lithuanian Sajudis, which had unified the people of that nation on its road to independence. Instead, numerous movements and parties had been formed in Chechnya under the influence of the various teips and the competing Islamic religious sects.

It was thus not very surprising that, for Moscow, the developing situation in Chechnya was becoming very important, especially after Ruslan Khasbulatov, himself a Chechen of the Charachoi teip and a deputy from the Chechnya-Ingushia Autonomous Republic, became the speaker of the Russian Federation's Duma, or parliament.

Khasbulatov had to be increasingly concerned for his own position. In the event that Chechnya seceded from Russia, his position as the Russian Federation Duma's opposition leader would itself have been put into jeopardy. Thus it had not been an easy task for him to choose whom to lean on to firm up his own support in Chechnya. This search for allies soon drew his attention to General Major Dzhochar Dudajev, who had earlier established close ties with the representatives of the Chechen separatist movement. Dudajev's main attractiveness at that time had been that, as yet, he had not had the opportunity to get caught up in the various Chechen political squabbles. This, therefore, had made him more acceptable to both the various movements in Chechnya and the individual party leaders.

Dzhochar Dudajev, formerly the commander of a Soviet Air Force Division in the city of Tartu in Estonia, had been assigned to Chechnya with Khasbulatov's help.[4] There, he had been reassigned to the reserve. It had been expected in Russian government circles that Dudajev would remain loyal to the Russian government because of the confidence it had placed in him during his earlier career. But once Dudajev became involved in the political passions then bubbling in Chechnya, he began to draw ever closer to Jandarbijev and Mamodajev.[5]

The First Chechen National Assembly (later renamed a Congress), was held on November 25, 1990. The assembly was a traditional general gathering of the Chechen nation. Its decisions carried great weight, and it was capable of granting authority to act in the name of the Chechen people. It was not, however, legally recognized by the government of the Russian Federation. Once convened, the assembly issued a declaration regarding the formation of the Chechen Republic of Nochchi-Cho (Ichkerija) and, with the active support of Mamodajev, elected Dudajev to the its executive committee.

Two days later, a session of the then still existing Chechen-Ingushian Autonomous Republic's Supreme Council (the Russian Federation's local governmental organ) also issued a Declaration of Sovereignty.[6] On March 11, 1991, this same Supreme Council also voted not to participate in the referendum then scheduled to be voted upon in the Russian Federation. Chechnya thereafter refused to participate further in any of the Russian Federation's referendums, but such refusal was also the beginning of its split with Ingushia. The Nazran, Malgobek, and Sunzha districts of the Chechen-Ingushian Autonomous Republic, inhabited mostly by Ingushians, chose to participate in the Russian referendum.[7]

The Second Chechen National Congress held in July of that year officially declared that the Chechen Republic of Ichkerija was not an integral part of either the Union of Soviet Socialist Republics or of the Russian Federation. Dudajev also strengthened his own position by being elected chairman of the congress.[8]

These, however, had been only declarative statements issued by an as yet unrecognized Chechen National Congress. Events were speeded up by the August, 1991, putsch in Moscow during which the putschists attempted to remove Mikhail Gorbachev from power and to revive the tottering dictatorship of the Communist Party. During the initial days of the putsch, Dudajev firmly declared that he would not support the putschists. Once the putsch was defeated, the stock of those who had stood up to the putschists rose markedly in the Russian political arena.

After the defeat of the putsch, the Soviet empire's days of continued existence were clearly numbered. In Chechnya, the defeat of the putsch also strengthened Dudajev's position. Actively supported by the speaker of the Russian Duma, Khasbulatov, who had returned to Chechnya especially for the occasion, Dudajev declared on September 3 that the Russian Federation's local governmental body, the Chechen-Ingushian Supreme Council, headed

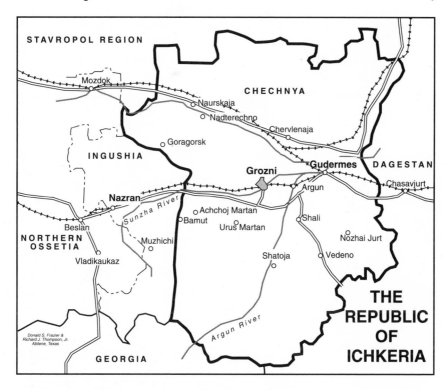

by Doku Zavgajev, was dissolved. Zavgajev, a member of the Nizaloi teip, re-treated to his home base in the Nadterechno region to wait and see what would happen next. Some time later, he was found a position in the Russian president's apparatus. Previously having been the Communist Party secretary of the Chechen-Ingushian region, he had lasted only a year in the post of chairman of the Chechen-Ingushian Supreme Council.[9]

On September 15, the Chechen-Ingushian Supreme Council voted to dis-solve itself. The Ingushian Assembly held in Nazran soon thereafter declared the reestablishment of the separate Republic of Ingushia.[10]

The Chechen Republic's presidential and parliamentary elections were held on September 27. Competing against two other candidates, Dudajev was elected president. Three Ingushian regions, two Cossack regions, and the re-gion of Nadterechno, however, did not participate in the elections. This fact and the fact that the division of Chechnya and Ingushia into separate re-publics had not been legalized in advance in Moscow induced the Kremlin not to recognize the elections. The day after Chechnya's Declaration of Inde-pendence, the Russian Parliament declared that the Chechen presidential elec-tions had not been valid.

On November 7, Boris Yeltsin declared martial law in Chechnya and Ingushia. An order for the arrest of Dzhochar Dudajev was also issued. To effectuate this order, a battalion of about one thousand Internal Affairs Ministry
troops were flown into Grozni on November 9, 1991. But angry crowds of
mountain people and Dudajev's Chechen National Guard blocked the airport
and the battalion was forced to leave Chechnya without even embarking from
their aircraft.[11]

The Russian president's order establishing martial law had an effect quite
opposite from what had been expected in Moscow. It raised all the Chechens
to their feet and immensely increased Dudajev's popularity. This gave him additional leverage to strengthen his government and to undertake measures to
solidify his country's standing as independent. Through his efforts during the
course of the next year, the formation of the Chechen Armed Forces was be-

gun and the Russian Army was withdrawn from Chechnya. Active measures were also undertaken to obtain recognition of the independence of Chechnya both internationally and in Moscow.

Not everyone in Chechnya was ready to recognize Dudajev's growing power, however. As these events were taking place, opposition to Dudajev was beginning to form. The first to declare his opposition was Umar Avturchanov, a former militiaman who had been elected in December as mayor of the Nadterechno region. Khasbulatov, who had maintained friendly relations with Dudajev until 1992, also now began to oppose Dudajev. This began especially after Dudajev ordered the recall of all deputies elected from Chechnya to the Russian Parliament. It increased even more after Khasbulatov's Chechen citizenship was taken from him.[12]

Opposition was also forming in Moscow against Yeltsin amid a flurry of parliamentary accusations of authoritarianism and blatant disregard of the parliament. Vice President Aleksander Ruskoj and Parliamentary Speaker Khasbulatov became the leaders of the Russian opposition. It had clearly not been to Dudajev's advantage to support the Russian opposition. After the August, 1991, putsch in Moscow organized by the supporters of a Communist Soviet Union against Gorbachev, Yeltsin turned all his energies to the effort of forcing Gorbachev from power and to the dismemberment of the Soviet Union. He had also initiated immense economic reforms. All this had precipitated an ongoing wrestling match with the Russian Parliament. In other words, the situation in Moscow was favorable for Dudajev, although his relationship with Russia remained very tense.

But friction could not be avoided. The first Chechen armed confrontation with Russia took place in late 1992. In October, during the Ingushian-Ossetian conflict, the Russian Army crossed over into the disputed Sunzha and Malgobek regions of Ingushia and approached Chechnya's borders. In response, Dudajev declared a state of alert in Chechnya and sent his army's tanks against Russia. Actual armed confrontation, however, was avoided. Vice Premier Yegor Gaidar flew in from Moscow and met with Chechen vice premier Mamodajev. They agreed upon the mutual withdrawal of forces.[13] This confrontation was profitable for Chechnya as with it began a period of negotiations with Russia. No treaty was signed, however, as Dudajev continued to hold firmly to his position concerning Chechnya's sovereignty, a position that clearly was unacceptable to the Kremlin.

During May and June of 1993, Dudajev succeeded in achieving exclusive rule: he had pushed out and dissolved the pro-Russian Chechen Parliament and Constitutional Court and had issued a decree prohibiting the activity of the pro-Russian opposition parties and their newspapers. Although his actions could be considered patently anticonstitutional, the situation in Chechnya at that time was so complex and the various political forces so split that such a one-dimensional evaluation should not be made. The problem was not simply an internal political matter. One side wanted to remain a part of Russia. The other side wanted to withdraw from its grasp. These were not reconcilable matters; only one side could win.

It was clear that the opposition forces would resist. Everything finally erupted when Dudajev's National Guard attempted to disperse the congregated followers of the Daimohk movement, which the capital's mayor, Beslan Gantemirov, also commanding Grozni's militia, vowed to defend. More than fifty people were killed during this confrontation, including several of Gantemirov's relatives and Dudajev's cousin Shamil.[14]

After these events, the distribution of forces in Chechnya became distinct. The Nadterechno district, with mayor and former militiaman Umar Avturchanov at its head, became the opposition's most important center. This district, dominated by Zavgajev's Nizaloi teip, refused to obey Dudajev's government in Grozni and declared the establishment of the Terek Chechen Republic. The former mayor of Grozni, Beslan Gantemirov, who was a member of the Chonchoi teip, was also forced to withdraw from Grozni and established himself in the Urus Martan district, his birthplace.

Twenty-eight-year-old Ruslan Labazanov, who had served for more than two years as the commander of Dudajev's personal guard, also went over to the opposition. He became the commander of opposition forces in Argun, located only some fifteen kilometers to the east of Grozni. According to Labazanov, his disagreement with Dudajev began only after documents came into his possession confirming Dudajev's apparent machinations involving the sale of oil and the fact that the president had received and kept for himself more than two billion rubles. Two days after Labazanov gave over these documents to the Chechen minister of Internal Affairs, the latter was killed. The Russian Federation's Prosecutor General's Office leveled criminal charges against Labazanov as well; Labazanov explained these on various occasions as involving "only" the illegal sale of automobiles.[15] (On May 31, 1996, Ruslan Labazanov and his personal bodyguard were killed by another opposition bodyguard who had begun to suspect him of maintaining contacts with Shamil Basajev's people.)

Each of the opposition groups had declared themselves in favor of Chechnya remaining an integral part of Russia. The opposition groups soon united and formed the Temporary Council, whose clearly stated purpose was to fight Dudajev and his followers—once Russia's support and assistance was obtained.

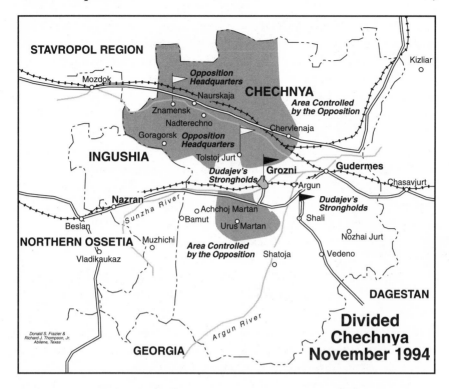

The results of these two years of activity were concrete: formerly united into an Autonomous Republic of the Russian Federation, Chechnya and Ingushia separated. Chechnya declared its independence from Russia, although Russia as yet did not recognize it. The Russian Army withdrew from Chechnya's territory. Dudajev's government took measures to defended its independence. The Chechen people divided themselves into two camps whose relations with each other were becoming ever more tense.

Dudajev's Battle with the Opposition

Although Chechnya's internal conflicts persisted throughout 1993, further open armed confrontations (with the exception of the June 5 incident in Grozni) were avoided until the summer of 1994. The opposition had not yet gathered sufficient strength to enter into armed conflict with Dudajev's forces. It continued to collect its strength, receiving material, technical support, and later weapons and military equipment from Russia. It was also being constantly urged to take resolute actions against Dudajev.

During this period, the various opposition groups also began to unite. They were forced to do this by the practicalities of the situation, as each oppo-

sition leader's individual armed formation was simply too weak to battle with
Dudajev's forces on its own. This unification process culminated in December, 1993, when the opposition forces formed the Temporary Council and appointed as its leaders Umar Avturchanov and the former minister of the USSR's
oil industry, Salambek Chadzhijev.

But by themselves, these actions were insufficient to enable the Temporary Council to declare itself as representing the Chechen nation. For this reason, yet another Chechen National Assembly was called together, this time by
the opposition. It took place on July 4, 1994, in the Nadterechno district. Obviously, who were to be the delegates at such a national assembly depended
upon who called it together. Although it was still called the Chechen National
Assembly and, purportedly, again spoke in the name of all the Chechen people, the composition of the assembled delegates and therefore its decisions
would vary greatly depending on who convened it.

After proclaiming that more than 2,056 delegates representing more than
two-thirds of Chechnya's communities were participating in the assembly, the
assembly first recognized the Temporary Council as the Republic's highest
governing body and, after issuing a demand that Dudajev resign, called for new
elections. It also authorized the sending of a petition to Ruslan Khasbulatov
requesting that he take over the leadership of the opposition movement.[16]

At Moscow's urging, on July 27, 1994, the Temporary Council petitioned
Russian president Yeltsin that it be recognized as the sole legal governmental
body in Chechnya. At the same time, it requested Russia for assistance in
reestablishing "law and order" and the creation of "more secure and more normal living conditions for its citizens."

On August 2, 1994, Russia quickly announced its open support for the
Temporary Council. By that time, opinion had formed in Moscow that the
use of Russian Armed Forces in Chechnya would be unavoidable. On August 11, Russian president Yeltsin spoke openly about the possible use of force
in Chechnya. From that moment on, the threat of an unavoidable war began
to hang over Chechnya.[17]

Having put in a major effort to form an anti-Dudajev coalition that could
be alleged to represent the Chechen nation, Moscow succeeded in furthering its own purposes. In actual practice, it was also much easier to support
a unified coalition than competing opposition forces. The well-known principle of "divide and conquer" was thus put to good use by Moscow. To divide
had not been a very difficult task, once the particularities of relations among
the teips were known.

The division of Chechens into two opposing camps was not accidental.
In the opinion of the well-known Chechen philosopher and political ana-

lyst V. Akajev, one of the main reasons for this was the growing friction between the mountain and flatlands teips. Many of Dudajev's followers had originated in the southern (mountain) districts of Chechnya, and for this reason the term "Ichkerija" had been included in the name of the new Chechen republic. As "Ichkerija" referred only to the two southern mountain regions, Shatoja and Vedeno, it thus had been possible to read into the use of the name "Ichkerija" an intent to grant primacy to the mountain teips over the flatlands teips in the new republic. This was negatively received by the flatlands teips, especially as the flatlands were populated mostly by the "intermixed teips" (having blood relationships with other nationalities). The opposition had been formed mostly from such mixed-blood teips and had sought support from Russia. Russian Security Services thus only needed to put these frictions to good use.

But perhaps the reasons for this friction lay not in any one event but in the relationships of the teips over the course of many years. As much that is determinative in the Caucasus is counted in terms of centuries, one has to go back to the time of Imam Shamil.

An overwhelming majority of Chechens are devout believers in the Islamic faith and belong to Sufi brotherhoods, or burdas. All such burdas belong to one or the other of the two rival Sufi tarikats, or ways, the Nakshbandia and the Kadaria. The first tarikat to reach the territory of Chechnya was the Nakshbandia. The teachings of this way had been used by Imam Shamil as the basis for the system of education that he instituted in the territories under his control and for the creation of his military clan theocracy. As a result, the proponents of the Nakshbandia tarikat gained ascendancy during Imam Shamil's reign and became its foremost elite.

After Imam Shamil's defeat and capture and his apparent willingness to comply with Russian demands, however, the authority of this tarikat quickly disintegrated. The burdas of the Kadaria tarikat continued to resist Russian rule even after Shamil's defeat and thus there began a massive transfer of allegiance among the teips to the Kadaria tarikat. After the end of Caucasus war, when the majority of the sheiks of the Nakshbandia tarikat also began to take a pro-Russian position, this campaign was also extended against these remaining followers of Imam Shamil.

Given the unavoidable Russian presence, the burdas of the Kadaria tarikat began to distinguish themselves by their self-imposed isolation and intense clannishness. Members of these burdas also began a campaign of violent resistance against the Russians. Throughout the Tsarist period and even during Soviet rule, the members of the burdas of the Kadaria tarikat also continued to express their resistance to Russian rule by not abiding by the laws passed by these regimes. (Hence the origins of the reputation of Chechens as not law-abiding, or at least as not willing to abide by Russian and Soviet laws.)

The deportation of Chechens to Kazakstan in 1944 gave a strong impetus for the reinvigoration of the Kadaria tarikat. During the 1950s, there appeared among the exiled Chechens in the Selinogradskii Oblast of Kazakstan the newest and most radical of the Kadaria burdas, the Vis-Chadzhi Zagiev. The Vis-Chadzhi Zagiev burda soon achieved among the Chechens the reputation of being the truest proponent of the Chechen nationalist idea. Among many of the exiled Chechens, the burdas of the Nakshbandia tarikat were also viewed as the "dens of the KGB." During his exile in Kazakstan, Dzhochar Dudajev's elder brother Bakmiraz belonged to this burda and was one of its teachers and mentors. Dudajev himself was apparently also a member.

With the return of the Chechens to Chechnya, the burdas of these tarikats distributed themselves in the country along a very clear territorial basis. In the 1980s, the Nakshbandia tarikat was based in Urus Martan. Aligned with it were Tolstoi Jurt and all the flatland regions north of the Terek River (later the regions controlled by the pro-Russian opposition). The burdas of the Kadaria tarikat relocated themselves mostly to the regions south of the Terek River (later coincidental with the regions aligned with Dudajev). As they had for at least a century, these two tarikats continued to differ politically: one was pro-Russian and assimilationist, the other was nationalist and in favor of an independent Chechnya.

According to people who express a knowledge of these matters, the teachings of the Nakshbandia tarikat have a "softness" that is no longer acceptable to the great majority of post-Soviet Muslims. The Kadaria tarikat has not yet taken on a conservative face, but much like the Nakshbandia tarikat under different circumstances, it plays the role of lawgiver. It apparently is not fundamentalist. The war against Russia and its "fellow travelers" has thus taken on a religious content.

Why did Russia resolve to take such resolute military action against Chechnya? Probably the most important reason was that Dzhochar Dudajev was practically unbendable and continued to insist that all questions of relations with Russia had to be conditioned on the recognition of Chechnya's independence. For Russia, Chechnya had become a wedge, threatening to tear apart its territorial integrity. If Chechnya was allowed to split off, the other autonomous republics would begin to demand the same, first in the Caucasus region, then elsewhere. Once the storm of national rebirth and independence gathered strength in this region inhabited by 25 million people, it would be practically impossible to contain it. The gusts of this separatist wind would then begin to blow in even the furthest reaches of the Russian Federation.

It must be remembered that the central Russian government had already experienced the same problems in its relations with Tatarstan. There, the first indications of a similar storm appeared, but Russia was able to deflect the storm's path and contain it as the president of Tatarstan lacked the resolve to stand up to Yeltsin. Both having formerly belonged to the same Party's elite caste, they came to an agreement. Tatarstan thus was satiated with only a grant of "wide" autonomy.

The most that the Russian government could have agreed to was to grant Chechnya the same "wide" autonomy as Tatarstan. But such status was unacceptable to both Dudajev and the Kremlin. For Russia, the problem was a dilution of power. The more republics that gained such "wide" autonomy, the weaker would necessarily become the Russian Federation's central government.

As to the actual reasons for Russia's decision to use force in Chechnya, most politicians and political analysts hold the same view: it was not only to protect the Russian Federation's territorial integrity but was also connected, in their opinion, with the fact that once Chechnya became independent, it would gain exclusivity as to the mineral wealth beneath its soil. The Chechens had taken over control from Russia of the existing gas and oil pipelines crossing its territory and the largest oil refinery in the Caucasus, which alone produced aviation fuel. Plans had also been made earlier by Russia to build additional oil, gas, and refined fuel pipelines from Azerbaijan to Europe across Chechen territory. Russia was still very interested in implementing this venture; it has been reported that agreements worth millions had already been signed and that even stock in such a venture had been issued. Thus, huge damages had been suffered and the threat of an international scandal was becoming imminent, a threat that needed to be liquidated at all cost. It was also very important for Russia to reestablish its broken communications and transportation links through Chechnya with its other regions.

A pretext was thus needed for the use of force by Russia. In Russia's view, the "criminal" situation in Chechnya was, in fact, quite critical, but this pretext was not sufficient by itself. A more workable one was that Dudajev had established an "anti-democratic, criminal regime" in Chechnya.[18] But for this, sufficiently convincing arguments were needed.

When the war in Chechnya began, Western journalists began to hear more and more about the "Chechen mafia." Although they had little idea of what the term actually meant, they began to repeat it in their articles. Ultimately, it became part of the color and defining context of this war. The term "Chechen mafia" is not new; it was first used by the Russian press in about 1988–89, when Gorbachev stepped onto the political scene and the first shoots of democracy began to sprout in the Soviet Union.

Political change was clearly coming, but the more immediate problem for the Soviet people still revolved around the problem of securing the food and staples needed for daily survival. The "Great Economic Experiment" had not worked and had only produced a population living on the edge of abject poverty. The Soviet Union's economic system was collapsing, and consumer goods were in ever shorter supply. Even the simplest goods such as flour, sugar, bread, conserved meats, sausage, clothing, shoes, and light bulbs were no longer readily available. Now these simple products became "deficit" goods. Soviet industry, still state owned, excessively centralized, and organized according to time-honored communist principles, was structurally unable to satisfy the needs of the population. To put it more concretely, there was almost no initiative in such industry to change, as the producers were simply not interested in producing such goods in any great quantities or of better quality.

Corruption was also rampant among those in power. The prevailing ideology and ethical norms had long died out and the nomenclatura, or ruling class, officially holding state property "in trust" for the people had long begun to view it as their own. As democracy began to take hold, there began to be heard more and more about the privatization (denationalization) of state property.

Without rules for equitably regulating this process, privatization began to be indulged in mostly by those in power having the necessary influence to push through their claims. Soon high government officials, leaders of the Communist Party, and members of the nomenclatura began forming consortiums for this purpose with industrialists and, often, clearly "underworld" personages and organizations. Together, they began to take advantage of their powerful positions to pile up immense personal wealth.

This "prichvatization" process (a Russian word meaning "to grab for oneself") had no territorial boundaries and was equally present in all the former Soviet Republics and even Chechnya itself. The process is still very much alive at the present time. But as long as it serves the interests of the powerful, very little is being reported about it in the press. In those few instances when journalists have investigated and written about it, they have often been killed. This "mafia" is quite like the mafia in the West.

There were also lower forms of mafia in the Soviet Union. In these same years, as newborn democracy began to loosen up the repressive bonds and strictures of the Communist regime, more freedom of action became possible and, inevitably, this also precipitated a greater amount of illegal activity. The basis of most of this illegal activity was the black market, which dealt in "deficit" goods. Given the moneylessness of Soviet society, there was pitifully little other activity where real money could be made. The only other viable alternative was government service and participation in its "legal" and "illegal" privileges.

Some of the black market goods were stolen outright. But such goods were most often obtained by bribing directors and managers of the state stores and others in the distribution chain. Obviously, for this trade to generate large profits, intricate "illegal" organizational infrastructures had to be formed that could produce better sourcing, bigger volumes, better distribution, and better protection against all those who would dare to interfere. The net result was that often deficit products, not available on store counters, would show up in open-air markets and the like.

As profits were better further north, the people of the Caucasus began to frequent the open-air markets of Moscow and the other larger cities of the Soviet Union. In every large city, such open-air markets were "conquered" or put under the control and protection of one or the other group. Of course, there was money to be made from this control. The Chechens, reportedly, were particularly good at protecting what they considered to be their own and quite often succeeded in chasing away the others. The participation of Chechens in this activity, however, was not larger in scale or more pervasive than that of the "Moscow mafia" or any of the other numerous illegal groupings attempting to compete for control of this black market trade.

In the last years of the 1980s, the competition between these various groups for control of the black markets precipitated a gang war. Reportedly, one of the more notable groups participating in this war, at least in Moscow, had been the "Chechen mafia," a term created by a journalist.

Most likely this term would have died out had it not been adopted by the government's spokesmen for quite other purposes. Attempting to mask the failures of its own economic system and the obviously empty store shelves, the government soon began to blame everything on the "mafia": "They have organized the theft of the goods, they bribe the store directors! They, the 'Chechen mafia,' are to blame for the shortages!"

Likewise, the term would most likely have died out if other, newer events had not intervened. Accusations of "undue" and "sinister" influences on the economy were still in vogue when the Soviet Union collapsed. But when Chechnya proclaimed its independence, the term regained a new vigor as part of the Russian propaganda campaign to label the Chechens as criminals and bandits. In the eyes of the Russian people, this was only confirmed by press reports that it was possible to buy practically anything in Chechnya: even weapons were being sold in Chechen open-air markets, and quite cheaply at that.

Although the "Chechen mafia" began to be discussed even more frequently in the press, few journalists have ever ventured to mention the dealings of the higher-level "mafia" in relation to Chechnya. The few who did, such as Igor Bunich in his book *Chronicles of the Chechen War,* generally accuse that illegal money was laundered through Chechnya and that illegal trading in metals, oil, and arms was taking place. Members of the Chechen government, even Dudajev himself, were accused of being involved in such dealings and of working in partnership with the highest Russian government officials and military leaders. Although profits of millions of U.S. dollars are always mentioned, these journalists have provided no hard evidence to back up their accusations.

Was there and is there a "Chechen mafia"? Most likely, there was and is. But certainly the "mafia" is no more present and on no larger scale than it is in any of the other former Soviet republics or, for that matter, in Russia itself. And most certainly, such "mafia" as there is, is not even imaginatively near to the "sinister and all-pervasive criminal organization" that is alleged, the destruction of which would justify the extermination of a nation.

But perhaps it was important only to make the accusation. Then the Chechen independence movement would have to try to negate the allegation and wipe itself clean of the stain. That, invariably, is a difficult and time-consuming process. Even if done successfully, chances are that it may not off-set the original propaganda advantage.

The best argument for Russia's use of force against Chechnya, of course, was blood. The open use of force to prevent the further spilling of blood would be justifiable in both the eyes of the Russian citizenry and the international community. So that blood would begin to be spilled in Chechnya, the opposition was hurriedly armed. In the space of half a year, the opposition was strengthened appreciably by Russian material support and began actively to oppose Dudajev's government. The first armed skirmish between the opposition and Dudajev's followers occurred on June 13, 1994, in Grozni. But this was only the first of many to come.[19]

The situation in Chechnya from this time on became complicated. Armed confrontations between the opposition's armed groups and Dudajev's military formations became more frequent. To trigger the conflagration, it had only been necessary that Dudajev begin to act more resolutely and participate more actively. To speed up the process, terrorist actions were organized during the spring and summer of 1994 in the Stavropol region of Russia. After four successive attempts to take buses filled with people hostage and to hijack and fly helicopters from Mineralnyje Vodi back to Chechnya, the Cossacks of the Stavropol region, traditionally opposed to the Chechens, became more active.

On August 5, three Chechen homesteads in the village of Galinganovsk, not far from the Stavropol region, were attacked. The Chechens living there were forced to leave everything behind and to flee to relatives in Chechnya. The next night, a group of armed individuals made an incursion from the Nadterechno region into the Naursk region. During the skirmish that followed, three Chechen border guards were killed. One situation followed another, and the tenseness grew. Chechens residing in Moscow began to close their businesses and make preparations to return to Chechnya.

Who had organized the terrorist acts—Moscow's Security Services, the opposition, or Dudajev's followers themselves—is itself not very important. What is much more crucial is that the purpose being sought had been accomplished. Chechnya began to smell of gunpowder, and Dudajev was being forced into taking resolute measures.

On August 10, yet another Chechen National Assembly took place, with two thousand delegates from seventeen regions participating. This time, the assembly was called together by Dudajev's followers and authorized Dudajev to declare a general mobilization. It also pronounced a death sentence for opposition leader Umar Avturchanov.[20]

The convening of a National Assembly was equally useful to Dudajev and to the opposition leaders. Making use of a National Assembly's traditional authority, even opposing political leaders could strengthen their positions and gain the ability to proclaim "officially" that they had obtained the necessary authorizations from the Chechen nation and thus were executing the "national will." It was important only to declare the fact that an assembly had convened. Not all the communities would be represented at each assembly. But neither side ever argued that the delegates to an assembly convened by the other side had come only by personal invitation and had not represented all the Chechen people, as it was self-evident that each side would invite only the community, regional, political movement, religious, and community leaders who supported their side.

It may also be surprising to many that a sentence, particularly a death sentence, would be handed down by a political assembly and not a court. But among Chechens, this is considered normal. Shariat (Muslim traditional law) was reinstituted, and the tradition of blood vengeance among the teips was reinstated. These traditions had lain fallow for a time but had never been forgotten.

Dudajev did not wait long to make full use of this assembly's authorizations. The next day, a general mobilization was proclaimed. It was also declared that from August 11, all aircraft flying over Chechen territory without permission from Dudajev's government would be forced by Chechen fighter aircraft to land in Grozni Airport. Martial law was declared in the Nadterechno region where the opposition had been attempting to recruit Dudajev's supporters and where five Chechen law officials had been killed during the previous week. Dudajev was finally taking resolute measures against the opposition.

On August 1, Dudajev's armed formations shot up Urus Martan, which was controlled by Gantemirov. Four days later, Argun was attacked and taken. When the village of Dolinsk, controlled by Avturchanov, was attacked for a third time, considerable losses were suffered by both sides. On August 17, Dudajev's forces also began their attack, supported by ten tanks and armored vehicles, on the community of Tolstoi Jurt, Khasbulatov's stronghold, killing and wounding many. The confrontations were becoming more fierce. The pretext for Moscow to openly use force in Chechnya was now becoming sufficient.[21]

In the opposition's armed formations, there was also an increase in the number of instructors sent in from Russia. They began to train the opposition's troops, who had no prior combat experience in the use of the modern weapons and equipment that had been arriving from Russia in ever increasing numbers.[22]

From about August, 1994, Moscow's politics regarding Chechnya became cloaked in secrecy. Sergei Shakhrai, who chaired the State Committee on Nationality Policy, was removed from any decision making regarding Chechnya, and his functions were given over to government official Nikolai Jegorov, who was new to these issues. Even assistants to ministers who were members of the Russian Federation's National Security Council were not briefed on the measures that were to be taken in Chechnya.[23]

For many, Jagorov's appointment as the government official authorized to deal with questions concerning Chechnya came as a surprise. But for those who were familiar with his disposition toward the people of the Caucasus, this said much. Jagorov was known for having acted resolutely when Russia initiated its war with the Caucasus mafia. When he headed the Krasnodar regional administration, the regional markets were swept free of peddlers from the Caucuses within days. This had not gone unnoticed. In May, 1994, Jagorov was appointed the Russian Federation's Minister for Nationalities and Regional Political Matters and in July to the President's Council for Cossack Affairs.[24]

CHAPTER 2

Preparations to Defend Chechnya's Independence

The formation of the Chechen armed forces was begun immediately after Chechnya declared its independence. The groundwork for this effort had been laid earlier in August and September, 1991, with the formation of the Chechen National Congress's Executive Committee's National Guard. The mobilization and civil defense systems previously maintained on Chechen territory by the Soviet Union were kept operating. Also, when the Soviet Union's army withdrew in 1990–91, it had left behind functioning military bases, training centers, and other facilities, as well as a large quantity of weapons and military equipment.

Chechen leaders originally envisioned that the primary core of the armed forces would be a regular army, formed taking into account the republic's geographic, national, and other characteristics. This regular army would be augmented by the National Security Service and the Internal Affairs Ministry's armed formations.[1] They also planned to form in the Army a mountain infantry brigade, a tank regiment, a motorized rifle battalion, an artillery battery, antiaircraft defense units, a military aviation force, as well as various special purpose units. The Army would consist of some 11,000–12,000 troops, equipped with approximately 40 tanks, 50 units of various armored equipment, and more than 100 artillery guns and mortars. During a second stage, a border brigade and a cavalry regiment were also to be organized. All three of the primary components of the armed forces would be put directly under the command of the president as the commander of the armed forces. The regular army was to be commanded through the Supreme General Headquarters.[2]

The formation and command of the National Guard and the self-defense formations were to be given over to the Defense Committee. According to information published in the Russian press, the republic's mobilization resources consisted of approximately 300,000 people between the ages of 14 and 65. The actual number was much smaller, perhaps even by half.

Upon a declaration of a general mobilization, the existing armed forces were to be supported by the formation of self-defense brigades or regiments in each of the eleven districts not controlled by the opposition. Each brigade or regiment was to consist of at least several battalions of three to four companies each, a tank company, and various support units (intelligence, communications, and the like). Each company was to be made up of 4 platoons, each having 27 to 30 people (100 to 120 people altogether). The platoons were to be subdivided into three squads each. Leaders planned to call up some 30,000 people into such self-defense brigades and regiments.[3]

The Chechen armed forces were formed very quickly. On January 11, 1992, Dudajev issued a decree declaring a state of alert in the whole republic. At the same time, a partial mobilization was ordered of veterans who had previously served in Afghanistan. They were organized into special-purpose detachments, marine infantry units, border forces, and Ministry of Internal Affairs armed formations.

By the end of 1992, Chechnya already had its own functioning army and a tested mobilization and training system. The republic also had available in its ranks a sufficient number of military professionals. But it still had a shortage of aviation specialists. Although its Air Force had 250 aircraft, it had only 41 trained pilots. Thus the Kalinovsk Aviation School was established to train pilots, and 40 people were sent to Turkey for additional training. Military training courses were set up in all the schools. Much attention was given to the training of newly formed units and the creation of a coordinated mutual-support system among the various military formations.

During the latter part of 1992, President Dudajev and the republic's military commander Denijev personally directed command and staff maneuvers. The theme of the maneuvers: "The call-up and bringing up to a state of readiness of the Military Forces, the Supreme Commander's Reserve, the Civil Guard Forces, the Security Forces, and the Self Defense Brigades in order to ensure the defense of the Republic against military aggression." Clearly the aggressor referred to in the maneuver scenario was Russia. For this exercise, the territory of Chechnya was divided into Central (the capital), Western, Eastern, and Southern Defense Zones. The National Guard, consisting of 62,000 people, also participated in these maneuvers. Its combat units, made up of

2,000 people each, were subdivided into formations similar to those of the regular army.[4]

By 1994, Dudajev and his supporters had succeeded in creating a sufficiently powerful national defense potential. The developing realities of the situation and the political, military, economic, and other factors affecting Chechnya, both internally and externally, had, however, forced changes of these earlier plans to a degree. In their final form, the Chechen armed forces came to consist of the regular army, the National Guard, the self-defense units, the presidential personal guard and personal guard units of the top military commanders, the armed formations of the Caucasus Nations' Confederation (the Borz special purpose battalion, the Abchaz battalion, and others were Chechen formations that had earlier fought in the Abhazija conflict and elsewhere), a separate special-purpose regiment under the command of the Internal Affairs Ministry, and the National Security Service's armed formations.

Tank, artillery, and antiaircraft artillery regiments were also formed within the armed forces, as well as a mountain infantry brigade, a Muslim "annihilation" brigade (an antidiversion, antiterrorist unit assigned to fight fifth-column subversion activity), two aviation training regiments, various special purpose units, and several training centers. The aviation regiments were deployed at Kalinovsk and Chankala Airports. Both aviation bases were defended by antiaircraft defense systems which consisted of ten Strela-10 surface-to-air missile systems, twenty-three other antiaircraft systems of various types, and seven Igla-1 portable antiaircraft weapons.

A National Security Service was organized and tasked to ensure the security of government officials. In the beginning, it was commanded by S. Chasimikov, then by Sultan Gelischanov. The service was subdivided into sections according to its five basic functions: foreign intelligence, counterintelligence, an internal security service, the presidential guard, and the regional Security Service commands. At its inception, this service consisted of 123 people, but later, at Dudajev's direction, it was reorganized by cutting the foreign intelligence and counterintelligence sections by almost half and by forming the Turnal combat operations detachment, a 30-man unit assigned with providing security for the highest government officials. After the reorganization, this detachment was to be enlarged to 160 people, but it was never brought up to full strength because of the shortage of appropriately trained specialists.[5] Most of the attention of the intelligence and counterintelligence sections was focused on the collation and analysis of intelligence information. Such information was provided by a large agent net. Later events indicated that the intelligence sections functioned very effectively.

Who Armed the Chechens?

When military activity began in Chechnya and Russia's federal forces met with fierce resistance, the question of who armed the Chechens quickly became one of the most relevant ones asked by the Russian press. Though different versions were suggested, there could be but one answer: to a large extent, Russia itself had armed the Chechens.[6]

By the beginning of 1992, few Russian military units were left in Chechnya. These were the 12th Motorized Rifle Training Division, the 173rd Regional Training Center, the Antiaircraft Defense Communications and Information Processing Center, the Armavir Military Aviation School's two air bases and military equipment warehouses, a radio communications detachment, a military hospital, medical equipment warehouses, and several other small units. The Russian Internal Affairs Ministry's 556th Convoy Regiment had also remained behind and was guarded by a Chechen OMON (Internal Affairs Ministry's Special Purpose Militia) unit.

According to official Russian information, the formations and units deployed on Chechen territory at that time had in their inventory 134 units of armored equipment (42 tanks, 34 armored personnel carriers, 14 armored vehicles, and various other equipment), 139 artillery guns and systems, 101 antitank weapon units, and 27 antiaircraft artillery guns and systems. They also had 426 aircraft, of which 5 were combat aircraft and 2 were combat helicopters. They had in their inventory 57,596 individual weapons, 27 railroad car loads of munitions, 3,050 tons of fuel and lubricants, 38 tons of military uniforms and ammunition, and 254 tons of stores. Even a number of Luna surface-to-surface rocket systems, having a range of 70 kilometers, were left, although these were without rockets and in disrepair.

When the organization of the armed forces was begun, one of the most pressing questions facing the Chechen Military High Command was how it was to arm its forces. For this reason, by the beginning of 1992, the Chechen High Command began to eye the Russian military forces still left in Chechnya and their equipment. On February 6–8, 1992, 4,000 weapons and 3 million rounds of ammunition were taken by force from various Russian military units. Three thousand more weapons and 3 million rounds of ammunition were also commandeered from the 556th Convoy Regiment. On February 7, the Chechens again took 554 automatic weapons, 494 pistols, 2 machine guns, 46 tons of munitions, 186 various types of motor vehicles, 40 tons of gasoline, and almost 20 railroad cars of food stores, uniforms, ammunition, and technical equipment from the various departments of the Armavir Military Aviation School.

Having foreseen the possibility of such self-help actions, the commander of the post-soviet Military Forces, Air Marshal Jevgeny Shaposhnikov, by his own admission, issued a directive instructing the Northern Caucasus Military Region's command to take measures to better safeguard its weapons and ordered the Land Army to relocate its weapons and combat equipment to central arsenals and weapons storage depots. A special commission, commanded by the assistant commander of the Northern Caucasus Military Region, General Igor Strogov, was appointed to negotiate the Russian Army's withdrawal from Chechnya with Dudajev.[7]

Not much could be removed in time, however. Only 2 antiaircraft artillery systems, 2 rocket control complexes, and 19,801 individual weapons are listed as having been evacuated. Almost everything else, about 80 percent, fell into Chechen hands. It is the prevailing opinion in Russia that the person most responsible for this result was Pavel Grachev, once he became minister of defense. On March 28, 1992, Grachev signed a directive, Nr. 316/1/0308s, obligating the Russian Army to transfer to Dudajev 50 percent of its weapons and equipment then still remaining in Chechnya.[8] But almost all of the other half of these weapons also fell into Chechen hands. Just as the evacuation of the Russian Army's weapons and equipment was begun, the Chechens succeeded in blocking off the aircraft transporting the weapons and the evacuation operation had to be called off.

Any further evacuation of weapons and equipment also became impossible because, by the end of February, 1992, almost all the enlisted troops, a large portion of its warrant officers,[9] and other officers had left their military units and scattered. Under the conditions then present in Chechnya, it became almost impossible to continue to remain in the army units. The Chechens blockaded all the military bases and began to shoot at them at night. They also issued constant threats and demands for the military units to give up their remaining weapons. Thus an inspection team arriving from Moscow at the 12th Motorized Rifle Division base found just a few officers and two soldiers remaining on the base. They also found the unit's combat equipment being guarded at each post by one Russian officer and two Chechens.[10]

In 1992, when Russia began its army's withdrawal from the Baltic states, an agreement had been made to transfer a part of the withdrawing army's military equipment and property to the armed forces of these newly independent countries. During their withdrawal, these army units had to give up possession of various buildings and other real estate to the new owners. The new owners on their part sought to ensure that such property would remain safeguarded and not be ransacked. Thus by mutual agreement between those receiving the property and the withdrawing army unit commands, a practice de-

veloped whereby both parties began to jointly guard the property to be transferred, with guards supplied by both sides. The commanders of the transfer-
ring military units were forced to agree to the new owners' demands for the
safeguarding of the property by guards from their own forces as ransacking
had become widespread. Seeking to profit from the transfer, Russian soldiers
were easily turning a good portion of the real estate into portable property by
selling off what could be removed to the local inhabitants. This same situation prevailed for a time in Lithuania as well. By early summer, 1992, there
were not enough Russian soldiers left in Chechnya to evacuate even a tenth
of the remaining combat weapons and equipment.

A part of the Russian military units' weapons and military equipment was
turned over to Chechnya officially. The other part, however, was taken by the
Chechens by force. Yet another version of how this came about allows that
a good part of the remaining military equipment and weapons was actually
transferred to the Chechens in return for certain payments. The conditions
being conducive, certain Russian officers apparently did not resist the temp-
tation to fill their own pockets with rather large sums of money and write off
the resulting shortages as the result of Chechen "robberies." [11]

By May, 1992, the largest part of Russia's in-theatre military units' weapons
and military equipment was already in Chechen hands. There was really nothing left for Russian defense minister Grachev to do but to issue orders to withdraw the Russian Army itself from Chechnya. The withdrawal of its practically
disarmed remaining units was completed by the end of the first half of 1992.

According to the Russian Military High Command's official information,
the Chechen armed forces were left 108 units of armored equipment (42 T-62
and T-72 tanks, 36 BMP-1 and BMP-2 armored personnel carriers, and 30
BTR-70 and BRDM-2 armored vehicles) and 153 artillery guns and mortars,
among them 18 BM-21 Grad rocket artillery systems and 30 old but powerful
122 mm D-30 howitzers. Besides these, 590 antitank weapons had been left
behind, among which were 2 portable Konkurs antitank units, 24 Fagot antitank missile control units, 51 Metis systems, and 113 RPG-7 handheld antitank
weapons.[12]

It is practically impossible to estimate how many firearms were left behind. Russian officers contend that this was 41,538 units: 18,832 AK-74 automatic weapons, 9,307 AKM automatic weapons, 533 Dragunov sniper rifles,
138 AGS-17 Plamia grenade launchers, 678 tank guns, 319 other large caliber
guns, and 10,581 pistols. It is even more difficult to calculate the munitions,
although it has been reported that left behind were not less than 740 rounds
for the antitank weapons, 1,000 82 mm rockets for the Grad rocket artillery
systems, 24,000 rounds for the D-30 howitzers, and about 200,000 hand

grenades. Large amounts of ammunition were also left: more than 11 million rounds of 5.45 mm, 2 million rounds of 7.62 mm, 500,000 rounds of 12.7 mm, and 140,000 rounds of 14.5 mm.

Under unexplained circumstances, the Armavir Aviation School also left behind all its aircraft at the Kalinovsk and Chankala air bases. At Kalinovsk, 39 L-39 training aircraft, 80 L-29 aircraft, 3 Mig-17 fighters, 2 Mig-15 fighters, 6 An-2 aircraft, and a number of Mi-8 military transport helicopters were left behind. At Chankala, the Chechens were left 72 L-39 and 69 L-29 aircraft. All the Czech-made L-39 and L-29 training aircraft were equipped with OB-16 weapons carriers (two each per aircraft, each weapons cassette being capable of holding 32 nonguided rocket rounds).

The weapons and military equipment obtained from the Russian forces were not Dudajev's military forces' only source of arms, however. A part of its heavy weapons were bought from Georgia and a part from former Soviet Union countries and other foreign states. A great amount of weapons also flowed into Chechnya without any control. During the 1992–93 period, Chechnya became a country through which large and small shipments of contraband weapons could be transported without any government regulation or interference. Automatic weapons and pistols could also be freely purchased at local marketplaces. That Chechens also bought weapons directly from factories in Russia itself is confirmed by the fact that in 1995, Russian federal troops often took from the Chechen fighters the newest manufactured Russian weapons and equipment as trophies. Such equipment had not yet been issued even to the Russian forces.[13]

According to the calculations of military experts, the weapons and ammunition left the Chechens by the Russians were sufficient for at least several weeks of intensive armed conflict. It was already clear in 1992 that such conflict would occur, as the reestablishment of independence from a colonial empire is almost never possible without an armed struggle. Even when independence is finally achieved, the new state's inviolability and its continued existence depends to a large measure on the guarantees of security provided it by its own armed forces. For this reason, Dudajev and his followers took all possible means to strengthen Chechnya's armed forces.

It was easiest to strengthen its forces by obtaining weapons from Russia. The conditions for this were extremely favorable, as Russia became filled to the brim with various weapons and military equipment after the withdrawal of the former Soviet Army from the countries of the defunct Warsaw Pact and from Lithuania, Latvia, and Estonia. In January, 1992, Russian president Yeltsin signed a decree by which the Russian Federation accepted full responsibility for the fate of the USSR's army and for all its property and weapons. But there had been no place left in Russia to store all the weapons, and the best alternative, of course, was to sell them off.

Allusions are made every so often to the fact that Russia actually signed an agreement with Dudajev for him to act as its intermediary for the sale of arms. Payment for services was to be made in the form of weapons deliveries to Chechnya. Dudajev has also been accused more than once in various publications of creating a criminal regime in Chechnya and of machinations involving the illegal sale of oil and weapons. Several of the versions pertaining to the sale of arms are interesting.

It is known that Russia's Internal Affairs Ministry accused the Chechens of organizing more than 900 raids against freight trains from the beginning of 1992 to August, 1994, during which time 6,498 railroad cars and containers were allegedly ransacked. Such accusations also intimate that this had been done with Dudajev's acquiescence. By Dudajev's order, from 1992 the transport militia along the railroad route through Chechnya was made no longer subordinate to the Russian Federation's Ministry of Internal Affairs. The function of guarding train traffic against robbers was assigned to Dudajev's assistants, who apparently took advantage of their delegated powers. At one time, the infamous Shamil Basajev, considered in Russia to be one of the greatest of terrorists, was responsible for this police function.

But robberies were often only a cover for what were, in fact, only illegal business transactions. Although robbery was written into the official documents, these were most often deliveries made by previous agreement. Who was sending what cargo and to whom was known only by a select few. Not without reason, all the 600 charges of train robbery that were filed continued to remain only on paper.[14] Criminal actions were filed, the appropriate formalities were taken, but further investigatory and prosecutorial actions were not pursued.

Part 2

The First Period of the War in Chechnya

CHAPTER 3

The First Stage of the War

The subject of the existence of a secret war in Chechnya is talked about very unwillingly in official Russian government circles. Little information can be found in the press either, as few have dared to speak about it openly. But what occurred has been impossible to hide, and by degrees, the cloak of secrecy that covered the beginnings of the war in Chechnya is being withdrawn.

When the decision was first made to use force in Chechnya, it was thought that it would be relatively easy to deal with the disobedient Chechen president Dudajev. The Federal Counterintelligence Service (formerly KGB) and the Russian Army General Staff's Intelligence Command (formerly GRU) reported that Dudajev's forces were as yet insufficiently organized and were not ready to resist a larger armed force. They also reported that Dudajev's regime was undergoing a serious crisis, that his government's control did not reach outside of Grozni, and that the presidential palace itself did not control much of anything. According to their information, the elders and the Chechen Army were dissatisfied with Dudajev and it would only be necessary to blow a little to cause his regime to collapse.

The same opinion was expressed in Moscow by Ruslan Khasbulatov after a visit to Chechnya. His purpose, however, was to return to a high position in government, which he had lost after he, together with Aleksander Ruskoj, had organized a putsch against Yeltsin. Released from jail after six months, Khasbulatov intended to start from Chechnya, where he was working in tandem with the opposition. Khasbulatov convinced the Russian president's Chief of Administration Filatov and the commander of the presidential guard, General Aleksander Korzhakov, who had been rumored to control the Russian Federation more than President Yeltsin, that Labazanov's and Gantemirov's armed formations would be sufficient to deal with Dudajev and his people. Of course, these opposition formations were as yet poorly armed and lacked training. For this reason, they needed to be strengthened with additional tanks, armored vehicles, aircraft, helicopters, and Russian crews.[1]

In October, 1994, Russian defense minister Pavel Grachev, executing President Yeltsin's instructions, issued orders that a General Staff Work Group be formed. He ordered it to prepare possible alternative scenarios for the use of armed force in Chechnya, including an incursion by Russian Army forces into Chechnya and the specification of further military actions while on Chechen territory. Appointed to this group were the General Staff's Operations Command's generals and officers. Besides other matters, this group was to coordinate the activities of the Federal Counterintelligence Service, the Ministry of Internal Affairs, the Border Army Command, and the Ministry of Defense in the Northern Caucasus Military Region during the planning and preparation stages of the incursion operation. The group was also tasked to collect and analyze information as to the strength of the Chechen armed forces, their deployment locations, and the arms available to them.

The Operations Command's assistant to the commander, General Lieutenant Anatoli Kvashnin, was appointed as leader of the group. The chief of the General Staff, General Colonel Mikhail Kolesnikov, also signed a directive obligating the staff of the Northern Caucasus Military Region to supplement the region's military units by means of a mobilization. The units were short of people and equipment.[2]

While considering the possible alternatives to the use of armed force in Chechnya, the Federal Counterintelligence Service suggested an intermediate variant: that the insertion of the Russian forces into Chechnya be done under the cover and with the assistance of the opposition. The opposition's armed forces were to storm Dudajev's headquarters; then, having taken the Chechen capital, the puppet Chechen Republic National Liberation Government was to legalize by special decree the Russian Regular Army's incursion into the republic's territory. Dzhochar Dudajev was to repeat the fate of Hafizullah Amin, who was shot in the presidential palace during the storming of Kabul.

To insure that the storming of Grozni would be successful, it would be necessary temporarily to strengthen the opposition's armed forces with armored vehicles and equipment and with crews made up of "volunteers" serving "under contract." It would also be necessary to support such combat operation with military helicopters and close air support aircraft. That it would be necessary to significantly strengthen the opposition's armed formations was indicated by their two previous attempts to attack Grozni, in October and in early November, which had ended in failure.[3]

Russian soldiers were recruited for this operation secretly. Only a few high-ranking military officials were even aware that an attack on Grozni was under preparation. For example, in mid-November, 1994, a military counter-intelligence officer reported to the Moscow Military Region's chief of staff, L. Zolotov, that an IL-76 aircraft was being prepared at Chkalov Airport to transport Russian officers to Chechnya. Upon receipt of such information, the Military Region's Commander ordered that an investigation be conducted immediately. It was then discovered that this flight was to carry tank officers from the Kamtemirov 4th Tank Division and from the Detached Motorized Rifle Brigade deployed at Serzen. All the officers had orders granting them vacation leaves. The commander of the military region ordered that the flight be terminated and that the officers return to their units.[4]

Recruitment was conducted under the direction of the assistant director of the Federal Counterintelligence Service (FCS) together with the commander of the FCS's command for Moscow and the Moscow district, General Major J. Savostjanov, and the Commander of FCS's Command for Fighting Terrorism, General Lieutenant A. Semionov.[5]

Most of the soldiers being recruited were from the Russian Land Army's elite formations and units: the Kamtemirov 4th Tank, the Tuman 2nd Motorized Rifle, the Tula 106th Paratroop Divisions, and a Brigade deployed in Teploje Stane, one of the regions of Moscow. Helicopter crews were recruited from military air bases near Moscow, including the Kaluga Air Base.

In recruiting the soldiers, FCS officers attempted to explain to them that Dudajev's regime was barely holding on, that his supporters were very poorly armed, that it would not be difficult to establish order in Chechnya, and that it would only be necessary to insert tanks and armored vehicles into Grozni. The recruits were told that they would not undergo any great risk and that they would be well paid. Each was promised an advance of 1 million rubles; for participation in an operation, an additional 5 million rubles; for a successful operation, 3 million more; for the knocking out of an enemy firing position, 3 million more; for the knocking out of a tank or an armored vehicle, 3 million more; and for the destruction of a self-propelled artillery gun, 5 million more rubles. In case of death, it was agreed contractually that the deceased's family would be paid 130 million rubles.

As this was significant money and as the payment of regular salaries within the army had already been delayed three months and more, the recruitment was sufficiently successful. Contracts were signed in the Tumanes

Division by 2 soldiers being transferred to the reserve; in the Kantemirov Division by 53 soldiers; in the Vystrel Advanced Officer Course by 8 officers and junior officers and by two junior officers being transferred to the reserve; and in the 18th Motorized Rifle brigade by 4 officers, 6 junior officers, and 3 soldiers. All these soldiers were tankers.[6] The dispatch of the recruited soldiers to Mozdok from the Chkalovsk Air Base near Moscow was commanded by the assistant to the minister for nationalities and regional political matters, General A. Kotenkov.

Without a doubt, divisional and other unit commanders knew that their soldiers were being recruited. A few had even attempted to protest but were told to keep quiet. Later when such secret recruitment came to light after the unsuccessful assault of Grozni, only one of them, the commander of the Kantemirov 4th Tank Division, General Major Boris Poliakov, put in a request that he be released to the reserve in protest against the use of his soldiers in a secret operation.[7]

Tank crews were formed in Mozdok at the Arsenal base, where forty brand-new tanks from the Northern Caucasus Military Region awaited them. Because of secrecy requirements, until the very start of the operation, the Russian units temporarily formed for the assault of Grozni made all their preparations at the Mozdok Military Base. Fifteen crews were organized using Russian soldiers, the rest using Chechens from Avturchanov's and Gantemirov's formations. By November, 1994, the opposition, with Russian support, already had approximately two hundred armored vehicles and tanks.

Minister Grachev and Defense Ministry officials continued to deny the participation of Russian soldiers on the side of the opposition in the war with the Chechen government forces, as well as any assistance of weapons or equipment to the opposition or even the constant flow of its own emissaries to the Temporary Council's Headquarters in the community of Znamenskoja. Even after the unsuccessful assault of Grozni when recruited Russian soldiers held prisoner were exhibited on television, Russian defense minister Grachev held to the line that they most likely had been recruited by the opposition itself and that there were no such soldiers in Russian Army rosters.[8]

The Opposition Attacks Grozni

Early on November 26, 1994, the opposition's armed forces, augmented by Russian soldiers and combat equipment and supported by Russian Military Aviation, began what they thought would be the decisive assault on Grozni. On the eve of the assault, a large group of Russian officers arrived at the military base in Mozdok. It was even mentioned that among them was the Russian Army's chief of the general staff, General Colonel Mikhail Kolesnikov. The assault took place simultaneously from three directions: from Tolstoi Jurt, from Argun, and from Urus Martan. More than 150 armored vehicles, 20 howitzers, 40 combat helicopters and aircraft, and 2,500 infantry participated in the assault.

Although it is still contended that the operation was commanded by opposition leaders Avturchanov and Gantemirov, more and more information indicates that the real commander was the previously mentioned assistant to the minister of nationalities and regional political matters, General Kotenkov, until then tasked with looking after the contracted personnel sent to Mozdok. The operation was also planned by Russia's Ministry of Defense, and the combat activities were commanded by the assistant commander of the 8th Army Corps, V. Zhukov.[9]

The opposition apparently expected an easy victory. Much hope was placed in the fact that Dudajev would not expect such large numbers of armored vehicles and equipment to participate in the attack. The 42-43 tank assault group formed up by the Russian Army moved out from Mozdok in the direction of Grozni only the morning of November 25 and received its orders and duty assignments on the eve of the assault while in the Tolstoi Jurt region.

It was planned to insert the armored vehicles and equipment, supported on the ground by infantry and from the air by helicopters, into the city. They were then to take up combat positions near the presidential palace, the Government, Security and Internal Affairs Ministry buildings, the television complex, and the newspaper complexes. It was expected that Dudajev's regime would then collapse. But things did not happen as planned. The armored vehicles attacked in column formation, but the opposition's infantry, being transported in buses, cars, and trucks, wound up not in front of the armored columns but to their rear. The helicopters also did not show up at the agreed-upon time.

The first armed confrontations occurred on the outskirts of Grozni that morning at about seven o'clock. By nine o'clock, one of the columns had already forced its way into the city, but then, almost immediately, two tanks were knocked out and the crews of the other three tanks surrendered and were taken prisoner.

It should not come as a surprise that the attackers succeeded with relative ease to take the National Security and Internal Affairs Ministry buildings, the television complex, and the presidential palace. Immediately, the opposition declared its victory, although this proved to be somewhat premature. They found the presidential palace empty. The Chechen president and his primary forces had redeployed to the capital's Oktiabrsk district.

Dudajev was prepared for the assault of Grozni. The night before, his intelligence chief had laid on his desk the opposition's maps for the assault, which had also contained notes regarding the attackers' planned moves and the distribution of their forces during this operation. Dudajev decided on a very risky move: to allow the armored vehicles and equipment to enter the city, then to surround and destroy them. It was easier to do this within the city than on its outskirts since in the city, antitank grenade launchers could be used much more effectively, especially if fire was opened up suddenly and from short distances.[10]

In making the decision, Grozni's particularities were taken into consideration. The Sunzha River flows through the city, dividing it into two parts. In order for the two parts of the city to communicate with each other, ten bridges were constructed to allow for the movement of motor vehicles and foot traffic. Another bridge was built to enable trains to cross the river. With the exception of the very center of the city, buildings were not very densely laid out. But in the center of the city, four- to ten-story buildings of concrete slab or monolith construction predominated. They had furnished basements that could easily be adapted into good defensive positions, all the more so as most of them housed government administrative agencies and community organizations. With the exception of several new housing projects, the rest of the city was made up of one-story buildings. Also significant was the fact that the center of the city was inhabited primarily by Russians while the rest was lived in by Chechens.

The Chechen General Staff set up an ambush in the center of the city. Dudajev's snipers positioned themselves on buildings adjoining those that were to be taken over by the opposition while antitank grenade launcher marksmen established themselves in their top floors and basements.

The battles that broke out that morning reached their fiercest point at about eleven o'clock as the armored columns reached the city's center. The opposition's tanks soon began to be enveloped in flames from such unexpected opposing fire, and its soldiers began falling from sniper bullets. The Chechen opposition's soldiers accompanying the armored columns apparently were not prepared to do serious battle. Instead of regrouping, they scattered in small groups throughout the city and soon were busy with more personal matters, mostly the ransacking of retail stores. The armored columns were left with almost no infantry support. The Russian soldiers became disorientated, as they too had not expected serious fighting. Besides, they had not even received specific combat assignments: they had been simply ordered to wait once they reached the center of the city.

Later, after they had been taken prisoner, Russian soldiers recounted that they were stunned into inaction when a tank showed up in front of them and suddenly opened fire. They had been told that Dudajev's forces did not have any tanks; therefore, it had not even dawned on them that the tank was not one of their own.

Not having made use of their apparent preliminary military success, the opposition forces were forced to withdraw. After seven hours of continuous fighting, the confrontations in the city quieted down.

Upon his return to the presidential palace, Dudajev announced that the aggression against the capital of the independent Chechen Republic had been repulsed. He had ample proof to charge Russia with aggression: among those taken into captivity were 68 Russian troops in ranks from enlisted man to major. In summing up the action, the Chechen government later reported that during the assault of Grozni, 32 tanks and 5 armored vehicles belonging to the opposition forces were destroyed and 12 more were taken as trophies. Four helicopters and 1 aircraft were also knocked down. Opposition losses included 300 troops killed and 200 taken prisoner. As to its own losses, the Chechen government reported only very minimal casualties.[11]

Some contend that, besides the Chechen government's regular forces, some 30,000 volunteers participated in the defense of Grozni. Although a head count could hardly have been made at the time, undeniably the assault of Grozni was expected and many volunteers gathered in the city from the surrounding cities and villages, especially when the confrontations with the opposition forces became more frequent. This especially occurred two days before the assault, after the Grozni Airport was bombed and groups of opposition troops began to block the majority of the roads leading into Grozni.

Judging from information appearing in the press, on the eve of the assault of Grozni, the relative strengths of the forces of both sides according to their numbers of heavy combat equipment were about equal. The opposition forces had more tanks and armored vehicles (the opposition forces had 200 tanks available while Dudajev's forces had 130) but fewer artillery guns and mortars. But during the Grozni operation, such general comparisons could have had little significance, as only a part of the Chechen government's combat equipment had been concentrated in the capital. The opposition also sent only a part of its available forces into Grozni. Although no exact figures are available, it is clear that the attacking force was clearly superior in the numbers of tanks and armored vehicles it had available. The basic advantage possessed by Dudajev and his supporters was in the numbers of fighters (about 40,000 – 42,000 government troops and volunteers) who participated in the action and in the numbers of individual firearms and grenade launchers available. This, in essence, was the deciding factor in the choice of tactics for the defense of Grozni. Dudajev's main objective was to destroy the attacking side's tanks and armored vehicles.

In repulsing the attack, tanks and armored vehicles were lit on fire using grenade launchers, regular antitank grenades, and Molotov cocktails. The Afghanistani Modzechadeen had taught Dudajev's troops how to fight against tanks and armored vehicles by attaching a napalm charge to a regular antitank grenade. Once the grenade exploded on the targeted vehicle, the napalm would be ignited and the burning liquid would make its way into the vehicle and set off the ammunition stores inside, destroying the vehicle.

Gazavat (holy war) fighters were also important in the defense of Grozni. These were kamikaze troops, volunteers who wore green bands around their heads. As many as eight of these fighters intentionally fell under the tracks of tanks and, while dying, blew up opposition tanks.[12]

Visiting Grozni in early December, Lithuanian parliamentary member Algirdas Patackas reported that, based on Chechen information, of the 67 tanks that entered the city, 43 were destroyed and 22 were captured by the Chechens. Thirty-five hundred opposition troops participated in the assault of Grozni. It was defended by only 300, according to the Chechens.

The leader of the Temporary Council, Salambek Chadzhijev, evaluated the assault group's actions somewhat differently. According to him, the attack was actually quite successful. Even the television tower was taken and held until morning. The Chechen opposition detachment formed up in Volgograd achieved the most success. They took the KGB building, but when they did not receive reinforcements after two hours, they abandoned it, taking with them a number of important documents, which they later turned over to their "ordering party." According to Chadzhijev, the assault failed because it was not adequately supported: the Russians failed to provide the 500 special-purpose troops that they had promised.

The overthrow organized by Russia had not succeeded. In evaluating the tactics used by the opposition forces while at the same time denying the Russian Army's participation in the assault, Russian defense minister Grachev stated that he never would have advised the use of tanks and artillery within a city, as that for him was the height of nonprofessionalism. According to him, several hours and one paratroop regiment would have sufficed for Russian military professionals to take the presidential palace.[13] This statement would later cost the lives of thousands of Russian soldiers.

It is now becoming obvious that the time chosen by the opposition for the assault of Grozni had not been convenient for the Kremlin and that insufficient preparations for it had been undertaken. Perhaps Russia would have been able to achieve its goals through the opposition had it not been feared that Ruslan Khasbulatov would then be able to take power in Chechnya without spilling blood. Events were speeded up in order to prevent this from happening. Khasbulatov's influence in Chechnya at that time had begun to strengthen appreciably, although he was not at all acceptable to Yeltsin.

The victory of the Chechen government's forces in Grozni was important from more than a political standpoint. For the Chechen High Command, the victory was also important in that it confirmed the correctness of the defense tactics that it had chosen. The Chechens had made use of the German army's experience in defending Berlin during World War II, adapting partisan warfare elements. This was in fact a new tactic for the defense of a city not written up in any of the tactical manuals or treatises published in the Soviet Union or in the Russian Federation. The Chechens would successfully use it many more times against a significantly more powerful enemy. The Chechens were becoming convinced that ambushes, antitank grenade launcher marksmen, and snipers were a very effective means of doing battle with armored columns in the streets of a city.

The Situation after the Failed Assault on Grozni

Having suffered a defeat, the opposition's forces withdrew to their primary dislocation areas. Although Khasbulatov, as one of the members of the Temporary Council, continued to threaten new assaults, these threats gradually died down. Further assaults were not repeated.

The assault's failure was especially felt in the opposition's capital, the community of Znamenskoja. Many of the opposition's troops began to lean in Dudajev's direction. The largest opposition group, headed by Avturchanov, still had sufficient forces and enough combat equipment to mount another military operation, but most of the opposition's leaders could not bring themselves to make such a decision. After the bombing of Grozni, that became impossible, as the Chechens would have considered them all traitors.

Disagreements also began to develop between the Temporary Council's leaders. Avturchanov, chief of the Nadterechno region, blamed the failure of the assault on Khasbulatov, accusing him of twice having split the opposition. According to Avturchanov, the first time had been in September, 1994, when, prior to the military assault, Khasbulatov took on the role of peacemaker. Opposition leaders Gantemirov and Labazanov had supported him. Gantemirov refused to participate in the assault, and Labazanov refused to obey the Temporary Council. The second time was in November, when Khasbulatov warned Dudajev of the tank assault and the pending air strikes. Using appeals and announcements over the radio, he also warned the people of Grozni.[14]

Grozni was relatively calm after the assault. Thousands of people continued to gather daily at public meetings held in the square in front of the presidential palace, demanding that the armed opposition be finished off. Dudajev also continued to issue demands that Russia officially admit that it participated in the organization of the overthrow and sent its troops, weaponry, and combat equipment into Chechnya. If Russia refused to make such an admission, Dudajev threatened to execute the Russian soldiers then being held prisoner.

The situation changed somewhat after the proclamation of Russian President Yeltsin's ultimatum of November 29. The opposition was already unable to take more active measures.[15] The Nadterechno region quieted down, and Gantemirov, one of the leaders of the Temporary Council, announced that the opposition was terminating further military actions against Dudajev. The opposition's armed formations at the community of Urus Martan scattered, a part of them withdrawing to the opposition's capital in Znamenskoja. A delegation of inhabitants from Urus Martan also made a visit to Chechnya's chief of the general staff, Aslan Maschadov, and offered him their services in organizing the defense of the republic.

CHAPTER 4

Preparations for Military Operations in Chechnya

After the opposition's armed forces' unsuccessful campaign in Grozni and their wholly unexpected shattering defeat, Moscow needed several days to reevaluate the situation and to make new decisions as to what future actions should be taken. The Russian government also had to put aside the press, radio, and television announcements that it had prepared in advance about the opposition's victory.

Having lost its secret war, Russia had no alternative but to use open force. All other alternatives had been dismissed earlier when it had been decided that no other means but force was able to influence the inflexible President Dudajev, who apparently had no intentions of giving up the idea of independence for Chechnya. For this reason, the plans prepared earlier for the open use of Russian armed forces in Chechnya were pulled out of the safes at the Defense Ministry and hurriedly finalized.

The Russian Federation Security Council's decision, made at a meeting held on November 29, 1994, to disarm the Chechen armed formations by force was only a formality. The Defense Ministry's plans were reportedly submitted and confirmed at the meeting. They called for actions in two stages: first, the blockade of Grozni, and, second, the disarming of the Chechen armed formations and the setting up of a local administration.

Whether such a meeting of the Security Council actually took place is highly doubtful. Well-informed sources report that only the proponents of the use of force participated in discussions with the president regarding the situation in Chechnya. Some of them were not even members of the Security Council. The decision to use force was made by a group of people from the president's innermost circle, and the information announced in the press about a meeting of the National Security Council was only a cover story intended to hide the real organizers of the war in Chechnya.[1]

Russian President Yeltsin made a decision about the actions to be taken in Chechnya and issued an ultimatum that same day, the Russian government's most uncompromising pronouncement to date. Yeltsin demanded that within 48 hours the participants in the armed conflict in Chechnya cease fire, lay down their arms, disband their armed formations, and release all persons then being held prisoner. Upon a failure to abide by these terms, martial law would be instituted in the territory of the Chechen Republic and all means available to the Russian government would be used to stop the further spilling of blood; to defend the lives, civil rights, and freedoms of Russia's citizens; and to reestablish constitutional justice, order, and peace in Chechnya. Yeltsin also stressed that armed confrontations in Chechnya were increasing and that the warring parties were beginning to introduce mercenaries from foreign countries into the conflict.[2]

Of the two sides to the armed conflict, only Russia had supplied weapons and equipment and had actively participated in armed aggression against the forces of the Chechen government. But there could be little doubt about which illegal armed formations were being referred to in the ultimatum. Dudajev's forces were the sole target. But the ultimatum signed by Yeltsin succeeded in preserving the continuity of the Russian political policies that had been previously set concerning Dudajev.

The day following the ultimatum's announcement, the president of the Russian Federation signed a decree, Nr. 2137s, authorizing the formation of a group that was to direct the disarming and liquidation of the "illegal armed formations," establish martial law in Chechnya, and look after its enforcement. Pavel Grachev was appointed the group's chairman. Minister of Nationalities and Regional Political Matters Jegorov; the head of the government's Customs Committee, A. Kruglov; minister of Internal Affairs Viktor Jerin; assistant minister of Internal Affairs and commander of the Internal Affairs Ministry's Armed Forces Anatoli Kulikov; commander of the Border Armed Forces A. Nikolajev; assistant to the prosecutor general V. Panichev; assistant to the minister of Foreign Affairs B. Pastuchov; general director of the Federal Agency assigned to the Presidency Responsible for Government Communications and Information A. Starovoitov; director of the Federal Counterintelligence Service Sergei Stepashin; chairman of the Federal Parliamentary Federation's Council's Committee for Security and Defense Matters

P. Shirshov; and chairman of the Parliament's Federal Parliamentary Federation's Defense Committee S. Jushenkov, were appointed as its members.

The group's chairman, Defense Minister Grachev, was granted wide authority by this decree. His directives and orders were to be obeyed by the executive government, the Internal Affairs and Counterintelligence (security) branches, the Internal Affairs Armed Forces, the Border Army, and all the enterprises, organizations, agencies, and officials participating in the operation in the Chechen Republic. Thus authorized to coordinate the actions of both the executive government's federal agencies and the government's forces tasked with ensuring security, while executing the operational plan and holding officials responsible, even to the point of removing them from their posts where necessary, Grachev had the right to use almost unlimited force in Chechnya.[3]

The same day, the Russian General Staff completed the coordination of its operations plan with the Ministry of Internal Affairs. Primary roles for the execution of the plan were assigned to the Internal Affairs Ministry's Armed Forces and the forces of the Northern Caucasus Military Region. The Russian General Staff planned during the assault and takeover of Grozni to use special units of the National Security Command to capture Dudajev and the people of his inner circle. The active use of military close air support aircraft and combat helicopters to suppress strong points and firing positions in this mountainous region was also included in the plan.

The military campaign was to be executed in four stages:[4] During the first stage and by December 6, Land Army and Internal Affairs Ministry assault groups were to be organized. They were to operate from three operating bases: Mozdok, Vladikaukaz, and Kizliar. Close air support aircraft and combat helicopters were to be deployed by December 1 to air bases closest to Chechnya. During this first stage, the Military Air Forces would be tasked with blockading Chechen air space.

During the second stage, December 7–9, three assault groups were to enter Chechnya along seven lines of march and blockade Grozni. Besides this internal perimeter ring, they were also to establish an external blockade along Chechnya's administrative borders. The Internal Affairs Ministry's forces were assigned the task of safeguarding movement and other communications along the lines of march and assuring the security of military forces during their entry into Chechen territory. The Federal Counterintelligence Service together with the Internal Affairs Ministry's special units were to locate and isolate Chechen government leaders and any opposition party leaders capable of leading armed attacks and diversions in the Federal Army's rear areas. The actions of military forces on the ground were to be supported by air strikes.

During the third stage, December 10 –13, federal Land Army units, attacking from the north and south, were to take the presidential palace, the government buildings, the television and radio buildings, and other important installations. After that, they were to continue disarming the Chechen armed formations and collecting their weapons and combat equipment.

The fourth and last stage of the Chechen military operation was to involve the stabilization of the situation using military forces and the transfer of the occupied territory within the next five to ten days to the control of the Internal Affairs Ministry's Army.

The preparation and planning of the operation was assigned to the commander of the Northern Caucasus Military Region. He was ordered to complete its detailed planning by December 5. The directive issued to the regional commander instructed, among other things, that he pay special attention to coordination between the units and ensure that the command was uninterrupted during all stages of the operation; ensure the thorough planning of the upcoming combat operations and its supply; organize the preparation of the troops, weapons, and equipment for the operation to a high level; pay special attention to the preparation of the troops for operations in large urban communities; ensure aircraft and artillery fire correction; ensure the readiness of supply units for the march; supply the troops with bulletproof vests, helmets, and warm winter clothing; ensure the necessary rear area support for the supply of front line units during the preparations for the operation and its execution; and organize and ensure medical care for the troops, paying special attention to the search for wounded, their evacuation, and the supply of medical assistance.[5]

It is now clear that such a military operation plan lacked reality. The Russian armed forces were simply not prepared to put it into action, and this was well understood by Russian defense minister Grachev. When the Russian president expressed doubts as to whether the Internal Affairs Ministry's troops were capable of accomplishing the tasks assigned them, Grachev simply assigned the primary role in the operation to his own paratroop forces.[6]

In reality, the situation in the Internal Affairs Forces was unenviable. According to its commander, now himself minister of Internal Affairs, General Lieutenant Kulikov, salaries to officers were being paid two to three months late. The Internal Affairs Army had only 50 percent of its allocation of weapons and equipment. Only certain units were in a better condition, having up to 80 percent of their planned weapons and equipment allotment. There were no fewer problems with unit personnel staffing. Officer and warrant officer ranks were filled only to 80 percent, enlisted and noncommissioned ranks only up to 62 percent. Reforms changing the Internal Affairs Army's function and structure were incomplete. Previously tasked primarily with guarding government installations, the Internal Affairs Army was reoriented to operational activity and its structures began to be dominated by operational units, fast reaction teams, and special purpose detachments. Its tactical and combat training changed accordingly.

The situation was not much better in the Defense Ministry's Armed Forces. This was confirmed by Grachev himself. Ten days prior to the start of the military campaign, he signed a top secret directive, Nr. D-0010, entitled "Concerning the state of readiness of the Russian Federation's Armed Forces and the correction measures to be taken for 1995."[7] The defense minister's conclusions were unequivocal: the Russian Army was unprepared for combat actions.

Noted in the directive was deep dissatisfaction with the army's level of mobilization readiness, serious failures in operational and combat actions planning, and the inability of various commanders and staffs to supply accurate argumentation for the correctness of their decisions. The defense minister expressed especially serious concerns for the low officer preparedness at the division, regiment, and battalion levels and for the poor training of troops. Maneuvers were being held under superficial conditions and with the assumption that all units are fully staffed and supplied with full complements of weapons, equipment, and necessary emergency supplies. The reality was that even the best formed units rarely had even 70 percent of the troops called for by their allotment. Most units had hardly 20–30 percent of their draftees. The shortage of junior officers was catastrophic. Bad living conditions, failure to pay wages on time, and rampant corruption in the army was forcing the best-trained officers to leave the military service to seek work in commercial ventures or at some other better-paid employment.

The Northern Caucasus Military Region's readiness was also evaluated in the directive. During the planning of the campaign, this military region was assigned the primary operations role. According to the evaluation report:

> The majority of the officers are not only unfamiliar with the combat readiness requirements set out by the controlling documents, they do not even know their personal assignments or what they are supposed to do during peacetime or war.
>
> The officers on watch in the majority of the inspected formations and units are poorly trained to take practical actions in response to combat command messages. Their instructions and other controlling documents are prepared in gross violation of General Staff requirements.
>
> Matters concerning the operational dispersion of the army's forces have practically not been made a part of their routine.

The military command sections have not been able to avoid superficiality in the planning and command of its army's use in regional armed conflicts.

The officers' professional readiness level is falling. For the most part, it is based on outdated views regarding the appropriate use of military formations and does not always reflect the real situation or changes in its formations' composition and supply in a combat situation when the tendency is for these to decrease.

In spite of such dire evaluations, Pavel Grachev and the other armed forces' commanders did not swerve from their concurrence with the decision to go ahead with the military operation. There is no adequate answer for this. Only one thing remains without doubt: compared with even combat-unready Russian forces, the Chechen armed forces apparently were still considered insignificant enough and could be played with. Besides, even in the worst case, there would always be the elite units available, and Russia certainly had tanks and other combat equipment in abundance.

The Russian Federal Army Deployed Near Chechnya

The deployment of Russian Federal Army units was begun on November 30. The haste was unfortunate, as clearly there had not yet been sufficient time to complete the operation's detailed planning. Grachev apparently had so few doubts that the operation would be approved at the highest levels that he decided not to linger. He ordered the preparations to proceed without waiting for official approval. Certain units had already begun their preparations in October and November.[8]

The airports at Mozdok and Beslan became the primary deployment bases for the assault force. A separate special purpose battalion tasked with intelligence functions was airlifted to Beslan. A Federal Counterintelligence Service Intelligence Group was already operating on Chechen territory. All intelligence units were placed under the command of Colonel A. Chramchenkov, who earlier had commanded the same battalion on Yugoslavian territory. A supply group was also sent.

The Internal Affairs Ministry's special Vitiaz detachment also arrived at Mozdok. This elite unit's primary mission was the performance of special missions under extreme operating conditions, such as when fighting terrorism or freeing hostages. There was, however, nothing unusual about the Russian government's decision to use it in Chechnya, and in fact it was the most appropriate unit to be tasked with the capture of Dudajev and to ensure his destruction. This was borne out by the unit's history.[9]

The detachment was created in 1978, when, by order of the commander of the Internal Affairs Army, a special-purpose training company was formed.

The company's tasking was expanded when "hot points" developed in the Soviet Union. In 1988, it was used in Sumgaiti and Baku. As the Soviet Union began to tear itself apart, these "hot points" increased in number and the company was expanded into a battalion. In 1989, it saw action in Baku, Fergena, Novi Uzenii, and Kizliar. In 1990, it was deployed to Stepanakert, Nachicevani, Jerevan, Tbilisi, and Suchumi.

When the Russian Federation left the Soviet Union, the Russian Ministry of Internal Affairs changed the battalion's organization only slightly. In May, 1991, it was reorganized into a special purpose detachment and given the name Vitiaz. Its tasking was not changed, as there were also sufficient "hot points" in the "new" Russia. In 1991, it was sent to Cchinvali, Grozni, and Vladikaukaz. In 1992, it was deployed to Machachkla, Nazran, and Nalchik; in 1993, it was again deployed to Vladikaukaz. This time it was to Chechnya.

That same day (November 30), the Russian General Staff's Operations Group, tasked with coordinating the activities of the Defense Ministry's units and the Internal Affairs Army in this operation, was brought to Mozdok. It was commanded by the Operations Command's assistant commander, General Lieutenant L. Shevcov. The group consisted of the chiefs and officers of the operations, intelligence, and organization-mobilization commands.[10] Measures were also quickly taken to return from Chechnya to their units in Russia the soldiers who had previously been recruited and had participated in combat operations on the opposition side.

In Russia, the Headquarters of the Paratroop Forces was put on alert status. A special work regime was instituted and the headquarters guard was strengthened. The headquarters commander, General Colonel Vladimir Beliajev, was assigned to head the planning for the use of paratroop forces in the military operation. General Lieutenant Chindarov, who had gained experience while commanding paratroop units in the Ossetian-Ingushian conflict, was assigned as operational commander.[11]

Combined regiments were hurriedly formed in each of the Paratroop Forces' divisions. The combined regiment was a new formation to Russian Army practice, with the possible exception of the revolutionary period. However, even the Paratroop Forces, which Grachev had attempted to shelter the most, had fallen into such a state of unreadiness that no other course was available. Real combat actions required at least somewhat capable units. But such regiments and battalions were not available even in the elite Paratroop Forces.

Thus companies were formed out of battalions, battalions out of regiments, and combined regiments from divisions, selecting from each at least somewhat capable soldiers and officers. For this reason, the formation of combined regiments was not left even to the division commanders. The assistant commanders of the Paratroop Forces were sent down to the divisions personally. Paratroop Forces assistant commander Zimin organized a combined regiment within the Pskov division, and the same type of regiment was formed by General Sigutkin in the Tula division. The Paratroop Forces Operations Group being formed was also augmented by two paratroop brigades, one of which was from Volgodonsk. It had been ordered that each combined paratroop regiment was to have 1,000–1,500 troops. The Paratroop Forces Operations Group was to consist of about 6,000 troops.[12]

On December 1, AN-12 aircraft carrying paratroopers began to land at the Mozdok and Beslan Airports. Columns of tanks, armored vehicles, artillery guns, field kitchens, and transport vehicles also began to move toward the Federal Forces staging areas. A unit of military doctors arrived in Mozdok from Moscow.

In the three regions bordering Chechnya, Russia began to form the Mozdok, Vladikaukaz, and Chasavjurt Assault Groups. These were made up of Russian Land Army, Internal Affairs Army, and special purpose units. The units hurriedly organized for this operation began to stream continuously to their deployment bases, and within a week, the formation of the Assault Groups was mostly completed.

An example of how this was done is indicated by the deployment of the Federal Forces Group at the Beslan Air Base in Northern Ossetia. During the first days of December, aircraft began to land there with units from the Tula Paratroop Division and the Internal Affairs Army's Don Division. The Don was a special-purpose division. Later an OMON unit, a special purpose militia detachment also arrived.

Officials of the Jekaterinburg OMON later recounted with heartache how everything really had taken place. Once the alarm was raised, their group of 101 troops were flown on December 2 to the Don Division regiment that was deployed at Rostov by the Don. On December 3 and 4, OMON groups from Cheliabinsk, Nizhnigorodsk, Samara, Saratov, and Moscow also arrived. The soldiers were ordered to change into regular militia uniforms without OMON insignia, and all nine hundred people were then flown to Beslan. Ministry of Internal Affairs general major Edvard Vorobjov, later killed in Grozni, was assigned as commander of the group. All the OMON troops were armed only with pistols, automatic weapons, and rubber truncheons. None of them had any idea that they would wind up in a war. No one had mentioned such a possibility to them when they were sent to Beslan.

Even with the myriad hardships, the war machine began to grind forward. That it would not be stopped became clear on December 5 when Minister of Defense Grachev, Minister of Internal Affairs Jerin, and director of the Federal Counterintelligence Service Stepashin, flew into Mozdok. The Chechens and the press correspondents were not at all mistaken when they associated the arrival of the Armed Forces commanders with the commencement of military actions against Chechnya in the near future.[13] A meeting, in which the minister of Nationalities Affairs, Nikolai Jegorov, also participated, was held that evening in Mozdok concerning the situation in Chechnya. That same evening, Grachev approved the operations plan submitted by the commander of the Northern Caucasus Military Region.[14]

Although everything had already been decided, several formalities were still necessary. Russian leaders wished to show to the world and the Russian people that Moscow had attempted to regulate the conflict by peaceful means so that later it could justify its act of aggression as being unavoidable.

The game rules for negotiating the regulation of the conflict having already been agreed upon by both sides, Grachev met the next day with Dudajev in the town of Slepcovsk in Ingushia. During the meeting, Grachev stated that if the sides did not agree to negotiations (that is, accept the terms of surrender being offered), martial law could be declared in Chechnya. Besides, the Russian president's decree had demanded that the opposing groups in Chechnya unconditionally lay down their arms by December 15. If peaceful means could not be found to regulate the situation, then harsher measures would be taken. The final decision regarding Chechnya would be made by Russia's Security Council, most likely on December 8.[15]

The ultimatum issued during this meeting was unacceptable to Chechnya. It had been clear from the beginning that Dudajev would not enter into any discussions watering down Chechen independence. Thus it could be said that there was only one road left, that of war. That war could begin in the near future was also indicated by the formation, pursuant to the Russian president's decree of December 2, of a Temporary Information Center tasked with "issuing information about the situation in Chechnya" (memories of the 1941 Sovinfoburo quickly come to mind).

On December 8, the Mozdok, Vladikaukaz, and Chasavjurt Assault Groups were declared to be in a state of combat readiness. The divisions began to prepare to take their starting positions. That day, the Russian Duma and the Federation Council met in closed session. Although there were also suggestions that the crisis be regulated peacefully, they decided to go the way of war. On December 9, Russian president Yeltsin signed a decree, No. 2166, which obligated the nation's government to use all means the government had at its disposal to "disarm" armed formations in the Chechnya, Ossetia, and Ingushia conflict zone.[16] All formalities were thus finally completed. The hands of Defense Minister Grachev were untied, conditioned only by the fact that the Russian president had given him only nine days to execute the operation. That was the length of time that Yeltsin had decided to recuperate in a hospital after an elective nose operation. Yeltsin felt that such hospitalization would be a calmer and more convenient way of avoiding questions, as nothing would then have to be explained to anyone. Grachev assured him that as to the military operation's success, it was not worthwhile having any second thoughts. The president's health was, after all, a much more important matter. Grachev, however, had to give in a bit, and he ordered that the special blockade operations plan for the Republic of Chechnya be finalized and submitted to him for approval by 10 A.M. on December 10.

Executing the President's orders, responsible Russian government bodies issued instructions that all crossing points along the Russian-Chechen border and access by air to Chechnya be closed by December 11. The Prosecutor General's Office also issued a declaration as to the legal situation in Chechnya, charging Chechnya with violations of law.

On December 10, while at Mozdok, Grachev confirmed the Northern Caucasus Military Region Commander's submissions regarding military operations in Chechnya. The operation was scheduled to begin early on the morning of December 11. At 10 P.M., the Military Region's Commander reported that all was prepared and ready.

Although the defense minister had stated on November 28 that one paratroop regiment and several hours would be sufficient to take Grozni, he assembled significant forces for the incursion into Chechnya. To defeat Dudajev, he brought in the Volgograd 8th Army Corps, commanded by General Leonid Rochlin, several divisions, combined brigades and regiments, the Northern Caucasus Military Region's air forces and special purpose, rear area, combat communications and radio location units. According to Grachev, Russia was ready to send 23,800 troops into Chechnya, 19,000 of which were Land Army troops and the rest Internal Affairs Army and OMON troops. More than 500 units of armor were also concentrated for the operation.[17] It should be noted that these were front line troops and, most likely, did not include support forces; thus the total force was, most likely, much greater.

Compared with the information that Russia's military intelligence submitted regarding Dudajev's armed formations, clear superiority of forces was created. There was now left only the waiting for the operations results.

The Continuing War against Chechnya

Two days after the failed assault of Grozni, Russian military aircraft renewed their attacks against Chechnya's cities and strategically important targets. Intelligence was also constantly being gathered from the air and on the ground from radio transmissions.

On November 29 at about 3 P.M., four jet aircraft attacked the Northern Airport 10 kilometers from Grozni and the other airports on its outskirts, shooting them up with rockets. They also bombed several districts of the capital. During these air strikes, six of the remaining eleven passenger aircraft left were destroyed. One of the attacking aircraft was shot down and crashed not far from the airport. At the Kalinovsk air base in the Naursk region, twelve of the L-29 training aircraft refit as combat aircraft were also destroyed by bombs.

The afternoon of the next day, sixteen aircraft and helicopters again bombed and rocketed Grozni and the Kalinovsk Airport. Most of the targets were Chechen defensive positions, armored equipment, and artillery massing locations, although bombs also fell on civilian neighborhoods. The runway of Grozni Airport was cratered. During these air strikes, Chechen antiaircraft defenses shot down two helicopters.

On December 1, Russian fighter-bombers again attacked the military airports, and that night bombs also fell on the Grozni housing districts. On the morning of December 2, Grozni and the airports on its outskirts were bombed. The Chechen tank regiment deployed in the city of Shali was also bombed, and the railroad yard at Gudermes was shot up with rockets. As a result of each strike, there were also many civilian casualties.

On December 3–6, only reconnaissance flights were flown. On December 7, the air strikes were renewed. Six jet aircraft shot up the capital's television tower with rockets and bombed the tank base located alongside the Grozni Airport. During the next several days, military aircraft continued to thunder over Grozni and the other cities.[18]

As Chechnya had almost no more military aircraft left, there was no doubt as to whose aircraft were executing the air strikes. But no officials in Russia were ready to admit that these had been Russian military aircraft, operating pursuant to a military operations plan. Such things cannot remain hidden for very long, however, and on December 5 during a press conference held in Mozdok, Grachev had to admit that Russian aircraft had attacked targets held by Dudajev's forces. But Grachev at the same time continued to deny that Grozni's civilian neighborhoods were being bombed. During this press conference, he admitted for the first time that Russian troops had participated on the opposition's side during the previous assault.

From the types of air strikes being flown, one can easily judge that, until the start of the incursion into Chechnya, Russian military air forces had been given three basic missions: 1) to destroy the Chechen Air Force, 2) to bomb the presidential palace and the television tower and, at the same time, if possible, to destroy Dudajev himself, and 3) to destroy the most important Chechen defensive positions and as much as possible of its heavy combat equipment. In this way, military aviation was tasked with ensuring that during the time that the federal forces were concentrating along the Chechen borders, Chechen armed resistance capabilities would decrease.

Although Chechen aircraft were of the outmoded type, they could still have preformed reconnaissance missions and bombed the army's troop concentration areas and armored columns on the move. Also very important was the fact that once the Chechen Air Force was destroyed, there would be no need for antiaircraft defenses for the federal forces.

Russian military aviation had most success with the first mission. Because of continuous air strikes against all four Chechen airports, Dudajev's aviation forces were almost completely destroyed by the beginning of the incursion of Russia's forces into Chechnya.

An almost contrary result was achieved while attempting to bomb the presidential palace and the Grozni television tower. Russian pilots had clearly not been sufficiently trained to bomb comparatively small targets accurately. For this reason, their intended targets were left almost untouched. Instead, their rockets and bombs fell mostly on civilian housing, causing numerous civilian casualties. This was not surprising, as almost no funds had been available for combat training and military pilots were being allowed to fly on the average of only fifteen hours per year. These hours necessarily had to be taken up mostly by takeoffs and landings.[19] The civilian casualties and the bombed homes only increased the Chechens' determination to resist the aggressors.

Not much was achieved during the attempts to destroy the Chechen government's most important defense positions and its largest tank and armor formations, especially the Shali tank regiment and the armored equipment base near the Chakala Airport. The bombing did not have the intended results since the Chechen fighters took defensive measures: they spread out the combat equipment over a large area and left the defense positions guarded by only skeleton watch crews.

The Chechen Preparations for Defense

The same day that Yeltsin issued his ultimatum, a hurriedly called meeting of the Chechen government was held in Grozni at which further government actions were discussed. The majority of the government's members were convinced that it would be necessary to stand and fight, although a portion also held to the opinion that the Chechen government had to seek a compromise with Moscow and begin discussions as to the possibilities of signing a federation treaty. Also discussed was the advisability of evacuating a part of the president's staff from the presidential palace in Grozni.

The situation in Grozni and in the other Chechen towns and villages was becoming tense. Refugees began to evacuate en masse from Grozni and the larger settlements to the outlying regions of Chechnya. Those choosing to remain in the cities took their families to the mountains. These people were for the most part ethnic Chechens, as the local Russian population had nowhere else to go. Those Russians who had retained any capability of withdrawing from Chechnya had already left.

A plan to take measures to repulse the aggression was also discussed during a session of the Chechen Defense Council. But there were few available measures that could be implemented centrally. Everything depended on each individual Chechen's personal decision to resist and his choice of means. Historically, this was every Chechen's right. Not without reason, not one of the several mobilizations called by Dudajev gave the intended results.

This time, however, the Chechens were united by the threat of war. By decision of the Chechen Defense Council, several "annihilation" groups, later referred to as battalions, were formed, and from December 1, they began to stand watch around Grozni. These were basically counterintelligence units looking for fifth-column activity and provocateurs. In the capital and in other cities, additional fortifications were hurriedly constructed and artillery positions were set up. Combat equipment damaged or captured during the earlier confrontation was repaired. Units manning the antiaircraft defenses were strengthened.

On December 2, by President Dudajev's decree, a special kamikaze group was created whose members wore black bands around their heads. The Gazavat (holy war) fighters who had played an important part in the defense of Grozni during the first assault wore green headbands and were the more traditional Islamic militants. This new formation with black headbands was to be even more militant and dedicated. According to Chechen beliefs, a soldier who pledges to sacrifice his life fighting for freedom becomes a saint and upon his death enters directly into paradise. Death in battle, however, is not to be sought needlessly. It has to serve a purpose and bring an advantage to the nation.[20]

On December 4, President Dudajev declared a general mobilization in the Chechen Republic. In almost all the communities, volunteer and self-defense groups were hastily formed. They were assigned the task of blockading the roads leading to Grozni. Military rule was established in Grozni. The

Chechen General Staff was given command of all armed formations. Military courts were also established. The Chechen government announced that thieves and looters caught at the scene of a crime would be shot without warning. The sale of alcohol was banned in Chechnya. Gas masks, stretchers, individual first-aid packets, and other self-protection measures were distributed to the Chechen populace.

Dudajev's numbers grew. Groups of volunteers began to stream into Grozni with and without weapons. They came not only from all the districts of Chechnya but also from the other regions of the Northern Caucasus and from more distant countries.

By the time the Russian federal forces initiated their incursion into Chechen territory, the Chechens were just about ready. When the battles began after the incursion, press and television reports began to be filled with pejorative references to Chechen fighters as hit men, a name used to mislead world opinion.[21] In reality, a very clear structure had been formed within the Chechen military during this short period of preparation.

All Chechen armed formations fell into three types of groups.[22] The first were the Chechen regular army forces. The second and most numerous were the volunteer forces. Volunteers were organized into military formations that later actively participated in combat activities alongside the regular army units. These formations consisted mostly of volunteers who had come from other towns and villages to defend Grozni. The third group consisted of the self-defense formations that had been organized by local inhabitants in almost every community. In Grozni and in the other larger cities, self-defense units were manned by the local inhabitants whose self-imposed mission was the defense of their own neighborhood, street, or even building. They armed themselves with whatever weapons they could get. In essence, these were territorial defense units formed on a volunteer basis. Later, when their home territory was taken over by the aggressors, the majority of their members joined the ranks of the volunteers.

The Chechen armed forces were thus formed of regular army units and volunteer units of two types. Each volunteer unit was mobile and had its own transport. Each also had good communications with the regular army units and among themselves. According to the Russian High Command's estimate, by December 11, 1994, Dudajev's regular army had grown to 15,000 troops and had been supplemented by some 30,000–40,000 volunteers. At that time, the Chechen army had 98 tanks, more than 150 armored vehicles and armored personnel carriers, and almost 300 artillery guns and mortars. This was a force to be reckoned with.[23]

Special Conditions Affecting Preparations for Combat Operations

The Russian military operations plan called for the deployment of federal forces along the Chechen border within five days. Realistically, however, this could not be achieved. Instead, it took almost two weeks, with the preparations stretching out until December 10. Even then, the deployment could not have been accomplished without using the simplest variant. The units were airlifted to their deployment areas with only light weapons and ammunition. Heavy combat equipment had to be supplied from the mobilization stores of the Northern Caucasus Military Region. The depots, however, failed to maintain the equipment to the required readiness standards, resulting in at least 20 percent of Russia's combat vehicles breaking down during the campaign against Grozni.[24]

In executing its deployment along the Chechen border, Russia once again acted in its traditional hurried manner, that is, without exhaustive preparation and with too much belief in its own military might. In international practice, it is customary that preparations for military operations take at least several months. For example, during the military operation against Iraq ("Desert Storm"), the NATO countries, for the most part the United States, conducted intensive preparations for almost half a year. During that time, the operation was planned out in every conceivable detail, the military units were deployed to the operating location, and supply lines were fully organized. In Chechnya, everything was done in less than two weeks. Similar planning was used in Chechnya as had been used in previous Soviet deployment actions to Tbilisi, Baku, and Vilnius, except on a much larger scale.

During the deployment of federal forces along the Chechen border, most of the Russian military command's attention was placed on the concentration of sufficient armored combat equipment and heavy weapons in the engagement zone. As was customary, comparative ratios between Chechen and Russian troop strengths and combat equipment assets were calculated. In the opinion of the Russian High Command, clear superiority of forces could be achieved using only the weaponry and combat equipment already available in the Northern Caucuses Military Region. This factor was decisive in how the Federal High Command chose to deploy its forces.

As events would later show, the Federal High Command failed to consider other relevant factors.[25] The first, as has been already mentioned, was the poor maintenance level and readiness of the equipment in the Northern Caucasus Military Region's depots. The second was the federal military command's dependence on the operating principle regarding tanks and other armored equipment that "more is better." This principle was later shown to be not as conducive to success as had been earlier believed. The efficacy of this principle was dependent on the assumption that Dudajev's forces would become frightened, lay down their arms, and not seriously resist, and that the operation would remain simply a demonstration of Russian armed might instead of turning into a war.

The third was the Russian High Command's mistaken view as to the probable character of combat actions. This was coupled with a disregard of the already well-known fact that tanks and armored vehicles could be very effectively fought using light weaponry such as antitank grenades and grenade launchers. It had long been taught in Russian military schools and academies how to use tanks and armored vehicles on a traditional battlefield and how to defend against them on a similar battlefield. But in Chechnya there would be no battles on what in any sense could be called traditional battlefields. No one in the Russian military command had dared to imagine that Chechen fighters would forgo traditional tactics or that tank and armored columns would lose their efficacy and be lit on fire from close range under battle conditions where they could not maneuver.[26]

A very important factor also proved to be the choice of the season when the operation was to be conducted. December in Chechnya is a time of snow, fog, poor visibility, and cold weather. Such conditions not only greatly increase the using up of stores but also lessen the effectiveness of combat equipment, especially that of aviation assets.

Additionally, the troops tasked to conduct this operation were, for the most part, recent draftees who had completed at best only short training courses. It should have been apparent that such soldiers could not be prepared for effectiveness in combat during such a short period of time. Soldiers called up earlier had not been trained to a much higher level because of the continuous lack of training funds.[27]

The question also arises as to whether the commanders at the regiment, brigade, division, corps, and army levels could have supplied better-trained soldiers. The answer is most likely not. For the Russian Army, the beginning of December is the time when the draft of new recruits is completed and soldiers drafted earlier are released into the reserve forces. During this period, the Russian Army normally weakens significantly. Thus this was the most inappropriate time for mounting the operation.

Another relevant issue is prisoners of war. Immediately after Dudajev made his announcement that Russian soldiers had been taken prisoner during the September 26 assault of Grozni, various efforts were made by the Russian Military Command to free them. However, a differentiation between the actions of political and community leaders and those of the Russian Military Command has to be made. Humaneness also has to be distinguished from operational necessity.

The Russian Military Command began to be seriously concerned about the release of prisoners only after it was forced to admit publicly that Russian soldiers fought on the opposition side and that Russian forces were secretly used against Chechnya. Given such an admission, it was apparently found to be of great importance to at least demonstrate to its own troops that the Military Command was concerned about those who had been taken captive, if only to bolster troop morale prior to the start of a second operation.

It should also be noted that during this whole period of preparations, many diverse political actions were mounted by the Moscow side, including ultimatums, proclamations, and various demands to begin negotiations. At the same time, Russia continued to set conditions that clearly were not acceptable to Dudajev and completely ignored Chechnya's own proposals. Having already made a decision to use military force in Chechnya, Moscow clearly lacked any real belief that peaceful means could be used to ameliorate the crisis that it found itself in. It made use of political means for the sole purpose of gaining the time required to get its military machine into gear.

Later the commission formed by the Russian Duma and headed by Stanislav Govoruchin to investigate the causes for the war in Chechnya and its results concluded that:[28]

1. The military operation had been planned without considering the fact that on Dudajev's side stood a regular and well-armed army of up to fifty thousand people.
2. The operation to regulate the crisis had not made use of political propaganda to gain the support of the local inhabitants. The assistance of the opposition was also not used in this regard.
3. The military formations and units had been so underequipped and undermanned during peacetime that it had become necessary to organize combined regiments and even to use marine infantry forces.
4. The maintenance level of the material and combat equipment had been very low and outmoded and worn out combat equipment was used in the combat actions.
5. Instead of expanding the command structure using the Northern Caucasus Military Region as an organizational base, a new combined command had been set up consisting of the commanders of the various forces. Realistically, overall command can be assigned to one leader but not to a "quartet of leaders." The tragic nature of this methodology revealed itself

when in 1995 Grachev gave a command to issue artillery shells to Internal Affairs Army units only after the shells had been paid for by their command.

6. Until the actual beginning of the operation, middle-level commanders had not been informed of their combat assignments, and coordination among them had not been organized.

In fact, the preparations for combat action took only eleven days. Eight days were devoted to the formation of the assault groups and their concentration in the engagement area and three for their deployment to their starting positions. Although the preparations for open combat were actually very brief, the classic indications that war was imminent remained. The political tension between the opposing sides increased, and both sides began to concentrate their military forces. As always, the actual beginning of combat actions was not accurately predicted. Actions were threatened to begin on December 15 but actually began early the morning of December 11. But was this unpredictable?[29]

CHAPTER 5

The Operation to Blockade Grozni

At seven o'clock on the morning of December 11, 1994, Russian Army units began their march toward Grozni. They were formed up in three assault groups and were to enter Chechnya along seven lines of march. It had been planned that the assault groups traveling in armored column formation from Vladikaukaz, Mozdok, and Kizliar would join up on the outskirts of Grozni at about 2 P.M. and then stop. Negotiations were then to begin with the Chechen leaders, and further actions were to depend on their outcome.[1]

But it had been sufficiently clear from the start what answers would be given to the Russian ultimatums. Shortly before the initiation of the military operation, the chief of the Chechen General Staff, Colonel Aslan Maschadov, clearly stated that his side was left with no choice but to fight. If it became necessary to give up Grozni, he said, the Chechens were prepared to take to the mountains and fight a partisan war from there.

The Russian federal forces met with unexpected resistance while yet in Ingushia and Dagestan. The assault group from Vladikaukaz was to cross Ingushian territory into Chechnya along three routes. These were along separate roads but actually quite close together. But the 76th Pskov Paratroop Division and the 21st Detached Paratroop Brigade moving along Route 3 were stopped near the community of Verchnyje Ashaluk by local inhabitants who blocked the road. As no provision had been made as to what to do in the event that local inhabitants refused to allow the columns to pass, the troops turned back.

The 19th Motorized Rifle Division moving along Route 4 found itself

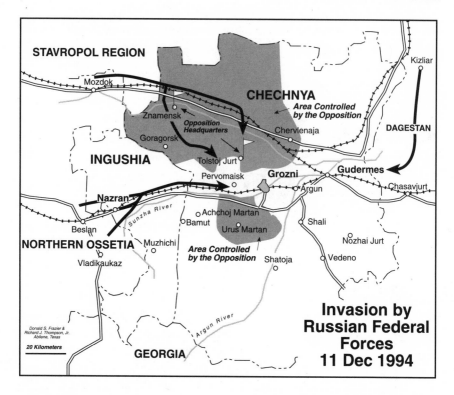

in a far more complicated situation. Not far from Nazran, its progress was
blocked by armed formations, militia, and local inhabitants. Here, near the
village of Barsuk, 68 units of combat equipment were seized by force or destroyed. The local inhabitants beat the armored vehicles with axes and cud-
gels and pierced the tires of the vehicles with sharpened metal stakes. They
also turned over automobiles and lit them on fire and took weapons away
from the soldiers. During this confrontation, one person was killed and seven
were injured. These were the first casualties of the war. Because of such organized resistance by civilians in other places along the route, the division was
only able to reach the community of Novi Sharoj by December 13, where it
was again forced to stop.[2]

Attempting to break the resistance in Ingushia, Russia had to resort to the
use of force against the civilian population. Gatherings of local inhabitants
along the columns' line of march were deemed to be Chechen-organized armed
resistance forces that needed to be liquidated by combat helicopter fire. Already during this first day of the war, a large gathering of people at the community of Gazijurt were targeted for punitive actions. Russian combat helicopters attacked, killing eighteen civilians.

The Kizliar Assault Group marching from the direction of Dagestan completely failed to enter Chechen territory. In the regions bordering Chechnya, local inhabitants, armed with bottles of flammable liquid, blocked all roads. In the Chasavjurt region, they had even succeeded in cutting off four armored vehicles and one motor vehicle from the main column and had taken 59 Internal Affairs Ministry troops prisoner, among them even 1 colonel. The Internal Affairs Army Command was forced to take immediate measures to free the captured soldiers. The assistant commander of the Internal Affairs Army flew in from Moscow to conduct negotiations with the local officials and gained their release. But only 38 soldiers were released. The others, for the most part officers, had been already been taken to Grozni by Dudajev's orders.[3]

The resistance of the local inhabitants in the territory of Dagestan was not as unexpected as it was in Ingushia. About 70,000 Chechens resided in the zone bordering Chechnya and because of their efforts and those of the other local inhabitants, the Kizliar Assault Group remained blockaded for an extended period.

It was expected that the Mozdok Assault Group would have the least problems in forcing its way into Chechnya. The group was to march from the Stavropol region to Grozni along two routes: from Mozdok through Dolinsk and from Mozdok by way of Tolstoi Jurt. Although these routes passed through the northern part of Chechnya, which was controlled by the opposition, even there the path of the columns was blocked by local inhabitants. That evening near the community of Tolstoi Jurt, a Chechen group attacked the Russian column. When two tanks were hit and lit on fire, the Russian column was forced to turn back.

All told, the Russian federal forces did not accomplish much the first day of their campaign, even though no direct confrontations with Dudajev's military forces took place. Their first engagement with Dudajev's forces was fought only the next day in the vicinity of the Dolinsk community. There the 106th Paratroop Division and the 56th Detached Paratroop Brigade were moving along route 2 when Chechen government forces fired several Grad artillery rockets into the Russian armored column. The Chechen positions were then attacked by combat helicopters and four Su-25 fighter-bombers. However, no further actions of any intensity occurred that day.[4]

Fierce confrontations began on December 13, the third day after the start of the campaign, when the Russian federal forces began to step up their pace. The largest engagements took place in the vicinity of the village of Chervlenaja and the community of Dolinsk, both located some 25 kilometers to the north of Grozni. Chechen positions near the village of Pervomaisk were also attacked. Russian combat aircraft also shot up Grozni and its outskirts and

Chechen positions in the village of Shamijurt. Russian military movements were supported everywhere by combat helicopters and close air-support aircraft when weather conditions permitted.

The first wave of the assault continued until December 17. The Russian federal forces, however, had not achieved any special successes by that date. The only exceptions were that they had succeeded in approaching some 7 to 15 kilometers from Grozni and had obliterated the village of Pervomaisk "almost from the face of the earth." (Actually, although Pervomaisk was left in ruins, it remained a center of resistance and would figure in later battles.)

With the announcement by the Russian president of yet another ultimatum, the Russian Army withdrew a short distance on December 17.[5] During the next two days, only isolated and minimal confrontations took place.

On December 19, the next assault wave began. Again Russian military aircraft began to bomb Grozni and the capital's more important targets. As they had prior to the ultimatum, the fiercest battles occurred for the village of Petropavlovskaja, where the Chechens had established strong defensive positions. The village became an important strategic target, since once it was taken, the Russian Army would gain control of the nearby bridge across the Sunzha River. This would open up the road to Grozni from the northeast. But during this new series of attacks, no significant successes were achieved, although the army again moved several kilometers closer to Grozni and the city could now be fired upon by artillery.

On December 21, Russia announced that it was closing Chechnya's borders and shutting down all air, rail, and sea communications with Azerbaijan and Georgia. This was intended to put pressure on Chechnya. Air transport was also stopped to Azerbaijan and Georgia from Ingushia, Dagestan, Northern Ossetia, Kabarda Balkaria, the regions of Krasnodar and Stavropol, and the Astrakhan and Rostov regional airports. Communications were also shut down with these territories from seaports on the Black, Azov, and Caspian Seas.

Ten days after the start of the military campaign, its apparent failure was beginning to worry Russian defense minister Grachev. After flying into Mozdok, he immediately removed a number of high-ranking military commanders. He fired almost the entire Northern Caucasus Military Region Command, including its commander, Aleksander Mitiuchin; assistant commander, V. Chirindin; and chief of personnel, V. Potapov. He also strongly suggested that his own assistant, G. Kondratjev, resign.

General Lieutenant Anatoli Kvashnin was appointed the new overall commander of the military operation, but only after the assistant commander of the Land Army, General Colonel Edvard Vorobjov, refused to accept the position. Vorobjov's refusal was grounded in the fact that the operation was commenced completely without preparation. The Land Army's Headquarters Staff had not participated in the planning and preparation of the operation.[6] He also failed to see its purpose. General Colonel Vorobjov learned personally how the operation was prepared for, how it began, and how it was being executed, when, unexpectedly, he himself received orders from Defense Minister Grachev to go immediately to Chechnya and participate in the mounting of the operation.

With the arrival of Grachev, the Russian federal forces became more active. Military units were ordered to begin the blockade of Grozni and to commence maneuver actions. On December 22, the 104th Paratroop Division's Combined Regiment skirted Grozni, moving from the north to the east, and took up positions to the west of Argun. Sensing the danger, Dudajev resolved to liquidate this force. He countered with his reserves from Grozni and Argun, which consisted of elite units, augmented by tanks, armored vehicles, and artillery. This was reported in the press as the first Chechen tank attack. This countering move, however, was already too late. The paratroopers had succeeded in fortifying their positions, and, after a fierce battle, the Chechens had to withdraw.[7]

To the north of Grozni in the Terek hills region, the 131st Maikop Motorized Rifle Brigade's Combined Assault Group began what were later termed "demonstrative" actions. Combat positions crept closer to Grozni. Russia had intended to blockade Grozni by December 26. Continuous battles took place along the approaches to Grozni from the northwest, the north, and the east. The Russian federal forces did not succeed in breaking through to the south of Grozni. Given the operational situation, the formulation of a different Grozni attack plan was begun. It became clear even earlier to the Russian Military High Command that the campaign could not be successfully concluded with the military forces then available. A decision was thus made to strengthen the existing federal forces by bringing in marine infantry units from the Northern, Baltic, and Pacific fleets and motorized rifle units from almost all the other military regions.

By December 26, the Federal Forces Group had been reinforced by the arrival of the Siberian Military Region's 74th Motorized Rifle Brigade, the Saint Petersburg (formerly Leningrad) Military Region's 45th Motorized Rifle Division's 129th Motorized Rifle Regiment, the Pavolga Military Region's 90th Tank Division's 81st Motorized Regiment, and the Ural Military Region's 34th Motorized Rifle Division's 276th Motorized Rifle Regiment.[8]

Defense Tactics

In preparing to repulse the invasion of the Russian federal forces into the republic's territory, the Chechen Military Command placed most of its attention on Grozni and on the city's defenses along approaches from the west,
north, and east. It had been useless to prepare for a positional war against a
much stronger opponent. Instead, since the opponent's choice of ingress routes
to Grozni was limited and all possible routes usable by military forces were
known, the choice was made to use perimeter defenses. Defensive perimeters
consisting of strong points and firing positions were established in the capital
itself, at its approaches and along the main highways leading to Grozni:
Mozdok-Icherskaja-Grozni, Vladikaukaz-Grozni, Nazran-Grozni, Chasav-
jurt-Gudermes-Grozni, and Kizliar-Chervlenaja-Grozni. The approaches to
Grozni from the direction of Urus Martan, which was controlled by opposition armed formations, were also fortified.[9]

Once the Russian federal forces began the military operation, the Chechen
Military Command, as had been expected, was forced to concentrate on repulsing the strongest assault group from Mozdok, which was attacking from
the northwest and north. The situation was relieved somewhat by the fact
that the Kizliar Assault Group tasked with attacking from the east had been
blocked and had been forced to remain in place. In the west, the Vladikaukaz
Assault Group also ran into a series of powerful strong-point defense positions
in almost every community along the road to Grozni. After several intense engagements, it also slowed its movement toward Grozni. As this western assault
group's purpose was to reach Grozni and not to take every community located
along the way, it was left with no choice but to change its tactics. Thus further on, wherever it met resistance, it bypassed such communities. But this resulted in a significant decrease in the column's forward movement, and news
about the column's progress practically disappeared from news agency press
releases. As the Chechens had blown up all the bridges along the main roads
to Grozni, the columns were forced to move along roundabout routes, the
passability of which under winter conditions was very poor.[10]

For the Chechen forces, the approaches from the northwest and north were
the most dangerous because the Russian columns passed through three regions controlled by the opposition and would be able to near the capital without hindrance to a distance of some 15 to 25 kilometers. The columns would
be engaged only when the Russian forces reached Chechen government-
controlled territories. Most of the battles thus occurred near the communities
of Chervlenaja, Pervomaisk, and Petropavlovskaja, and this continued right
up to the assault of Grozni itself. The Chechen regular forces were augmented

mostly by volunteers from the powerful Argun and Gudermes armed formations. The Chechens chose as their primary northern defense line the Karpinski hill formation not far from Grozni. The defensive positions established all along the crests of these hills were so strong that during the daily morning-to-night bombings by nine aircraft and three helicopters that had been constantly in the air, none of the Chechen defenders were killed and only one machine gunner was wounded. During this same period, the defenders succeeded in knocking down two Russian aircraft with a machine gun taken from a tank.

Ambush parties were also sent out far in front of the defense positions in the direction of the Russian federal forces, and guard posts were set up on the dominating heights while the enemy was still far away. Strong-point positions equipped for long-term defense and where combat equipment and weapons were stored were guarded only by watch teams. Chechen fighters occupied these positions only when the opponent neared. For this reason, air strikes were able to inflict little damage to the Chechen defense system.[11]

The roads along the Russian columns' lines of march and the approaches passable by military units to the communities along the way were also mined. The roads themselves were obstructed by cut-down trees. Heavy trucks were placed across narrow roads and blocked the intersections.

As the Russian columns moved forward, Chechen fighter groups finding themselves at the enemy's rear reverted to partisan war tactics. For this reason, almost every Russian column experienced resistance from their front and as well as constant attacks from their rear and flanks.

As the enemy columns approached, Chechen fighters usually did not open fire immediately but let them draw near. Operating from up close and suddenly opening up withering cross fire from all directions, the Chechen fighters found that the effectiveness of their attacks was markedly greater. Often the maneuvers of attacking from the columns' rear and counterattacking were used. They also often set up what were called "killing fields." On December 21, a reconnaissance unit from an operational regiment supported by tanks stepped into such a "killing field" as it entered the Petropavlovskaja community. Eleven soldiers were killed and seven wounded by unexpected and intensive grenade launcher and automatic weapons fire from short distances and from several directions at once. The unit was almost completely destroyed.

The Chechens' most important weapon was surprise. Chechen fighters did not engage in battles of any duration, their primary tactic being the maneuver of "attack and retreat." Even heavy weapons were used according to this principle. The Grad salvo firing rocket artillery systems in the Chechen inventory were most often aimed in advance onto a specific target area. When Russian units entered the targeted area, lethal fire was suddenly opened up. The Grad systems were then hurriedly withdrawn to another location.[12]

The tactic of "attack and retreat" began to be used more and more after the Chechen Military Command became convinced that resistance from strong-point defensive positions and other fortifications was not providing the intended results. In positional warfare, the Russian Army was clearly far superior, especially when it was also able to concentrate aircraft and artillery fire. Strong points and other fortifications could only slow down the movement of the opponent's columns while the primary purpose of the Chechen armed forces was to stop by combat actions the opponent's movement toward Grozni. Surprise attack tactics were thus more appropriate for this purpose. Whenever Russian military units succeeded in surrounding an attacking group of Chechen fighters, they continued to resist only until nightfall and then, being thoroughly familiar with the surrounding area, they dispersed, sneaking through the enemy's combat positions in small groups.

Having suffered considerable losses to intense Russian aviation and artillery fire, the Chechen armed forces began to change their tactics involving the use of heavy weapons and equipment. They would fire a few rounds from their artillery guns, self-propelled mortars, and combat vehicles from positions prepared in advance and then quickly withdraw and dislocate to another location. They also began to emplace mortars and recoiling grenade launchers on truck bodies and even inside automobiles. In such cases, they cut holes in the roofs and fired while moving.[13]

Very great attention was also paid to intelligence. Intelligence was gathered by local inhabitants and by special intelligence-diversion teams. Artillery targets were reconnoitered and artillery fire was corrected by specially trained specialists.

The organized resistance brought results. The Russian Combined Federal Forces were unable to put their planned blockade of Grozni into effect.

The Causes for the Federal Forces Failures

As mentioned earlier, the hastily concentrated Russian Combined Federal Forces were unable to operate effectively during the opening stage of the military operation. Prior to the actual beginning of the military operation, a large majority of the federal forces officers and troops had been fully convinced that they only had to march to Grozni, surround the capital, and then wait for further orders. In the participating units, formations, and various services, preparations were undertaken for only this course of events. This was clearly noted by reserve colonel lieutenant Aleksander Frolov, who participated in the march to Grozni as a member of one of the units from the Pavolga Military Region, which had been attached to the Northern Assault Group, commanded by General Lieutenant Rochlin.[14]

While yet in Mozdok, Colonel Frolov observed that there was no discernible order in the troop concentration areas, that even primary and reserve deployment areas had not been designated. There was no road commandant service or guard organized, no regime created for controlling admission to unit deployment areas, and the areas themselves had not been prepared from an engineering standpoint to receive the deployed troops. Transportation of units, the movement of transport, and rear support services reminded him more of a torn-apart beehive than a functioning army. Thus, excellent conditions were created for Chechen intelligence to operate in, and it was able to learn in advance the planned movement routes of all the units and their routing schedules.

Units also made no efforts in the troop concentration areas to prepare for the eventuality of combat, and combat equipment had not been readied for such contingency, although tanks had been brought up from depots where they had been in storage since 1989. Armored equipment crews were formed hastily, for the most part, of untrained raw recruits.

All this became all the more clear with the start of the operation. Two out of every ten units of armor were unable to make their way under their own power all the way to Grozni and had to be towed. Already worn-out motor transport vehicles constantly broke down along the road. Gasoline and diesel fuel brought from depots proved to be unusable as it had been mixed with water to hide prior thefts of fuel.

The supply of troops was also totally chaotic. For the most part, hot food was being prepared only for the Internal Affairs Ministry units. Elsewhere, one tin of food quite often had to feed five soldiers during a whole 24-hour period. The situation was not much better with rest facilities during the march. Most often, troops were forced to sleep wherever they found available place, in tanks, in armored vehicles, and in the cabs of motor vehicles. Engines were almost never shut off, and fuel supplies were used irrationally. This affected not only costs but also efforts to supply supplementary fuel.

Intelligence during the march to Grozni was organized even more poorly. Those tasked with gathering tactical intelligence worked ineffectively, and the information gathered was mostly inaccurate. Normally for battalions and larger formations, area and detailed reconnaissance is organized to track enemy activity. Area reconnaissance usually covers an area of 10 to 100 kilometers from the operating unit and is performed from the air. Detailed reconnaissance is done at a distance of 5 to 25 kilometers from the unit and is normally conducted by reconnaissance teams operating on foot. However, a lack of knowledge of the locale and the capability of Chechens to maneuver secretly impaired intelligence effectiveness. Reconnaissance was done only according to the rule "What I see, I will report," though the purpose of intelligence is to gather and report sufficient information to ensure that the opponent's actions will not come as a surprise.

The march to Grozni was itself badly organized. During it, its guard was executed poorly, with guard units distancing themselves no further than eyesight distance from the main force. During rest breaks and stoppages, the combat vehicles and troops made no efforts to disperse and made no use of camouflage. If Dudajev's forces had been able to make use of even one complete Grad rocket artillery battery, Russian federal forces' losses would have been appreciably larger. (One Grad battery—eighteen combat vehicles, each having 40 tubes—can "plow" a 10-hectare area with one salvo.) There were also no efforts made to suppress the enemy's intelligence-diversion units.

The largest negative effect on the troops, however, resulted from the lack of a clear chain of command. Often, high-ranking commanders issued orders not through the chain of command but by directly contacting specific unit leaders, bypassing their commanders. Quite often, the orders or instructions received conflicted with each other.

The high-ranking commanders also issued so many restrictions on the use of fire that lower-rank commanders could only instruct their troops either to throw their weapons at the enemy physically or to put up their hands. For example, a Russian helicopter crew spotted a Chechen Grad artillery vehicle and, while attempting to get further instructions by radio as to what to do next, were themselves shot down by the Chechens. Only later did the units obtain permission to answer Chechen fire with fire.

In actual combat situations, the Russian federal forces showed themselves to be quite different from what had been previously envisioned by their commanders. In the opinion of Russian military experts, the primary reasons for this were the Armed Forces' poor state of combat readiness in general and the fact that the military operation had been begun without appropriate preparation.

The Defense Ministry and the General Staff, however, were fully informed of this state of affairs. One report concerning the army's state of readiness fell into the hands of the staff of the Russian newspaper *Novaja Ezhednevnaja Gazeta* (New daily newspaper) and was published on January 25, 1995. It was written by a high-ranking officer expressing his opinion as to the readiness of the Russian Army for this military operation. Although the author's name is not mentioned in the report, it is not hard to guess that it was prepared by General Colonel Vorobjov. The report read, in full: [15]

REPORT

As I worked with the generals and officers of the General Staff (GS) and the Northern Caucasus Military Region (NCMR), I ask permission to express my opinion about the preparations of the various headquarters and military commands to organize combat actions and to execute them.

I. COMMAND PREPARATIONS

NCMR Commander General Colonel A. Mitiuchin was assigned command of the joint forces operation.

The first stage of the planning for combat actions was performed by the General Staff under the direction of General Lieutenant L. Shevcov and the General Staff's Operations Command (OC).

Overall, the special operation plan was prepared competently as had been required; however, detailed planning identified a number of shortcomings, which were later not taken into consideration:

First, the command organization was unable to change over into a wartime conditions work regime. Parade field attitudes and superficiality were not avoided by even the lower-ranking officers. Division and operations-tactics group commanders' attitudes were negatively affected by Russian defense minister Grachev's declaration that "he would take Grozni with one paratroop regiment."

Second, there was not one training exercise conducted for the command, and concrete combat tasks were not assigned. The NCMR commander did not sign even one document outlining the organization and execution of combat actions, especially rules for the opening of fire and use of air strikes. All documents were signed by the NCMR chief of staff general lieutenant V. Potapov.

Third, the NCMR Headquarters and the commander himself showed themselves to be unprepared to organize and plan combat activity. The commander's direction of the people under him was very weak, and he refused to hear out their proposals. All his "instructions" were issued mostly in the form of uncensored curses and abuse. A planning group for the use of fire and atomic weapons was not formed.

Fourth, coordination between the participating forces was not organized. On December 5, 1994, the defense minister ignored the NCMR commander's report that the command organization, command posts (CP), and the army in general were not ready to conduct combat actions.

Fifth, in organizing, planning, and executing combat actions, no attention was paid to weather conditions (fog, rain, etc.) and the time of year. It should have been mandatory that there be conducted exercises using communications equipment for the command organization, the purpose of which would have been to ensure the coordination of their actions under combat conditions. More specifically, there should have been conducted command and staff exercises of a three-to-five-day duration. Besides these, an additional ten to fifteen days should have been allotted for the preparation of forces. Combat actions should not have begun earlier than December 20–25, 1994.

II. STAFF PREPARATION

1. In preparing for this operation, there was not conducted even one exercise or instructional session for the commanders and staffs at all levels.

2. Staffs proved to be not ready for work under combat conditions, and staff work was organized at a very low level.

3. The operation was planned and prepared very superficially, which later resulted in indefensible weapons, equipment, and troop losses.

4. The enemy's situation, composition, and the probable character of its actions were not analyzed.

5. In planning military actions, no consideration was given to the actual situation, state of readiness, supply, and capabilities of its own forces. Lower-echelon commanders were not informed as to their neighboring units' missions and the character of their actions.

6. Conclusions as to the developing situation, proposals, and mandatory calculations were done superficially. Besides this, the command as a rule ignored them.

7. Continuous and harmonized coordination was not organized.

8. Previous combat experiences were not summarized, and these were not passed on to the combined formations and units.

9. Accounting of personnel, weapons, and other equipment was done carelessly. For this reason, the identification of soldiers killed in action was made difficult, and it was hard to deal with soldiers taken prisoner or missing in action and to account for equipment falling into the hands of the enemy.

10. The work atmosphere at the various staffs was very emotional and agitated. The tension was created by the High Command and personally by General Colonel A. Mitiuchin.

III. THE ARMY'S READINESS

1. The personnel were poorly prepared psychologically and physically for the execution of combat actions under harsh weather conditions.

2. The army was not trained to march, attack, and defend.

3. Weapons and equipment were used unprofessionally due to poor personnel training.

4. Soldiers' work habits were weak while acting individually or as part of a unit under combat conditions.

5. Troops were unused to firing weapons individually or as part of a unit.

6. Mechanic-drivers and drivers were poorly trained to drive combat equipment.

7. Armored personnel carrier (APC) gunners and tank gunners did not know the rules for firing at suddenly appearing targets or at moving targets and acted indecisively. (There were instances when tank and APC weapons were not even put into use.)

8. Troops were not trained in administering first aid on the battlefield and did not know how to use preparations against shock.

9. The units were not trained how to concentrate fire or to change fire to another target.

10. Smoke cover to camouflage movement on the battlefield or to evacuate the wounded was used very poorly.

11. Sniper teams were not organized to suppress artillery guns, howitzers, recoiling antitank grenade launchers, and grenade launcher teams. There was also no counterfire organized against snipers.

12. Troops were also not trained to mark battle lines or to designate targets for aircraft with smoke rockets.

13. There was not sufficient use made of turning force tactics, and ambushes were not set up.

14. Troops were not trained in methods of movement on a battlefield.

15. Assault groups were not formed to take out firing positions, strong points, and other fortifications. Flamethrowers and grenade launchers were poorly used.

16. The troops did not have personal identification badges (dog tags), and this made identification of the dead difficult.

17. Sergeants were not trained to lead on a battlefield and were not able to replace an officer when he was killed.

18. Special purpose units (Intelligence Command, Defense, and Internal Affairs Ministries) were not sufficiently trained to execute their assigned missions.

19. Combat training of units is not conducted in regular dislocation areas. As a rule, this is done in unfamiliar surroundings, lacking any material base.

20. Experience gained in the Afghanistan conflict was not used in the combat actions.

IV. COMBAT SUPPORT

a) *Intelligence*

1. Probable locations of resistance along the columns' movement routes were not foreseen in time.

2. Intelligence units did not perform route reconnaissance in advance.

3. Intelligence was conducted passively and was limited to observation. Enemy artillery positions and changes in dislocation positions were not identified in time.

4. During combat actions, intelligence units did not take even one prisoner who could be interrogated. For this reason, the capabilities of confirming acquired intelligence information decreased appreciably.

5. The Command of the Assault Forces used for the most part intelligence information acquired by the Federal Counterintelligence Service, the General Staff's Intelligence Command, the Internal Affairs Ministry Army's and the Internal Affairs Ministry's Intelligence Commands.

6. The execution of combat assignments by intelligence units was performed poorly.

b) *Camouflage*

1. Insufficient attention was paid to camouflage, which is a form of combat support.

2. The personnel were not trained in camouflage methods.

3. Firing positions and troop positions were not camouflaged, and for this reason troops were killed.

4. Camouflage measures were not used.

5. Weapons and equipment were not camouflaged according to the local environment's background.

c) *Engineering support*

1. Troops were not trained to dig in, construct trenches, or appropriately cover entrenchments.

2. In constructing positions, sandbags were not used.

3. Not all personnel were supplied with entrenching tools.

4. Personnel were not trained in the setting up of mine fields, their removal, and in the destruction of explosives.

5. Movement support sections and mine removal units worked poorly.

6. Troops were not trained to build bridges speedily and well and to construct crossings.

7. Engineering intelligence was not gathered as to the locality and the enemy.

V. TECHNICAL SUPPORT

1. Combat equipment was brought to the combat zone in an unprepared-for-combat condition.

2. There was a lack of spare parts for certain types of weaponry (armored personnel carriers, armored vehicles, tanks, artillery guns).

3. Much of the equipment lacked antifreeze and did not have batteries, necessary fuel, and lubricants.

4. The control of the technical condition of the equipment was very poor; the evacuation of damaged equipment was badly organized.

5. Ongoing repair of damaged and burned-up equipment was practically not performed.

VI. REAR AREA SUPPORT

1. Rear area support of combat units was organized at a very poor level.

2. Not all troops were issued warm underclothes, leggings, and felt boots, for which reason many troops suffered from frostbite.

3. Troop food supplies were insufficiently organized. (For periods of six to eight days, troops did not receive hot food; their rations had no fruit or vegetables.)

4. Baths and the washing of clothes was not organized for troops, and for this reason, troops suffered from lice.

5. Warming stations were not set up where troops could get warm.

6. Body armor vests were issued to troops in an uncompleted condition (they lacked the protective plates).

7. Troops were not supplied with helmet liners, warm gloves, canteens.

I consider it mandatory that the command be informed about the deficiencies identified above so that they would not be repeated in further planning to send units and detachments into Chechen territory.

Perhaps under different circumstances, the listed reasons for failure would have been sufficiently decisive, but in this war, other factors also played a part. The Chechens had no doubts that a war had begun. They had prepared themselves both spiritually and psychologically for this and were able to act decisively. On the other hand, Russia's propaganda machine continuously argued that this was in fact only an operation to disarm illegal Chechen armed formations. This message lulled the Russian soldiers themselves, and only their first losses forced them reevaluate their situation. The soldiers were constantly told that the operation was proceeding successfully and that the disarming of Chechens in some communities had already begun, although this did not at all reflect reality. Although various rumors were heard, the soldiers had to believe their leaders, as no one yet knew what their real mission was.

President Dudajev's ally in this war was Russian aircraft. Bombs falling on the communities increased the civilian casualties and at the same time enlarged the Chechen fighters' numbers. Cursing Yeltsin, Grachev, and even Dudajev, those who earlier had not considered fighting on Dudajev's side now took weapons into their hands.

But Dudajev's fighters' numbers were increased even more by leaflets scattered around Grozni that contained Grachev's order to take measures to deport Chechens. It is contended that these leaflets were scattered from planes. It is, however, not even clear whether such an order was ever issued. Perhaps the leaflets were intended to frighten the Chechens into obeying, but for Dudajev, their appearance was extremely useful as Chechens knew very well what deportation was. They did not need to doubt whether it was intended or not; the bitter lessons of history were still much too clear in their memories. And for them, it was not all that important whether this, in fact, was a provocation or not.[16]

The First Results of the War in Chechnya

According to official information from the Russian High Command, from the start of the military operation until December 25, 44 troops were killed and 116 wounded. The Chechen information services reported that 1,850 Chechen soldiers and civilians died during this same period. Most of the civilians were killed from air bombardments and by artillery and mortar fire.

The losses of both sides, however, were considerably larger. It was commented in the press that the Russian Military Command was reporting inaccurate, greatly reduced casualty figures. The press from the democratic world reported that from December 11 until the end of that month 800 Russian soldiers were killed.[17] This is confirmed by various sources, although the same conclusions can be reached by analyzing official Russian information.

It is also well known that the fiercest battles took place near the communities of Dolinsk, Pervomaisk, Petropavlovskaja, and Chervlenaja. The press reported on December 16, 1995, that Russia had lost 250 troops in battles near Pervomaisk. Even if one assumes that this figure includes both killed and wounded, it indicates much larger losses than were reported in the official information bulletins issued on December 25, 1994.

On December 19, 1994, the press also reported information received from medical personnel at the Mozdok field hospital commanded by Colonel Lieutenant L. Raff. The field hospital registered 509 dead and was receiving 60 – 80 new wounded each day. During eight days, 150 medical operations were performed. This does not correspond even remotely with the official information that was issued.

In Russian military organizations, there exists a casualty determination system that makes it almost impossible to obtain accurate information. Only soldiers who die on the battlefield are considered killed. If a wounded soldier later dies in a hospital, he is not calculated among the number killed. Every service also has its own hospitals, which engenders many disagreements. For example, troops under the command of the Defense Ministry are not admitted to Internal Affairs Ministry hospitals.[18]

It is also almost impossible to calculate the combat equipment losses taken by one or the other side during this early stage of the war. In part, this is because damaged equipment is normally repaired and returned to service.

But this is also owing to the fact that neither side wanted to supply information as to its own combat equipment losses. This is understandable as it is a wartime necessity to disinform the enemy.

Calculating from information reported in the press, which, of course, may or may not be accurate, by December 25, the Russian Army had lost not less than 150 units of combat equipment (tanks, armored vehicles, mortars, artillery, trucks, and so forth) and two helicopters. The Chechens on their part had lost 32 – 40 units of combat equipment.

During this first stage of the military operation, two aspects characteristic of attitudes in the Russian Army were becoming apparent. The first concerned the military forces from the Northern Caucasus Military Region. Even before the start of the military operation, the Caucasus Nations Confederation announced their solidarity with Chechnya. Many of the inhabitants of this mountain region were also disposed against Russia. For this reason, the officers and sergeants of the NCMR units could not show even the least initiative in the fight against Chechnya for fear of revenge against their families left in their permanent dislocation areas. Thus almost half of the officers and warrant officers of the 19th Motorized Rifle Division deployed to Vladikaukaz signed requests asking to be released from military service. Additionally, a majority of the participating soldiers were drafted into military service from this same region. Wanting to help the Chechens, they began to desert, and some even went over to the Chechen side. According to press correspondents, there were instances of soldiers being forced to go on the attack at gunpoint.

The second clear aspect was that many officers and generals in the Russian Federation Armed Forces refused to participate in the military operation in Chechnya as they failed to recognize any valid purpose to waging war against the people of their own federation. They also understood that this war would bring great harm to Russia. These attitudes were prevalent among all the officer ranks, even at the highest levels. Criminal charges were brought against many of them, and the Defense Ministry–controlled Russian daily *Krasnaja zvezda* (Red Star) even attempted to label them as traitors to their country's interests.

From December 22, the press began to publish numerous articles about the assistant commander of the Russian Land Army General Colonel Edvard Vorobjov's resignation after Grachev offered him command of the operation to disarm the Chechen forces. Similarly, the press published many commentaries about the 76th Pskov Paratroop Division commander's refusal to begin combat actions without written orders from Defense Minister Grachev.

Such disagreements were widespread. Even before the start of the operation, high-ranking Russian officers not agreeing to the use of force in Chechnya were removed from their posts. Among them was Assistant Defense Minister Boris Gromov, who had also refused to command Russian armed forces fighting against Chechnya.

General Aleksander Lebed, commander of the 14th Army and, like Gromov, one of the most popular Afghanistan conflict commanders in the Russian officer ranks, began to criticize harshly the military operation in Chechnya. In his opinion, it was purposeless to fight with the people. It was also impossible to regulate such a conflict using military means since Russia could not win this war.

There is, however, a well-known Russian proverb: "When one cuts a forest, chips will fly." In this instance, the people became the chips. These were completely innocent civilians: women, children, and old people, their fate totally unrelated to whether they were Chechens or Russians. Perhaps someday the purposeless losses shall be accurately calculated. But as history speaks so loudly, what are thousands and even hundreds of thousands of casualties to Russia, a nation of millions, bent on furthering its own interests and defending its colonial empire?

There were also other losses. As soon as the Chechens began to resist, the Russian repression machine began to function. Wherever a Russian soldier stepped foot, there all male Chechens were hunted down. Anyone capable of raising a weapon was suspected, regardless of whether they were fourteen-year-old youths or sixty-five-year-old men. They were all herded into what were called "filtration camps," which differed little in their character and cruelty from Nazi Germany's concentration camps.

The war in Chechnya touched not only the countries adjoining it but also territories and countries further off. This could be called the war's "zone of influence." It is impossible to delimit this noncombatant zone's specific borders, but it is quite possible to specify those regions where the influence of the war was felt in political, economic, social, military, and other sectors. A stream of refugees flooded neighboring territories. In such territories, stricter population control regimes were introduced, the security of buildings and other complexes was strengthened, and military units and internal affairs ministry forces were put on a higher level of combat readiness.

By the end of December, about 37,000 refugees had left Chechnya because of military activity. Other reports indicate that 35,700 had gone to Ingushia, 7,000 to Dagestan, the rest to the regions of Stavropol, Northern Ossetia, Krasnodar, Kabarda Balkaria, Karachoi Cherkesia, and elsewhere.

The effects of the war were also felt even in faraway Moscow. This was not only because Moscow families were soon receiving news that their son, husband, or brother had been killed or wounded but also because of threats arriving from Chechnya about possible terrorist acts. In Moscow itself and around it, the control regime was soon strengthened.

CHAPTER 6

The Assault of Grozni and Its Defense

Upon his arrival in Mozdok on December 22, 1994, Russian defense minister Grachev quite correctly concluded that to set up a complete blockade of Grozni would require a lot more time. But any such further delay ran counter to his plans and could also strongly affect the prestige of the Russian Army: How would it appear if one of the world's mightiest armies showed itself incapable of waging war against such a small country's only recently organized armed forces? Thus the original plan had to be quickly adjusted to the realities of the developing situation.[1]

For the storming of Grozni, four battle groups were created, each designated according to its planned line of attack: the Northern Battle Group commanded by General Major Konstantin Pulikovski, the Northeastern Battle Group commanded by General Lieutenant Leonid Rochlin, the Western Battle Group commanded by General Major V. Petruk, and the Eastern Battle Group commanded by General Major N. Staskov.

On December 25, the plan for the assault of Grozni was finalized. The operations plan called for the primary assaults to be made concurrently from the north, east, and west. Then, together with the Internal Affairs Ministry's and the Federal Counterintelligence Service's specialized units and detachments, the battle groups were to take the presidential palace, the government buildings, the television and radio stations, the railroad station, and other important objectives located in the center of Grozni. The central part of the city as well as the Zavodskaja and Katajama districts were to be blockaded.

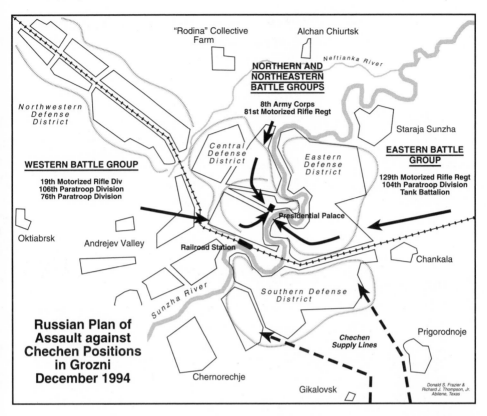

"Rodina" Collective Farm

Alchan Chiurtsk

Neftianka River

NORTHERN AND NORTHEASTERN BATTLE GROUPS

8th Army Corps
81st Motorized Rifle Regt

Northwestern Defense District

Staraja Sunzha

Central Defense District

Eastern Defense District

EASTERN BATTLE GROUP

WESTERN BATTLE GROUP

19th Motorized Rifle Div
106th Paratroop Division
76th Paratroop Division

129th Motorized Rifle Regt
104th Paratroop Division
Tank Battalion

Oktiabrsk

Andrejev Valley

Railroad Station

Presidential Palace

Chankala

Sunzha River

Southern Defense District

Russian Plan of Assault against Chechen Positions in Grozni December 1994

Chechen Supply Lines

Prigorodnoje

Chernorechje

Gikalovsk

Donald S. Frazier &
Richard J. Thompson, Jr.
Abilene, Texas

Attacking from the north, one Northeastern and two Northern Assault Groups were to block the northern part of the city and the presidential palace from the north. Their route was to be along Juznaja, Majakovski, Krasnozna-menskaja, and Miro Streets on the right and along the Sunzha River on the left. From the west, two Western Assault Groups, attacking along the railroad tracks and Papovic Street were to take the railroad station, then turn north and block off the presidential palace from the south. Once these assault groups attacking from the north and west accomplished their assigned tasks, the main roads would be blocked off and a corridor would be opened up through the city.

Paratroop units were to block off the Zavodskaja and Katajama districts of the city. From the east, two Eastern Assault Groups attacking along the Gudermes-Grozni railroad tracks, then along Lenin Prospect, were to reach the Sunzha River, take the bridges crossing it, then unite with the units at-tacking from the north and west and block off the central part of the city from the east.

Once Grachev approved the assault operations concept, measures were taken to put it into effect. Their purpose was to redeploy the various units to their initial attack positions. The bombing of Grozni and the pounding by artillery of the outskirts of Grozni was intensified. Confrontations in the regions to the north and northwest of Grozni also intensified. The 129th Saint Petersburg Motorized Rifle Regiment initiated the assault by starting its move from northwest of Grozni eastward to the Chankala Airport.

The Russian Federation's Security Council quickly approved Grachev's decision. At a meeting held December 26, the council made the decision to commence the assault and occupation of Grozni. Shortly after the meeting, Yeltsin announced that the first stage of the Chechen operation had already been completed and that Moscow was planning to recreate its government institutions in this region.

It should be noted that at the same time that it approved the initiation of the war, the Security Council also confirmed the membership of the delegation that was to negotiate with separatist Chechnya. Appointed to the delegation were Vice Premier Nicolai Jegorov; the director of the Federal Counterintelligence Service, Sergei Stepashin; and the commander in charge of the operation, General Lieutenant Anatoli Kvashnin, who had been blamed for the failures of the operation to date.

Orders were issued the same day extending the deployment of Internal Affairs Ministry troops and officials to the conflict zone. For example, the assistant commander of the Russian Internal Affairs Ministry command, Colonel Ziurikov, extended the deployment dates of the OMON units to January 26. (Russia's Internal Affairs Ministry regulations require that members of the OMON be deployed no longer than one month to a given location to accomplish their assigned mission.)

On December 26 and 27, armed confrontations eased somewhat. Because of bad weather, military aircraft almost did not fly that day. More intense engagements were fought only in the vicinity of the Ichkerija bridge across the Sunzha River and in a region not far from Argun that lay to the east of Grozni.

The assault group commanders received advance instructions for the assault on December 25. The operational commander, General Lieutenant Kvashnin, personally participated in the briefings of the battalion commanders and the staff of the 81st Samara Motorized Rifle Regiment, tasked with operating along the primary line of attack.

The main assault of Grozni was begun on December 28. Russian forces succeeded in taking Kirovsk, an industrial suburb of Grozni some ten kilometers to the northeast of the center of the city and not far from the Chankala Airport. Engagements were fought for the community of Petropavlovskaja. Before morning, the oil drilling facilities in the community of Katajama were also taken. Fighting continued near Pervomaisk, Alchan Kala, Argun, near the strategic Karpinski heights, and in other locations.

Russian military aircraft bombed Argun, Gudermes, and the Prigorod-noje suburb of Grozni. Bombs and rockets also fell on almost seventy hamlets and villages. The bombing of the communities to the east of Grozni was intended to weaken the attacks of Chechen Armed Forces from the rear against the Russian Assault Group, which had taken positions at the Chankala Airport. The next day, although the battle lines slowly crept closer to Grozni, the most intense battles occurred in much the same locations. Chechen forces tried to counterattack, but their attacks were repulsed.

The results of the first two days of the assault apparently satisfied Grachev. At a press conference held in Mozdok on December 30, he announced that the first stage of the assault had been accomplished and that further actions would be conducted by the Internal Affairs Army. During the second stage, Land Army forces would assist the Internal Affairs units to liquidate the Chechen armed formations. All regular army units would then be withdrawn with the exception of the motorized rifle troops who would take over the military bases in Grozni previously occupied by Russia's Motorized Rifle Training Division and the Tank Regiment. After this announcement, Grachev, together with Internal Affairs Minister Viktor Jerin, left Mozdok, where they had been staying for more than a week and returned to Moscow.

The assault of Grozni itself began the next day. Apparently, too much faith had been put in the successes of the first days of the operation, and Grachev decided to assault Grozni and finish the operation off in one blow, despite the fact that advance preparations had not been made for such a move. The blow was to be a huge surprise to the Chechens, and there certainly were sufficient forces deployed for such a strike. Reportedly, the order to mount the assault was given by Grachev while celebrating his own birthday.[2]

The purpose of this unexpected decision to storm Grozni immediately is sufficiently clear. Unable to blockade Grozni successfully, Grachev made the decision to forgo the blockade for the time being. Instead, Russian forces would take the center of the city by mounting an unexpected assault and in one step liquidate Dudajev and the government officials supporting him. Even the Vitiaz special-purpose unit tasked with capturing Dudajev was unprepared for this. But it was becoming impossible to delay the assault for any length of time. The ranks of Grozni's defenders were increasing daily.

The Organization of Grozni's Defense

Chechnya's General Staff concentrated in Grozni its largest and best organized armed formations. During the early part of December, 1994, there had been deployed to the capital the Borz special-purpose detachment (60 men, 2 tanks, 1 armored vehicle, 1 armored personnel carrier, and 1 D-30 122 mm howitzer), the Grom special-purpose battalion (200 men), the personal Presidential Guard (300 men, four tanks, 7 armored vehicles, and 2 artillery guns), a special-purpose police unit (more than 300 men, 12 tanks, 2 self-propelled artillery guns, and several armored vehicles), and a number of other armed formations and self-defense units, each numbering from a few to several hundred men.[3]

With the beginning of combat activity and especially as Russia's Combined Federal Forces began to approach Grozni, the defenders' ranks began to grow continuously. The defenders began to man strong-point defensive positions and prepared defense fortifications that until then had been held in readiness.

According to information then available to the Russian Military Command, the Chechens for the defense of Grozni had gathered together almost 15,000 regular army troops, 60 artillery guns and mortars, about 30 Grad rocket-propelled artillery units, and about 150 antiaircraft systems of various types. They also had available sufficient individual weapons and grenade launchers. No one has even attempted to make an accurate count of the number of volunteers who came to defend the capital. The press, however, has suggested that the number was thirty to forty thousand. The Chechen fighters later contended that so many volunteers gathered that they could not supply them all with weapons and had to send some of them home.[4]

According to Chechen chief of the General Staff, Aslan Maschadov, the city was defended by no more than five to six thousand government forces troops. This is quite believable, as prior to the assault of Grozni, international news correspondents in Chechnya observed that armed Chechen groups began to withdraw to mountain strongholds in the regions of Bamut, Asinovskaja, and Achchoj Martan. The Chechen military command clearly understood that, sooner or later, Grozni would be taken and that further resistance efforts would by degrees have to take on a partisan warfare character. For this reason, it was necessary to conserve already diminished regular army forces and to prepare for fighting under new conditions.

The Chechen Regular Army was better armed, better trained, and better led than the spontaneously gathered local self-defense forces. The regular forces could also be used where they were the most needed, as determined by the highest levels of command. Unavoidably, the haphazardly gathered volunteers acted mostly according to their own decisions, gathering where, in their own opinion, they were most needed. The local self-defense forces operated mostly in their own localities. According to Chechen chief of staff Maschadov, the prime weakness of the volunteer and local self-defense fighters was that they invariably left their positions at night to go home and then returned the next morning. Commanders attempted to oppose this, but their efforts for the most part proved to be futile.

Only a part of the elite Chechen Regular Army units remained in Grozni, mostly to defend the city center and the presidential palace. The primary forces tasked with the defense of the center of the city were the Abchaz and Muslim battalions and the special-purpose brigade. The defense of the other sectors of the city and the territories on its outskirts was left to the volunteer forces.

To repulse the coming attack, the Chechen military command set up three defense lines. The innermost defense perimeter was established at a distance of about 1 to 1.5 kilometers from the presidential palace. The middle defense perimeter was placed in the northwest at a distance of about 1 kilometer from the inner defense line and in the southwest and southeast at a distance of about 5 kilometers. The outermost defense perimeter ran along the outer borders of the city and extended further out in the area of Dolinsk.

Along the inner defense perimeter surrounding the presidential palace, strong-point defense positions were set up in buildings in which all the floors and cellars had been prepared for the firing of grenade launchers, automatic weapons, and heavy machine guns. Along Ordzonikidze and Pobeda Prospects and Pervomaiskoje Street, tank and artillery positions were prepared from which direct, straight-line fire could be applied. Concentrated within this defense ring were some 2,000 fighters, 34 armored units, several Grad rocket artillery units, and self-propelled artillery guns. Along Kopernik and Altajskaja Streets, teams of fighters were deployed, each numbering about 80 to 100 fighters and equipped with 2 armored vehicles and at least 60 antitank grenade launchers.

The middle defense perimeter consisted of strong-point defense positions at the beginning of Staropromyslovski highway and defense positions at the bridges across the Sunzha River, in the Minutka district, along Saichanov Street, and in the area of the Lenin-Seripov Refinery. The outer defense perimeter consisted of strong-point defensive positions along the Grozni-Mozdok and Dolinsk-Katajama-Tashkala highways and in the suburban districts of Neftkiansk, Chankala, Staraja Sunzha, and Chernorechje.[5]

The plan to assault Grozni using three armored columns, the number of armored vehicles in each column, their basic lines of march, and intended incursion points into the city were no secret to Dudajev. For this reason, where the incursion of Russian forces was expected, the Chechen High Command organized defenses in depth. At these positions and at the most vulnerable approaches, tanks and other armored vehicles were dug in up to their turrets.

Later events would show that Chechen preparations for the defense of Grozni were conducted by experienced military specialists who knew their profession.

The New Year's Assault of Grozni

The Russian Combined Federal Forces began their assault of Grozni on New Year's Eve. The night before, Grozni had been pounded by artillery, and on Saturday, the morning of December 31, Russian military aircraft flying out from the Jiesk, Krymsk, Mozdok, and Budionovsk airports, pounded the city with bombs and rockets. With these actions, the final assault of the city began.

In order to ensure that air strikes would be conducted continuously, the commander of the Air Forces, General Colonel Piotr Deinekin, suggested before the start of operations that two crews be assigned to every aircraft. This was also attempted for the SU-24 fighter bombers armed with RPK-500 guided rockets, which after release, home in on their intended targets. But it was almost impossible to find pilots in the North Caucasus Military Region capable of aiming such rockets, let alone able to avoid colliding with each other in the course of battle. Thus it was necessary to call up pilots from the Achtiubinsk Flight Center. They were only able to form a five-SU-24M fighter-bomber squadron with two crews per aircraft.[6]

In spite of such efforts, the effectiveness of air strikes during the first day of the assault was close to zero because of bad weather. Grachev ordered that Grozni be taken by January 1. Later, on January 9 while in Alma Ata, he announced that the "the operation to take the city had been planned within very short time constraints and had been executed with minimal losses ... And the losses, I want to tell you frankly, occurred only because a portion of the lower echelon commanders had faltered. They had expected an easy victory and then quite simply had caved in under pressure."[7]

The operation's success depended primarily upon the battle group moving in from the north. As planned, the primary thrust was left to the 81st Motorized Rifle Regiment and the 131st Motorized Rifle Brigade. The regiment consisted of three battalions, and the brigade was made up of two motorized rifle and one tank battalion as well as an artillery battery equipped with six Tunguska self-propelled antiaircraft gun units. The Russian military command had planned to augment the battalions' fire power with these units, and they had been assigned two units each to the two brigade battalions, one to the third battalion of the 81st Motorized Rifle Regiment, with the remaining

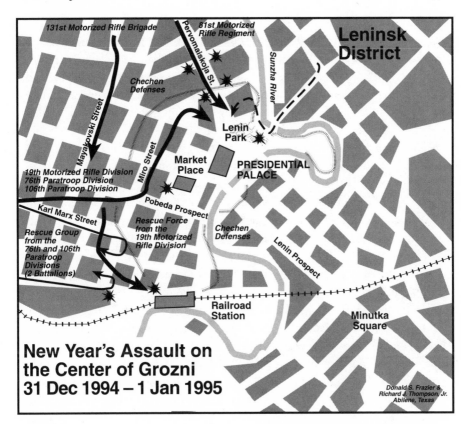

131st Motorized Rifle Brigade
81st Motorized Rifle Regiment
Pervomaiskoja St.
Sunzha River
Leninsk District
Chechen Defenses
Mayakovski Street
Lenin Park
Miro Street
19th Motorized Rifle Division
76th Paratroop Division
106th Paratroop Division
Market Place
PRESIDENTIAL PALACE
Karl Marx Street
Pobeda Prospect
Rescue Group from the 76th and 106th Paratroop Divisions (2 Battalions)
Rescue Force from the 19th Motorized Rifle Division
Chechen Defenses
Lenin Prospect
Railroad Station
Minutka Square
New Year's Assault on the Center of Grozni 31 Dec 1994 – 1 Jan 1995
Donald S. Frazier & Richard J. Thompson, Jr. Abilene, Texas

unit left for the defense of the Brigade Headquarters. This was an attempt to make use of the experience gained in Afghanistan, where Shilka antiaircraft gun units were used for this purpose. Such guns were not appropriate for combat within a city, however, their minimum range being much longer than the effective firing range of grenade launchers.

The columns began to move toward the city early that morning. The 131st Motorized Rifle Brigade's assigned task was to take the railroad station and prepare a bridgehead for the assault group storming the center of the city from the west. The brigade was able to accomplish this by 1 P.M. It reached the railroad station and took it almost without opposition, except for a small skirmish fought that morning. Shortly after 9 A.M. its scout company had encountered a small Chechen guard force and it had been necessary to go around this obstacle by turning into Majakovski Street. Although the column came under Chechen fire once more, no larger skirmishes were fought right up to the railroad station.[8]

Columns of the 81st Motorized Rifle Regiment, tasked to establish a bridgehead in the center of the city, also came under grenade launcher and mortar fire while yet on the outskirts of the city near the bridge over the Sunzha River. Later, after entering Grozni, its armored personnel carriers formed columns of three and moved almost unopposed down the streets of the city up to Gospitalnaja Street. But there they suddenly met with fierce Chechen grenade launcher fire. Immediately two tanks began to burn and three more began to crawl sideways. The armored vehicles speeded up but then ran into a column of paratroop armored personnel carriers moving in the direction of the Presidential Square.[9]

Fierce Chechen opposition was met only around 1 P.M. After the assault's disastrous defeat, both sides argued that the operation's overall plan and its starting time had not been unexpected by the Chechens, but facts indicate otherwise. Apparently, the Chechens did not really expect that the assault would begin before the New Year. If the situation had been otherwise, the attacking units could hardly have been able to take the railroad station and get to the center of the city without at least some opposition. That Dudajev would have dared to repeat the tactics used on November 26 is also not fully believable. This was not the same situation and certainly not the same enemy. By 1 P.M. the Chechens apparently had evaluated the developing situation fully and effectively reorganized their resistance. A do-or-die battle then broke out.

The fiercest engagements took place in the northern part of the city where Russian columns forced their way to within three to four blocks of the presidential palace and in the area of the railroad station.[10] The counterattack of the assault group forcing its way into the city from the north was organized faultlessly. Its further progress was blocked by Chechen forces commanded by Shamil Basajev.

The armored columns moving down narrow secondary streets were most often stopped by knocking out the first and last armored vehicles. Afterwards, the combat vehicles stuck in the middle were fired at from the surrounding buildings, knocked out, and set on fire. Those tanks able to break out from the columns then began breaking into the adjoining concrete buildings by smashing through them in reverse. They then attempted to return fire from encirclement. Some of the tanks were also able to force their way from the streets into the larger inner courtyards of the buildings and to establish perimeter defenses. But the major portion of the armored vehicles were either knocked out immediately or forced to fight while encircled and without any hope of breaking out.

The greatest forward movement was achieved by the 81st Motorized Rifle Regiment of the 20th Motorized Rifle Division. Tanks and armored vehicles moving down the main thoroughfares succeeded in forcing their way through to the very center of the city and even to the presidential palace. But unsupported by infantry (they were riding on the tops of vehicles), they were all destroyed by antitank grenade launcher fire.

During the day and evening battles that followed, the assault force was able to organize sufficiently dependable defenses while encircled and under attack. One of the regiments of the Volgograd Corps was surrounded and took cover in the hospital complex area.[11] During these battles, the assault force lost up to seventy units of armored equipment.

The 131st Motorized Rifle Brigade, after having successfully taken the railroad station, found itself in an even worse situation. According to this brigade's officers, they fell directly into a trap. At about 3 P.M., Chechen grenade launcher and sniper teams opened fire from all the attics, floors, and cellars of the surrounding buildings. During just the first hour of the battle, thirteen tanks and armored personnel carriers were knocked out and left burning. Their brigade commander, Colonel Ivan Savin, was wounded in both legs. By 3:30, the brigade was forced to go on the defense. Cut off, it had to continue fighting until the next morning. When their ammunition began to run out, the brigade commander decided to attempt a breakthrough, but this did not succeed.

The brigade commander ordered his assistant, Colonel Andrijevski, who had been left with the remainder of the regiment at the northern approaches of the city, to break through the encirclement ring from the outside. By early dawn, Colonel Andrijevski succeeded in organizing a column of some forty combat vehicles and by six o'clock that morning had begun to move toward the railroad station. The rescue column was forced to change its route somewhat and move along Majakovski Street as it could not traverse the other streets because of Chechen fire.

At about eleven o'clock that morning, the column neared the railroad tracks. But with only several hundred meters left to the railroad station, it was halted when the column's first vehicle was knocked out. Colonel Andrijevski was forced to order the column to turn back and move toward the station along Rabochaja Street. But at the intersection of Komsomolskaja and Rabochaja Streets, the column again met with antitank grenade launcher fire. In order to avoid withering fire, the rescue column turned toward the circus building, away from the railroad station.

According to the participants in the battle, a grenade launcher antitank shell then knocked out the column's command vehicle and the column lost any effective command. The tank immediately lit up like a torch. The shock wave from the explosion swept the special purpose detachment from Bertsk

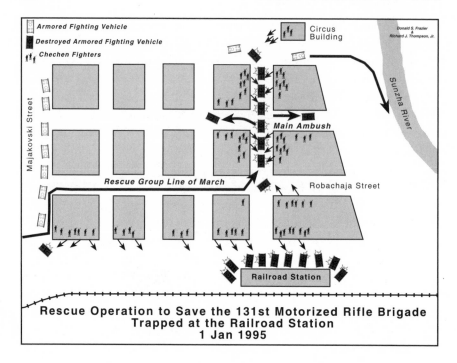

**Rescue Operation to Save the 131st Motorized Rifle Brigade
Trapped at the Railroad Station
1 Jan 1995**

from the tank. One of its soldiers, thrown to the asphalt minus a leg, began firing his weapon in a frenzy at the surrounding windows. Each window answered almost immediately with a hail of bullets. Each of the group's armored personnel carriers was pierced by at least five antitank grenades. The asphalt was soon covered with a carpet of bloodied infantrymen. No one had told them what to do in the event their commander was killed, so they continued to fall by the platoon, and the wounded were finished off by snipers. Only two tanks were able to break out, later hiding on the far side of the railroad station building. The rest, left in place, kept burning and crashing into each other in the confusion.

Perhaps one more armored vehicle could have succeeded in breaking out. But, in fright, the driver stepped so hard on the accelerator that the vehicle was unable to complete the turn from the circus building toward the Sunzha River and ran off the embankment into the water. Only two soldiers were able to swim out.[12]

According to the local inhabitants, the Chechens lost forty fighters during the battle with this column. Two other rescue groups were sent to the rescue of the brigade. One of them, from the 19th Motorized Rifle Division, was to have operated in coordination with Colonel Andrijevski's group, but it was unable to force its way to the area of the railroad station.

The brigade commander Ivan Savin finally received permission after 3 P.M. to retreat toward the area of Lenin Park. But to break through with sixty wounded proved to be impossible. There was no other alternative left, particularly when one more rescue group, made up of units of the 106th and 76th Paratroop Divisions, also turned back at 3:20 P.M., unable to break through to the area of the railroad station. Finding himself in a hopeless situation, the brigade commander decided to break out at any price. During the first attempt, the survivors from the assault group were able to reach only the Sortirovochnaja station. After a short pause to regroup, they decided to break through to the "Rodina" Collective Farm, where it was thought there would be no Chechens.

But the brigade's unit commanders were not familiar with the city. Not even having maps, they became lost and, unexpectedly, came out near the presidential palace. They continued to try to force their way toward the Sodovyja neighborhood. It was then that almost all the brigade staff officers as well as their commander, Colonel Ivan Savin, were killed. Seventy-four soldiers, among them the brigade staff's chief of operations, were captured by the Chechens.

Only on January 23, three weeks after the battle, were the soldiers of the brigade able to return to the scene of the battle and begin searching for their dead. During that time, the bodies of the dead soldiers had lain in the places where they had met their deaths. Only skeletons remained of some of the bodies, which had been devoured by stray dogs. A bit earlier, the body of the brigade commander, Colonel Ivan Savin was found. A bullet had struck him in the forehead. Besides him was the stiff body of a medic.

Prior to the assault, the brigade consisted of 446 soldiers. It is impossible to provide an accurate count of how many of them were killed since, as of February 9, 120 were still listed as missing in action. But of its 26 tanks, 20 were set on fire. Of its 120 armored troop carriers, only 18 returned from Grozni. All 6 Tunguska self-propelled antiaircraft guns were destroyed. Later, this became known as the tragedy of the 131st Maikop Motorized Rifle Brigade.

Despite all this, the Russian Army would most likely still have succeeded in accomplishing the operation's mission if not for the assault groups attacking from the east and the west, which had been unable to accomplish their assigned tasks. The assault from the east had been conducted by the battle group commanded by the assistant commander of the paratroop forces, General Major Staskov. The battle group consisted of the 104th Paratroop Division, the 129th Motorized Rifle Regiment, a tank battalion, and a special-purpose paratroop detachment. However, only a small portion of the paratroop division, previously deployed in the area of the Chankala Airport, participated in the attack. The commander of the 104th Paratroop Division refused to participate in an assault for which adequate preparations had not been undertaken.

The attacking column consisted of the 129th Motorized Rifle Regiment, a tank battalion (20–25 tanks), 5 Shilka self-propelled antiaircraft guns, 3 D-30 122 mm howitzers, about 10 paratrooper armored personnel carriers, and a special-purpose paratroop detachment (2 armored vehicles and 1 Ural truck).

On December 31 at 11 A.M., the column began to move toward Grozni and at about 1 P.M. neared the bridge over the railroad tracks. Here the column was met with a barrage of grenade launcher shells and automatic fire. The paratroop armored personnel carriers were cut off from the column, and almost all were soon left burning. The column, coming under Chechen fire, then turned to the right by mistake, as no one had known the way. The column then turned around once more and at 4 P.M. had reached the Rodina movie theatre. There, it again came under heavy fire. It then retreated to an open area nearby. Continuously battered by Chechen fire, it remained there until morning. From 9 to 10 A.M., it was bombed by its own SU-24 aircraft, which succeeded in knocking out five more armored vehicles.

After this attack, the battle group was attacked once again by the Chechens and was forced to retreat to the area of the Chankala Airport. But it retreated so fast that it left its dead and wounded as well as a portion of its equipment behind. When it finally reached the Chankala Airport at 2 P.M. on the first day of the New Year, the 129th Motorized Rifle Brigade calculated that it had lost 150 soldiers.[13]

The battle group attacking from the west was commanded by General Major Petruk. Within this group, the 19th Motorized Rifle Division commanded by Colonel G. Kandalin was not able to keep up with the tempo of the attack. With the Chechens mounting a fierce defense, this division's lead regiment was stopped while yet on the outskirts of the city. This faltering took place despite the fact that the actions of this regiment were directly controlled by the Northern Caucasus Military Region's assistant to the commander for combat readiness, General Lieutenant S. Todorov.

By midnight, units of this regiment were able to break through almost to the presidential palace and had only about 300 meters left to go. But unable to withstand Chechen fire in the vicinity of the central marketplace, one of the battalion commanders decided to turn toward Lenin Park. The other battalions followed. Stopped also were the units of the 76th and 106th Paratroop Divisions of this battle group.

By January 1, 1995, at 1 P.M., it became obvious that Russia's Combined Federal Forces had suffered a disastrous defeat. Almost 6,000 soldiers and

350 units of armored equipment had participated in the assault. During its course, 200 units of armored equipment had been knocked out, of which 25 had been taken by the Chechens as trophies.

Russian defense minister Grachev later reported that 534 soldiers had been killed during this stage of the operation. But on the evening of January 1, the Chechen chief of staff, Aslan Maschadov, announced that 800–1,000 Russian soldiers had been killed during the battles for Grozni and that 81 had been taken prisoner. In any case, at least one of every ten soldiers participating in the assault was killed, plus many wounded. Also, more than half of the armored equipment participating in the assault was destroyed. The world had not witnessed such a bloody battle since the end of World War II!

Could the Assault of Grozni Have Been Successful?

According to military theory, battle within a city is one of the most complex forms of warfare. In fact, battles for a city on this scale have not been fought since the end of World War II. For this reason, military theorists base their analyses for the most part on that war's experiences.

During World War II, the majority of operations to assault cities resulted in great losses in men and equipment to the attacking force. As a rule, the success of such operations depended upon advantages in strength and means, upon the level of troop readiness and the completeness of their preparation, and upon well-organized and uninterrupted command, coordination, and supply. One of the most important aspects of such preparations was a complete blockade of the city, thus cutting off all the defenders' supply routes. In Grozni, insufficient attention was paid to the latter aspect. The roads out of Grozni to the south were left open for the defenders. The operation was also begun in great haste, without exacting preparation.

Let us assume that the operational conception for the assault of Grozni was appropriate at the time it was conceived. What was not taken into account was the fact that the army was completely unprepared to carry it out and was in fact incapable of doing that which had been planned for it by its commanders. This is confirmed by the participants in the assault.[14]

As was related by a captain in the 81st Samara Motorized Rifle Regiment, up until December 14, his unit's primary activity had been snow removal. On December 14, his unit was placed on alert by an "alarm" signal and was sent to Mozdok. At Mozdok, their regiment was hurriedly supplemented with new people and equipment and then hastily underwent preparations for military operations. The soldiers were in fact completely unprepared; some did not even know how to use sniper rifles. They only learned they were entering Grozni when they saw its multistory buildings. Having entered the center of the city from various directions, their armored columns then stopped and, almost immediately, were riddled without mercy by artillery shells and grenade launcher fire.

Likewise, according to a lieutenant, on December 30, his unit was moved by forced march from Mozdok to Grozni and on the night of New Year's Eve reached the outskirts of Grozni. There a skirmish developed that lasted forty minutes, during which time two of their armored vehicles were knocked out and burned. Later, they found out that they had engaged forces from their own side. Their opponent, an Internal Affairs Ministry unit tasked with controlling the roads out of Grozni, also had considerable casualties. Because of coordination and communication failures during the assault, federal forces destroyed considerable numbers of their own soldiers and equipment.

The operation was mounted by the Russian High Command totally without accurate knowledge of the real situation. Coordination between the various units and the artillery was not organized. Recognition signal training was superficial, hurried, and done without the participation of the commanders of units and armored vehicles that had to operate along the primary lines of march. Reconnaissance, especially of the defenders' antitank defense positions, was not conducted.

Unit and subunit commanders had not been familiarized with the layout of the city, the features of the main thoroughfares and streets and their configuration, or with the features of the buildings' underground construction and the layouts of utility and sewer tunnels. Before the start of battle in what was an unfamiliar city, commanders were issued only 1:100,000 scale maps. In assaulting a city, maps of a scale of 1:25,000 are clearly necessary, or at least schematics of the city district in which the unit is assigned to operate.

Before the assault, field manuals apparently were not even glanced at. For this reason, specialized assault groups were not formed and the city was not stormed in sectors. All forces were used simultaneously, without leaving a reserve for contingencies. There was also no determination made of what were to be the most important sectors and buildings to be taken or of the primary direction of the assault thrust. One can fairly draw the conclusion that available forces were not concentrated along the most important attack courses.

Infantry operated not in infantry formations on foot but riding on the tops of tanks and armored vehicles. Combat vehicle crew commanders had not been trained to operate in coordination with infantry, that is, to have the infantry search out and designate targets for them. Besides this, the majority of the tanks during the course of the assault operated completely without infantry support.

Interior Ministry troops who were supposed to follow the armored vehicle columns did not do so. Falling back, they instead began to organize blocking posts. For this reason, the houses, other buildings, and cellars left to the rear of the columns were not searched. The routes of march were reconnoitered either not at all or very superficially.

The fact that the armored vehicle mechanic-drivers were inexperienced also had a negative impact. After the columns sustained fire, barriers of debris formed on some streets. The drivers were unable to get around these. This forced the columns to slow their movement and to stretch out. The drivers simply were not trained to maneuver in city conditions.

It must also be noted that many of the units were so unexpectedly thrown into battle that there was not sufficient time to prepare the soldiers psychologically for combat. Many of them simply had not understood that they had found themselves in a war. A good example of this was reported in the press: during the New Year's assault, one tank got lost near the presidential palace. Stopping at one of the squares, the tank port opened up and a young tanker asked some Chechens standing nearby where he could buy some cigarettes. Instead of an answer, he received a burst of automatic fire. The tank was hit with grenades, and the tanker slumped over.

The 131st Maikop Motorized Rifle Brigade's chief of staff later labeled this Grozni assault operation a pure misadventure, an opinion held by a large number of other high-ranking officers. Perhaps the harshest evaluation of the Grozni assault was made by the Russian daily *Moskovskij komsomolec* (Moscow young communist) in an article published January 6, 1995, and entitled "Operation 'New Years'": "Grozni was bombed by diesel mechanics, the targets were picked by pontoon operators."[15]

Without a doubt, this New Year's armed forces operation will never be written in gold letters into the annals of Russian military victories.

Tactics of the Chechen Forces Defending the Capital

In planning the defense of Grozni, President Dudajev and Chief of Staff Maschadov used the experience they gained during the prior assault of the capital. They deployed the Chechen forces not along the borders of the city but in the city itself. Outside the city, the Russian Combined Federal Forces were obviously vastly superior. But upon entering the city, the federal army had to divide itself into a large number of threads stretched out along the streets of the city. The effectiveness of its heavy weapons, especially tanks, necessarily decreased. The defenders' ability to use the element of surprise increased dramatically.

The Chechen tactic to fight armored columns played the greatest role. By hitting the first and last vehicles, the whole column was effectively stopped. Then the stationary armored vehicles caught in the middle were methodically destroyed. This was achieved in various ways.[16] One was through the use of antitank grenade launcher snipers. The majority of such snipers were military professionals. As their numbers were not large, once they accurately hit the first and last armored vehicles of a column, they hurried off to another location, leaving the final destruction of the helplessly stuck column to the less proficient.

Another method used when there was a shortage of experienced grenade launcher gunners was to set up grenade launcher traps. As the armored column neared, an antitank round would be launched in the column's direction. As the federal soldiers were untrained to fire from moving vehicles, the column invariably stopped and opened fire in the direction from which the grenade was fired. The standing column was then fired upon with antitank grenades launched from the surrounding buildings.

The third and main method for engaging the enemy's armored columns was by the maneuver of well-prepared grenade launcher, machine gun, and sniper teams. These teams moved to their targets by automobile or truck or operated on foot, using their intimate knowledge of the city—its underground utility tunnels and the like—to their advantage.

Also of great importance to the Chechens was the tactic of cutting off the armored vehicles from their supporting infantry. This succeeded largely because the Russian soldiers simply were not trained for battle in the streets.

Chechen tactics were quite simple but effective. Their advantage lay in their comparatively light equipment, their portable antitank weapons, and their mobility. Being mobile, the Chechens were able to concentrate their forces quickly where they were most needed.

The Chechen Military Command placed no less importance on snipers. They also operated very effectively. Russian officers confirmed that in just the 8th Volgograd Army Corps, practically all the platoon leaders and company officers were taken out by snipers. In one of the battalions of the 81st Regiment, only one officer and ten soldiers survived sniper fire.

The Chechens also had an advantage in that they operated in small groups. The federal army units were confronted with an almost invisible enemy. They were being constantly fired upon, but as the Chechen fighter groups were very mobile, it was never very clear in what direction they should fire back. It was characteristic of the conflict that there never were any clear battle lines.

The Russian Army was trained to fight regular army units. If the Chechen forces had been organized in regiment or division formations, they most likely would have been destroyed in several weeks. But the Russians Army was not trained to fight with small armed groups.[17]

The factor of surprise was, again, of great importance. The first echelon of the armored columns were allowed to pass through to the center of the city almost without hindrance. Concentrated fire was applied only when the city's streets became filled with columns of armored vehicles. When the armored vehicles began to be hit on all streets at almost the same time, the columns began to jam up and lost their maneuverability.

The defense of Grozni was commanded by the Chechen General Staff and Dzhochar Dudajev himself. Later, for his excellent organization of the defense of the city and its successful command, the chief of the General Staff, Colonel Aslan Maschadov, was awarded the rank of general by decree of President Dudajev.

The command of the Chechen forces was not especially centralized. Each force knew only the general situation and its basic assignments. The most important aspect of command was the distribution of forces, each group being assigned to a specific territory. During the repulsion of the assault, the Chechen forces operated almost independently. Many small groups of Chechen fighters in the city also found themselves appropriate places in the city's defenses. Everyone's basic purpose was, after all, the same: to destroy the enemy. These mobile, completely independent groups chose their targets themselves and, being always on the move, created for the Russian units the appearance of a unified Chechen attack. The coordination among the leaders of the Chechen fighter groups was, however, exceptional. Even without centralized command, they succeeded in fighting their opponent all over the city simultaneously. Their level of coordination often was such that Chechen groups would themselves pick as targets for attack enemy units that at that moment were not even being fired upon. The command principle chosen for the defense of Grozni of "less centralization, more coordination" proved to be totally justified.

Little information is available on the Chechen mid-level field commanders. The older military commanders, such as Maschadov, had served in various posts and had attended various academies, and thus at least some of their history before the war is known. The younger commanders—aged twenty-eight, thirty-two, thirty-six, and so on—had obtained normal civilian educations not only in Chechnya but in Russia, but little of their earlier experiences sheds light on their actions in this war. They rose, for the most part, to the ranks of commanders because of their own talents and the experiences accumulated during the war itself.

The Chief of Staff, Aslan Maschadov, forbade his forces to operate in large units or to use combat equipment in city conditions. The Chechens, however, quickly adapted to effective use of their small group advantage. Their tactics were very simple, especially when fighting Russian units fortified in buildings. Whenever the Chechens succeeded in forcing the Russian soldiers from a building, they left at most five of their fighters in the building. After some time, the Russians would counterattack and concentrate at least a company against the building. They would then shoot it up with artillery, try to set it on fire with flamethrowers, and then attack it according to all the tactical rules. But having taken back the building, they invariably found in it only a few bodies of Chechen fighters. Also whenever the Russian soldiers took up defensive positions, they customarily positioned several people in every building, thus diluting their forces. The Chechens then concentrated several fighter groups into a "fist," or single strike force, and struck a single target.

Before attacking, they first shot into every window a "fuga." A fuga was created by attaching two 400-gram pieces of trotyl explosive to a RPG-7 grenade launcher round with adhesive tape. This had been the invention of the commanders of the Abhaz battalion. The results of the fugas were very impressive. But not less effective were the antitank grenades, tinkered with by the same "inventor." When napalm was attached to them, tanks would immediately flame up. And if an armored troop carrier was hit by such a fuga, it would blow a huge hole in its armor, the munitions would detonate, and the turret would fly off, just as if grass was being cut with a scythe.[18]

The Taking of the Presidential Palace

For the Russian Army, the assault of Grozni was a failure. But, not having yet evaluated the situation or discerned that the battle for Grozni was already lost, Russian defense minister Grachev announced on January 2, 1995, that it would take only five to six more days to clean the city of Chechen armed formations and collect the weapons from the Chechen volunteers.

Meanwhile, the Russian Combined Federal Forces' primary attention was still focused on the rescue of encircled Russian assault groups and on the security of its remaining armor and equipment.[19] Russian forces withdrew heavy combat equipment from the center of the city while still attempting to hold on to positions they occupied around the center. Fierce engagements continued, however, at the railroad station, the central marketplace, and in the vicinity of the hospital complex. Aircraft were also used very intensely.

Some of the most apparent shortcomings were reacted to quickly. Already by January 3, unit tactics were changed. The Russian forces began to operate in small groups, using tanks, armored vehicles, armored troop carriers, and artillery supported by infantry. The Northern, Baltic Sea, and Pacific Ocean Naval Commanders were ordered to prepare and send their marine infantry to Chechnya.

Blame also had to be apportioned. The Russian High Command quickly blamed the failures of the Grozni assault on the battle group commanders. By January 4, General Major Petruk was replaced as commander of the Western Battle Group and General Major Ivan Babichev was assigned in his place. Colonel V. Prizemlin took over as commander of the 19th Motorized Rifle Division. The Northern and Northeastern Battle Groups were combined into one. The new Northern Battle Group was formed, and General Lieutenant Rochlin was appointed its commander.[20]

On January 4 and 5, the Russian Army began to redeploy its forces. The 129th Motorized Rifle Regiment marched by a skirting maneuver to the northern part of Grozni and pushed the Chechens out of a military base located on the east bank of the Sunzha River. The purpose of the move was to strengthen the Northern Battle Group. All-out assault was abandoned and a decision was made to take the city building by building and neighborhood by neighborhood using street battle tactics. The forces in position around the Central Square were also strengthened. The intensity of the fighting decreased.

According to official information announced by the Russian High Command, 2,500 Chechens had been killed since the start of the conflict. Russian forces had also destroyed 150 Chechen aircraft, 26 tanks, 40 units of other armored equipment, and 63 artillery guns. In other words, the Russians had destroyed the whole Chechen Air Force and about a quarter of all the combat equipment possessed by Dudajev's forces at the start of the operation. At least 108 Chechens had also been taken prisoner. According to official reports, about 250 Russian troops had been killed in Chechnya, among them 116 Land Army soldiers, 100 paratroopers, and 40 Internal Affairs Ministry troops. However, news agencies reported quite different figures. In their estimate, the numbers killed were much larger: about 2,000 Chechen and 1,800 Russian soldiers had died in the assault.

On January 5 and 6, the assault of Grozni was renewed. An attempt was made to encircle and block off the defenders still fighting in the center of Grozni and to expand the territory of the capital under its control. The center of the city was again assaulted from the west from the railroad station, from the north from the central marketplace, and from the northeast. Reacting to political pressure, Yeltsin ordered that the bombing be suspended from January 5.

Besides these measures, Russia attempted to strengthen its armed forces in Grozni. Columns of armored vehicles and other equipment began to move

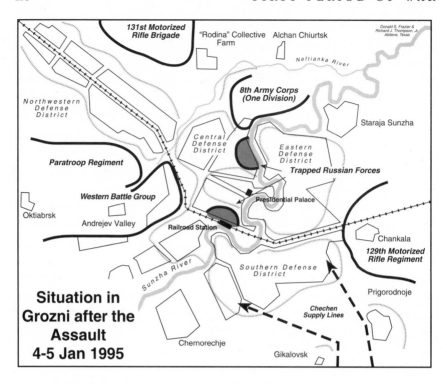

Situation in Grozni after the Assault 4-5 Jan 1995

across Ingushia towards Grozni through January 18. The airlift of marine infantry units to the conflict zone began on January 9.[21] Five Il-76 aircraft airlifted in the Baltic Naval Fleet's marine brigade's paratroop battalion, commanded by the brigade's commander Colonel J. Kocheshkov from Chabarovsk Airport to Mozdok. Seven Il-76 and one An-124 aircraft airlifted in the Northern Naval Fleet's marine battalion from Olenegorsk Airport. Seven Il-76 and six An-12 aircraft brought the 165th Marine Regiment from the Pacific Naval Fleet. Together with the soldiers, sizable amounts of combat equipment, weapons, and munitions were brought into the conflict zone. About 90 tons of munitions were airlifted from just the Northern and Baltic Naval Fleets alone.

From January 10 through 12, a cease fire was conditionally agreed to by both sides. A forty-eight-hour truce was offered by the Chechen side. Many more cease-fire agreements would be made later, but this truce is noteworthy in that exchanges of prisoners were begun. During this cease fire, Russian military counterintelligence officers in Grozni received from the Chechens thirteen Russian prisoners from the 503rd Motorized Rifle Regiment of the 19th Motorized Rifle Division.

The preparation of a new military operations plan also began at this time. Again the greatest attention was placed on completing the taking of Grozni. Because of the need for absolute secrecy, this plan was prepared by a narrow circle of generals and colonels. The plan provided that once the Combined Federal Forces in Grozni were strengthened, the blockade of the city was to be completed from the south and the southeast. This was intended to finally cut off the supply lines of the Chechen fighters in Grozni. The Eastern Battle Group was renamed the Southeastern Battle Group, and the Pavolga Military Region's assistant commander, General Lieutenant Popov, was assigned as its commander.[22]

The plan was put into operation without calling off the prior assault. On January 14, Russian forces succeeded for the first time in breaking through to the presidential palace, although not for long. Again air strikes were renewed. Air forces were used to bomb not only Grozni but the other communities as well.

The columns of armor and other units arriving daily in Grozni took up combat positions after short preparation and began to participate in skirmishes. Although the Chechens continued to resist fiercely, by degrees the initiative was taken over by the Russian forces. An airbase was set up at the Northern Airport and helicopters were redeployed there.[23]

On January 18, the Chechen High Command made a decision to leave the presidential palace, the defense of which had become purposeless. The palace had been pierced from the roof down to its cellars by powerful delayed-action bombs and had become a ruin. That night, the Chechen fighters abandoned the palace, whose bunkers had housed the city's Defense Headquarters, about one hundred Russian prisoners, a first aid clinic, and several journalists. The headquarters was moved to a reserve bunker, the prisoners were taken to another secure area, and the wounded Chechens were evacuated.[24]

The next day, Russian military units took the abandoned palace. They were opposed by only two Chechen fighters. The Russian flag was raised over the palace. Participating in the flag-raising ceremony were motorized rifle regiment commander Colonel S. Bunin, reconnaissance platoon leader Lieutenant A. Jurchenko, Sergeant I. Smirnov, enlisted man A. Zakirov, Northern Fleet marine battalion commander Colonel A. Chernov, and assistant squad leader Sergeant G. Azarychev.[25]

Coincidence or not, the flag over the presidential palace was raised by the soldiers of the 33rd Motorized Rifle Regiment, the same regiment in which, serving fifty years before, Jegorov and Kantarija had raised the red flag over the Reichstag.[26]

With the taking of the presidential palace, the third stage of the Chechen war was completed. The city, however, was left untaken. Also left untaken were the other Chechen communities that remained outside the control of the opposition forces. The occupation of the presidential palace was just one more threshold that was crossed in the war in Chechnya but it was only of political significance. As almost all heavy weapons firepower in Grozni had been concentrated onto this minute piece of the earth's surface, a continuation of the defense of the palace would have meant only purposeless losses for the Chechens.

CHAPTER 7

Preparations for Military Operations in the Other Regions of Chechnya

The day after the Russian Federation flag was raised over the presidential palace in Grozni, President Yeltsin announced that the taking of the palace factually meant the cessation of hostilities. The Land Army was to be withdrawn by degrees and order was to be maintained by units of the Internal Affairs Ministry.[1]

The announcement was, of course, premature. The essence of the January 25 announcement was corrected during a meeting of the Russian Security Council with an explanation that the situation as yet did not allow the Russian Army to be withdrawn. The council decided that the Land Army would stay on, although the most important operations would be conducted by the Internal Affairs Army. The council also congratulated Defense Minister Grachev for "successfully concluding the military operation in Chechnya." At the end of January, assistant Internal Affairs minister General Anatoli Kulikov was made commander of the military operation in Chechnya.

President Yeltsin's announcement and the Russian Security Council's actions can be interpreted only as a wish to strike out reality. As of January 20, the Chechens still held two thirds of Grozni—the western, southern, and eastern districts, as well as strategic positions near the Sunzha River. They had only withdrawn from the area of the railroad station. The maps used by General Rochlin's headquarters contained notations that the Federal Army's Northern and Western Battle Groups controlled only a tenth of the city's territory.[2]

According to Russia's own military intelligence information, a 3,500-member Chechen fighter group was still left in Grozni, with ten tanks and armored vehicles, five Grad rocket artillery systems, and five or six artillery guns. The Chechens also had forces elsewhere. The strongest groups were concentrated in the cities of Argun, Gudermes, and Shali, in the communities of Bamut, Achchoj Martan, Novij Sharaja, Samanshk, and Sernovodsk, in the villages of Shchelkovskaja and Grebenskaja, and in the area along the Dagestan border.

But the operational situation in the Chechen capital had changed. From the north, General Rochlin's units had neared the center of the city and were spread out among the damaged buildings of the Republican Hospital. General Rochlin's headquarters had been established there in fortified dugouts and in the basements of these buildings. Collocated with the headquarters were the intelligence battalion and the special-purpose units. The rest areas for troops coming back from blocking posts were also located there.[3]

From the west, General Babichev's units had wedged themselves in towards the center of the city. What was tactically the most significant, however, was that an open road to the south of Grozni still remained in Chechen hands. Along it flowed additional Chechen fighters, food, ammunition, and explosives.

Constant confrontations continued in Grozni. Even the presidential palace, which Russian troops had abandoned after taking it, was fought for again after several Chechen snipers took positions in it. Small Chechen fighter groups also kept attacking Russian posts so that in one or another location, street battles were constantly erupting. But Chechen fighters were being forced to begin their withdrawal. Their main forces in the city began to concentrate in the southern, southeastern, and eastern districts of Grozni. The strongest group, more than 1,600 fighters commanded by their field commander, Basajev, was concentrated in Chernorechje. This group still had several tanks and Grad rocket artillery units.

The fiercest battles occurred for the positions and the bridges across the Sunzha River. The 165th Marine Infantry Regiment, which just arrived from Primore, suffered its first losses in engagements near the Sunzha River. One of the 3rd Battalion's Company Commanders, Senior Lieutenant Maksim Rusakov, was killed by a mortar round, five more troops were wounded, and eight were taken prisoner. Later, the Chechens exchanged them for the bodies of eight of their fighters.

The reports of the Russian military medical units give an indication of the intensity of battles during the second half of January. Each day, 60 to 100 wounded were brought to the field hospital set up in the shelters of the former Civil Defense Headquarters. According to the calculations of the medical personnel, during 18 days of fighting, the Northern Battle Group alone had lost about 1,000 soldiers killed, and 5,000 more wounded. It was said that while storming the presidential palace, General Rochlin had "laid down" the Volgagrad Corps' 255th and 33rd Regiments.

The Chechen positions in Grozni were constantly being bombarded from the air and pounded by artillery, even heavy artillery. The Akacija self-propelled 152 mm artillery guns were especially actively used for this purpose. One of these self-propelled howitzer batteries brought in from the Ural Military Region was used to prevent the Chechens from nearing the approaches of the bridge across the Sunzha River. Another was set up on the northern outskirts of the city near the airport and was used to support the activities of the 276th Motorized Rifle Regiment.

On January 24, the Russian High Command once again announced that the capital of Chechnya had been taken and that it was time to go on to a new phase of the campaign. This was a strange announcement, particularly as the Federal Army Groups in Grozni were still being reinforced, and all the more so as the Federal Army's combat activities became even more intense the next day. This was interpreted the most realistically by journalists, who viewed the Federal Army's increased combat activity as the last assault of Grozni after which the Chechens would have to give up the city.

The Chechen Armed Forces in Grozni became more active, especially after Dudajev called together the first Chechen Defense Committee meeting in his alternate headquarters. The confrontations in the suburbs of Oktiabrsk, Chernorechje, and Aldi, at the Minutka square, and in the areas neighboring the Sunzha River became more intense. Counterattacks were mounted even in the center of the city, where several streets as well as the tramway station were taken over. Russian troops were also attacked near the Chankala Airport.

But these were only temporary successes. On February 3, three Russian tanks broke through Chechen defense positions to the south of Grozni and neared the main highway. The Russian force succeeded in almost surrounding the Chechen capital when they took the strategically important crossroads to the south of it.

Although Grozni and its suburbs were still being fought over, the Chechen Forces High Command decided to withdraw the largest portion of its forces from the city in order to conserve them. It also decided to transfer its headquarters to one of the suburbs. On February 9, the commander of the Chechen Headquarters, Aslan Maschadov, announced that the giving up of the capital to the Russians did not mean a Chechen defeat or an end of the war with Russia. In his opinion, the Chechens had learned to fight and had become more disciplined. According to President Dudajev, the withdrawal from Grozni meant that a new stage of the war, the spring and summer campaigns, were beginning.

The Transfer of the Conflict to Other Regions

Although by the end of January, 1995, Grozni had not yet been taken, the character of the war had changed. Such large Federal Army Forces and so much armor and combat equipment had been concentrated in the city that few doubts remained that Grozni would be taken sooner or later. The Russian High Command also began to prepare for military operations against Chechen armed forces in the other Chechen communities. Besides, it was necessary to justify President Yeltsin's January 20 announcement by at least feigned combat actions elsewhere. Apparently for this reason, on January 21,

Russian military aviation began for the first time to concentrate its fire not on Grozni itself but on the surrounding communities. Confrontations and air strikes also took place in further off communities. This can be interpreted as the start of the transfer of combat activity by perceptible degrees to the other regions of Chechnya. From this date, continuous bombardments by artillery and rocket strikes from the air were directed against Bamut, Samashk, Zakan Jurt, Argun, Gudermes, Shali, and other Chechen communities. Ingushia was also struck along its border with Chechnya.

By the beginning of February, the primary objectives of the Federal Army outside of Grozni were also becoming clear. Attempts were being made to take over the communities neighboring Grozni to the south, southwest, and southeast and to cut off the roads still open to Grozni from the mountain regions. Bombed and attacked most often were Jermolovka, Alchan Jurt, Alchan Kala, Chechen Aula, and the Grozni suburban districts.

In the west, the main thrust of Federal Army attacks was against the village of Samashk and the hamlet of Asinovskaja. In the east, Argun and Gudermes were also targeted. Only the communities in the mountain regions were still not being subjected to more intensive efforts.

It was becoming clear to the Chechens that they would not be able to keep Grozni under their control for very much longer. Their forces continued to suffer considerable casualties during the intense fighting for every building, street, and block. Whereas at the beginning of the operation the Federal Forces had been equipped with outmoded heavy weapons and equipment long held in storage, whose technical condition had been poor and subject to constant breakdowns, now the Federal Forces had not only changed their tactics but had brought in more effective equipment for the street fighting, such as Shmelj flamethrowers.

Having decided to withdraw a part of their fighters from the city, the Chechen High Command immediately began to make preparations for the defense of the mountain regions. The forces left in the city were concentrated in the Chernorechje district and in the southern and southeastern districts of Grozni. It was easiest from there to maintain communications with the other regions of the country. Having suffered considerable losses, the Chechens also began to supplement their numbers by organizing the formation of new forces and their training. Although this was done in practically all the communities, the primary centers for troop mobilization and training were Argun, Shali, Jermolovka, Shamijurt, and Meskerjurt.

President Dudajev offered the Russian High Command a cease fire a number of times and to begin negotiations to regulate the conflict by political means. The Russian answer had always been the same: the Chechens must put down their arms and capitulate. The Chechen field commanders then began to evaluate other possible forms of armed resistance. Expressing their opinion publicly on January 28, Dudajev for the first time openly threatened to transfer the war in Chechnya to the cities of Russia and added that this would most definitely happen if the fighting lasted for one more month. According to Dudajev, "No tanks will then be able to defend Moscow. Besides the capital of Russia, there is also the Northern Caucasus, Krasnodar, Stavropol, and the Astrakhan region."

Later, this possibility was repeated a number of other times. Having made the decision to leave Grozni, Dudajev once more called together the Chechen National Assembly on February 10. The assembly voted to continue the fighting if the Russian High Command further ignored the Chechen offer of a cease fire and negotiations. The Chechen High Command communicated their plan to the Russian commanders as to how the conflict should be regulated by political means.

The Grozni takeover phase of the operation was concluded by the start of negotiations between the military commanders of both sides. First agreeing that the political terms would remain open, both military commanders, without the direct participation of politicians, then concluded an agreement to cease the firing of heavy weapons in the city and to begin negotiations for an exchange of prisoners.

On February 13, at the Ordzhonikidzevskaja railroad station in Ingushia, the commander of Russian Combined Armed Forces in Chechnya, General Kulikov, met with the chief of the General Staff of the Chechen Armed Forces, now General Maschadov. The negotiations took place under the intermediation of the president of Ingushia, Boris Agapov. Also participating in the meeting was the commander of the Russian Defense Ministry's Armed Forces in Chechnya, General Kvashnin. The railroad station was guarded by dozens of Russian, Chechen, and Ingushian soldiers.

During a second meeting that took place several days later at the Slepcovskaja Airport, the terms of the first agreement were expanded. The Russian side agreed to allow into Grozni an unarmed group of Chechen fighters who, together with Russian soldiers, would remove the bodies of the dead. An offer was also made to the Chechens that a demilitarized zone be created in Grozni. The Chechens agreed to consider this plan but refused to agree to limit the use of their heavy weapons.

With the beginning of negotiations, combat activity in Chechnya died down somewhat. Grozni was formally passed into the hands of the Federal Army, although many groups of Chechen fighters still remained in the city. The negotiation, however, resulted in only a temporary truce.

The Transformation to Partisan War Tactics

The Chechen Defense Committee decided at its first meeting at its new head-quarters to give more attention to a changeover to partisan tactics. The experience in defending Grozni, gained at the price of so much blood, had showed that the most appropriate and effective means of doing battle with the Russians was by mounting partisan actions using small units. Large fighter forces operated ineffectively; besides, such groups usually sustained larger losses.

The partisan warfare consisted of attacks against Russian units in their deployment areas or at their posts, ambushes along roadways, sniper actions, diversions along the railway line, attacks against small groups of Russian soldiers or individuals, and attacks against means of transport. The Chechens began to avoid engagements with strong groups of federal forces in Grozni and in the village communities. In withdrawing after surprise attacks, the Chechens always carried away all their dead and wounded, leaving behind neither weapons nor documents.

In those areas of Grozni that were occupied by the Russian Federal Forces, the city was divided into sectors and an attack group was assigned to each. Such fighter groups, armed with individual weapons and grenade launchers, operated in subunits of four to six people, usually a commander, a radio operator, a sniper, a grenade launcher operator, and riflemen.

By the beginning of February, a radio communications link was established with every Chechen attack group. The groups conducted sudden attacks against Federal Army positions and later began to mine buildings usable for the housing of troops. The combat groups operated in shifts: a group would arrive in the city at night, operate for several days, and then withdraw at night to their rest camps. Then another group would take their place. Sometimes the Chechens would wear Russian military uniforms.[4]

The headquarters of the Russian Land Army evaluated the tactics of the Chechen fighters as follows:

> The armed forces of the Chechen Republic consist of Chechen "hit men" and foreign mercenaries. They number about 6,000 people. Their primary method of attack is by ambush or an "attack and retreat" tactic. The hit men operate as a rule in groups of 15–20 people. Some assignments are carried out by smaller groups of 3–5 people, among whom are a sniper, a grenade launcher gunner, and a machine gun operator. Such group is armed with individual weapons, RPG-7, RPG-18 antitank weapons, and often bottles filled with flammable liquid. To maneuver, they use trucks and automobiles. The "hit men" sometimes dress in Russian military uniforms. For communications, they use foreign-made portable radio transmitters. An amateur

"ham radio" net is also used to collect intelligence information and to issue commands. Snipers operate very actively in Grozni. Primarily they attempt to position themselves along the perimeters of areas occupied by Federal Army units. They take firing positions on the roofs of houses and on the upper floors of multistory buildings. They fire not directly out of the windows but out of the inner depths of the apartments, away from the windows, which makes it difficult to detect and suppress them. Artillery is fired from ambush using solitary guns. Grad multiple tube rocket artillery and mortars are pre-aimed and pre-positioned. After a salvo from a Grad rocket artillery system or a round from an artillery gun, the firing positions are changed. Those tasked with fire control and correction operate in the Federal Army unit rear areas as peaceful citizens or refugees. There have been instances where Russian-speaking inhabitants, especially women, have been forced to reconnoiter Russian Army forces. Their cooperation is usually achieved by taking their family members hostage. For the gathering of intelligence and for artillery fire control and correction, people are often sent into Russian units as apparent supporters of the opposition. The Chechen "hit men" listen in on the command radio communications net very intelligently and use the information received for the purpose of destroying Russian objectives.[5]

The continuous attacks of the Chechen forces forced the Russian Federal Forces units to take additional defense measures. The Chechens reacted to this by introducing several new tactical elements. One of these was to provoke the Russian units into firing at each other. Chechen commanders noticed that coordination between Russian units adjacent to each other was poor, especially if they belonged to different ministries or were from a different service. Quite often, there were no direct communication links between the Russian unit commanders, and thus provocation tactics could be put into effect very simply. A small Chechen fighter group would slink in the dead of night into the territory in between the Federal Army units and open up grenade launcher, machine gun, and automatic fire in the direction of both Russian forces units. In order to set up the appearance of a larger attack, trotyl explosives were sometimes attached to the antitank grenades. These "combined" munitions imitated artillery and mortars rounds, as the explosions of the "enhanced" grenades sounded much more powerful. As soon as the Russian units opened up answering fire, the Chechen fighters would withdraw. The Russian units would sometimes continue to fire at each other for a long period of time before realizing that they were firing at their own forces. Quite often they kept firing at each other until the next morning when helicopters called in to assist flew to their location and helped them to unravel the situation.

Sniper tactics were also changed somewhat as the increased watchfulness in the Russian units decreased the effectiveness of individual Chechen snipers. Snipers began to operate not alone but in groups supplemented by two additional fighters armed with grenade launchers and automatic weapons. In engaging the intended target, they would first shoot it up with automatic weapon fire. When Russian soldiers returned fire, a Chechen sniper in position some four to six hundred meters from the target would easily pick them off. If an armored vehicle or other combat equipment began to advance toward them from the Russian position, it was hit by the grenade launcher gunner. The team would then quickly withdraw.

In village communities, there was an increase of occurrences where Russian soldiers were shot up from speeding automobiles. The Chechens also began to attack the enemy's armored vehicles and combat equipment differently. From the start of the incursion until the middle of January, the Chechens had simply attempted to destroy such vehicles. Later, because of their own combat equipment losses, attacks began to be prepared much more carefully and with a view to picking out in advance the equipment in the columns that they themselves needed. Thus it was attempted to shoot out the tires or to damage the wheels of such vehicles. The damaged enemy equipment would then be towed to a secure location and repaired.

The Chechen High Command also paid great attention to intelligence, especially to reports from its own military formations and from local inhabitants, giving much attention to the analysis of the information gathered. Of great importance was the interrogation of Russian soldiers taken prisoner and the gathering of information as to Federal Army unit movement control. Upon sighting a column, Chechen scouts passing themselves off as local inhabitants, would drive along in light cars at either the rear or the front of the column. As they passed the column, they would count the equipment and heavy weapons and make an approximate estimate of the numbers of personnel accompanying the vehicles. When they found themselves in front of the column, they would turn to the side and stop at a convenient location to observe.

Chechen communications intelligence operated especially effectively. For this were used Russian-made military radio transmitters (staff command vehicles KShM R-142 and R-161 and portable outdated R-105M and R-109 radio transmitters) and the amateur ham-radio transmitter net. For the immediate transmission of intelligence information, foreign-made radio transmitters, mostly Motorola handsets, were used. The Chechens knew the Russian Federal Army units' communications radio net practices and frequencies and could get in touch with even the Russian combined unit commanders. The Chechens used their knowledge of the Russian military radio communica-

tions system for more than intelligence purposes. There were also notable instances when, having attacked federal military positions and after Russian
commanders had called in helicopters for close air support, the Chechens
"corrected" the targeting information being passed on to the helicopters by
connecting into the radio frequencies. In one instance, after the Russian aircraft intensively pounded Russian positions, they even thanked the Russian
pilots by radio "for a job well done."[6]

Evaluations in Russia of the Actions of the Federal Army

It had taken the Russian Federal Army two months to take Grozni. The Russian General Staff's first operations plan had called for this to be done in no
more than two weeks. And by that time, not only was Grozni supposed to
have been taken but also the whole of Chechnya was to have bent to Russia's
will. Instead, only a conditional transfer of Grozni into Russian hands was
achieved.

In Russia, much attention was beginning to be given to the analysis of
the situation in Chechnya and the reasons for the Russian Army's failures during this campaign. This was the most important subject discussed during the
January 16 session of the Russian Federal Parliament's lower house, at which
President Yeltsin gave his yearly report. He noted in his report that in order to
preserve Russia's sovereignty, the government had the authority and had been
required to use force, having used up every other means of influencing events
in Chechnya. He admitted, however, that they had not been prepared to use
force effectively.

During the first stage of the planning of the operation, superficiality was
rampant and effective cooperation between the various Armed Services was
lacking. Russian military forces were also insufficiently ready to regulate local
conflicts.

The Chechen operation showed that the political and military system
of planning and decision making was outmoded and that it was necessary to
change this system's structure and personnel. The conflict also caused great
social damage in the country.

The results of the military operation in Chechnya were further discussed
at a conference at the Russian Defense Ministry held on February 28. Attending were the ministry's and the General Staff's senior Chiefs of Sections and
the commanders of the various military services, the military regions, the
corps and divisions participating in the Chechen campaign.

In discussing the results of the Chechen operation, Defense Minister
Grachev evaluated the actions of the Russian Army favorably in his report, al-

though even he was forced to admit that the level of its state of readiness had been unacceptable. In the course of his address, he mentioned the most important weaknesses:

> During the incursion, the units had almost never made use of their own available information or of information gathered by their own intelligence and had completely relied on the aviation forces to accomplish this function;
>
> The commanders had not been prepared to execute their functions, to command under field conditions, or to make use of the equipment and the communications means available to them;
>
> Almost no attention had been paid to unit and subunit technical supply and support, especially when the units were from the other Military Services;
>
> The supply of combat equipment and weaponry, for example, night vision glasses, munitions rations, and munitions supply, had been unrealistic under combat conditions.[7]

Defense Minister Grachev's report was also very critical of the Federal Counterintelligence Service for its submission of inaccurate information about the Chechen armed forces. The director of this service, Sergei Stepashin, admitted this for the first time on January 21, stating that his service had made many mistakes during the intervention into Chechnya and that the Russian Army had in fact not been superior to the Chechens armed forces.

The conclusions of the Russian military experts are also worthy of notice. During a conference on February 20 in the Kubinka Military Complex in the suburbs of Moscow, the senior commander of the Armor Command, General Colonel A. Galkin, stated that 2,221 units of armored equipment (tanks, armored vehicles, armored personnel carriers, self-propelled artillery guns, and so forth) were deployed to Chechnya. Of these, 225 armored equipment units, among them 62 tanks, were totally destroyed. (This should be understood to mean that a much larger number of armored equipment had been hit, as this figure does not include armor units that had been repaired and returned to service.) Most of the armored equipment had been hit in Grozni.

In the opinion of the military experts, this could only be compared to the operation to take Berlin in April, 1945. At that time, the Soviet Army had lost several hundred tanks (almost two tank armies). If the comparative relationship between the attacking and the defending forces is taken into account, the conclusion must be drawn that, percentage-wise, the armored equipment losses in Grozni street battles had been even more severe than in Berlin.[8]

Most of these losses were sustained because of the use of antitank weapons by the Chechens. It has been calculated that the Chechens were able to concentrate the fire of six or seven antitank weapons against each tank, armored vehicle, and armored personnel carrier. The Chechen fighters also made unconventional but effective use against armored vehicles and armored personnel carriers of hand grenades to which napalm had been attached.

The Russian losses were unjustifiably large. For this reason, the military experts suggested that special attention be paid to unit tactics. Thus a "checklist of combat procedures for soldiers in units and subunits in the Republic of Chechnya" was drawn up in the Land Army Headquarters. This brought back memories of the Soviet Army's experience during World War II and during the postwar years, when checklists had been almost the primary manuals for theoretical military training, especially since they could be quickly prepared and distributed. The following checklist was one of the first that was distributed to the army operating in Chechnya. It devotes most of its attention to the particularities of unit and subunit combat actions under various circumstances. Checklists are almost always boring because they tend to state the obvious. Ordinarily, if the company officers have been drilled in the performance of such actions during training, these things would be part of standard operating procedure. But apparently the officers at the company level were as green as the troops and needed guidance as to what they should do. Thus, "rules of thumb" were issued.

Travel to assigned regions (combat zones)

Units and subunits shall only travel to their assigned regions (combat zones): upon completion of their move by convoy, from their disembarkation areas after arrival by rail transport, from designated airports after arrival by air transport, and from the Assault Force assembly areas in rear areas. They can also relocate in the territory of the combat zone itself.

The movement of units and subunits is to be done along designated routes along which blocking posts have been organized and blocking positions established. Officers from the various Headquarters or units to whose area of deployment the move is being made shall be assigned to accompany the assembled columns.

Besides issues that can be decided in accordance to standard procedures, in organizing movement, it is mandatory to additionally: set up a stable radio communications link with the commander of the unit to whose deployment area the move is being made, also with the commanders of the blocking posts along the way, and internally within the column itself. During the movement, radio sets shall be kept in the receiving mode. Notification of the crossing of boundaries and of arrival to the assigned zone shall be made by short, pre-agreed signals. During the move, observation of the surrounding area shall be organized in every armored vehicle. Observers shall be ready to open fire at a moment's notice in the event the column is fired upon. Every transport vehicle's technical condition shall be painstakingly checked before the move and all defects found shall be corrected before the column begins its move.

When moving at night, only night vision apparatus is to be used. The use of the regular headlights is strictly forbidden. During the period of the move, unknown people are not to be allowed to near the column. In the event of sudden individual weapon and grenade launcher fire at the column, soldiers on the tops of armored vehicles shall open fire and suppress the attackers. It is mandatory that damaged vehicles be towed to the assigned deployment area. If this is impossible, they are to be towed to the nearest blocking post where they are to be guarded by the units manning the blocking post until repair and evacuation units arrive. Upon arrival at the assigned deployment area, immediate dispersal of unit (or subunit) troops to their assigned positions shall be organized.

Assault group combat actions

The conditions under which fighting is done in the cities and the communities are characterized by limited observation and fire zones, complex maneuvering, and the extreme necessity to maintain coordination not only between the units and subunits executing combat assignments but also with the units deployed in neighboring regions. In battles to take communities, assault detachments shall be formed as parts of a strengthened battalion in the regiments assigned the objectives. The first assault detachment assignment can be the taking of a strong point firing position and one or sometimes two or three blocks.

The assault detachment shall attack as a rule along two streets, one of which shall be a main street. From combat experience in Grozni, an assault group attacking along a main street can be made up of the following: Three motorized rifle platoons, one tank company, one flamethrower platoon (nine flamethrower operators), two Tunguska ZSU-23-4 guns, two IMR engineering-intelligence vehicles, one UR-77, one engineering, mine removal team, one technical repair and supply section, and a medical team consisting of one doctor, one doctor's assistant, three nursing instructors, and twelve orderlies.

An assault group attacking along the adjoining street can be made up the same way or have less reinforcement means. Besides the listed forces, the assault group shall also include a "cleaning out" group made up of several squads which shall search and clean out enemy fighters from the buildings, also a convoy group.

The first assignment of the assault group can be the taking of one building, several small buildings or one city block. Artillery units and helicopters shall be assigned to support the assault groups. Collocated with the commander at the command post shall be an air forces fire controller and an artillery fire controller. The assault group shall be supplied with explosives, incendiary devices and signaling equipment. The assault group's subunits shall be subdivided by twos and threes and complete coordination and mutual support shall be organized among them.

Given an assignment, the assault detachment (group) commander, besides dealing with issues to be decided in accordance with standard procedures, shall additionally: analyze and become familiar with the situation along the direction of the attack (which objectives have already been taken by his own army's units, methods of communicating with them, the locations of blocking posts, possible enemy breakthrough directions, where and what assignments are being conducted by special purpose units and mutual recognition procedures with them, and possible enemy firing positions and sniper locations during the period of the assault), issue concrete assignments to units under his command, units attached to his command and units supporting his forces, organize the coordination of all these units, give the units under his command the necessary time to accomplish the detailed preparations necessary to accomplish their combat assignment and to check their readiness by the assigned time.

As various units, including Internal Affairs Ministry forces, are included in the composition of the assault group and as aviation, artillery and neighboring units are assigned to support it, the commander's primary task becomes the organization of clear and uninterruptable coordination among all parts of the group.

It is mandatory to organize coordination between: all units of the assault group, the motorized infantry operating on foot, the assault detachment's (group's) artillery and supporting artillery and aviation, the assault groups and subunits defending the blocking posts and the buildings already taken, the assault groups and subunits operating in the vicinity and the assault group units and special purpose intelligence groups conducting assignments along the same attack direction.

One can expect success in battle only after detailed preparation is completed as to all these questions concerning the execution of upcoming combat assignments and this knowledge is passed down, even by means of several variants, to the commanded units.[9]

CHAPTER 8

Warfare in the Flatlands

The Russian Federal Army renewed combat activity on February 21. Confrontations took place at the approaches of Grozni, in the regions of Goichi, Alchan Kala, Samashk, Asinovskaja, and Sernovodsk. Argun, Gudermes, Shali and other communities were bombarded.

Although, after taking Grozni, the Russian High Command wished to prepare for operations to liquidate the other resistance centers, the primary Federal Army forces in Chechnya were still tied up in Grozni and along its approaches. The Chechen forces that remained were still putting up especially fierce resistance in the city's suburbs and even in the center of the city. Without an increase in manpower and equipment, the Federal Army units were incapable of achieving any significant results in the other communities.

It was thus necessary to finish up with Grozni before deploying the Russian forces to other objectives. This was the primary purpose of the commencement of a new wide-ranging operation. It was especially important to expand the territory under its control to the southwest, to the south, and to the southeast of the capital. The sooner Grozni was cut off from the other territories controlled by the Chechens, the faster resistance would be broken within the city.

Already during the first day of the operation, Federal Army units attacking Chechen forces in the Promyslovsk region were able to take the strategically important heights near the village of Gikala, about three kilometers to the southeast of Grozni, and to cut off the Baku-Rostov highway.

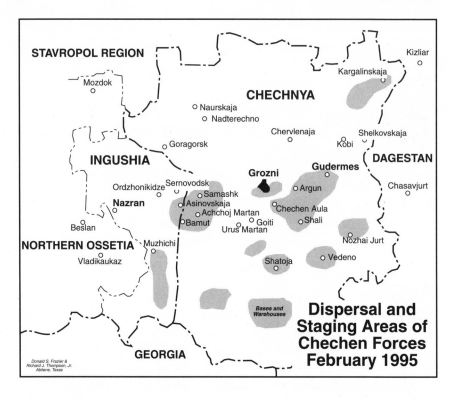

Dispersal and Staging Areas of Chechen Forces February 1995

Fierce confrontations continued until March 6, when the Chechen High Command decided to withdraw from Grozni its last still active Chernorechje group, commanded by one of its most renowned field commanders, Shamil Basajev. By this date, the Federal Army had succeeded in expanding the zone under its control a distance of eight to ten kilometers to the southwest, south, and southeast of Grozni. In the western part of Chechnya, the Federal Army also succeeded in cutting the highway connecting the communities of Samashk, Achchoj Martan, and Bamut.

Once the strategic situation changed, the intensity of the combat activity also decreased. No homogeneous Chechen defense line existed, although, in a discontinuous fashion, it stretched from the border of Dagestan in the east through the large cities of Gudermes, Argun, and Grozni along the strategic Baku-Rostov highway to Ingushia in the west.

Chechnya also began to break up into a number of "Groznis." The primary Chechen forces became concentrated into two groups, Western and Eastern. The strongest was the Eastern Group, uniting the Argun, Gudermes, and Shali Defense Regions. The Western Group's defense line stretched through Samashk, Bamut, and the village of Asinovskaja.

Accordingly, the Russian High Command also decided to separate its forces into two groups, the Sever (Northern) and Jug (Southern) Groups. The Sever Group was to operate against the Eastern Chechen Group and the Jug against the Western Group. General Major Genadi Troshev was assigned as commander of the Jug group. This group was to attack from Grozni along the road to the west, then unite with the 100th Internal Affairs Army Division in the Samashk forest region and liquidate by degrees the Chechen armed formations in the western part of Chechnya.[1]

The units assigned to the Sever Group were withdrawn from Grozni and its suburbs and concentrated in the region of Chankala Airport where the headquarters of the group's commander, General Major Babichev, was located. Here the plan for operations against the Eastern Chechen Group was being developed, and from here units were deployed to their assigned starting off positions.

By March 15, the control of Grozni's approaches were transferred into the hands of the Internal Affairs Ministry's Dzerzinski Division. The control in the city itself and the task of liquidating the small Chechen fighter groups still remaining were given over to the OMON (Internal Affairs Ministry's special purpose militia). In preparation for the new phase of the military operation, the Federal Army units continued their redeployment until March 20.

According to the Russian High Command, the Chechens still had 30 tanks and 15 Grad rocket artillery systems left. Its forces also still had some 14,000–15,000 fighters, of which about 5,000 were "mercenaries." The Federal Army Group had concentrated almost 200,000 troops in Russia along Chechnya's borders. Approximately 25 percent of these forces were in Chechnya itself. Assigned to only the Sever Group were 3 paratroop divisions, 3 motorized rifle brigades, 4 motorized rifle regiments, a marine infantry regiment, and other units.

From the second half of February, a positional war for the most part took place in the other communities. Federal Army units refrained from active assaults and instead set up their positions some 400–600 meters from the Chechen positions. In this way the Russian Army attempted to avoid losses from Chechen light weapons fire and to use its own heavy weaponry and equipment, of which it had superior numbers, more effectively. Chechen positions and communities were thus constantly pounded by artillery and mortars and bombed from the air.

Even in battles from dug-in positions, the Federal Army continued to suffer substantial losses as both sides continued to intensively shoot up each other's positions. The relatively small numbers of heavy weapons that the Chechens still had available were used especially effectively using "nomad" tactics.

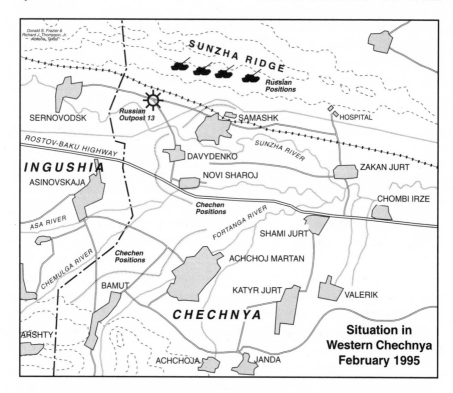

Using the cover of darkness, a tank or artillery gun would take up a position chosen in advance and open fire for a short time. Then it would hastily be withdrawn. Answering fire would be concentrated at an already empty position.

The Federal Army's positional war was one of the primary elements in its preparations for the new combat operations phase. In this way, the operation in Grozni was finished off and its forces freed up and dislocated to new regions. At the same time, the threat of new attacks constantly hung over the most important Chechen defense positions in the surrounding communities.

The Taking of Argun

Argun was the most important objective for the Federal Army's Sever (Northern) Battle Group in preparing for combat operations against the Eastern Chechen Fighter Group. It was the gateway to Gudermes and Shali. The first bombs on this small city had already fallen on December 4. On December 22, the Argun group was forced to defend against the 104th Uljanovsk Paratroop Division, which forced its way into this region. From that time on, the situation remained unchanged, although Argun was assaulted five times.

In the beginning of March and before the beginning of the Argun assault operation, the division occupied territory along a line from the community of Petropavlovskaja through Komsomolskaja up to the outskirts of northern Argun. The forward edge of their positions lay some 300–400 meters distant from the positions of the city's defenders. These positions were separated by the Argun River.

During confrontations near Argun, the division lost 30 troops killed and 122 wounded. The Chechens also knocked out 14 armor units and 9 motor transport vehicles. These were the official numbers from the division, although according to information reported by the Argun defenders, 41 units of armored equipment and 6 trucks were hit. The city's defenders' losses had been 7 killed and 40 wounded.[2]

According to information from the Sever Group's headquarters, a 2,000-member Chechen fighter group was positioned in Argun, supported by 10 tanks and 15–20 mortars. The commander of the Argun defenses, S. Aslanbekov, reported that the city at that time was defended by a small group of Chechen fighters even though it called itself a regiment. The regiment had been formed haphazardly from local inhabitants and volunteers who arrived from Dagestan, Kabarda, Azerbaijan, and elsewhere.[3]

In preparing for the assault of Argun, one of the battalions of the 165th Marine Infantry Regiment succeeded on March 12 in taking some very important heights from which the environs of Grozni and Argun opened up. The Chechens were unable to retake these heights. Although small, this victory later helped the units of the Sever Battle Group to take Argun.[4]

On March 19, the Russian forces received orders to assault Argun. Early that morning, the attack was begun by forcing the Argun River from two directions. The 106th Paratroop Division's Combined Regiment neared Argun from the north, at the same time cutting the Baku-Rostov highway. The same type of regiment from the 104th Paratroop Division went around Argun from the south. The marine infantry took the heights, and the 506th Motorized Rifle Regiment went around the city from the south and west. On March 21, the Russian forces succeeded in closing the encirclement by bringing up the 276th Ural Motorized Rifle Regiment. At the same time, two Internal Affairs Army brigades completed the closing of the internal encirclement ring.[5]

On March 22, the Federal Army's High Command issued an ultimatum to the inhabitants of the city. It demanded that the inhabitants leave the city in order to avoid the city's complete destruction and new civilian losses.

Chechen fighter groups from Gudermes and Shali attempted to break through the encirclement into the city but did not succeed. The defenders of the city then abandoned their positions and left the city. Although abandoned by its defenders, the city continued to be shelled by artillery and mortars. Only on March 23 did the commander of Russian forces in Chechnya, Anatoli Kulikov, announce that at five o'clock that evening federal troops had entered the city, although confrontations on the outskirts of the city still continued for several more days. The occupation of well-fortified Argun and the loss of the Gojten Kort heights near it, which had been taken March 22 by the 165th Regiment's marine infantry, broke the Chechen Eastern Front defense line. The roads to Shali and Gudermes were thus opened up.[6]

It is not known at what cost the Federal Army took Argun. It announced that this was done with minimal losses: 3 soldiers killed and 9 wounded. However, these losses were suffered by only the 106th Paratroop Division's Combined Regiment.

The Russian High Command announced that it had taken Argun, but it would have been more accurate to say that they had simply entered it. In Argun, the Grozni presidential palace takeover variant was repeated. After methodical, long-term pounding by artillery and extensive bombardment from the air, the city was so destroyed that there was not much left to defend. Every day about a thousand artillery and mortar rounds fell into the city, not counting bombs and rockets that were dropped or shot at it from the air. In deciding to withdraw its forces from the city, the Chechen High Command chose to conserve its people and equipment.

The Federal Army column entered the abandoned city along the Grozni-Vedeno highway almost without opposition. It then took over the railroad station and eventually reached the central street of the city. Further events were very much like those in Grozni: during the day, the OMON actively operated in the city; at night the Chechen partisans continued their attacks.[7]

The Taking of Gudermes and Shali

The taking of Argun and the dominating Gojten Kort heights markedly eased the course of the next stage of the Federal Forces' military operation. The forces planned to take over Gudermes and Shali in the same way that Argun had been taken, after intensive and continuous bombardment by artillery and bombing from the air. Thus Gudermes was continuously pounded by an artillery regiment from positions in the recently taken Terek hills heights. Shali was barraged by long-range artillery, among them the Grad and Uragan artillery systems. Having taken Argun, the Gudermes and Shali assault operations were executed simultaneously. Federal Forces had planned earlier to blockade Shali, approaching it through Chechen Aula, about six kilometers away.

The 324th Motorized Rifle Regiment from the Ural Military Region was assigned to take Chechen Aula and to blockade Shali. Having arrived in Chech-nya in the beginning of February from Jakaterinburg, the regiment was read-ied for a week in Tolstoi Jurt for the execution of its assignments and was then attached to the Jug (Southern) Battle Group for the operation to blockade Grozni from the south. The regiment accomplished its preliminary assign-ments by cutting off the road and taking the livestock breeding-farm center near Chechen Aula. But it did not succeed in taking Chechen Aula itself or in coming out near Shali. It was forced to stop in the vicinity of its approaches, where the regiment suffered significant losses: in only the battle for the milk farm, one of its companies lost all its officers and nine more soldiers were wounded.[8] When this variant for the assault of Shali did not succeed, the plan was changed since once the Gojten Kort heights were taken, the road to Shali from Argun opened up. The 506th Motorized Rifle Regiment was then sent against Shali.

During preparations for the operation to take Gudermes, the Federal Army Battle Group was reinforced by the 131st Maikop Motorized Rifle Brigade and the 276th Ural Motorized Rifle Regiment. The city was also blockaded from the east by the 76th Paratroop Division and from the west by the 129th St. Pe-tersburg Motorized Rifle Regiment and the 74th Siberian Motorized Rifle Brigade. The 165th Marine Infantry Regiment was tasked to take the domi-nating heights near the city.[9]

The Chechens established their main strong-point defense positions near Gudermes along the approaches where they most expected the enemy to come: along the Baku-Rostov and Argun-Gudermes highways and near what are known as the Gates to Gudermes. However, the main assault came not from these directions but across a swampy area.[10] The strategy proved to be unnecessary. With the exception of some small engagements at the approaches of the city and in the city itself, Gudermes fell into the hands of the Federal Army almost without opposition on the evening of March 30. By decision of the Chechen High Command, the Chechen fighters had left the city before the encirclement was completed.[11]

In Gudermes, the Chechens again repeated the Argun variant, only this time much more decisively. The conditions here were also more favorable, as the city almost melts into a forested region on the Belorechje side. When the Russian columns entered the city and stopped, the Chechen fighter groups re-entered the city and began continuous attacks. They cut units off from one another and succeeded in completely surrounding some units. In the city, armored equipment and artillery again became almost powerless. During just the first and second days of April, the Federal Army lost 43 units of ar-mored equipment. The Federal Army was able to survive and then force the

Chechen fighters out of the city only by a major effort and at the price of significant casualties.

Federal Army positions on the dominating heights near Gudermes were also attacked, but the Chechens were unable to take them back. The Russian Army newspaper *Krasnaja zvezda* (Red Star) wrote in great detail about the city's blockade and the takeover operation, including the fact that the city had been entered without suffering casualties. But the article failed to mention the battles that boiled over afterwards and the losses that were eventually suffered.

The assault of Shali was begun the same day, March 28, as had been the assault of Gudermes. However, the units of the 506th Motorized Rifle Regiment were first ambushed and then blocked by a mine field, stopping the attack. Only the next day did this regiment, together with the 503rd and 324rd Motorized Rifle Regiments, the 166th Motorized Rifle Brigade, and the 165th Marine Infantry Regiment, succeed in blockading the city. They then issued an ultimatum to the defenders of Shali. No answer was received.[12]

The Chechens fiercely fought only at the approaches of the city where defense positions were prepared. Almost 3 kilometers of entrenchments had been dug just to set up these positions. But when the defense of the approaches and suburbs of the city became hopeless, they decided to withdraw from the city, leaving in it only a handful of defenders. They also decided to transfer the Command Headquarters to Vedeno, which was further into the mountains.[13]

Although the defenders of Shali withdrew, the city continued to be barraged by artillery and mortars for a day and a half. Federal Army units entered it only on March 31 at 2 P.M. They hurriedly announced that the city had been taken, although this again did not totally reflect reality. Fearing that the same would also happen here as had happened in Gudermes, only the Internal Affairs Ministry units were left in the city. The Defense Ministry's troops were withdrawn almost immediately and moved out in the direction of the village of Dermachiuk. Taking over a tractor station on the other side of this village, they set up an artillery battery and began to shoot up the area surrounding Shali. The Internal Affairs Ministry troops left in the city also took up fortified positions, but only in one part of the city. In fact, the city itself was left untaken, and firefights in it and in its suburbs continued for a long time afterwards.

The Tragedy of the Village of Samashk

The Chechen defense forces, renamed the Southwestern Front and operating in the western part of the country, were able to repulse all Federal Army attacks and to keep its communities in its own hands until almost the end of March. It succeeded not only in keeping the enemy at bay but was also able continuously to mount attacks against its opponent, causing it great damage. However, confrontations of larger scope did not take place while the primary Federal Army forces in Chechnya concentrated on the operation to take Grozni. The communities of Samashk, Achchoj Martan, Bamut, Davydenko, Novi Sharoj, and Asinovskaja all continued to be subjected to bombing from the air and to artillery barrages. Fiercer battles only began at the beginning of March and especially from the middle of that month when the Russian High Command made a decision that it was time to liquidate the Western Chechen Forces Group.

The fierceness of the ongoing confrontations was graphically described in a report of the chief of staff of the Chechen Southwest Front, published in the Russian daily *Moskovskij komsomolec* (March 23, 1995):

To the Southwest Front Commander, Colonel R. Gelajev:
Report.
Russian army losses during the military operation:
Near Shami Jurt: tanks—1 unit, BMPs—6 units, BTRs—5 units, "Ural"—2 units, Zil (trucks)—1 unit; soldiers—from 30 to 70 people.
In the community of Bamut: BMPs—3 units, soldiers—unknown;
In the community of Alchan Jurt: BMPs—1 unit, artillery gun (100 mm)—one unit, "Niva" (four-wheel-drive light transport vehicle)—1 unit;
In the community of Atagi: 1 Mi-24 helicopter knocked down, scouting party destroyed—5 people
Chechen losses:
In the village of Shami Jurt: 1 killed, 3 wounded;
In the village of Bamut: 1 killed;
In the village of Atagi: 1 wounded.
Southwest front chief of Staff Captain Alpakov.

On March 24, the Federal Army succeeded in entering Achchoj Martan, but after the Chechens counterattacked, it was forced to leave the city. A special military operation against the western Chechen forces was begun April 7. That day, Samashk, Achchoj Martan, Bamut, Davydenko, and Novi Sharoj were attacked simultaneously. Before each assault, an ultimatum was issued to the community being attacked, but no replies were ever received back. After fierce engagements, Federal Army units succeeded in taking only three communities: Samashk, Davydenko, and Novij Sharoja.[14]

The 100th Internal Affairs Army Division had been operating in the region of the villages of Shamashk, Davydenko, and Novi Sharoj. General Lieutenant Anatoli Antonov commanded the operation, which was conducted by the Internal Affairs Army. (Antonov is Anatoli Romanov's pseudonym. For a time, many of the Russian senior officers used pseudonyms in Chechnya, not wanting their real names to become known.) During the operation to take Samashk, the Internal Affairs Army and its specnaz units operated under the cover of the 659th Motorized Rifle Regiment.

As was announced by the Russian High Command, during the battle for Samashk, 130 Chechen hit men were killed and 124 taken prisoner. Federal Army losses were listed as 13 soldiers and 1 tank knocked out. However, other numbers were submitted later: 16 killed and 56 wounded. According to Chechen sources, 4 of their fighters were killed in the battle.

The circumstances of the taking of the village of Samashk drew the special attention of not only journalists but the Russian population at large and even the deputies of the Russian Duma. This was primarily because, even five days after the takeover, the Federal Army refused to allow anyone into the village, even the deputies of the Duma.

On April 6, the village was issued an ultimatum. The same day, units of the Internal Affairs Army began to move toward the village to set up a blockade. However, as they neared one and a half kilometers to the north of the village, a tank and then an armored vehicle ran over mines and were blown up. As they continued their approach, another armored vehicle was blown up by a mine.

Although the time set by the ultimatum had not run out, Russian forces then began to shell the village with artillery and mortars. The barrages continued through the night and into next morning. The village was then bombed from the air and periodically shot up again by artillery from a point-blank range of one kilometer. The center of the village and many houses around it were totally destroyed. Russian soldiers supported by tanks and armored vehicles began to force their way into the village.

The village was entered by a 350-man combined force made up of the Internal Affairs Army's Sofrin Brigade (250 soldiers), the Moscow and Pamoscow OMON (84 people), and the Orenburg Quick Reaction Special Detachment. The Vitiaz Special Purpose Detachment also participated in the operation. For the attack, they were formed up into ten assault groups.

The Russian force was resisted by only the local Chechen self-defense detachment, numbering about 40 people. One 10-man self-defense formation took up defense positions near the school. But early that morning they had exited the village, moving out in the direction of the village of Zakan Jurt. Another 12-man group attempted to return the fire of the Russian forces but then

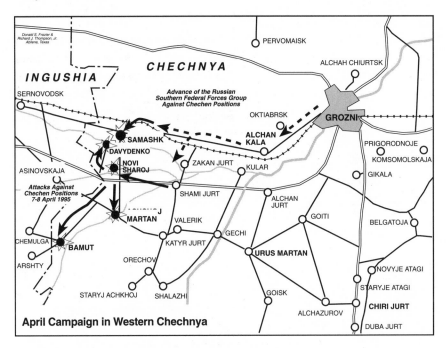

April Campaign in Western Chechnya

withdrew almost immediately to the nearby forest. Only a few fighters chose to remain in the village. After witnessing the actions of the Russian soldiers, these decided to fight on to the end.[15]

The Russian assault force moved into the village along Proletarskaja, Sharipov, Vygonaja, and Rabochaja Streets. They first shot up each house from their armored vehicles, then threw grenades into the cellars of the houses and into the adjoining structures. They also lit the houses on fire with rounds from grenade launchers. Along these four of the ten streets that stretched through the village, almost every second house was burned to the ground. In the final tally, 371 houses were burned, 100–150 villagers were killed, and a large group of men between the ages of 15 and 73 were taken away to the Mozdok Filtration Camp. According to witnesses, no mercy was shown to children, old people, invalids, or women. Drunken soldiers threw grenades into cellars and rooms, knowing that unarmed people were hiding there.

It was reported that not only dead bodies but also live people were burned.[16] Bodies were either thrown into the burning buildings or were doused with gasoline and set on fire. Flamethrowers were also used for this purpose. People were not permitted to leave the burning buildings. Sixty-seven-year-old S. Surchashev, who was paralyzed, died in this manner as well

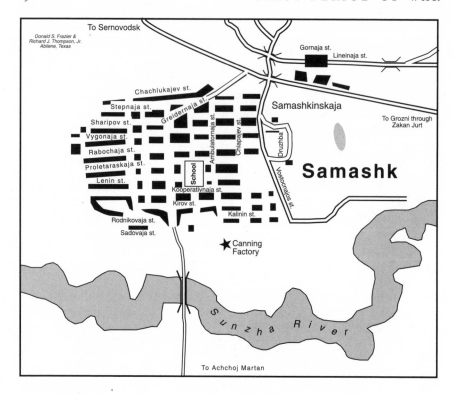

as the father and daughter of the Bazujev family. Ch. Tachajev's son Rezvan was laid in front of a tank and crushed to death. These are just a few of the witness reports.

Accurate information is available about the deaths of only about 112 of the civilians killed. Of these, 103 people (90 men and 13 women) were registered as living in the village. The youngest was 15 years of age, the oldest 96. According to the information gathered by Russia's Memorial Civil Rights Defense Center, 18 people died during the artillery and mortar barrages, 5 died during the strafing of the streets by armored vehicles, and 7 died from sniper fire. Another 30 people were shot in their homes or courtyards, and 5 died from grenades thrown into the cellars of their houses, adjoining structures, or living quarters.[17]

The commander of the operation, Internal Affairs Army General Antonov (that is, Romanov) later contended that the assault began only after 450 peaceful inhabitants had left the village. He also argued that the attack began earlier than the time set by the ultimatum because the Chechen hit men decided to kill the village elders who allegedly demanded that all weapons be laid down, that the requirements of the ultimatum be met, and that the Russian troops be allowed to enter the village unopposed. His arguments are, however, spurious, as village elders in Chechnya are greatly esteemed and no Chechens would ever dare to kill or even threaten them.

The Russians also attempted to justify the harshness of the attack by arguing that the village did not abide with the ultimatum's demand that it give up 264 automatic weapons, 2 machine guns, and 1 armored vehicle. But this demand was impossible for the villagers to meet as the defenders had taken their weapons with them while withdrawing. The Russian High Command further contended that the village was filled to overflowing with Chechen fighters. After the takeover, more than 30 defense positions were found. These had been constructed by the Abchaz battalion and the remnants of the Grozni and Gudermes armed forces but had been abandoned for some time.

On April 11, a group of local village women were finally allowed to reenter the village. Only several dozen inhabitants were found alive in the village. Duma deputy Anatoli Shabad succeeded in entering the village along with the women and was shocked by the effects of the attack. His videotapes indicate the Russian soldiers' exceptional cruelty toward the local inhabitants.[18]

One of the grimmest locations in Samashk was the forest nearby. Local inhabitants reported that some 150 people withdrew from the village into the forest, where they were later rocketed by helicopters. Many bodies remained in the forest, but it was impossible to remove them because of mines and unexploded rockets. An accurate count of the total casualties suffered at Shamanshk will most likely never be made since not only local inhabitants but also many refugees were killed in the vicinity of the village. In the opinion of Chechens, the operation was the work of some special punitive unit.

As soon as information about the cruelties inflicted by the Russian forces on the civilian inhabitants of Samashk appeared in the press, the Russian Defense Ministry hurriedly issued denials. On April 12 in the daily newspaper *Krasnaja zvezda,* the Russian Defense Ministry's information and press office categorically denied that rockets and bombs were used against the village of Samashk. It contended that the inhabited areas of the village were not struck, only the assembly areas of the illegal armed formations, mostly in the forested area to the southeast of Samashk.[19]

After visiting Samashk, a group of deputies from the Russian Duma concluded that the operation against the village was a totally new form of Russian Army action in Chechnya. It was a typical punitive action against civilian inhabitants, done for the purpose of instilling fear into the inhabitants of not only Samashk but also the communities of Achchoj Martan, Bamut, and elsewhere.

Why, in fact, did Shamashk become the first target for Russian punitive actions? There are several possible reasons for this, not counting the rage that had steadily built up among the Russian forces during almost five months of intense Chechen resistance.[20] As one Russian officer contended, the Chechen fighters were like cockroaches: you smoke them out in one place, they appear in another. You smoke them out in that place, they reappear in yet another. You smoke them out once again, they reappear in the first place.

The ultimate answer, however, is that the operation was conducted by Internal Affairs Ministry units. This was in fact the first operation that had been independently planned and executed by the Internal Affairs Ministry Army since the beginning of combat operations.[21] Russian Internal Affairs Ministry units had already distinguished themselves by their cruelty, propensity to rob, and other harsh behavior toward the local inhabitants. The Internal Affairs Army's 100th Division operating in the western part of Chechnya had withstood continuous attacks by Chechen forces. They had also sustained significant losses, most of which had been suffered in the region of Samashk. The division considered itself an elite, privileged unit whose mission was to control civilian populations by force. It had not yet gotten accustomed to the fact that someone would dare to resist it. Confrontations in the Samashk region had been occurring since the middle of December. Although the village itself had been attacked several times in an attempt to break the resistance of the Chechen fighters, it had remained an exceedingly hard nut for the Federal Army to crack.[22]

At the start of the campaign, the basic mission of the Russian Combined Federal Battle Group was to reach and take Grozni. It was considered purposeless to allot large forces to "reestablish constitutional order" in the rest of Chechnya. Thus a "no peace and no war" situation developed between the Russian military units operating outside of Grozni and the Chechens. One of the regions where this situation prevailed was the western part of Chechnya, which encompassed the villages of Achchoj Martan, Samashk, Bamut, Asinovskaja, Melchi Jurt, Novi Sharoj, Zakan Jurt, and Shami Jurt. Also concentrated along the border with Ingushia were tens of thousands of Chechen refugees from Grozni.

The Russian federal forces took positions along the line Samashk–Davydenko–Novi Sharoj–Achchoj Martan–Bamut. About 4–5 miles from Samashk on the road to Sernovodsk, the Russian Internal Affairs Ministry forces established a blocking post, designated as the 13th Outpost. As the federal forces were forced to go around to the north of Samashk and to proceed on to Grozni along the low Sunzha ridge, they constructed a bypass road along this ridge. Federal Army units and columns with military cargos used this secondary route for travel to Grozni. To defend this new road, a military unit was positioned several kilometers to the north of it and set up firing positions along the southern slope of the ridge facing the village.

Another road joining Ingushia with Grozni was the Rostov-Baku highway. However, a part of this highway was not accessible to the Federal Army and columns were forced to turn from it and go by way of Sernovodsk and the 13th Outpost, established on Samashk's shoulder. They then would get back onto the Rostov-Baku highway further on. Samashk thus became the connecting point through which movement flowed in both directions, although it did not have to go into Samashk itself. This portion of the Rostov-Baku highway was used mostly by civilian traffic since military column traffic had ceased to use it.

Civilians were constantly being detained at the Internal Affairs post designated as the 13th Outpost and then sent to the so-called filtration camps. For this reason, the conditional truce between the two sides periodically broke down, confrontations broke out, and the post was fired upon. From December 11, 1994, to the end of March, 1995, about thirty Russian soldiers were killed near Samashk. In the early part of January, 1995, the Chechens knocked out a Russian armored vehicle that had gotten lost near the village. On January 18, an armored personnel carrier attempting to enter the village was hit and 6 Russian soldiers who jumped out were killed by the Chechen fighters.

Slowly the situation became more intense. On January 27, 1995, 6 helicopters rocketed the village and the area around it. The next day, this was repeated by 7 more helicopters.

The first major assault of the village was begun on January 31 when the Chechens destroyed a Pacific Fleet marine infantry column of armored vehicles and trucks that had attempted to enter the village. Three Russian soldiers were killed and 17 wounded (other figures in another report indicate 9). Several armored personnel carriers and an armored command vehicle were burned. The Chechens also took several of the wounded Russian soldiers prisoner.

For several days thereafter, shots and explosions were heard in the village, but the federal forces were unable to maintain their positions and were forced to withdraw. The Chechen fighters again returned to the village. Later, Samashk was again shot up a number of times by weapons of all types and was bombed, but it held on tenaciously. The village, even though it was in territory controlled by the Russian forces, remained under Chechen control. In the opinion of the Russian High Command, the Chechen forces fortified in the village of Samashk had become especially dangerous at the end of January when they and the forces in Bamut and the surrounding communities were reinforced by Chechen fighter groups withdrawn from Grozni.

On March 3, 1995, the federal forces High Command delivered an ultimatum to the village of Samashk demanding that the Chechen fighters lay down their arms. The Chechen fighters withdrew into the adjoining forest and were able to avoid the artillery barrage and bombing of the village that followed. As was previously mentioned, only the 40–50-man local self-defense force remained in the village. The situation became even more tense when, in the middle of March, the Chechen fighters destroyed an Internal Affairs Special Purpose Detachment and its armored equipment. This led to the tragedy of the village.

There are two other possible reasons for the unbridled cruelty inflicted during the takeover of Samashk. One is that the mass destruction of the village and its inhabitants was a convoluted form of retribution against Dzhochar Dudajev himself. A portion of the inhabitants of this village belonged to the teip from which Dudajev originated. Using this fact, some of the Russians contended that all the villagers belonged to this teip and that this was the reason why it had resisted so fiercely. The final reason may be simply naked revenge for Grozni. During the tragic New Year's assault of Grozni, the fighter forces from Samashk participated in the defense of Grozni and were responsible for burning many Russian tanks and armored vehicles in the center of that city.

The massacre at Samashk did not quickly disappear from the news, if only because it was an indication of events to come. On March 15, 1996, it was already being reported by the Russian High Command that not 150 but only 68 inhabitants, mostly men, had died in the takeover. The accuracy of the numbers is not as important as is the cynicism being shown. It is as if, by decreasing the figures, the killings could be written off as a quite ordinary military operation against the usual hit men.

In truth, the character of the conflict had already changed drastically. The war, previously proclaimed as being fought merely to "disarm illegal Chechen formations," in fact, turned into a campaign of genocide against the Chechen people. By 1996, the Chechen communities, surrounded by triple encirclement rings, were repeatedly destroyed by artillery and rocket fire after pro forma announcements that no civilian inhabitants were left in them and that they had become nests of hit men. Such tactics had been first tried out in Samashk, but apparently even there the killing had not been fully completed.

The second, even more terrible stage of the Samashk tragedy was begun on March 16, 1996, almost one year after the earlier punitive action. On this decisive Saturday, the village was again shaken by explosions from artillery rounds. The next day, eleven Mi-24M helicopters attacked the village with rockets, followed by Su-24 fighter-bombers. In the opinion of Russian Duma deputy A. Mironov, a punitive action of such cruelty had not been conducted since the very beginning of the war.

The commanders of the 19th Motorized Rifle Division and the Internal Affairs units were convinced that about 250 hit men were concentrated in the area of the village, some of whom had arrived from Bamut and Sernovodsk. In fact, by then only women, old men, and children were left in the village, as about seven thousand people had already withdrawn into neighboring Ingushia and the surrounding communities. The village was encircled and a corridor was then created for the civilian inhabitants to exit. But the corridor was kept open for only half an hour, and a majority of the people of the village were unable to get out.

The attack was commenced after Chechen fighters shot up federal forces positions from the food packing factory on the outskirts of Samashk, the one industrial facility in the village, and inflicted a painful blow. After sweeping the village almost from the face of the earth by artillery, Internal Affairs Ministry units entered at about noon on March 18 and began to comb the village. Tanks and armored vehicles participated in the assault.

The village was kept blockaded, and even journalists were not allowed to get near. "There witnesses are not needed!" Russian soldiers at the Chechnya-Ingushia border post remarked to *Izvestija* correspondent I. Rotar.[23]

The Chechen fighters withdrew from the village when the attack began but did not surrender. According to Chechens, 35- to 45-year-old Russian "contractors" then began to operate in the village with great cruelty. Already ransacked property was ransacked once more and people were killed without regard to age or sex. (Recruits are generally 18 to 21 years old. The Russian military sometimes hires "supplementary" troops for work that the recruits would balk at or refuse to do. The suspicion is that a special detachment of hardened criminals had been brought in.)

The village burned for more than a week, and the air above it was covered with smoke. Only on March 27 did the commander of Russian Army Forces in Chechnya, General Viacheslav Tichomirov, announce that the military operation in the village of Samashk was completed. According to him, more than 110 Chechen fighters had been killed, although apparently these were mostly male civilian inhabitants. Various sources indicate that more than 600 civilian inhabitants were killed during the assault. There are no accurate figures available as to Federal Army casualties.

What happened in Shamashk was only a prelude. Later, the whole of Chechnya was turned into a series of large Samashks, and the village's fate was repeated in Pervomaisk, Novogroznensk, Arshty, and many other communities.

Tactics for the Defense of the Communities

During the assault operation conducted by the Russian Federal Army from the second half of March until the middle of April, the communities controlled by the Eastern Chechen Group, as well as a majority of the communities in the western part of Chechnya, were taken over. Especially fierce fighting took place in the foothills zone of western Chechnya. This had to be admitted by the Russian Military High Command. According to the Commander of the Russian Federal Army Group in Chechnya, General Anatoli Kulikov, during these battles, the Internal Affairs Army suffered almost half of all losses that it sustained from the start of the Chechen campaign.

In the middle of April, the Federal Army Group operating in western Chechnya redeployed its forces. Attacking in three directions, it then continued the assault operation: about 300 units of armored equipment were directed against Bamut, about 80 against Orechov, and about 100 against Jandy Chutor.[24]

The most important objective was Bamut. Here, in the Bamut-Chemugla-Arshty triangle, the largest number of Chechen fighters was concentrated. The last two villages lay in the territory of Ingushia. Russian intelligence was of the opinion that the village of Arshty had become the fighters' rest and recuperation base. For this reason, it was bombed a number of times, although officially Russia was not conducting any military actions against Ingushia.

Official Russian sources contended that almost 80 percent of Chechen territory was already under the control of Russian forces and that the primary mission of the military operation, the disarmament of the Chechen formations, was proceeding quite successfully. On April 19, Russia's military daily newspaper *Krasnaja zvezda* reported that in the last several days, 78 people had given up their weapons in Achchoj Martan. In Gudermes, there had also been collected 161 individual weapons, a mortar, and a number of mines and grenades. In Urus Martan, 23 automatic weapons, 1,180 bullets, 64 grenades, 27 mines, and 3 grenade launchers had been collected. Chechens who turned in weapons were issued amnesty certificates in which their names were not entered. They were to write in their names themselves. Without doubt, the Chechen fighters soon began to make use of the opportunity to obtain such certificates. There was no problem in obtaining additional individual weapons, as they could easily be bought from the Russian soldiers. Such amnesty certificates, however, later helped Chechen fighters to reenter Grozni and the other cities, where they again formed into groups.

But the Federal Army Command's collection of weapons procedures were simply an attempt to create the image that the Federal Army Group's operation was succeeding. In reality, it did not control much Chechen territory except for those areas where the Russian forces units were themselves dislocated.

The Federal Combined Army's occupation of communities was conditional at best. During the protracted battles for the communities, the Chechens were able to make use of the fact that upon entering the cities, tanks, armored vehicles, artillery, and mortars lost their superiority and become powerless against small, fast-moving fighter groups.

The Chechens refused to make use of positional defenses for their communities. Protracted pounding by Federal Army heavy weapons would turn these communities into piles of ruble. Besides, in positional battles, the enemy was able to avoid larger losses.

The tactics used by Russian army units for the takeover of the communities were simple and in most instances conducted in identical fashion. Before entering the settlements, an attempt was always first made to encircle and blockade them. Responding to this tactic, the Chechens would fight only until the Federal Army forces completed half of their encirclement ring and then would quickly withdraw. They would reform in the adjoining regions and then reenter the communities at night and attack the occupying forces, administering significant losses. The situation thus quite often became reversed, with the Federal Army forces fighting from encirclement. The Federal Army units were thereby forced to take over the same communities a number of times. As the Chechens gave up a majority of their communities without a battle, official Russian announcements reported that they were taken with minimal losses. However, nothing further was reported about losses suffered from Chechen counterattacks after the occupation of the settlements.

Leaving their most important communities in the flatlands areas of Chechnya, the Chechen fighters intensified their diversion and sabotage activities. Small fighter groups, mostly at night, lit buildings on fire and shot up Russian positions and posts in the Federal Army's rear areas, even in Grozni. Diversion teams were inserted into all the largest settlements. Larger or smaller attacks were executed almost every night.

During this period, a psychological war was also begun against Russian officers in an attempt to frighten them. Lists of combat pilots and known rapists were made up. Combat pilots bombed civilians and thus killed innocent noncombatants, mainly old people, women, and children. Soldiers who raped also raised a special fury among Chechens. Chechen tradition requires that women be greatly honored; however, a raped woman loses her right to live and is either killed or has to commit suicide. Information was collected about the families and home addresses of these two types of perpetrators. There apparently were no real problems in making up lists of the pilots who had bombed Chechen communities. Chechens reported that such information could be easily bought from the Russian troops.[25]

It is hard to say even now how events and the course of this war would have developed further had the celebration of Victory Day not neared. On May 9, Russia was preparing to celebrate the fiftieth anniversary of the end of World War II and was intending to invite many honored guests from the major foreign countries to its celebrations. These celebrations were greatly hindered by the war in Chechnya. For political reasons, it was impossible to continue fighting during the celebrations of an end to a war.

On April 26, Russian president Yeltsin signed a decree, No. 417, declaring a moratorium for the use of armed force from April 28 to May 12. In the event of Chechen provocations, units were to react according to the given circumstances. The federal forces' assault operation was thus suspended before all the main Chechen communities could be taken over. Preparations had begun to conduct a large operation in the eastern part of Chechnya in an attempt to cut this part of the country off from Dagestan. Fierce engagements were also being fought along the approaches of Serzhen Jurt. The road to Vedeno, the most important Chechen fighter base, ran through Serzhen Jurt. In spite of this, Russian defense minister Grachev ordered that combat activity be suspended for a period of ten days starting May 1.[26]

During the period of this last assault, the combined Federal Army's total losses as of April 19 had grown to 1,518 killed, 4,891 wounded. Another 267 were listed as missing in action, and 80 had been taken prisoner. During this period, 153 prisoners had been returned from Chechen captivity, among them 25 officers. The basic means by which prisoners were released was through informal exchanges with the Chechens, quite often trading live Russian soldiers for the bodies of dead Chechens. Left unidentified were 260 bodies of Russian soldiers. These reported losses were, however, only the official Russian Military High Command figures. In reality, these figures should have been as much as two times higher.

The fierce engagements and continuous air strikes against Chechen settlements in April also enlarged the stream of refugees from the flatlands and foothills territories. The officially registered stream of refugees grew to 480,000. Of them, about 100,000 stayed on in Chechnya, 232,600 went on to Dagestan, Ingushia, and Kabarda Balkaria; 40,000 went to the Krasnodar and Stavropol regions and the Rostov and Astrakhan territories; and 7,000 moved to Russia's central regions.

In the opinion of the Federal Army commander, General Kulikov, by the end of April, Dudajev's Armed Forces had been almost destroyed, with not more than 7,000 soldiers left in its ranks. A majority of the fighters were concentrated in the Vedeno, Nozhai Jurt, and Shatoja regions, the rest scattered elsewhere.

The Chechens thought otherwise. One of the field commanders, Shamil Basajev, who had been awarded the name of Hero of Chechnya for his part in the defense of Grozni, declared during a television program that the Chechen Armed Forces were about to begin active operations in the flatlands territories and in the mountains. A mobile army with all the necessary structures was being created, and bases were being established in the mountains.

CHAPTER 9

Warfare in the Mountains

Russian president Yeltsin's announced moratorium and the temporary halt of combat actions in Chechnya took effect on April 28. Politicians and commentators considered it entirely a politically induced announcement. No one, in fact, believed that combat actions would be completely stopped, particularly as many of the Chechen field commanders announced that they would not honor the moratorium. Large-scale military operations were, however, suspended.[1] The moratorium was useful for both sides. During it, attempts were made to begin negotiations for the regulation of the crisis by peaceful means. The Chechen forces made use of the moratorium to relocate their units, to reorganize their formations, and to reestablish their weapons and ammunition reserves. Both sides continued to prepare for new battles.

The situation, meanwhile, remained very tense. The Chechens continued to carry out diversions against Federal Army units. The Federal Army also continuously violated the moratorium. Information reported in the press vividly describes this conditional "cease-fire":

April 30. In the region of the Giliana community, Chechens knocked down a combat helicopter with fire from an antiaircraft machine gun, forcing it to land in Dagestan. The crew was not hurt.

May 1. A Chechen fighter group attacked a 6-vehicle column moving toward Grozni. The column was halted when the lead armored vehicle and the truck bringing up the rear were knocked out by grenade launcher fire. Afterwards, the column was raked by automatic and machine gun fire. The battle lasted three hours. The Chechens withdrew after Russian reinforcements arrived. Three internal affairs forces soldiers were killed, 8 were wounded. Chechen losses are unknown. Command posts in Grozni were also attacked, leaving them to operate under siege conditions. During the night, in just the 3rd Headquarters, which was manned by about 100 soldiers, 9 soldiers were wounded, 2 were hurt seriously. Because of continuous Chechen attacks, martial law was enforced from 9 P.M. to 6 A.M.[2]

May 2. All night, the Chechen hit men attacked the Federal Army's headquarters in the Leninsk region of Grozni. The military unit in Chankala was also attacked; 4 Russian soldiers were killed and 13 were wounded.[3] During confrontations near Ichkhoj Jurt, 1 Russian soldier was killed and 5 more were wounded during the night.

May 3. During the night, five Federal Army control posts were attacked in Grozni, killing and wounding an unknown number of soldiers. Chechen positions were bombarded by artillery and bombed from the air along the whole front line.

May 4. Chechen attacks were conducted in Grozni against Federal Army objectives. In the Leninisk neighborhood, located in the northwest part of Grozni, heavy weapons were used. During the previous week of the announced moratorium for the suspension of hostilities, the revolutionaries attacked Federal Army units in Grozni 92 times. Nine federal soldiers were killed, 33 were wounded.[4]

May 5. The nightly confrontations in Grozni continued to intensify. During the night, twenty Federal Army posts were shot up. One officer was killed and 2 soldiers were wounded. Thirty-two Chechens were killed. The floor of the bank where money had been kept for the bank's reconstruction was blown up. The village of Valerik, 20 kilometers from Samashk, became the arena of confrontations. Helicopters attacked Chechen positions near Bamut. Heavy artillery operated all night until four o'clock in the morning. Near Serzhen Jurt, the Chechens knocked down a Russian SU-25 military aircraft. The pilot was killed.

May 6. Confrontations took place between the Federal Army and the Chechen forces. These were mostly near Shali, Bamut, Orechov, and Alchan Jurt. According to the Russian High Command, 2 Russian soldiers and 41 Chechens were killed.

May 7. Fierce confrontations occurred in Grozni; Russia labeled them as attempts to darken the World War II victory ceremonies. The Chechens reported that during the night they had taken over a part of the Russian positions, but the Russians denied this. The Chechens shot up the guard posts near the Grozni headquarters. Russian aircraft bombed Chechen positions in the eastern and western parts of Chechnya.

May 8. Fighting occurred mostly near Bamut and Serzhen Jurt. During this 24-hour period, Chechen groups of 10–30 fighters attacked Russian posts in Grozni 12 times. Chechen information minister Movladi Udugov denied Russian Federal High Command reports about dozens of Chechens killed. According to him, only 6 Chechen fighters had been killed during the past week. The Russian High Command reported that the Chechens were planning to mount a major attack against Grozni on May 9. At the same time, the Chechen chief of staff, Aslan Maschadov, stated that he had issued orders to limit military operations as much as possible that day.

May 9. Small engagements occurred along the front line, although in Grozni it was calm.

May 10. Russian president Yeltsin announced that no combat actions were taking place in Chechnya and that regular military forces were not participating in the conflict. Only the Internal Affairs Ministry forces were continuing to confiscate weapons still possessed by several small groups of mutineers.

Meanwhile, 5 Mi-24 combat helicopters attacked Serzhen Jurt. During the attack, 7 inhabitants of the village were killed and 8 wounded. The communities of Vedeno, Shatoja, and Gudermes were rocketed and bombed. Eight inhabitants were killed, 12 were wounded.[5]

A representative of the Federal Forces High Command in Chechnya reported that during the past 24 hours, Chechen hit men shot up Russian positions twelve times, especially fiercely in the Bamut, Orechov regions, along the Gudermes-Chasavjurt highway, and in the suburbs of Grozni. During the confrontations, 1 Russian soldier was killed and 11 were wounded. Russian units killed 38 hit men and destroyed 1 armored vehicle, 10 automobiles, and 9 firing positions. The commander of Federal Forces in Chechnya, General Colonel Jegorov, stated that Chechen fighters had intensified their actions against the Federal Forces during the last several days. The most intense battles had been fought near the settlements of Aleroja, Novogroznensk, Suvorov Jurt, Koshkeldy, and Ichkhoj Jurt. Udugov accused the Russians of using chemical weapons during their daily bombing of the Shali region.

As the moratorium drew to a close, the intensity of the confrontations grew. The Russian High Command reported that during the period of the moratorium, the Chechens had attacked Russian positions 180 times. During these attacks, 38 Russian soldiers had been killed and 223 had been wounded.[6]

On May 11, some 8 hours before the end of the cease-fire, the Russian Army began to move out from their positions. Their purpose was to cut the road leading to the southeastern part of Chechnya, particularly to Vedeno. The commander of Federal Forces in Chechnya, General Colonel Jegorov, stated that his forces were prepared to destroy the rebellious groups completely when the announced truce was called off at midnight. Although the truce had been useful from a military standpoint, no instructions were received to extend it. On May 12, the assault was renewed.

The Situation in Chechnya at the Start of the New Assault

Although the Federal Forces High Command continued to contend that the Chechens controlled only three mountain regions in the southern part of the country and this was only about 20 percent of the whole territory of Chechnya, the Chechen partisans continued to conduct attacks in regions occupied by the Russian Army, in Grozni, Shali, Gudermes, and elsewhere.

Grozni itself, in fact, remained partially controlled by the Chechen forces. The commander of the 3rd Headquarters, Major A. Krivolapov, told a reporter from the Russian daily newspaper *Konsomolskaja pravda* that it was very tense in the city: The command headquarters set up in an old, partially destroyed school building was being shot up every night. The soldiers were afraid to go out at night even to smoke and were opening up fire at every sound. The numbers of wounded were increasing daily. In his opinion, of the 100 soldiers manning the headquarters, not one would be left alive after their two-month assignment.[7]

With the institution of martial law in Grozni, everyone who refused to obey the command "stop" was shot at. The city was full of returning refugees who were refugees by day and fighters by night. No one could say how many Chechen hit men were in the city.

Russian soldiers and the OMON conducted daily searches, arresting almost every male Chechen between the ages of 18 and 30. All the suspects were taken to the filtration compound set up in the Staropromyslovski region, where they were treated harshly. They were interrogated using brutal physical force, deprivation of sleep, hunger, and all the other means developed by the security forces. Some were released after it was determined that they did not pose a threat to the Russian forces. Others were kept in primitive conditions for indeterminate periods of time.

The pro-Moscow Chadzijev Opposition Government succeeded in forming its own 340-man Chechen militia to keep order. Although it patrolled together with the Russians, neither side trusted it.

Because of the nightly firefights, the local inhabitants were afraid to come out their cellars or to turn on the lights in their apartments at night. There was also a great shortage of food. The local inhabitants attempted to buy food from the Russian soldiers. The other communities occupied by the Federal Army were in a similar situation. In territories left under the control of Dudajev's government, life continued according to its own laws. Shariat courts operated in Vedeno and the other regions.

The Chechens had very few heavy weapons left and were short of light weapons and ammunition. In their attempts not to use up their weapons and ammunition, the Chechens fought mostly at night and after the enemy objectives had been well scouted out. According to Chechen sources, weapons and ammunition were being bought mostly from the Russian soldiers for alcohol and hard currency.

Imran, the leader of one of the Chechen detachments in the mountains, told reporters that one commander succeeded in purchasing an armored vehicle and a large amount of ammunition from the Russian soldiers in return for two cases of vodka and a promise that Russian positions would not be shot up for a week.[8] According to him, Chechen losses in the mountains had decreased markedly. His detachment previously consisted of 80 people, of which only 11 were left. Almost all had died defending Grozni or in battles in the flatlands areas. During the month that they were in the mountains, only one fighter was killed.

Chechen chief of staff Maschadov and one of his five field commanders, Shamil Basajev, contended that it was still too early to talk about a partisan war, although such a war would be conducted once the enemy took the initiative. However, the Chechens had still not released the initiative from their own hands. The Chechen units were deployed in positions according to their own plan of attack. Each larger city occupied by the enemy was divided into sectors. There, the fighter groups were organized into strictly defined formations, although there were also groups operating independently. Commanders of Russian and Chechen units sometimes were able to agree on temporary truces, during which prisoners, the wounded, and the dead were exchanged.

Federal Army units had for some time already limited themselves to the use of one tactic: The settlements were bombarded by artillery and mortars regardless of the presence of civilian inhabitants. The communities were taken when they were completely destroyed and no people were left alive in them. This was done because of the army's poor military training and because of the soldiers' own fear of being killed or wounded. The local inhabitants were being sacrificed to ensure the soldiers' safety. During conversations with journalists, an artillery commander, Russian colonel M. Nikolajev, openly admitted that "scorched earth" tactics had been grabbed at in order to finish off the Chechens as soon as possible, although the fighters' losses from such tactics were minimal.[9]

The Russian use of this tactic changed Chechen tactics as well. Because of the fierce artillery bombardments and air strikes, the Chechens refused to enter into direct confrontations with the Russian forces. Most of their attention was directed to the use of "flying" fighter detachments and attacks against Russian patrols, outposts, and operating bases throughout the whole territory of Chechnya. In this way, they attempted to scatter the enemy's forces. They thought quite correctly that the Federal Army would not be able to maintain substantial forces in every community. Small forces were no challenge to the Chechens, as they could be annihilated at night by sniper and grenade launcher fire and surprise attacks. It was also becoming apparent that air strikes were not effective under such circumstances, as the fighters could find cover among the Russian units themselves. The new tactics allowed the fighters to "melt" in among the inhabitants. The gathering of intelligence and the supply of food and medicine also improved.

Thus the new assault wave began in the background of continuous Chechen attacks in the territories occupied by the Federal Army. It was begun with the intensive bombardment by artillery and air strikes of the Chechen fortified defenses near the villages of Duba Jurt, Chiri Jurt, and Serzhen Jurt in the south and near Bamut and Orechov in the west.

At the same time, Chechen activity in Grozni, where the Chechens had been able to concentrate significant forces during the truce, was intensified. On May 14, the Chechens carried out almost thirty attacks. New attacks were planned in the cities of Gudermes, Argun, and Shali. On May 15, at a conference in Nozhai Jurt, the Chechen field commanders decided to take back Gudermes.[10] Fierce engagements flared up after the middle of May.

The Assault in the Region of the Mountains

After several days of intensive pounding of Chechen positions by artillery and air strikes, the Federal Army began its attack on May 17. In the eastern part of Chechnya, the assault was mounted in the direction of Vedeno, Shatoja, and Agishta. The most important objective, however, was Vedeno, and to get to it, it was first necessary to take Serzhen Jurt, whose defenses were commanded by Alistan. During an attack that lasted several hours, 6 Russian soldiers were killed. Three Chechen fighters were also killed and 2 wounded. Unable to take Serzhen Jurt, the Russian Army was forced to withdraw. The attacks against Chiri Jurt and Duba Jurt also did not succeed. Only by May 20 were the Russian Army units able to take up positions on the outskirts of Chiri Jurt and to take the cement factory located there.

In the west, Bamut and Orechov were the primary attack objectives. Each day of fierce engagements brought considerable losses to both sides. According to Russian military experts, the official daily summations of killed and wounded for that period reminded them of the Sovinformbiuro announcements of 50 years before.[11]

The first assault wave had been unsuccessful. The second assault wave began May 24. The Russian High Command announced that the assault would be continued until the president's order to disarm the Chechen formations was accomplished. The confrontations only became fiercer. This was admitted by the commander of Russian Federal Forces in Chechnya, General Jegorov, according to whom during just the first day of the new assault, 8 Russian soldiers were killed and 20 wounded. The Chechens had lost 123 fighters.[12]

A special attempt was made to take the heights designated as 541.6 near Serzhen Jurt. For two months, Chechen fighters entrenched upon them had not given the Federal Army units any peace, shooting up their transport along the Gudermes-Chasavjurt highway with artillery. These heights also controlled the oil wells from which Chechens pumped raw petroleum by hand and then processed it into gasoline. On the morning of May 27, one of the Russian companies succeeded in taking the heights. During the attack, four Russian soldiers were wounded. While withdrawing, the Chechens were forced to leave one of their dead behind, a very rare occurrence for them. During the previous weeks, Russian soldiers had paid very dearly for these heights: 20 soldiers had died there. But having taken the heights, Russian units were able to creep one kilometer closer to Serzhen Jurt.

Battles took place along the whole southern front line near the communities of Orechov, Bamut, Agishta, Serzhen Jurt, Bachi Jurt, and Mesket. It was attempted through Bachi Jurt and Mesket to break through to Nozhai Jurt. The fiercest fighting took place near the settlement of Agishta, five kilometers to the south of Shali and in an area not far from the villages of Aleroja and Ichkhoj Jurt. According to Russian Defense Ministry information, just on May 28, the Chechens lost 138 fighters and 3 armored vehicles. Six of their defense positions were also destroyed. Federal Army losses were listed as 4 killed and 9 wounded. Near Serzhen Jurt, 11 soldiers from the Pacific Fleet's Marine Infantry Detachment were killed. The Chechens reported that near Serzhen Jurt, 30 Russian soldiers and 11 Chechen fighters were killed and 10 Russian armored vehicles were destroyed.

During these battles, the Federal Army succeeded in cutting the road from Shatoja to the other southern communities. By degrees, the Federal Army began to push the Chechens in the direction of Vedeno and Agishta. But in the vicinity of Serzhen Jurt, it became necessary to change tactics and to use a turning maneuver, striking the Chechens from the rear. After this maneuver, the heights designated as 319 and 312 were taken, and Federal Army

The Joint Federal Forces Mountain Operation 17 Apr-4 May 1995

Donald S. Frazier & Richard J. Thompson, Jr. Abilene, Texas

units positioned upon them began continuously to pound the communities of Vedeno, Shatoja, Beni Kotar, Agishta, and Mesket with artillery.

The approach to Agishta was strategically important for both sides. The Federal Army intended for the assault to separate the Vedeno and Shatoja Chechen fighter groups. On May 31, the Federal Army succeeded in reaching the Argun and Hurihulan River gorges through which it could reach Shatoja and Vedeno. Thus their further assaults were concentrated in these gorges. However, the Chechens surrounded and destroyed one of the Federal Army armored columns in the Argun gorge. The enemy's ability to maneuver was constrained by the Chechen fighters entrenched on the dominant heights along the Duba Jurt mountain range.

The Russian forces were able to take the villages of Kirov Jurt, Chatumia, and Machet on the road from Vedeno to Shatoja after only two days of fighting. A favorable situation developed to mount an attack on Vedeno. This was begun June 3 from two directions: from Dachas-Borzoja-Agishta and from Dachas-Borzoja-Machet. Besides these thrusts, paratroopers were also airlifted to a location near Vedeno and given the mission of cutting off the movement of Chechen reinforcements from the regions of Shatoja and Nozhai Jurt. Before beginning this part of the operation, the commander of the Combined Federal Army Group, General Kulikov, issued instructions that fire be temporarily suspended and that sixteen roads be opened up along which peaceful inhabitants from the mountain communities could leave the combat zone.

Early on the morning of June 4, the Federal Army succeeded in taking Vedeno. The primary Chechen forces withdrew a distance of 7 to 12 kilometers from the city, but the bombardment of Vedeno continued for a long time afterwards.[13] The 245th Motorized Rifle Regiment, the 165th Marine Infantry Regiment, and units of two paratroop divisions participated in the Vedeno assault operation.

During the operation to take Vedeno, 17 Russian soldiers were killed and 36 were wounded, according to official Russian High Command figures. It was also announced that 300 mutineers had been killed. Also destroyed were 8 of their tanks, 9 armored personnel carriers, 3 armored vehicles, 1 armored scout vehicle, 3 howitzers, 1 Grad rocket artillery system, 2 artillery guns, 6 mortars, and 28 automobiles. Besides these, 1 armored scout vehicle, 1 artillery gun, and 2 grenade launchers were captured, and 16 firing positions, 10 strongpoint defense positions, and 2 "pillboxes" were destroyed.

The Russian High Command considered the takeover of Vedeno to be a very important victory. However, the Chechen field commanders maintained that it did not change the basic military situation. Earlier the fighting had been conducted in the flatlands areas in open battles under battlefront conditions. Now partisan war tactics would be employed. The Chechens lost only an important strategic location. According to Chechen information, during the two-day battle for Vedeno, the Russians lost more than 400 soldiers, 1 Su-24 bomber, 2 Su-25 fighter bombers, and 4 helicopters.[14]

Vedeno having been taken, Dudajev's Headquarters was transferred to the small town of Kiri in the mountains not far from Shatoja. The Chechen Armed Forces were split into two groups, one in Shatoja, the other in Nozhai Jurt. These communities then became the primary Russian Army attack objectives. Chechen positions were attacked in the Machet-Elistanzhi region in the direction of Vedeno and from Vedeno in the direction of Charachoja high up in the mountains. Intense combat actions also took place near the villages of Verchotoja and Elistanzhi and near the settlements of Agishta, Serzhen Jurt, Bamut, Orechov, Staryj Achchoja, and Jarysh Mardy.[15]

Although the Chechens attempted to minimize the significance of the loss of Vedeno, this was for them a very severe blow. Noncoordination of their activity was clearly apparent from that time on. Each Chechen fighter group began to operate almost independently.[16]

The operation to take Shatoja began on June 10. The evening of the next day, paratroopers were airlifted to the northeast of Shatoja. These were units of the 7th Paratroop Division that had previously been based in Lithuania with headquarters in Kaunas, Gediminas prospect 25. The last regiment of this division left Lithuania on September 31, 1993.

The 324th Motorized Rifle Regiment emerged near Shatoja from the north and the 245th Motorized Rifle Regiment from the east, thus blockading the city. The Chechens decided to leave it. On June 13, Federal Army units entered the city. The next day, Nozhai Jurt was also taken, the last of the twelve regional centers. At the same time, the flag of the Russian Federation was raised over Shatoja.[17] The Russian High Command reported that during the June 13–14 assault of Nozhai Jurt and Shatoja, 6 Russian soldiers were killed and 18 wounded. Chechen losses were 70 killed and 300 wounded.[18]

It is not known what losses were suffered by both sides during this last assault, which had begun on May 27. The information reported in the press is very contradictory. According to Russian High Command reports, Federal Army units lost almost 100 soldiers killed and 200 wounded. They had also killed about a 1,000 mutineers. However, a different picture was reported in the press. One medical staff member from the military field hospital located at the Grozni Airport told reporters that just during the last two days of May, 50 Russian dead and 235 wounded were brought to the hospital. Chechen information sources indicate that the Federal Army, counting the wounded, lost hundreds of soldiers each day.

CHAPTER 10

The Tragedy of Budionovsk

Having taken Nozhai Jurt and Shatoja, the commander of the Northern Caucasus Military Region, General Colonel Kvashnin, announced that "the last phase of the war in the mountains of Chechnya had drawn to a close." According to him, the remnants of Dudajev's Armed Forces could be divided into four already not centrally controlled forces. These were located to the south of Shatoja, in the Darga gorge, in the region of Nozhai Jurt, and near Bamut.[1]

The Russian Military High Command already saw a victorious end to the military campaign. However, President Dudajev, while confirming the takeover of Nozhai Jurt and Shatoja, remarked that "the battle was not ended, it had just taken on new forms."[2] He did not explain what forms it had taken.

But by the next day, Russia was already shaken. Having unexpectedly made their way into the city of Budionovsk in the district of Stavropol (Russia), an armed group of Chechens commanded by Shamil Basajev forced their way into the mayor's office and the buildings housing the militia, the bank, municipal communications, and the military headquarters. A portion of the hit men turned into the streets of the housing quarter and began shooting at passersby and at the windows of the buildings. Blood began to flow, and the city was frozen in horror. After taking hostages, the Chechens fortified themselves in the buildings of the city hospital. The armed Chechen group had begun a terrorist operation of yet unseen scope and character.[3]

The exact infiltration route of the Chechen terrorist group is unknown. It is thought that they had come from the Vedeno area through the territory of Dagestan making use of the fact that the majority of the various roads and byways along the route were not controlled either by the Russian Army or by Internal Affairs outposts. They chose the most appropriate method of covering their movement: their two covered Kamaz trucks (Russian-produced cargo trucks) were passed off as transporting "cargo 200," which signified that bodies of dead Russian soldiers were being transported. The trucks were escorted by a Ziguli-6 (Russian-made passenger) automobile repainted with militia markings and equipped with flashers. It was driven by Chechen fighters who had Slavic-looking faces.[4]

This unusual operation's further course is known in somewhat greater detail: on the morning of Saturday, June 14, the column made up of the "militia" Ziguli-6 automobile and the two covered Kamaz trucks containing the Chechen hit men neared Budionovsk. There they were stopped by a police outpost, but the two uniformed, Slavic-looking "militiamen" only slowed their Ziguli vehicle and informed the police that they were escorting a "cargo 200." They drove on without stopping. As the trucks passed through without inspection, a command was given to the other outposts further on to stop the column and inspect it.

At about 12:15 P.M., as the column was leaving the city, another militia post near the village of Praskovjev stopped it. The pseudomilitiamen did not have the required documents but refused to allow their escorted trucks to be inspected. They instead offered to go to the local militia headquarters to explain. The column then turned in the direction of the center of the city. An additional local police Ziguli automobile positioned itself at the head of the column, followed by a Moskvic (Russian-made passenger) automobile containing two local militia officers. As the column arrived at the militia building at about 12:30, the Chechens suddenly opened fire. Three of the Russian militiamen escorting the column were killed and one was wounded.[5]

The hit men acted swiftly after that. Immediately automatic and grenade launcher fire was opened up, and the militia building was attacked. The building was quickly taken, but Basajev's group did not linger there; even the dead militiamen's weapons were not taken.

Just as quickly and decisively, Basajev's fighters attacked and took the military headquarters, the municipal communications and bank buildings, and the mayor's office, all located in the same city center. Two other fighter groups moved out toward the marketplace and the youth center building. There they spread out in small groups, either moving on foot or driving commandeered motor vehicles, mostly automobiles. They then began shooting at everything in sequence. Buildings and cars were shot up with grenade launcher fire. Bullets and grenades swept everything before them. Most of the local people were

killed near the marketplace square. Later, witnesses told journalists that the
Chechen women snipers had been the most cold-blooded, calmly and professionally picking off their targets.[6]

One group of the Chechen battalion also shot up a bus carrying officers
from the helicopter and assault regiments deployed near Budionovsk. Some
of the hit men also attempted to force their way into this military base, but
they had to withdraw as the base had instituted security measures against terrorist attacks.

Having taken the mayor's office building, the terrorists raised above it the
Chechen flag. It became clear only then as to who was conducting this harsh
terrorist act. Practically all the city's administrators, including the vice mayor
and several technical workers, were taken hostage. All the drivers found in the
garage were shot.

Resistance to the Chechen battalion also quickly formed. When the militia building was attacked, the higher administration levels and the neighboring military units were informed immediately. Preparations had been taken
earlier against possible Chechen terrorist actions; the militia assigned the full
responsibility for fighting terrorists had been reinforced. Once information
was received at about 12:40 P.M. by the helicopter regiment near Budionovsk,
a 32-officer reinforcement group, commanded by the regiment's chief of staff,
Colonel J. Kovaliov, was quickly formed. They hurriedly arrived at the city cen-

ter by automobile and immediately began a firefight with the terrorists. During this skirmish, 8 aviators were killed and 8 others were wounded. Among the wounded was the regiment's chief of staff. The wounded, both the militiamen and the aviators, were taken to the hospital.

An Internal Affairs Ministry Special Detachment was immediately sent from Stavropol. Helicopters began to hang in the air above the city. But the Chechens intermingled with the local inhabitants, making it impossible to fire at them.

Meanwhile, it was becoming continuously more difficult for the Chechens, particularly as their numbers of wounded grew. Basajev decided upon one more step. Observing in what direction the wounded inhabitants of the city had been taken, he gathered his groups on Kalinin Street and ordered them to move toward the hospital located on the outskirts of the east side of the city. During the taking of the hospital, several more civilians were killed. About 450 medical workers and 500 patients were in the hospital at that time. The Chechens also brought along 300 more people they had taken hostage en route. The total hostages being held thus numbered about 1,200. Basajev's people then began to distribute the hostages, including the hospital personnel and the new people who had been brought in, throughout the wards of the hospital. A portion of the hostages were also locked in the cellar. The Chechens then began to mine the hospital building. They set up two heavy caliber machine guns on the hospital roof and began to shoot up everything around. Local inhabitants attempting to fight fires in the burning buildings came under fire, as well as the firemen who had come to help them and all others who ventured into view. In the machine gun fire, a commuting bus became the coffin for six people. The wounded militiamen and military aviators who had been brought to the hospital an hour and a half earlier were also executed by the terrorists.

No one dared to come near the hospital. In this way, by three o'clock, the first stage of this bloody terrorist military operation was concluded. It had lasted a bit more than two and a half hours, during which time 40 people had been killed and 69 wounded. The Chechens suffered 6 killed and 12 wounded, among them Shamil Basajev's brother Shervani.[7] Three Chechen fighters were captured.

Not all the members of the battalion had been able to get to the territory of the hospital. During the confrontations, one of the fighter groups attempted to take several Ikarus (Hungarian-made) buses and their passengers hostage. When this did not succeed, they commandeered a GAZ-66 (Russian-made cargo truck) and forced their way out of the city in the direction of Mineralnyje Vodi. But near the village of Orlovsk, about twelve kilometers from Budionovsk, their progress was blocked and they were surrounded. There was also some indication that one more small group forced their way out of the city in the direction of the village of Pokojnoja. It is thought that these groups did not come to Budionovsk with Basajev and did not have time to join up with the battalion's primary forces. One and a half hours after the takeover of the hospital, soldiers from the Blagodarnensk regiment arrived in Budionovsk. But it was already too late.

The Purpose of the Military Terrorist Operation: To Stop the War in Chechnya

The tension in Budionovsk mounted. The Internal Affairs Ministry's Special Detachment, even though it surrounded the hospital's territory, did not dare to attack it. Shamil Basajev had announced that for every 1 of his fighters killed, he would kill 10 hostages, 5 if 1 was wounded. More than 1,000 people were being held in the hospital.[8] The worst element in the situation was the complete lack of understanding by the Russian side of what was going on. They did not know who commanded the terrorists or how many terrorists there actually were, although it was suspected that there were perhaps twenty to thirty. It was also not clear at the beginning why the terrorists were there or why they had chosen Budionovsk as their target.

Meanwhile, the condition of Shamil Basajev's brother grew worse. Only a transfusion of blood could save his life. One of the hostages, an assistant commander of the local firefighter brigade, a major, was found to have the correct blood type. He soon found himself lying next to Shervani Basajev, giving blood. But according to Chechen tradition, having given blood to another makes one that person's blood brother. For this reason, the terrorists not only let the major live but also appointed him as their intermediary during the negotiations that followed, entrusting him to pass on their demands to the representatives of the Russian government.

Shamil Basajev, without identifying himself, soon issued demands that the Russian government begin negotiations with President Dudajev and that it terminate its war in Chechnya and withdraw from it the Russian Army. That evening an emergency session of the Russian executive government was hurriedly called together. Vice Premier Oleg Soskovec had to act as chairman as Premier Viktor Chernomyrdin was on vacation at that time. The government officials pondered the situation that had developed and the measures that had to be taken almost immediately. An action group was formed in the Russian Federation's Ministry of Internal Affairs, and the assistant minister of Internal Affairs, Mikhail Jegorov, was appointed its leader. It made the decision to send Internal Affairs and Defense Ministry operational forces to Budionovsk. At ten o'clock that evening, Vice Premier Nikolai Jegorov, Internal Affairs Minister Viktor Jerin, and the director of the Federal Counterintelligence Service, Sergei Stepashin, flew in to Budionovsk.[9]

In Stavropol, an action group was also hurriedly formed in the local Internal Affairs Ministry Headquarters. Everywhere, not only in Budionovsk, the security of government installations was reinforced and additional Internal Affairs outposts were set up along all the roads and approaches of the cities throughout the country. Antiterrorist measures were also taken in Moscow. The government began investigating all citizens of Chechen origin.

As there were many wounded in Budionovsk and the hospital itself was in terrorist hands, several first-aid brigades were sent into the city, not only from Stavropol but also from Zelenokomsk, Georgijevsk, and even from Piatigorsk. The wounded were transported to Zelenokomsk.

The night passed relatively calmly. The terrorists even let the medical personnel answer the telephones, although in the morning they forbade this and began answering the telephones themselves. The federal government's action group issued a demand that the hostages be released and threatened that the terrorists' own families would be taken hostage. The action group was told by Basajev's group to do whatever it wished.

The negotiations with the terrorists for the freeing of the hostages began early the next day, Thursday, June 15. At 7 A.M., Federal Army general Vacha Ibrahimov, formerly Internal Affairs minister of Chechnya and Ingushia arrived at the hospital. He was allowed to meet not with Basajev but with his assistant, Aslambek Ismailov. During the hour-long negotiations, General Ibrahimov pleaded that the women, children, and more seriously sick patients be released. Aslambek refused to agree to this, repeating the terrorists' earlier political demands. He added an additional demand that an immediate press conference be organized.

Although the commanders of the Russian forces were leaning toward the use of force against the terrorists, they decided to keep to the tactic of negotiations for the time being. The local action group in Budionovsk agreed to allow one more meeting. At about 11 A.M., Internal Affairs Minister Jerin himself arrived to participate in the meeting. But the Chechens refused to allow him into the hospital building, stopping him 100 meters away. No concrete results were achieved at this meeting. The hospital's attackers only agreed to allow food and medicine to be brought in for the hostages. Basajev also refused to listen to a delegation of elders who arrived from Chechnya or to the local Chechen representatives.

By that time, powerful operational forces were being concentrated in Budionovsk: the Alfa and Vega Special Purpose Units, Internal Affairs Ministry units from the Moscow and Northern Caucasus Military Regions, the famous Dzerzhinski Division's Special Group, the Stavropol 21st Assault Paratroop Brigade, and a brigade from the 68th Army. The city and the hospital were surrounded by a double security ring. Special attention was given to the security of the Stavropolimer Chemical Plant, which was located in this city. The Russians thought that this plant might be the terrorist objective since, if it were blown up, it would result in a huge ecological catastrophe for the Stavropol region. Given this critical situation, Russian premier Viktor Chernomyrdin cut short his vacation in Sochi and came back to Moscow.

All the world's news agencies began to report the events in Budionovsk. Chechen president Dudajev telephoned the ITAR-TASS News Agency that same night and informed them that no unit in the armed forces under his command had received instructions to conduct terrorist actions on Russian territory.

Meanwhile, the tragedy in Budionovsk continued. Basajev apparently came to the firm conclusion that issuing ultimatums to the Russian government was insufficient. It was necessary to speak to the whole world and to tell about the Chechen tragedy as he and his compatriots saw it. He demanded through Aslambek that a press conference take place at 2 P.M. When the press representatives failed to arrive at that time, Basajev twice put off the time and then, at 6 P.M., ordered that 5 hostages be shot. He then sent an ultimatum to the action group: if the journalists did not arrive to the press conference by 8 P.M., 10 more hostages would be shot. In spite of this threat, the 30 press representatives were late in arriving at the hospital.

During the press conference, it finally became known what until then had only been guessed at. For the first time since the start of Basajev's operation, clear information about its purposes reached Russia, its leaders, and the world. Finally it was confirmed that the terrorist military operation was commanded by one of the most famous Chechen military commanders, Colonel Shamil Basajev himself.[10]

At the start of the conference, Basajev stated that he planned and executed the operation without the knowledge of Dudajev and Maschadov, since once Vedeno was taken, communications with them were cut off. The original purpose of the operation was to reach Moscow and to do there what was done in Budionovsk. But, because they ran short of money to bribe the militia outposts, the battalion was not able to reach Moscow. Thus Budionovsk was only a chance target. Defending the Chechen communities had become purposeless, as the civilian inhabitants kept getting killed by the Russian bombs and artillery rounds. The Chechen fighters shot at the Russian soldiers, but the

Russians attacked the villages and their civilian inhabitants instead. Having given up all the communities, there had been no other course left but to go to Russia itself. The purpose of this excursion was either to stop the war in Chechnya or to die. Shamil Basajev referred to his group as an intelligence-diversion battalion and stated that it had 210 people. He had not expected a counterattack in Budionovsk, and for this reason alone, he ordered that as many hostages as possible be taken. He turned toward the hospital because many in his battalion had been wounded. He did not want to leave the wounded to their fate, although it had been agreed by all in advance that they would not stop for the injured. He decided to establish a filtration camp in the hospital of the type that had been established by the Russians for the Chechens.

Because of the frequent firefights with the Russians, his battalion had taken casualties, even at the hospital. For this reason, hostages were shot. This practice would continue, though in the future the military personnel, militiamen, and members of the OMON would be shot first. Women and children would not be shot unless this was done by the Russians themselves while storming the hospital. The negotiations with the action group to free the hostages were only irritating him. The action group threatened, in exchange, to shoot two thousand Chechens living in the Stavropol district. This did not concern him, as they were Russian citizens. In taking the hostages, he ordered that the Vietnamese and Turks be released but that the local Chechens be kept as hostages as they had equal rights and obligations as the rest. Asked about the civilian casualties during the first hours of the incursion into Budionovsk, Basajev did not allow himself to be drawn into the discussion but curtly stated that his forces had fought against the militia and the military and that civilian casualties had only been incidental.

In closing the press conference, Basajev repeated the conditions of his ultimatum: that the war in Chechnya be terminated, that negotiations with President Dudajev be started, and that the Russian Army be withdrawn from Chechnya.

The Unsuccessful Storming of the Hospital

On Friday, June 16, the events then occurring in Budionovsk were debated during the whole morning session of the Russian Parliamentary Duma. At the same time, the commanders of the Russian Armed Forces gathered to discuss possible ways of using its forces against Basajev's battalion. They could not bring themselves to make a decision to use force, especially since just prior to flying off to Halifax for a meeting with the leaders of seven of the most powerful countries in the world, Russian president Yeltsin promised personally to deal out justice to the persons responsible for this tragedy.

Russian vice premier Jegorov attempted to find one more way out. Through an intermediary, he offered the terrorists a special airplane, a choice of whatever route and destination they designated, and as much money as they wanted if only they agreed to leave Budionovsk. Basajev in answering this offer only repeated the requirements of his earlier ultimatum.

The well-known human rights defender Sergei Kovaliov, having decided to act as an intermediary in the negotiations with the terrorists, flew to Stavropol. He likewise condemned the terrorists' conduct but declared that Basajev's demands for negotiations between the Russian leaders and Dudajev were fully justified.

Since the highest heads of the Russian government had not come to any firm decision, the Federal Forces decided to storm the hospital. Assistant Internal Affairs minister Jegorov took command of the assault operation. The operation plan called for the following: once they forced their way into the hospital's territory, the Alfa Group was to attack and take the main hospital building; the Moscow District Special Quick Reaction Detachment was to take the trauma building; the city of Moscow Special Quick Reaction Detachment was to take the infectious diseases building; the Internal Affairs Ministry Special Quick Reaction Detachment was to take the garages. The Vega Detachment and the Specnaz Group and 14 armored personnel carriers were to provide covering fire for the Alfa Group. Four armored vehicles were to provide covering fire for the Specnaz. Places were also assigned to snipers. But very little time was allowed to prepare for the operation, which began at five o'clock on Saturday morning.[11]

At the beginning, it appeared that everything was going along as planned. The first group came out near the garages, the two other groups took over the trauma and infectious illnesses buildings. Eighty-six hostages were found there but no hit men. Just as the first group began to move from the garages toward the main hospital building, Basajev's soldiers opened up with hurricane-like fire from machine guns, grenade launchers, and automatic weapons. The other two groups met intense fire as well. Five soldiers from the group that had taken the infectious diseases building succeeded in getting to the wing of the main hospital building where a cafeteria was located, but they could not get inside as grenades were thrown at them, which they miraculously survived. It was possible to get inside the main building only through the doors or through the second-floor windows as almost all the windows on the first floor were covered with protective metal grates. The attackers could not take any further active steps for almost three hours, as they did not have the necessary

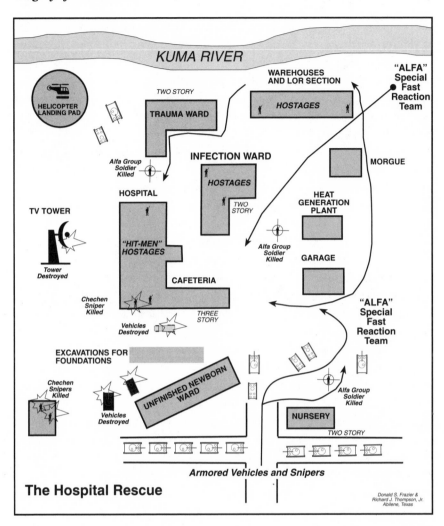

The Hospital Rescue

Donald S. Frazier &
Richard J. Thompson, Jr.
Abilene, Texas

covering fire support. The armored equipment did not arrive on time. When they finally did arrive, it was already too late. The hit men by that time had positioned hostages in the second- and third-floor windows as a human shield. The hostages, pale from fright, were waving white flags and screaming at the Russian soldiers not to shoot.

The assault did not come off. Although sporadic shooting continued, soon discussions began for a truce and negotiations. At 9:20 A.M., the assault was called off. The hostages that were freed were allowed to come out of the hospital territory. Some of them came out screaming at the Russian soldiers that they were murderers.

Three Russian soldiers, V. Solovov, R. Riabkin, and D. Burdiajev, were killed during the assault. Ten more were wounded. There were also casualties among the Chechen fighters. The press reported that 6 were wounded. Many hostages were also killed.

Russian Duma deputies then arrived to negotiate personally with Shamil Basajev. They were joined by General Vladislav Achialov, one of the participants in the October, 1993, putsch and himself a native of Grozni. The negotiations were unsuccessful. The parliamentarians again offered Basajev's forces an airplane and permission to fly without hindrance to any country that would agree to accept them. Again, this offer was refused and the earlier demands concerning the war in Chechnya repeated. Regarding the hostages, Basajev declared that his forces were not intending to do battle with women and children. In spite of the assault, not one further hostage was shot by the terrorists. At 12:40 P.M., the Russian negotiators left the hospital.

Despite this turn of events, Shamil Basajev decided to release some of the hostages. During the short truce that followed, the Chechens released 154 hostages, mostly women and children. They were allowed to leave the main hospital building in two columns.[12]

But the truce lasted only five hours. At 2:30 P.M., the assault of the hospital was renewed. It lasted for about an hour until an order was received to terminate it and to await further orders. That there would be no further assaults was confirmed by Russian president Yeltsin during a meeting with journalists in Halifax. Five Russian soldiers died during the two assaults.[13] With this order began the new stage of Basajev's operation in Budionovsk.

Russia Is Forced to Agree to Shamil Basajav's Demands

Russian premier Chernomyrdin spoke that evening by television to the Chechen hit men fortified in the hospital. He asked that the spilling of blood be stopped and that these totally innocent people be released. He stated that he was in favor of securing the freedom of the hostages without the use of force but added that his country would not allow the war in Chechnya to spill over into the whole Northern Caucasus region.[14]

That night, Basajev again held a press conference, which 10 journalists were allowed to attend. He stated that thirty hostages had been killed during the two Saturday assaults and that their bodies lay in the cellar. He did not, however, permit the journalists to view the bodies. He refused to say how many Chechens had been killed, only assuring the journalists that no civilian hostages were executed because of the assault. He stated that the total number of hostages executed to date was 11.

After the press conference, thirty-two additional hostages were released by the Chechens and allowed to leave the hospital together with the journalists. The body of a dead Alfa soldier was also released.[15] That night, negotiations for the release of the hostages were continued with the assistant chief of the Stavropol District Administration, A. Korobeinikov. With Basajev's agreement, 25 additional women and children were released.

That night Russian premier Chernomyrdin personally began negotiations with Basajev. During the two telephone conversations that followed, they tentatively agreed that the Chechens would release the hostages except for a small number to ensure the safety of the hit men during the course of their return to Chechnya. Basajev raised three conditions: that Russian combat actions in Chechnya be completely terminated, that official peace negotiations be started immediately, and that transport be provided for his group and their safety be guaranteed until they arrived at their desired destination. The remaining hostages would be released once the peace negotiations began. He also demanded that a referendum regarding Chechnya be held in Russia but later retracted this requirement.

For his part, Premier Chernomyrdin promised to carry out all such conditions and stated that a delegation for the negotiations had already been formed and was ready to fly to Chechnya. Vice Premier Nikolai Semionov; the commander of the Federal Army in Chechnya, General Anatoli Kulikov; and the representative of the Union of Public Organizations, Arkadi Volski, were appointed as members of the delegation. The Russian premier refused only to agree with the demand that the Chechen delegation be led by President Dudajev, as his whereabouts and how he could be reached were unknown.[16]

Shamil Basajev did not immediately give his final agreement to the offer, saying that he had to discuss it further with his side. They agreed to wait until ten o'clock the following morning to finalize the agreement. Despite all of Chernomyrdin's promises, a firefight again broke out that morning between the Russian soldiers surrounding the hospital and the Chechens.

At 10 A.M., Sunday, June 18, Basajev communicated that he had not yet come to a final decision. The two sides agreed that he would call again in an hour. Kovaliov, accompanied by O. Orlov, had arrived at the hospital together with 5 Duma deputies to complete the drafting of an agreement.

Later Basajev again corrected his demands: war activity in Chechnya had to be terminated immediately and peace negotiations begun. Chechen prosecutor general Usman Imajev was to represent Dudajev in the negotiations. He also demanded that the Russian premier make an official announcement as to the termination of war activity in Chechnya and the beginning of the peace negotiations. After such announcement, Basajev promised to release 100 more women and children immediately.

Premier Chernomyrdin agreed to these conditions, stating that the order to terminate war activity would be immediately prepared. He, however, asked that the Chechens prepare to release the promised hostages and avoid getting drawn into any further provocations. The order would be issued in the next several hours and the start of its execution would be communicated afterwards to Basajev by telephone.

Shamil Basajev continued negotiations with the representatives of the administration of the Stavropol district as to procedures for the release of hostages and his battalion's return to Chechnya. He demanded that an airplane be provided by 5 P.M. but was told that it was impossible to arrange this in such a short period of time. Instead, Ikarus buses were offered. Basajev stated that he would take 130 hostages with him and asked that Kovaliov accompany him and the hostages. They also discussed allowing journalists to accompany them. At 3:30 P.M., Sergei Kavaliov and the other deputies left the hospital, and 126 hostages were allowed to leave with them.

On June 20 at 8 P.M. Moscow time, war activity in Chechnya was terminated by order of the commander of Russian Federal Forces in Chechnya, General Kulikov.

The Return to Chechnya

During his conversation with Chernomyrdin that night, Basajev promised to release the hostages at five o'clock the next morning. However, because of misunderstandings that arose in finalizing the procedures for the departure of Basajev's men and the release of hostages, the hostages were not freed at the agreed upon time.

All such details were being negotiated with Basajev by the commander of the Internal Affairs action group in Stavropol, General Viktor Medvedickov. Finally, they reached an agreement as to the column's return route, the number of volunteer hostages who would make the trip, and the transport and movement procedures. All the journalists wanting to go with the column were issued leaflets stating that they were going along as volunteers without any guarantees as to their safety.[17] Seven red Ikarus buses were provided to transport Basajev's troops and the hostages. A refrigerator truck was brought to transport the bodies of the Chechen fighters who had been killed.[18]

On Monday at 3:10 P.M., the passengers were loaded into the buses. Seated in each bus were 8–10 Chechens, 1 or 2 deputies of the Russian Duma, 1 or 2 journalists, and about 20 hostages. The hostages were placed along the windows, and the hit men took the seats in the middle. Weapons and ammunition were loaded in the aisle between the seats. Drivers were picked from among the hostages, and alongside each was seated one of the battalion's fighters. The wounded were put into a separate bus so that, if necessary, the rest could operate according to the developing conditions without being burdened by the wounded. In all, 114 hostages were loaded into the buses, along with 11 journalists and 9 Duma deputies. Among the volunteer hostages was the mayor of Budionovsk. No one really stopped to count how many fighters had exited the hospital with Basajev. According to Shamil Basajev himself, there had been 127 fighters in his formation before setting out on the operation. During the operation 16 were killed, 15 were severely wounded, and 10 suffered less severe wounds.

The column began to move toward Mozdok at 3:15 P.M. It was accompanied by a militia automobile escort. Helicopters and aircraft constantly patrolled overhead. The road was kept completely free, as had been prearranged by the militia for security.[19]

The column calmly passed through the communities of Stepnoja and Kurskaja and was nearing Northern Ossetian territory when it was suddenly stopped. Its way was blocked by armored vehicles and two helicopters that had landed nearby. Apparently, the Internal Affairs ministers of Kabarda Balkeria and Northern Ossetia had made a joint announcement that they could not guarantee the security of the column in the territories of their republics because of the hostility of the local inhabitants. General Kulikov decided to change the route and have the column go to Vedeno by way of Dagestan, a route that was some 300 kilometers longer.

Although Basajev fiercely protested any divergence from the agreed upon route, he was forced to give his consent to this change. The column turned back and by 10:30 P.M. was back at the Stepnoja community. From there it turned and proceeded toward the community of Achikulak, located in the region of Neftekumsk. At five o'clock the next morning, the column finally neared the administrative border of Dagestan, where it was again stopped, this time only for two hours. Having passed through Kizliar, the column finally arrived at Chasavjurt (Dagestan) at 8:30 and stopped at one of the town squares. Thousands of people met them there, all shouting in celebration: "Shamil! Shamil!" "Hurrah for the heroes!" "The war is ended!" The column was immediately surrounded by the militia and a ring of OMON soldiers. Basajev also set up his own defense posts.

It was not clear when the column would be allowed to move on again. After prolonged and painful waiting, Basajev finally made an official announcement to the press. In it, he stated that it was unclear why the column was held up in Chasavjurt or whether this was a provocation. He announced that he was taking onto himself all further responsibility for the continuation of the journey. They would now proceed to the Chechen village of Zandak where

Baasjev Group's
Return Route
to Chechnya

they would release the hostages. Then the Chechen fighters would go on to
Vedeno. He further stated that he could give no guarantees for the safety of
the hostages in the event of further provocations from the Russians, adding
that no guarantees had been given for the safety of his battalion's fighters and
himself.

Finally, after eight hours of excruciating waiting, the column began to
move once more at 4:50 P.M. At 7:10, it finally arrived in the village of Zandak, one of the last five villages high in the mountains that still remained
in the hands of Dudajev's fighters. There the column was met by a jubilant
crowd, armed Chechens, and Basajev's brother. At a public meeting Shamil
Basajev addressed the crowd. He stated that their operation had not been conducted as an act of vengeance but rather as a step that had been forced upon
them in order to try to stop the war and the annihilation of the Chechen nation. As they had done upon leaving the hospital, Basajev and his assistant,
Aslambek Ismailov, once again asked the people of Budionovsk for forgive-
ness for what they had done. They also asked them to try to understand that

his group had been left with no other choice. The column with the hostages was then allowed to return to Russia. The tragedy of Budionovsk was drawing to a close.[20]

But did it really end? As soon as Basajev's battalion and the hostages moved out, the hospital territory, buildings, and especially its cellars were carefully searched. Six more bodies of those killed were found. Budionovsk then began to bury its dead. Russian Defense Ministry and Internal Affairs soldiers and officials also buried their dead. According to the Internal Affairs Ministry, 124 inhabitants of Russia had been killed (other sources reported 119). Another 126 wounded lay in Stavropol hospitals, among them 22 military personnel. Besides these, 53 sick people had also suffered from the events in Budionovsk. Later, a Day of Mourning was proclaimed in Russia.[21]

Shamil Basajev also buried his dead soldiers, but they were not allowed to lie in peace even in their graves. The day after the burials, the Russians bombed the community of Zandak, with many of the bombs exploding in the area of the cemetery.

War and Terrorism

The Chechens met Shamil Basajev and the fighters of his group as heroes.[22] Shamil Basajev's name had rung around the world. Some condemned him, but others understood him as they finally began to appreciate the extremity of the conditions that had forced Basajev and his group to go the road of terrorism.

Although the raid in Budionovsk had all the standard features of a terrorist act, there is also no question that Basajev and his group accomplished an operation that was unique from both a military and a political viewpoint. This military-diversion operation conducted by, at best, a company of soldiers succeeded in stopping a vastly more powerful country's savage war of annihilation against a much smaller nation whose forces were hovering on the brink of defeat. It forced Russia to begin negotiations for a settlement on equal terms, which up to that time Russia had refused even to contemplate. Without doubt, this action was planned and prepared by the Chechen High Command at its highest levels.

Basajev's Budionovsk operation was conducted at the most appropriate moment for both Russia and Chechnya. By taking Shatoja, the Russian military forces completed the consolidation of their hold on all the primary Chechen communities and regional centers. The oil pipelines running through Chechnya also were finally brought back under Russian control, which, in fact, was what the Russian government had been seeking in the first place. Also, judging from official Federal Army reports, Dudajev's remaining Chechen forces were no longer being considered as much of a threat to Russia.

If Russia had continued combat operation, it would have only compromised itself even more. By then, it had become quite clear that regardless of how long the Russian forces continued waging the war, they would not have been able to vanquish the Chechens completely. Unable to gain a clear victory, they inevitably would have bogged down. The resilience of the Chechen forces were shown quite clearly in Bamut. There the Chechen forces were being led by Shirmani Alpakov, who, just two years prior, had himself been a captain in the Russian Army. Thus the time had come to terminate further combat activity and to find the most appropriate way of ending the fighting.

For this reason, Russian premier Chernomyrdin made quick use of the opportunity provided him by the Budionovsk tragedy. He remained undecided for only two days, and that was really only the time needed to weigh all the pros and cons before making a decision. By agreeing to terminate combat activity and to begin peace negotiations, Chernomyrdin was actually able to strengthen his own position at the top levels of the Russian government.

The Chechens had also vitally needed to stop further combat actions. Regardless of how well they fought, their forces were gradually melting away because of the casualties suffered during the constant confrontations with the Russian Federal Forces. The continuous bombing and artillery bombardments were destroying the Chechen communities one after the other and killing their civilian populations. The surviving civilian population was being driven from their homes in ever increasing numbers and was being forced into refugee camps elsewhere. In an effort to limit such civilian losses, the Chechen forces gave up further tactical efforts to defend the communities. Under these circumstances, few alternatives were left the Chechens. Efforts to preserve the remaining structures of the Dudajev government also gained prime importance.

Because of Budionovsk, Russia was forced to begin negotiations with Dudajev. In effect, the operation stopped this powerful country's war efforts. It was obvious that a small country like Chechnya could not win the war by the traditional methods, and clearly it would only have lost if the war had been protracted. For these reasons, Chechnya decided on the unusual method of "military terrorism."

But was this method of "military terrorism" really all that unusual? In ordinary usage, the term "terrorism" is understood as an act of violence perpetrated against civilians by civilians for a criminal purpose. The term "military terrorism" has to be understood as an act of "terrorism," that is, an act of violence against civilians, which is conducted by a military force as part of an overall military campaign or for a military purpose. It still retains the criminal connotations.

Terrorism evokes a singular horror among civilian populations. Thus the governments of the industrialized and militarily powerful countries continue to be quick to condemn any form of terrorism as a wholly unacceptable means of waging any conflict for fear of releasing this "evil genie" out of its rightful imprisonment. Their arguments are usually grounded on the proposition that terrorism lies outside the international conventions proscribing the use of military force. Thus actions not allowed by these conventions are criminal and therefore punishable under civilian or other criminal statutes.

As terrorism, for the most part, is conducted against civilian populations by civilians or at least by "nonuniformed" forces of unclear identity or purpose, it is seen as arbitrary and purposeless violence. Moreover, as civilian populations have few, if any, real defenses against such acts, they are also considered despicable, cowardly, and dishonorable. Because of the massive and wide-scale injuries that are often caused by such acts of violence, condemnations of "terrorism" are also replete with phrases such as the "inhumanity" of the acts and the "senselessness" of the losses inflicted on innocent civilian victims.

But while expressing their condemnation of terrorism, larger countries do not condemn the use of their own armed forces during conflicts and their own use of "conventional" weapons of destruction against primarily civilian targets. Thus armed actions undertaken by conventional military forces still have a legality attached to them, and the destructive effects of their actions on civilian populations, whether inflicted directly or indirectly, are for the most part condoned.

In evaluating situations such as Budionovsk, questions as to the workability and even viability of such conceptual and legal frameworks inevitably force themselves to the surface. Although such legal frameworks may be truly laudable regulatory efforts to limit the more extreme effects of warfare, they do not stand up very well in light of the harsh realities of modern warfare.

Ever since man decided to crack his neighbor's skull in place of trying to reason with him, the essence of war has always been violence against the opposing party and inevitably his supporters. But to the victims of such violence, it is of little practical importance whether they are first taken hostage by terrorists and then shot or are suddenly blown up by an intended or even misplaced bomb from a roving military aircraft. It is obviously not the organizational form that the inflicting party takes on that is of prime importance.

The more persuasive argument would be that military forces should fight military forces and leave the civilian populations alone. Obviously, a small terrorist group would hardly be able to take a larger military force hostage. It is mostly the civilian population that bears the brunt of terrorism, and thus the proscription should remain in place.

But war, even conventional war, is almost never simply a battle between regular military forces. Statistics show that during all the wars since World War II, for every soldier of a country defending itself that is killed, ten civilians also die. And what about the wounded, the maimed, the refugees, and the communities and homes that are destroyed? During a war, any war, the civilian population always suffers the most.

So are there any material differences? In its effects, hardly. The conclusion that forces itself through the present legal maze is that war itself is in essence a form of terrorism, only on a larger scale. This is even more so from the attacking rather than the defending side. Since the war zone is almost always on the defender's territory, the attackers inevitably do the most damage to the civilian population. World news agencies and the more influential analytic publications generally avoid the word "terrorism," as it is thought to be quite difficult to separate "terrorism" from armed resistance. Such a label is used with great reservation and only in those extreme circumstances where the means used and the damage inflicted far outweigh the sought-after results. The "reasonableness" of the act seems to be the key.

Unavoidably, the Russian war effort in Chechnya by this same definition must also be considered a form of "terrorism" being conducted by that country against the Chechen nation, although, to be more precise, the correct label would be "military terrorism." By even the terms of the prevailing conventions, Russia's terrorist acts were multiple: they included the holding for years of thousands of innocent hostages in filtration camps. Russia also made use of extortion backed up by deadly force. It continued to demand that the Chechen nation abandon any hope of freedom and self-determination that was their right under international law and the United Nations Charter. When they refused, Russia bombed Chechnya's civilian communities from the air and bombarded them by artillery and mortars from the ground, killing untold thousands of civilians. According to Russia's plan of action, the Chechens were simply to be forced to lay down their arms by any means necessary, including the massacre of its civilian population. It was to bend to Russia's will, with or without a surviving Chechen population.

In essence, the "military terrorism" conducted by the Russians differed only in its scale. However, while all this was taking place only on Chechen soil, not one Russian public official ever publicly entertained the thought that his own military forces were conducting terrorism. What is more, the international community remained in much the same stupor. But as soon as a similar act, only on a much smaller scale, was executed on Russian soil in response, immediately cry was made about "terrorism."

At the beginning, Shamil Basajev's battalion's operation was categorically labeled a terrorist act, with all the condemnation and abrogation that goes with the label. But later, this view imperceptibly began to change. In time, particularly in Russia, the opinion gradually took hold that, although Basajev's operation was a terrorist act, the terrorists' demands were wholly justified. Again it would seem that "reasonableness" was the key preventing its condemnation.

Basajev's side used violence only to the degree necessary to achieve the operation's purposes. This was understood even by those who spent five days with his group as hostages. They later recounted that the hit men had not shown any unnecessary antagonism or animosity toward them and had not used any gratuitous steps to harm them. But because of the sacrifice of civilians at Budionovsk, it was possible to stop, at least temporarily, the killing of many more thousands of people. A terrorist act stopped a much larger terrorist act.

Many of the sacrifices at Budionovsk could have been avoided had the hospital not been assaulted. The Russian assault was done without any great regard as to the safety of the hostages being held inside. Not without reason, the hostages screamed at the Russian soldiers, calling them killers.[23] Unavoidably, blame for the deaths in the assault also has to rest, at least partially, on the consciences of the Russian forces commanders.

When considering the tragedy at Budionovsk, a final troubling question forces itself to the forefront: Could it have been possible to stop the war in Chechnya without resorting to such a harsh terrorist act as was committed by Basajev's battalion? The Russian side most likely will continue to say "yes," although they had contemplated no means other than the complete destruction of Dudajev's forces and the resisting Chechen communities. Up to Budionovsk, all talk of truces and negotiations had been but empty words. The Russian guarantee of later peace would have been only the newly formed 58th Army, that is, peace again through the use of force. This hardly would have satisfied the Chechens who would have been the targets of such suppression actions. Had Russia gone further along its chosen course, more deaths and suffering would have awaited the Chechens, along with a life without shelter in destroyed cities and villages or in the mountains. This, without question, would have resulted in the inevitable annihilation of the Chechen nation.

A final form of the question has to be posed: What are the limits of the use of force by a small nation that is threatened with a harsh occupation or even annihilation by a larger, more powerful attacking force? It obviously cannot hope to oppose such a force by conventional military means alone. This is particularly true when the attacker has available modern weapons and military technology not available to the defender in any comparable degree. Is terrorism against the attacking forces' civilian population then the only alternative left? Clearly there is a right to defend oneself. But what if everything else fails or is rendered ineffective?

The tragedy at Budionovsk was a unique event in that a small group, by executing a military diversion operation, succeeded in stopping a powerful country's war against a small nation on the verge of losing. It forced Russia to begin negotiations upon equal terms. The first period of the war in Chechnya was drawing to a close.

CHAPTER 11

Results of the First Period of the War

Before the start of combat activity, almost a million people lived in Chechnya. During the first half year of the war, about 40,000 of these people were killed. About 370,000 people were officially registered as refugees (some sources indicate that this figure was closer to 480,000). According to information gathered by the Russian civil rights organization, Memorial, 27,000 civilians died in Grozni alone, among them 2,000 children. Of the 400,000 people who had lived in Grozni, only 280,000 continued to reside in the city.[1] Because of combat activity, the population of Chechnya decreased by between 410,000 and 520,000 people, or almost 50 percent. Of the 427 communities in Chechnya, 380 were either partially or completely destroyed.

The losses suffered by the Chechen armed forces cannot be accurately accounted for since some fought independently rather than under the Chechen high command. Besides, the numbers of personnel in the various units were never constant. According to official information reported by the Chechen side, by April 12, 1995, 2,230 Chechen fighters had been killed and some 5,000 wounded. Information submitted by Russia one day earlier as to its own losses indicated that 1,690 Russian soldiers had been killed, of which count 300 bodies could not be unidentified. Another 6,263 had been wounded. Thus the losses declared by both sides were comparatively equal. In reality, both sides sustained much greater losses.

During this period of combat activity, the Chechens lost virtually all their

heavy weapons and combat equipment. Judging from Russian official pronouncements, the Chechens apparently lost more heavy weapons and combat
equipment than they possessed in their inventory at the beginning of the war.
Apparently, these Chechen losses included commandeered Russian equipment that had been hit and left on the battlefield and that the Chechens were
not able to repair.

The economic losses sustained by the Chechen Republic because of the
war activity are almost impossible to calculate. Although official Russian government pronouncements have mentioned huge sums that would be needed
to reconstruct the republic's economy, it is hard to accept the accuracy of these
statements. At best, these sums reflect the costs of rebuilding basic infrastructure rather than replacing what had actually been lost. Thus the peoples' personal losses—that is, their accumulations over lifetimes—do not quite enter
this figure. Even if the figures are correct, it is even harder to believe that Russia would be capable of appropriating such vast sums even if it wished to do
so. One may recall the earthquake in Armenia; money for its reconstruction
could not be found even in the whole of the Soviet Union, which was much
stronger economically than is present-day Russia.

According to official Russian military forces figures, during these first six
months of the war, approximately 1,700 Russian Federal Forces soldiers died
and 7,000 were injured. The Chechen Information Center, however, reported
much larger figures, counting 25,000 Russian soldiers killed. In the opinion
of independent military experts, it would be more appropriate to set the loss
figures somewhere in the middle of these two counts.

There is sufficient proof that the Russian High Command continuously
submitted decreased loss figures. A journal kept by one of the commanders of
a paratroop battalion speaks most graphically about the subject of troop losses.
Excerpts from it were published in the Russian daily *Komsomolskaja pravda* on
January 16, 1996. According to this journal, of the battalion's 400 soldiers who
actively participated in combat operations from December 11, 1994, the following were left by February 2, 1995:[2]

7th PC (paratroop company): 2 officers, 1 soldier.
8th PC: 2 officers.
9th PC: 2 officers, 3 soldiers.
Intelligence platoon: 2 soldiers.
Communications platoon: 2 soldiers.
Grenade launcher platoon: 1 soldier.
Rocket artillery platoon: 2 soldiers.
Mortar battery: 13 soldiers.

Anti-tank battery: 14 soldiers.
Rear area support group: 24 people.
In all: 68 people.

During almost two months of battle, the battalion lost 332 people, or 80 percent of its personnel. Some were killed, others were wounded, others were missing in action or deserted. A similar situation existed in the majority of the battalions. Even if the average losses in the other units were cut by half or were deemed to be not more than 30 to 40 percent, the losses of the 55,000-man Russian battle force in Chechnya would be still be three to five times higher than those listed in official reports.

The medics of the various field hospitals and morgues also calculated that the number of Russian soldiers killed was much higher than that reported in official sources. Again, it is suspected that the official reports were based only on the number of soldiers who actually died on the battlefield. Soldiers who died later from their wounds were not included in their figures.

In all cases, the Russian Federal Forces during the first half year of the war in Chechnya suffered greater losses than the Soviet Army sustained during ten years of war in Afghanistan. The Russian president and the Defense and Internal Affairs Ministry commanders all mentioned that the most important factor was that the powerfulness of the Chechen armed forces had not been sufficiently appreciated. The Chechens were better prepared for combat activity than their opponents estimated. They also had greater numbers of military professionals who had gained their experience in more than one war.

The other obvious reason for the large losses sustained by the Russian Federal Forces has already been mentioned: the military units were sent off to fight in Chechnya completely without preparation. They were formed up for the most part from untrained recruits who were then forced to gain their military experience at the price of their own blood.

Perhaps an even more important reason was that the Russian Armed Forces were simply not organized for this type of military action. Most of the Russian military forces' training had been focused on larger unit tactics, starting at the platoon and company level. It later became apparent that the training of individual soldiers and the training of action at the squad level had been omitted. This became very important under the conditions that the federal military forces found themselves in Chechnya. Squads and individual soldiers had not been trained to act independently against the fast-moving Chechen fighter groups.

Additionally, many casualties were suffered during confrontations and firefights among the federal units themselves. This fact was well illustrated in the above-mentioned battalion commander's journal. A notation entered in a military report submitted in January, 1995, concerning his unit's activity in Grozni reads: "We are being bombarded by both our own and the opponent's artillery. We are being fired at from three sides." One of the war correspondents visiting the federal military units fighting in Grozni early in 1995 came to the same conclusion: "Today there is no soldier or officer in Grozni who has not been under fire from his own forces. Everyone is hitting our forces: aircraft, artillery, tanks and snipers." The commander of a motorized rifle regiment, Colonel Lieutenant Vladimir V. openly admitted that, "Every second person killed in the regiment was killed by fire from our own forces." [3]

Such confrontations and firefights occurred for a number of reasons: because of poor training of both the individual soldiers and at the unit command level, because of the fear of Chechen attacks, and because of poor unit coordination. In addition, Chechen fighter groups often intentionally provoked such confrontations.

The fact that the Combined Federal Forces in Chechnya were not a unified structure also had an impact on the number of losses. The Combined Federal Forces were made up of Defense Ministry and Internal Affairs Ministry units and the Federal Counterintelligence Service's detachments. Mutual antagonism had grown up among these services, and, sometimes at the slightest provocation, this antagonism resulted in the opening up of weapons' fire against each other.

The antagonism was actually stimulated at the highest Armed Forces levels, as well as in the lower ranks. At the higher levels, it showed up in the continuing attempts of each service to blame the failures of the military operation in Chechnya on the others. The Russian Defense Ministry, in an attempt to justify its own huge losses, constantly emphasized the fact that its units had been forced to operate where it was the most dangerous, although the opposite was supposed to have been the case: their mission had been only to assist the Internal Affairs Army.

At the lower levels, the antagonism was brought on by the different actions of the troops in their dealings with the Chechens. The Ministry of Defense units would take the communities at the price of large losses and then turn them over to the Internal Affairs units and the OMON. The latter invariably would act very harshly toward the local inhabitants, most often robbing and pillaging everything that fell into their hands. This only raised the Chechen level of antagonism against the Russian troops. Thus the Chechens also viewed the various Russian troop formations differently. For example, soldiers of the Defense Ministry units, except for certain "contract" personnel, were regularly taken as prisoners of war. Internal Affairs troops and the OMON were most often executed on the spot.

The federal military units also suffered many losses from bombs dropped by their own aviators.[4] According to reports, these losses were as great as those suffered from Chechen artillery and mortar fire. As fog almost always hung over Grozni and the other communities, Russian pilots most often released their bombs from an altitude of 6,000–7,000 meters. The free-falling bombs and unguided rockets would disperse to a large degree, and the chances of them hitting the Chechen positions was about equal with the chances of them hitting friendly troops. Even with aircraft such as the Su-24, which was equipped with aiming devices, the bombs invariably fell about 150 meters to either side of the intended target.

The Russian casualties suffered from its own air forces resulted not only from a gross lack of accuracy in the placement of bombs. The kill radii of the X-29, X-25, and C-25 guided rockets used in Chechnya were also relatively large, about 280 to 400 meters. Heavy bombs were also used, whose shock waves traveled up to 300 meters and whose shrapnel flew up to 1,200 meters. In other words, there was always sufficient shrapnel for all.

Friendly positions were also hit by aircraft because of the lack of sufficient pilot combat training at their home bases and because of the pilots' psychological unpreparedness for combat actions. Whenever the pilots attacking the Chechen forward positions had information that the opponent possessed hand-carried antiaircraft rocket weapons, they hurriedly fired off their unguided rockets and pulled out of their attack runs as fast as possible, thus intentionally minimizing their own abilities to deliver the weapons accurately.

Quite often, the commanders of the Russian infantry units also made a practice of refusing to indicate their front lines with signal rockets to the attacking aircraft so that this information could not be used by their opponent. Friendly positions were also often inadvertently fired upon because of defects in the aviation weapons themselves. In many cases, instead of flying the several kilometers as intended, the rockets fell directly under the helicopters onto friendly positions.

Furthermore, the Russian Federal Forces' units became a source of arms for the Chechen fighters. There always could be found soldiers and commanders in the Russian ranks who, for alcohol and dollars, would sell not only light but also heavy weapons. They also often agreed to exchange weapons for soldiers from their units who had been captured by the Chechens. In Grozni, the price of a soldier or an officer became common knowledge. It was self-apparent to the Russians that these weapons would be later turned upon their own forces.

The Russian Federal Army's Weapons and Equipment Losses

Information about what weapons and equipment losses were suffered by the Federal Army in Chechnya is also insufficient. Statements of high-ranking military officers that have appeared in the press may help us determine the numbers.

The assistant commander of the Land Army for Weaponry, General Colonel S. Majev, who had been charged with the supply of equipment for all the forces participating in the Chechen operation, stated that more than 4,000 units of armor and other combat equipment were forced out of service. Of these, about 2,500 units were withdrawn because of technical deficiencies and about 1,500 were knocked out during combat. Totally destroyed were 800 units: about 400 of these were armored equipment (tanks, armored vehicles, artillery, and so on), about 600 were motor vehicles of various types, and about 80 were rocket artillery systems. The total number of completely destroyed heavy weapons and combat equipment was about 900 units.[5] (The apparent contradictions in the sum of these figures results from how different equipment is lumped together in a category for accounting purposes. The overall figure, however, gives a good indication of the real losses.)

During this period of combat operations, the Federal Army's service units repaired more than 2,700 various types of heavy weapons and combat equipment. Evacuated from combat positions and from along the lines of march were more than 2,000 heavy weapons and combat equipment, about 600 of these were from Grozni. The more severely burned and knocked out weapons and combat equipment were evacuated to permanent repair facilities.

These figures do not make clear the total number of heavy weapons and combat equipment used in Chechnya. During preparations for the military operation, about 4,000 heavy weapons units and other combat equipment and 2,500 tons of munitions and technical military goods were supplied from the Northern Caucasus Military Region, from other military regions, and from the central supply depots. Additionally, from the beginning of the operation until December 28, 1994, another 4,000 weapons units and combat equipment were taken from the supply depots, brought to the combat zone and prepared for combat use. Thus it would appear that almost 8,000 units of heavy weapons and combat equipment were brought into the combat theater, about 50 percent of which were forced out of service because of technical deficiencies and combat actions.

The Russian Air Forces Group in Chechnya consisted in essence of the 4th Air Army reinforced by reconnaissance, close air support, bomber, and long-range aviation units. This group lost two Su-25 attack aircraft in combat (one was knocked down on February 4, 1995, near Chechen Aula, the other on May 5 near Serzhen Jurt). Fourteen other aircraft were also hit but made their way back to their bases and were repaired.

Two squadrons of Mi-24 combat helicopters and 2 squadrons of Mi-8 and Mi-26 transport helicopters also participated in the campaign. During 6 months of combat operations, the Land Army's aviation forces lost 4 Mi-24 and 3 Mi-8 helicopters. There is no information as to how many helicopters were hit but survived.

Ethics of War

It is quite difficult to determine what were the Federal Forces' ethical and moral views concerning this type of operation prior to the start of military operations in Chechnya, especially when they were being conducted on its "own" country's territory. After experiencing failures and trying to justify themselves, high officials of the Russian Military Command later stated on a number of occasions that its army had been unprepared to fight against its own citizens.

The question of whether the army was fighting its own citizens had not been debated, although Moscow's official position throughout this conflict was that Chechnya was a part of the Russian Federation. It is well known that Chechnya was inhabited not only by Chechens; a large number of ethnic Russians also reside there, especially in the cities. A widely accepted but unofficial view in 1992 was that the Russian government recognized the Chechen Republic de facto. It even transferred a portion of its weapons to the Chechen forces before withdrawing its army from the country in exactly the same manner as it had done in the other newly independent republics that split off from the Soviet Union. An agreement was even signed in the summer of 1993 between the Russian Federation and the Republic of Chechnya, recognizing the sovereignty of the Chechen Republic. That Russia recognized the independence of Chechnya was also indirectly confirmed by the fact that the Russian Federal Army had first chosen to participate in aggression against Chechnya in secret, when Russian tanks and aircraft without identification markings had supported the opposition forces against Dudajev.

Russian officers, soldiers, and others hold many different opinions about the "rightness" of the actions of the Federal Forces in this now blood-saturated land. It may be more accurate, however, to separate these views according to the actions of the Military High Command, the units, subunits, and even the soldiers themselves.

Two aspects concerning the Military High Command must be singled out, namely, the nature of the combat operation in Chechnya itself and the tactics used during this operation. As has been mentioned previously, the officers at the higher levels of the High Command did not have a unified view as to the operation in Chechnya. Many of even its highest-ranking officers spoke out against it and refused to participate in the operation, especially those who previously fought in the war in Afghanistan.

During this period of combat operations, many of the top commanders attempted to act circumspectly, not wanting to turn the operation to "disarm the illegal armed formations" into a war against Chechnya. Such commanders were later intentionally removed from their duties, with the removal disguised as either the reorganization of the battle group or under a different bureaucratic cloak. In this way, the Military Command pyramid at various levels was filtered out so that everything would move in the direction intended by Moscow's plans, at least when viewed from the side.

But perhaps more important is the question of the tactics used during the combat operations. Journalists, the Chechens, and even Russian soldiers labeled them as "scorched earth" tactics. They had not been determined by the politicians or by the political parties; in other words, the use of such tactics had not been predetermined by either the country's parliament, the executive government, or the other institutions of the civilian government. Their use was decided upon by the Military High Command alone.

According to the statements of Chechen fighters, the "scorched earth" tactics did not inflict much damage to the Chechen Armed Forces, as the fighters almost always were able to take cover in prepared shelters, leaving only observers outside.

The Russian bombs and rockets, artillery rounds, and mortar shells for the most part hit civilians, turning whole communities into rubble. In essence, the whole Chechen nation was being punished because its government and Armed Forces chose to resist the Russians. The operation to "disarm the illegal armed formations" became in effect one huge punitive action. The achievement of the purposes of the military operation was being sought regardless of price and with total disregard for the harshness of the results. Although in the opinion of the majority of the military commanders, the civilian government and not the army was responsible for the war in Chechnya, the methods chosen to achieve the military operation's purposes, including the choice of "scorched earth" tactics, were determined by the ethics and consciences of the military commanders themselves.

The use of such harsh military tactics and their purpose were not fully understood by the soldiers. Their continuing question was: Why and for what are we fighting? At the same time, the war affected their behavior. It negatively affected the army's prestige, unleashing all that was the worst in it.

The spilling of blood during wartime induces further cruelty and a disregard for other peoples' suffering and pain. The press reported on many occasions the Russian soldiers' harsh behavior toward the Chechens and various cases of robbery, rape, and pillage. Yet no resolute efforts were ever taken to punish this behavior. Only 286 criminal actions were filed in this surge of massive ongoing criminality by the Russian troops. One of the opposition leaders, Beslan Gantemirov, even remarked publicly in April, 1995, that while only four Russian robber-soldiers had been executed in Grozni, this should have been 4,000 or even 40,000. In his opinion, all Russian soldiers in Grozni, without any exception, were robbers and thieves.

One of the four Russian soldiers taken prisoner by the Chechens in the town of Shali, an 18-year-old from Briansk, recounted how 2 officers and 4 warrant officers raped and then shot several Chechen women. This had been watched by the whole company in formation. One video showed how Russian soldiers in Grozni's Prigorodnoje district raped Chechen women in front of their husbands and fathers and then shot them.[6]

A woman from the village of Asinovskaja also recounted how her three children died after her house was burned down. After entering the village, the Russian soldiers demanded that the older women provide them with young girls for the night. They told the mother that if she cooperated they would not shoot her and would not wreck her house. When the mother refused to turn over her twelve-year-old daughter to members of the OMON, they shot the child in the head before her mother's eyes.[7]

Robbery and pillaging became prevalent to such a degree that some local inhabitants attached notes to their doors saying, "Please do not bother us. This apartment has already been robbed three times." The situation became so out of control that, in the warehouse district of Grozni in early March, 1995, a Russian special purpose detachment fiercely fought a Russian paratrooper unit for two days. The object of the battle was a large oriental carpet warehouse.

Such were the ethics of the Russian troops during the war in Chechnya. Several hundred thousand soldiers were affected by the war. Returning home to Russia, were they not going to revert to the same methods in peacetime, especially during their country's economic depression? And not only in Russia but also in the countries neighboring Russia? And how many illegal weapons found their way back to Russia along with the soldiers returning from the battlefield?

A criminal war breeds criminality.

The Press and Propaganda

For almost the first time in Russian history, a free and independent Russian press was reporting the news as it happened and reporting it objectively. It was also asking pointed questions and getting answers from the Russian military brass. The frequent unpurged reports of the military's actions that were appearing in the print and electronic media were a totally new experience for Russian government officials. At the same time, however, many of the old propaganda mills were still attempting to participate in the creation of public opinion and to put whatever spin on the news that the government deemed appropriate at the time.

The Russians hold that Dudajev won the information war and that Chechnya's information minister Malvadi Udugov gave so many interviews that as soon as anything happened, he was already inserting his slant on the news. According to this widely held opinion, he functioned more successfully than the whole Russian propaganda machine.

Udugov had two and sometimes three assistants. As soon as a battle or an event took place, they immediately gave out printable information, much more quickly than the Russian information officers. Also, Dudajev and the other Chechen military leaders gave interviews quite willingly on television and on the radio. Even though he was himself constantly being hunted, Dudajev succeeded in getting onto the airwaves on a regular basis. The Chechens were thus able to communicate their slant on the news and to show the cruelty and atrocities of the Russian military, thereby affecting public opinion more than the Russians.

In Russia, there were basically two directions of reporting that were appearing in the news media. One set of newspapers took the position that the war was legal and justified and that the Russians were the forces of good. But these newspapers were not large in number. The others, the sizable majority of newspapers and news agencies with the widest publication, understood the war not to be good in itself or for Russia and began to criticize the Russian incursion into Chechnya. Criticism was even indulged in by former military officers who had been released to the reserve. Associated with newspapers, official journals, or analysis publications, they wrote critically, and most often quite objectively, about the war. The majority wrote negatively about Russia's politics and about Russia's military actions in Chechnya.

Understandably, there were efforts made to control the press, but the government's power was, for the most part, limited. The authority of official newspapers such as the military newspaper *Krasnaja zvezda* was much less than before, and, on the whole, few, even among the military, tended to believe them.

The newspaper *Moskovskij komsomolec* wrote the most about the war and its reporting was perhaps the most objective. Also reporting objectively was the newspaper *Nezavisimaja gazeta.* Comparable was the newspaper *Kom-*

somolskaja pravda. The newspaper *Izvestija* covered events quite widely but printed much less commentary. It often published political statements as well as interviews with officials but was somewhat neutral. The newspaper *Pravda* practically did not write about the war at all. When they did publish something, most often there was nothing in the article that was new or incisive or that would shed light on the subject.

The greatest amount of reporting against the Chechens and in support of the army was published by *Krasnaja zvezda,* as such propaganda was its function. The newspapers *Zaftra* and *Sovietskaja Rosija* wrote in much the same mode.

Most useful were the articles written in military journals and in journals that reported political events, although their audiences were much smaller. The volume of articles published in these journals was large and the information contained in them was significant. In these journals many events and actions were analyzed objectively and comprehensively. As the journals were being used professionally by the various services, accurate reporting was necessary so that the Russian Army could determine how to function more effectively.

As for the disclosure and the publication of classified military documents, there is every indication that journalists, for the most part, purchased these quite easily. Were any efforts made to prevent such disclosure or to punish the people who disclosed? Most likely, there were attempts, but it was very easy to make a copy of a secret document under the prevailing military document handling practices. For example, the document quoted in this book about the readiness situation in the army, which had been given to Grachev, was in the possession of every regiment and therefore did not have to come directly from the safes of the general staff. It would be almost impossible for officials to determine from which regiment it was obtained. And if a journalist had friends and acquaintances, copies were not hard to get. Besides, this was a very unpopular war and many in the military, including high-ranking officers, actually volunteered documents for publication, often intending to correct the abuses that were listed in them.

On the mass-media front, many able reporters and photographers were finally able to work according to their consciences. Their work covering the Chechnya war was superb, which has great importance for the future.

Besides the mass media, other means were used to influence public opinion. These were the more standard fare of propaganda and included leaflets delivered mostly from the air, as well as intentionally skewed announcements on radio and television. But given the presence of other uncontrolled information sources occupying the same air waves and servicing the newspaper reading public, as soon as an event was reported on television, in print, or else-where, the Chechens responded that it was not that way at all. If an event was intentionally skewed to favor the Chechen side, the Russian side would of course show it differently.

Russia's propaganda machine showed itself to be very ineffective. Natu-rally, if Russia had been fighting a defensive war, its propaganda might have been more effective. But in Chechnya, Russia was attacking, and the people, both in Russia and Chechnya, instinctively felt that something was wrong with Russia's actions. The feeling in Russia was "What do we need those Chechens for anyway? And what will we do when we finally win this war and occupy Chechnya?" When the people instinctively feel this way, propaganda cannot be effective.

Part 3

The Second Period
of the War in Chechnya

CHAPTER 12

Negotiations for Peace

Peace negotiations began on June 19, 1995, after Russia announced that it was suspending combat actions.[1] The Russian delegation was led by the assistant minister for Nationalities, Viacheslav Michailov, and included Vice Premier Nikolai Semionov, the director of the Union of Public Organizations, Arkadi Volski, and assistant Internal Affairs minister Anatoli Kulikov. Dudajev was represented at the beginning of the negotiations by Usman Imajev, Aslan Maschadov, and one of the field commanders; later this delegation was enlarged.

During the first day of talks, little was achieved. The sides did, however, agree to extend the truce for several more days and to take measures to prevent new terrorist acts. Negotiations also began for the exchange of prisoners, whom the Russian side labeled "individuals being held by force." It was understood that the term was to cover only Russian soldiers who had been taken prisoner by the Chechens.

The next day, the delegations agreed that negotiations would be held separately concerning three "blocks" of issues subdivided into military, political, and economic categories. Within the confines of the military block of issues, negotiations were to be held for the complete cessation of war actions, for the withdrawal of the Russian Federal Forces, temporarily leaving three units in Chechnya, and for the dissolution and disarmament of the Chechen units. The Russian government's delegation later also demanded that the delegation representing Dudajev publicly condemn the terrorist act in Budionovsk and give over Shamil Basajev to the Russian authorities, threatening that if this was not done, it reserved the right to terminate the negotiations and the moratorium for the cessation of combat actions.[2]

The main political issues were the definition of Chechnya's status, the dates for local government and Chechen parliamentary elections, and Dudajev's participation in them. The most important economic issue was the liquidation of the economic effects of the war.

An agreement regarding the military issues was reached quickly, and a protocol was signed late at night on June 21.[3] Each side agreed to withdraw its forces a distance of some 3 to 4 kilometers from each other. The Chechens agreed to disarm a major portion of their formations in three disarmament stages: the first was to be the dissolution of the larger formations defined as units of 50–500 fighters. After that, it was to dissolve its mobilized non-regular army. The third stage was to effect the disarmament of individuals. The Russian delegation agreed that self-defense detachments of 15–25 people could remain in the communities on the condition that a list of these people together with the serial numbers of their weapons be provided to the Federal Army.

The sides further agreed that two Federal Army brigades would remain on Chechen soil: one Internal Affairs Army brigade composed of four battalions (2,000–6,500 people) and one motorized rifle brigade (also 2,000–6,500 people). Both would be part of the newly formed 58th Army, which would be deployed in Grozni. Both sides also obligated themselves to release all prisoners and people being detained and to continue the negotiations in Grozni.

After the signing of the protocol, the Chechen delegation at an arranged press conference condemned terrorism and agreed to help Russia find Shamil Basajev and the members of his battalion who had participated in the Budionovsk raid. It was self-apparent that this was an empty declaration and would not be taken seriously by either side.

For the Chechens, the political issues block was the most important, but they did not succeed in pushing it the least bit forward. The delegations' positions were especially far apart on the question of Chechnya's status. Imajev, the leader of the Chechen delegation, demanded that the 1991 Chechen Constitution be recognized as the fundamental law of the republic. The Russian delegation held that Chechnya was an integral part of the Russian Federation. For this reason, the two delegations' views as to Dudajev's participation in the elections also differed: If Chechnya was in fact a part of the Russian Federation, then, according to Russian law, Dudajev could not participate in the elections since there was still an outstanding warrant for his arrest.[4]

The negotiations became deadlocked when the Russian delegation found they did not have sufficient authority to decide the political issues. Both sides declared a recess on June 24 and left for consultations with their respective governments. In this way, the first round of the negotiations drew to a close.

The negotiations were renewed on June 28 after Russian president Yeltsin gave the leader of the Russian delegation supplemental authority to negotiate and to sign protocols as to the political issues.[5] This time, the most important issue during the meetings of the delegations was the political question, but only regarding elections in Chechnya and the preparations for them. The Kremlin refused to enter into any discussions concerning the question of the complete independence of Chechnya, holding that Chechnya could only expect economic autonomy.

During this round of talks, the sides reached an agreement about holding elections for all levels of government. These elections were to take place on November 5 and were to be observed by both international and Russian observers. It was also agreed in principle that, in the future, all problems would be resolved without resort to the use of force and that the political status of Chechnya would be negotiated only after the elections.

Russia made its wish known that until the elections a Coalition National Council made up of Dudajev's and Chadzhijev's people should govern. Dudajev was offered a "zero" variant under which he, the leader of the opposition's Chechen National Justice Committee, Umar Avturchanov, and the prime minister of the opposition's Chechen National Rebirth Government, Salambek Chadzhijev, would all resign at the same time. Dudajev refused to accept this "zero" variant, remarking that he would resign only when Russia recognized the independence of Chechnya. He refused in the same way Russia's offer that he leave Chechnya.[6]

The question of the political status of Chechnya was still the primary obstacle to the parties' reaching a final settlement. Russian president Yeltsin, in appraising the results of the negotiations, stated with optimism that what was missing in the agreement between the Russian Federation and the Chechen Republic were only four lines that would define the relationship between Russia's territorial integrity and the Chechen peoples' rights to self-determination. For Russia, an acceptable solution was that Chechnya be granted "wide autonomy" status as this would not conflict with Russia's Constitution and would guarantee Russia's territorial integrity. But Dudajev continued to base his arguments on the fact that Chechnya had never signed any document legalizing its inclusion in the Russian Federation.[7]

By the beginning of July, the deadlocked status of the negotiations were completely obvious: Further discussions as to Chechnya's status were useless, as neither side was willing to concede anything. The debate on political questions had lasted almost forty days, not counting the recesses.

Finally the positions of the delegations neared each other somewhat, and a compromise was reached. The question as to Chechnya's status was put off when they agreed that Chechnya would continue to live under its 1991 Constitution as a sovereign country but that its sovereignty would be conformed to Russia's Constitution. In other words, Russia agreed to separate the military issues from the political.

With Russia consenting not to condition the military issues block on the question of Chechnya's status, the delegations signed an agreement on the night of July 30 "for the peaceful regulation of the situation in Chechnya" (the military issues block). The agreement consisted of four parts:

1. The cessation of combat actions;
2. The release of persons being held by force;
3. The disarmament of the Chechen forces and the gradual withdrawal of the Russian Army.
4. The cessation of terrorist acts and diversions.[8]

In fact, this agreement only legalized the protocol concerning the military issues that had been signed on June 21, several days after the start of the negotiations. It contained no material changes from the first protocol. The only concrete result achieved during that whole time had been Russia's agreement to proclaim an amnesty for all the "rebels" or "separatists," as the Chechen fighters were now being characterized in the press. The references to Chechen fighters as "rebels" instead of "hit men" began to appear in the press only after Russia was forced to begin negotiations with the Chechens.

The guarantors for the execution of this agreement would be the representative of the Russian Federation in Chechnya and a Special Observers' Commission. The commission's leaders were to be the commander of the Joint Federal Forces Group, A. Shirokin, and the chief of the Chechen General Staff, Aslan Maschadov.

Forced to negotiate with the Chechens, Moscow stubbornly attempted to demonstrate during the negotiations that it was still the master of the situation. Although the negotiations were conducted quite calmly, the Russian delegation sought at every opportunity to put pressure on the Chechens, constantly threatening to call off the negotiations and to renew combat actions if the Chechens did not agree with the specific terms the Russians offered. This had a negative effect on the course of the talks but was not decisive. Even better results might have been obtained had three unfortunate circumstances not affected the talks.

The first and apparently the most decisive was that on July 3, before the negotiations were concluded, Yeltsin signed an order for the permanent dislocation of the Russian armed forces in the Republic of Chechnya.[9] By this order, the Russian forces were tasked to ensure political and military stability in the Northern Caucasus region. In fact, this was to be done by the newly formed 58th Army (the 19th Motorized Rifle Division and three brigades). Two brigades were to be permanently dislocated in Chechnya itself. Together with the border units, the Russian forces in Chechnya were to consist of almost 15,000 troops.

It was clear that for Dudajev and the Chechen negotiations delegation the issuance of such an order meant the complete disregard not only of their opinions but also of the negotiations themselves. The president did not even politely await the results of the negotiations before demonstrating that the Kremlin was not abandoning the use of force in Chechnya in the future. While the Chechens could discuss disarmament, they had to keep in mind that, under such circumstances, they could not very well lay down their arms while the Russian Army remained on Chechen territory.

The second circumstance affecting the talks was the continuing criminality of the Russian troops while on Chechen territory. In the beginning of July, three civilian inhabitants were murdered and burned near the village of Pervomaisk. In Grozni, a Russian family of two elderly pensioners were murdered. The Chechens were especially enraged by the killings in the village of Prigorodnoje. There a family of seven was murdered, including three young children. The negotiations were put off several times until the circumstances of these murders could be investigated and the culprits found. When the investigation of the latter tragic incident was completed, it was determined that drunken Russian soldiers had committed the murders. It is unclear whether this was a specially organized provocation or simply uncontrolled criminal behavior on the part of Russian soldiers. But its effect on the course of the negotiations was apparent.[10]

The third circumstance was that the negotiations were conducted in the background of small but constant armed confrontations. Although a ceasefire had been declared, this truce was being violated by both sides. Each day the Chechens continued to shoot up the posts and positions of the Russian units, killing or wounding several Russian soldiers each day, even in Grozni.

In the mountain regions, only the intensity of the confrontations decreased. But there was no actual cessation of combat activity, and the Chechens had even gradually taken back the initiative. For example, the 245th Motorized Rifle Regiment in the vicinity of Shatoja spent the month of July practically besieged by the Chechen fighters. One step to the side and Chechen sniper fire invariably exploded. Here the commander of the Chechen forces was I. Madajev, who had fought in Grozni until the end of February. The

Russian units also continued to shoot up Chechen positions, even using heavy artillery. Of particular note, because of their intensity, were the confrontations in the region of Bamut.

However, both sides found it necessary to reach a compromise and to sign an agreement demonstrating at least their intentions to terminate combat actions and to continue the regulation of their relationship by peaceful means. To this end, the Russian delegation found it advantageous to make use of the Federal Army's Intelligence Command's own evaluations regarding the Chechen attacks against Russian positions to show that not all the Chechen fighter groups were fully under the control of the Chechen General Staff and that some were continuing to fight during the period of the truce on their own initiative. About 700 fighters were attributed to such independent, uncontrolled forces. The Russians submitted that General Maschadov's control over his own forces was weak and that, for this reason, the situation in Chechnya would remain unstable even after the agreement was signed. This, of course, meant that the permanent dislocation of the Russian Armed Forces in Chechnya would be justified as a guarantee of the country's stability.

Each side clearly considered the signing of the agreement to be a concession to the other. The Russian delegation considered it a concession to the Chechens that they had agreed to separate the military issues from the political. The Chechens believed that they had conceded by agreeing to the permanent dislocation of two brigades in Chechnya. One of these was to be an Internal Affairs Army brigade, the other a brigade belonging to the Ministry of Defense. They were to be equipped with about a 100 tanks, 200 armored vehicles and armored personnel carriers, heavy howitzers, Grad rocket salvo artillery systems, and other weapons and equipment. Although a brigade ordinarily consists of about 2,500–3,000 troops, each of these brigades was to be manned by up to 6,000 soldiers.[11]

Differing Opinions on Enacting the Agreement

The Chechen High Command did not linger to show that it was ready to enact the agreement that had been so hard to reach. On August 1, an order of the chief of the General Staff was issued instructing all Chechen armed formations to cease fire as of August 2 at midnight. The Chechen formations were also ordered to exchange maps with the Federal Army units. On these maps, they were to indicate the positions of both sides, radio communications links, and call signs. They were also instructed to organize continuous communications and coordination with the Federal Army units, to set up collection points for the surrender of their combat equipment and weapons, and to work out procedures for the destruction of those weapons.[12]

During the meeting of the Chechen Defense Council held on August 2 and chaired by Dudajev, the agreement signed for the resolution of military issues was confirmed. During this meeting, Usman Imajev was removed as leader of the negotiations delegation, apparently for undue concessions to the Russian delegation. Ch. Jerichanov, previously a member of the delegation, was appointed as the new leader of the negotiations team. Experts were consulted for the enactment of the agreement. In Grozni, work group meetings began for the closed Special Observer Commission, the Commission for the Exchange of Prisoners and "Individuals Being Held by Force," and the Commission for the Resolution of the Political Issues. At the Russians' initiative, most of the attention of the Commission for the Enactment of Military Issues was given over to the prompt release of prisoners and the disarmament of Chechen formations.[13]

Although the first prisoners were exchanged on August 2, both sides almost immediately began to level harsh charges at each other for alleged refusals to honor this portion of the agreement. They agreed to exchange the prisoners on an "all for all" basis but disagreed as to just how many prisoners each side was actually holding.[14]

The Russian representatives contended that there were 36 prisoners still being held by the Chechens (there were 90 according to other information) and that in Vedeno alone 20 prisoners had been counted. The Russians also conceded that they were holding 1,350 Chechen fighters prisoner.

The Chechens contended that they had only a few prisoners left. There had been 181 officially registered prisoner exchanges completed, and another portion of the prisoners had been given over directly to their parents without any formalities. The Chechen central government alleged that it did not have any more information about other prisoners.

The Chechens also submitted to the Russians a list of 1,308 fighters missing in action. Undoubtedly this was done in an attempt to free their countrymen then being held in the filtration camps, since, as was well known, Chechen fighters almost never surrendered unless they were captured after being seriously wounded. The Chechens listed by the Russians as having been taken prisoner and submitted by the Chechens as missing in action were, in fact, simply civilians being held by the Russians. But according to information gathered by correspondents, more prisoners existed than was being admitted by the Russian representatives—about 2,000–4,500, including those held in the filtration camps.

The Russian representatives categorically denied even the existence of such "so-called" filtration camps. At most, they admitted there was one such collection point in Grozni where only about 30 Chechen fighters were being held for questioning. According to the Russians, all other prisoners had been taken to Russian prisons, and some had even been jailed in far-off Chabarovsk.

Most journalists following the prisoner issue held opinions that differed from those of the parties to the negotiations. According to their calculations, almost 300 Russian soldiers were still being held prisoner by the Chechens, but not all of them, in fact, wanted to be returned to their units. Some of them were masking their desertions in this manner and were attempting to stay alive by avoiding further participation in combat. Many soldiers were, of course, missing in action from both sides. But many Russian soldiers also were not being held by the Chechens but were simply hiding out among the civilian inhabitants.

The exchange of prisoners issue reached a stalemate when the Russian representatives, believing that the Chechen forces were purposely holding back Russian prisoners, refused to free the Chechen prisoners that they were holding. The Chechen fighters' reaction to the Russian refusal to free their people was very direct: If what we have is insufficient to satisfy the Russians, then we will simply have to take more Russian soldiers prisoner.[15]

Not much was achieved with the disarmament of the Chechen formations issue either, although formally the voluntary surrender of weapons began. The first such official ceremony took place on August 7 in the village of Zandak in the Nozhai Jurt region. The commander of the Combined Federal Forces Battle Group, General Romanov, and the Chechen chief of staff, General Maschadov, both participated in the ceremony.[16]

Both sides felt it necessary to demonstrate that the disarmament process had started. For the Russian commanders, it was necessary to demonstrate to the brass back home that they were getting results. The Chechens also had to demonstrate their willingness to abide by their obligations under the agreement. The Chechens, however, were unwilling to disarm fully before better assurances of an appropriate and lasting peace were received. This was particularly important because the negotiations were only beginning and could be called off at any moment. Thus maneuvering room was sought within the wording of the agreements.

The agreement called for the disarmament of "illegal armed formations." But what specifically did this term include? For example, Dudajev's armed formations had officially been referred to as "illegal armed formations," and the Russian delegation, of course, had them in mind when they signed the agreement. But Dudajev's view was different. For him, "illegal formations" were all those that were opposing his legally constituted government. Foreseeing the results of the negotiations, Dudajev made use of the possibilities given to him by the truce in order to hasten the passage of the Chechen Defense Law, which redefined Avturchanov's opposition formations and the Russian Federal Army units as "illegal formations." This in effect changed the essence of the agreement and allowed the preservation of his forces for the time being.[17]

In early August, all hopes that the Chechens would voluntarily disarm began to fade after Dudajev announced that during the first stage of enacting the military block, weapons were to be taken away only from "criminal armed gangs and individuals." In other words, the Chechen negotiations delegation had not sought in vain to ensure that the agreement would legalize the local self-defense detachments. The agreement had provided that upon a surrender of weapons, local self-defense groups of up to 25 individuals armed with individual weapons would be established in each village. One of the most important Chechen defense purposes was to prevent Russian armored vehicles from entering the villages. General Maschadov therefore included in the signed order for the establishment of self-defense forces that each such self-defense detachment was to be equipped for that purpose with two machine guns and one grenade launcher since, obviously, without grenade launchers, armored vehicles would be able to enter the villages unhampered.

But so few weapons were being surrendered that an avid imagination was needed to characterize this process as disarmament. This became apparent during a weapons surrender ceremony in the village of Arshty in the Shali region. There 100 weapons were turned in, but of the 40 automatic weapons collected, 25 were immediately turned over to the village's self-defense force. When the Chechens surrendered only 221 weapons of various types during the first 20 days of the disarmament process, their intent became obvious.

However responding to even this purported progress, the commander of the Northern Caucasus Military Region, General Kvashnin, agreed that Russian units would be withdrawn from the communities and that their blocking posts would be liquidated. As the inhabitants were afraid to give up their weapons, Kvashnin also agreed to allow them to keep their weapons at home as long as they did not walk around with them publicly. He felt that this would help regulate the Federal Army's relationship with the local inhabitants.[18]

The Russian side, nevertheless, soon charged the Chechens with not honoring the agreement as to the military issues block, especially as to matters related to disarmament, and on August 14 issued an ultimatum threatening to use force once again.[19] The situation was ameliorated somewhat when Romanov and Maschadov reached an agreement the same day for a plan to disarm Dudajev's armed formations. To enact it, four joint groups were created. Weapons would first be surrendered in the Achchoj Martan and Sunzha regions and then, by August 30, the Russian Army would withdraw from that region. They also agreed to prepare a time schedule for the withdrawal of all armed formations from the mountain regions.[20]

Neither War nor Peace

The signing of the agreement gave both sides a certain amount of optimism that combat activity would be terminated, but the soldiers of both sides were less convinced that this would be the case.[21] Thus it was apparently not coincidental that on the same day that the Russian delegation signed the agreement and flew out of Grozni, the Federal Army units near Shatoja and Vedeno were encircled by the Chechens. Confrontations also intensified near the communities of Bachi Jurt, Mairtup, Kurchaloja, Shali, Guni, Resht, and Chidi Chutor.

The first night of the "peace" in Grozni was marked by the intensive shooting up of all the Russian Command Posts and blocking posts. As a result, 8 Russian soldiers were killed and 32 were wounded. The Russian military High Command again expressed the hope that this was not the doing of the Chechen delegation but that the Chechen central government was not in full control of the situation. But in fact this was only a temporary intensification of combat actions. After the signing of the agreement, such actions did decrease.

During the truce for negotiations, the Chechens did not simply sit on their hands, awaiting the results of the talks. In their opinion, the conditional peace was at best only temporary and, for that reason, they used it to redeploy and reconsolidate their forces. Once the negotiations were begun, the Chechens were able to freely move around in large armed groups throughout the whole territory of the republic, as the Federal Army units and their blocking posts had been issued orders not to hinder them.

After the agreement was signed, the Chechens began to operate even more openly. An especially visible example of this was a public meeting that took place in the city of Shali in the beginning of September. More than 100 armed fighters drove to the meeting in 40 automobiles. At the meeting, one of the field commanders, Abu Movsajev, even addressed the crowd in Dudajev's name and spoke in favor of the division of Chechnya into two parts separated by the Argun river. The part consisting of the regions of Argun, Gudermes, Nozhai Jurt, and Shali, he proposed, was to be controlled by the supporters of the president of Ichkerija. Its capital was to be Shali.

The renewed concentration of Chechen fighters in the communities was also looked upon with distrust by the Russian Federal Battle Group Command in Chechnya. The concentration of Chechen forces in the communities of Roshni Chu, Asinovskaja, Slepcovsk, Sernovodsk, Shali, Shatoja, Achchoj Martan, and Urus Martan, in their surrounding regions and along the approaches to Grozni was looked upon with anxiety.

The situation began to become even more tense when the Federal Army High Command began to make attempts on its own initiative to disarm the Chechens by force. This was especially felt in the regions of Gudermes, Sernovodsk, Achchoj Martan, and Shali and in the village of Kurchaloja. While such attempts to effect disarmament did not take place in Gudermes and Sernovodsk, the situation was also not helped by the pounding of Achchoj Martan by artillery or the bombing of the village of Roshi Chu by Russian aircraft. The Chechen negotiations delegation soon informed the Russian side that their unilateral attempts to disarm the formations by force would not work.

The situation was heated up even more by Russian military intelligence, which constantly reported potential Chechen attacks against Grozni. The reports mentioned various dates for the attacks and even claimed that such operations had been approved by President Dudajev. In the beginning, such an assault was expected on September 7 and 8, later in the middle of the month.

But Argun became the center of events.[22] On August 20, a group of 250 Chechens from the mountain village of Targo in the region of Vedeno came openly into Argun and, without resistance, took over the militia building. The Chechen column consisted of two Kamaz trucks carrying stores and weapons, a field kitchen, two rocket launchers set up on truck cargo beds, and about ten light automobiles. If the column had traveled along the main roads, it would have had to pass thirteen Russian blocking posts. But it was widely assumed that the Chechens were so thoroughly familiar with all the roads and byroads in the area that it had apparently not been all that difficult to travel unimpeded from the mountains into the city. The group was commanded by 39-year-old Alandi Chamzadov, who declared himself the military commandant of Argun, stating that he was acting under Dudajev's direction. However, until the war, Chamzadov had been with the armed opposition, together with Labazanov.

While taking the militia building, the Chechens beat up the militia officer of the day and drove him out of the building. Some of the Chechen fighters spread out into the neighboring buildings and set up defense positions.

The next morning, this district located near the center of the city was surrounded by Federal Forces units. Twenty to thirty armored vehicles and other combat equipment were concentrated just on Titov Street next to the militia building. Three more T-60 tanks were positioned to cover the bridge across the Argun River and two more armored vehicles were positioned at the nearest intersection, some one hundred meters from the Militia Building. Ten to fifteen helicopters also continued to hover in the air over the city.

According to Chamzadov, the assignment of military commandants was an internal Chechen matter and the operation being conducted was not directed against the Russian Federal Army. The mission of the new Military Commandant's Office was to observe how the Russian military units were being withdrawn and to maintain order in the city.

This operation greatly impeded and brought confusion into the negotiations. Apparently it was not expected by the Chechen chief of staff, General Maschadov, as he twice took time to meet with Chamzadov. After these meetings, Maschadov announced that the situation was under control and that Chamzadov had promised to obey all his instructions and to lay down his weapons.[23]

In spite of such assurances, on the afternoon of September 21, Russian Internal Affairs Army units surrounded the militia building and began to shoot at it. A special-purpose detachment supported by tanks, artillery, mortars, and helicopters later also assaulted the building. The Russian side contended that the decision to take more active measures was precipitated by the aggressive actions of the Chechen fighter group. Apparently, on the same evening that the militia building was taken, four passersby were killed by bullets from a passing automobile without license plates. The Russians attributed this action to members of the Chechen fighter group.

Although the militia building was shot with artillery for four hours and by rockets from helicopters, once it was finally taken, only the bodies of three Chechen fighters and two civilians who had not been able to withdraw in time were found. The Chechen group had disappeared without a trace, having calmly left the building in the direction of the main housing area of the city. They had left behind their automobiles and field kitchen and had disappeared in spite of the fact that all the roads out of the city had been blocked.[24]

The incident was strange not only because the Chechens succeeded in disappearing without a trace. Although the bombardment of the militia building was quite intensive, not one round hit it; at least 50 nearby buildings were, however, lit on fire and all the buildings next to it were demolished. During the operation, 6 civilians were killed and more than 100 head of livestock were requisitioned.

For the Chechens, the Argun operation was seen not only as a test of its reconstituted forces but also as an attempt to demonstrate to all the inhabitants of the republic who still had the upper hand in Chechnya.

The deadlocked negotiations, the refusal by both sides to abide by the agreement as to the military issues, the constant threats by the Federal Battle Group Command, its continuing attempts to take weapons away by force, the regrouping and reconsolidation of the Chechen armed formations, their renewed strength, and the gradual general heightening of tension all brought the renewal of combat activities closer.

The relationship between the two sides grew even colder between September 15 and 20. The Chechens were accused of increasing the intensity of their attacks against the Russian positions. According to the Russian High Command, from the signing of the agreement on July 30 until August 15, the Russian military units were shot at 200 times. This resulted in 10 soldiers being killed and 37 wounded. From September 1 through 18, the number of times that the Russian positions were shot up doubled: during this latter period, they were attacked 408 times. But this was done much more intensively, and the Russian losses tripled: during the attacks in September, 26 Russian soldiers were killed and 153 were wounded.

The tension began to grow even more when Russia's representatives stopped attending the work group sessions after charging the Chechens with not abiding by the military agreements and refusing to submit information as to how many armed formations they had, where they were dislocated, and what weapons the units possessed. They also accused the Chechens of having intensified their actions in preparation for new battles in Roshni Chu, Kadi Jurt, Azamat Jurt, and the other foothills communities. The numbers of their self-defense posts increased significantly, and the movement of the Chechen formations intensified throughout the country. One of the examples the Russians submitted was the newly established self-defense outpost in Shatoja near the bridge across the Argun River.

In the opinion of the Russian High Command in Chechnya, this was the result of wide-ranging consultations among the Chechen field commanders that took place on September 19 in Roshni Chu and the next day in the community of Aleroja. At such conferences, the transfer of the war outside the borders of Chechnya was discussed, among other issues such as the dragging out of the disarmament process and the combat tactics used against the Russian operational forces within the country. The commandant of the Russian Militia Force in Chechnya, General Lieutenant A. Baskajev, contended that the Chechens had also increased their intelligence-gathering activities involving the movement of military transport, especially command vehicles, and were mounting attacks against such vehicles. Submitted as an example was the shooting up of General Popov's automobile on September 21 in the vicinity of the 16th outpost of Grozni's 21st Commandant's Headquarters.

The tension was increased even more the morning of September 20 by the assassination attempt against the Russian president's representative in Chechnya, Oleg Lobov, who had been assigned these duties after the signing of the agreement. As a column traveling from the Northern Airport to Grozni neared the bridge across the Neftianka River, a powerful explosive charge of about 200 kilograms of trotyl explosive was set off under the bridge. Although no one was hurt, the attempt gave the Russian government the pretext to charge the Chechens with an increase of terrorist activity. It is not very clear even now who conducted this terrorist act, but, without doubt, it was directed against the peaceful regulation of the situation in Chechnya.[25]

Although terrorist acts by then had become a daily occurrence in Grozni, they began to be stressed even more by the Russian High Command after the attempt against Lobov. This was especially so after four armed men entered the Federal Military Commissariat in Grozni that same day, ordered the military personnel there into automobiles, and took them in an unknown direction. The next day, one of the oil storage tanks in Grozni was also blown up.[26]

On September 24, the negotiations were put off for an unspecified time. The Chechens were prepared to continue the talks, but both sides were unable to reach any further agreement as to the self-defense detachments.

In spite of all these circumstances, the Russians were determined to disarm the Chechens by force. The Russian Federal Army Command issued several ultimatums to give up weapons and threatened to call off the negotiations if this was not done. On September 22, Russian Army forces issued an ultimatum to the inhabitants of Semovodsk to give up 250 weapons in four days. When this was not done, they threatened to assault the village. A unit of armored equipment and artillery was readied for this purpose. But as the ultimatum was issued at the initiative of a lower military unit's commander, the village was not assaulted after the intervention of Lobov, Internal Affairs minister Kulikov, and General Romanov. Semovodsk continued to be blockaded despite the fact that the commander of the Combined Federal Battle Group in Chechnya, General Romanov, had prohibited any further blockading of communities during the middle of the summer.[27]

The situation in Chechnya at this time was very aptly described by Liudas Dapkus, correspondent for the Lithuanian daily, *Lietuvos Rytas,* who was reporting from Chechnya at that time: "After the signing of the agreement as to the military issues, Chechnya is now more like a battlefield on which the opponents are attempting to take up better positions during the truce and to make preparations for the upcoming battles. The Russians are gradually withdrawing their unnecessary units but are digging entrenchments around the cities. The Chechens are giving up hunting rifles and buying rockets."[28]

Once the peace process started, Dudajev's forces, previously driven into the mountains, once again took over the primary positions in the majority of the communities and in Grozni. Russian intelligence reported on more than one occasion that the Chechens in essence were preparing once more for war. The conditions for the renewal of combat actions had become ripe.

If, in the middle of April when both sides had not known how to terminate the war, the Budionovsk action conducted by Shamil Basajev's forces saved the situation, now in attempting to terminate the negotiations, the attempt on the life of the commander of the Combined Federal Battle Group in Chechnya, General Lieutenant Romanov, provided a way out of the negotiations. On October 6 as a column in which Romanov was traveling entered the tunnel in Minutka Square, a powerful explosion ripped through the tunnel. Ten people were killed by the explosion and several were injured. A commuter bus that had also entered the tunnel at the time of the explosion was damaged. Severely injured, Romanov was hurriedly flown to Moscow.[29]

The Secretive "Third Force"

The attempt on the life of General Lieutenant Romanov had a negative effect on the situation in Chechnya. He was the only one of the high Russian military officials who actually attempted to resolve the issues of the withdrawal of the Russian Army and the disarmament of the Chechen formations. Certain successes had been achieved and a dialogue had been started, but after the attempt to kill him, both sides put off the negotiations.

Some blamed Dudajev for the assassination attempt, others the opposition. Also accused were the Russian forces, for whom the continuation of the war was advantageous, mostly because they had been able to convert Chechnya into a transit base for the sale of weapons. Moscow began to consider sterner measures.

The negotiations that Russia had been forced into lasted 109 days. It was clear to both sides from the very start that positive results would most likely not be achieved. The conditions raised by the Chechens were clearly unacceptable to Russia, and Russia's conditions were likewise unacceptable to Dudajev and his people. Both sides based their positions on their own respective constitutions. But during this same period, a "third force," which, according to political observers, was interested in the continuation of the war, began to dominate in the press. This force had shown itself both in Chechnya and in Russia.[30]

One of the variants being debated was that this "third force" was represented in Chechnya by Moscow's stand-ins and by the commanders of the Chechen armed formations that were not under Dudajev's command. The most important of these were obviously the mayor of Grozni, Gantemirov, whose armed formations had fortified themselves in the Urus Martan region, and Labazanov, whose forces had taken up positions in the region of Tolstoi Jurt. During the war, these pro-Moscow Chechen opposition forces had maintained neutrality and observed the course of events from a distance, awaiting the right opportunity.[31]

In Russia, only on occasion did hints appear as to the existence of such a "third force." This "third force" did not express itself anywhere openly. But then why would a representative of such a "third force" appear publicly and take a position in favor of the war and its continuation by whatever means? Who in fact would dare to say openly that millions of people in the Russian Federation should continue to await with anxiety another "cargo 200"? And who would dare to say openly to the Chechens that they would have to be destroyed?

Whether such a "third force" in fact ever existed is debatable. However, a great stir was created by a document dated July 12, 1995, which had been prepared by one of Russia's analytical groups whose work is closely followed by individuals having real power and influence in the Russian government.[32]

This analytical report consists of four parts. The first part, containing an analysis of the developing situation in Chechnya and an evaluation of its decisive causes, states that Russia, having won the military portion of the Chechen campaign, did not succeed in gaining any political results from its military victory and was, in fact, totally defeated on the political front. According to the document, this became particularly apparent from the moment that Russian premier Chernomyrdin took over the initiative during the Budionovsk action in an attempt to regulate the Chechen crisis by peaceful means. But it was not the premier's wish to peacefully regulate a critical problem that was criticized. It was the concessions that had been made by him and others to the Chechens. Until that time, Dudajev's government had been considered a "criminal regime," and he and his followers had been considered terrorists and national enemies who needed to be arrested and put in jail, not negotiated with.

The second part, in which the results of nonintervention in this developing process are analyzed, suggests that positive results would depend on the consistency of the federal government's appraisal of Dudajev's regime and such public figures as Dzhochar Dudajev, Shamil Basajev, and others. The Russian president had more than once declared Dudajev's government to be a criminal regime permeated with banditry. He had also characterized Dudajev, Basajev, and other such figures as not only enemies of Russia and the Chechen people but also narcotics dealers and terrorists on an international scale.

Such an evaluation served to justify in part the Chechen operation in the eyes of the Russian people, the military, and other force structures and before the international community. Chernomyrdin's agreement to negotiate with them was, in effect, an admission that Dudajev's regime was in fact not criminal and that Dzhochar Dudajev himself was not a bandit. The negotiations themselves were clearly purposeless if recognition of Dudajev's government did not eventually follow. Unavoidably, the question would then be raised as to why this cruel war had been fought, blood had been spilt, and huge casualties suffered. Who then would shoulder the responsibility?

To lay the blame on the Armed Forces was impossible in principle. Also, two stereotyped views of Chechnya had developed at all levels of the Russian populace. The first, favorable to Yeltsin, was that the Dudajev regime was an absolute evil and that no negotiations with it were possible. The second, a contrary view, was a characterization of Yeltsin and his "clique" as the executioners of the Chechen people. They were looked upon as soaked in blood and deserving of punishment at the hands of a war crimes tribunal.

But if Dudajev or even his field commanders were recognized as worthy partners for negotiations, the unstable balance of these stereotypical views would be damaged to the disadvantage of the first view. The second view would then gain such ascendancy that it could tear apart the organization of the Russian State. In the background of the central government's and the presidency's loss of face, the country would begin to break apart. The resonances of anti-Russian feeling would spread throughout the Northern Caucasus region and could effect even the loyal Russian regions.

According to this analysis, the army and the other force structures in Russia were already close to a condition where they could easily distance themselves from the president in whom they had previously believed. The use of large forces to keep the Russian Federation together would then become impossible, and the country would unavoidably begin to break apart. All hopes of reestablishing a "Great Russia" would then be buried. Russia would repeat the Gorbachev episode when the Soviet Union broke apart for this very reason.

The third part of the document holds that Russia's political situation was not getting any better. Its influence in the Newly Independent States (former republics of the Soviet Union) was getting weaker, and a real possibility was opening up that the borders of the NATO block would eventually near Briansk. Russia was being forced to enter into compromises.

In this situation, Russia's "strange" negotiating stance in Chechnya threatened to become the drop that overfills the glass. This was all the more true as all such questionable regulation procedures ripe with unequal concessions were leading to the establishment of a protégé relationship with the European Community. The pressure upon Russia could thus become systematic.

From all of this, a conclusion followed that the course of the negotiations in Chechnya should be corrected at least to the extent that the "Gorbachevian" tendency regarding Russia's territorial integrity and political stability would be cut off. Strategic decisions had to be made that could become the principal basis for a new direction in the negotiations.

The fourth part suggests a time schedule and model for the regulation of the conflict. The document notes that in seeking to regulate the conflict, it was first necessary to reestablish the legal norms in Chechnya and then to establish a control mechanism by which such norms could be put into effect.

To force the situation back into an acceptable legal framework, the following was suggested:

1. The total completion of the war effort. This was connected with the assignment of a military commander who was strong, unyielding and yet sufficiently flexible, able to work productively in the whole of the Caucasus region, and to whom special authorization could be given in the southern region (southern Russia and the Northern Caucasus) even, given the necessity, of instituting special summary courts/martial courts. The commander and the strategic military forces group had to become the guarantee that elementary order would be established and the preconditions of the previously mentioned legal norms would be re-created. The strategic military forces group would establish sole rule, independent of the subordination of the agency involved.
2. It was impossible to establish legality without first destroying the terrorist regime and punishing the guilty parties.
3. Compromise in Chechnya was impossible, as this was a trap from both the political and legal standpoint. There was only one possible road: to liquidate the Dudajev regime, to acknowledge it as illegal, and to take measures to ensure normal living conditions in Chechnya.

Seven stages were listed for the regulation of the crisis in Chechnya. The first stage: The destruction of the Dudajev by military means and the handing over of the leaders of the regime to a military tribunal.

The second stage: The reestablishment of norms for the inhabitants ensuring an elementary living standard while under the control of the military-economic administration. The administration was to punish marauding, terrorism, and any refusal to carry out instructions and orders according to the norms of the special reconstruction period.

The third stage: The political processes were to be regulated. However, only those development variants that recognized Chechnya as a federation subject within Russia would be considered. The normal Chechen populace would choose its own political structures and would form something akin to a government, for example, a council of elders, a council of the teips, or the like.

The fourth stage: A military-political administration would be set up from the military government structures and the newly formed council. The changeover to a local, purely political government would be done gradually, while withdrawing the army but leaving a limited military contingent.

The fifth stage: Elections were to be held. Relapses that occurred were to be coordinated with the local (pro-Russian) self-defense detachments and the limited military contingent's troops and dealt with in accordance to Russia's martial law statutes.

The sixth stage: Elections were to be held and the military-political administration's functions were to be gradually transferred to an elected government, elected in accordance with Russia's laws.

The seventh stage: Fully normal "democratic" institutions were to begin functioning and legal norms would be reinstituted.

As can readily be seen, this document leaves no room for negotiations, as they did not even enter into the conception for regulating the issue of Chechnya. The war was to continue until the complete destruction of Dudajev's armed formations was achieved. Later events would show that future Russian policy did not deviate greatly from this conception's guidelines. The conception was only corrected according to the requirements of the developing situation.

But apparently no unified "third force" ever existed, although two basic forces interested in the continuation of the war were clearly felt. One consisted of those for whom the war was a continuing source of profit. The other was made up of those who firmly believed that without a victorious war, "Great Russia" would disintegrate.[33]

Legal Concepts Affecting the Right to Secede

The goal of preserving a "Great Russia" was always at the heart of the Russian Federation's efforts. The basic contours of this policy had remained unchanged since tsarist times with only the tools of modern warfare being added to the methodology. All the old ramifications of empire went with it and, in essence, hegemony by force of arms remained its key ingredient. The threat of the sheathed sword thus underlay all of Russia's efforts to "negotiate" the acquiescence of its non-Russian subjects.

In the summer of 1990, when Mikhail Gorbachev promised to change the Soviet Union into a "real federation" based on a "voluntary" basis, there was little agreement or understanding as to what this, in fact, would entail. There was even less clarity as to what legal principles this would require. On its face, Gorbachev's proposal was almost a call to reorganize the USSR on a democratic basis and to start from a clean slate. But given the experiences of the last seventy years and the traditions of empire permeating the Kremlin, such a clean slate was clearly unavailable. Unavoidably, the subject non-Russian republics continued to suspect that negotiations with the Kremlin would again be illusionary, with the Kremlin as always reserving for itself the last word as to any division of power.

Hardly anyone believed that the Kremlin would cede power. In any real sense, Gorbachev, in spite of all his talk of reform, was still speaking of preserving the primacy of the Communist Party, of "socialism," and, inevitably, of the centralized institutions of the existing system. These institutions, notably the Party, the Security Forces, the military, industrial, and military-industrial sectors were all products of empire and, by all appearances, were still bent on preserving the hegemony of the center over the republics by any means necessary. Gorbachev's continued inability to free himself from tendencies to use the repressive power of the center to gain tactical advantage also raised questions as to his real intent. Most of the republics, or at least the people constituting them, wanted to get out from under this continuing threat of forced submission.

Tsarist Russia had been created by conquest. Such rights acquired by conquest eventually evolved into the legal basis for its subsequent claim to the conquered territories. Preservation of such claims inevitably depended upon the continued use of force by tsarist Russia to suppress all those wanting to break away.

Once the Bolsheviks established themselves as successors to the tsarist regime, the new Soviet government was quick to establish its own rights over the former tsarist territories. These rights, originating on the basis of conquest, inevitably had to be reestablished with the help of the Red Army and without any regard to the wishes of the subject peoples.

Soviet ideology, however, placed great importance on the apparent willingness of its subject peoples to abide by its rule. It was to be, after all, a "free union" of the "worker classes" without regard to narrower national interests. Although union, in most instances, had been the result of "requests to join" voted upon by quickly installed puppet governments in the wake of Soviet armed occupation, the resulting legal framework, in almost all cases, took on the appearance of democratic or at least legal processes. The Communists strived to provide the formal appearance of acquiescence, and the Stalin and Brezhnev constitutions had even gone so far as to provide its member states with a right to "secede." It was said, however, in Soviet legal texts that the presence of the Communist Party in each of the subject republics was the guarantee that such states would not make use of such legal right.

The USSR Constitution defined the union republics as "sovereign" in a provision that read: "A Union Republic is a sovereign Soviet Socialist State that has united with the other Soviet Republics in the Union of Soviet Socialist Republics." But "sovereignty" as a legal concept remained unclear both as to content and limits and was illusionary in practice.

The Soviet Union, in fact, had always been a unitarian state, ruled from its center. Centralized control from Moscow of all aspects of its subject territories' political and economic life was its essential feature. Republican governments were left with only the function of executing instructions from the center. "Elected" from "single candidate" lists approved by the center, such governments were minutely overseen by the local Communist parties and, in a real sense, were merged with such parties. As fully subservient agents of the center, the local parties themselves had little independent say as to the political or economic policy in their own republics.

Although in time, especially during the Khrushchev and Brezhnev eras, numerous non-Russian Communist parties managed to add national content to their party organizations, they inevitably continued to represent the interests of the center as opposed to the people of their republics. Their leaders had never been elected by their own people in open and free elections, and what legitimacy they had clearly depended upon the continuation of their grant of authority from the center. Moreover, any "autonomy" gained by them and, consequently, by their republics had, in fact, been purchased by the parties from the center in exchange for political loyalty or gifts. Such "autonomy" had also been used, in most instances, for the benefit of the local party elites rather than the people.

Thus the legitimacy of the "authority" of such parties to represent the people of their republics in the upcoming negotiations with the center remained open to question. Such representatives obviously lacked authority granted by their constituents, and their own interests inevitably conflicted with those of the people they were purporting to represent. And thus, in most cases, the upcoming negotiations were in danger of again reverting to internal party bartering sessions between dominant and subservient "cliques" of ruling elites for better positions near the economic larder. Unless drastic restructuring occurred, the people of the republics were again going to be left out of the process.

Making use of the chaos resulting from the impending disintegration of the empire, new "nationalist" interest groups began openly to form in the republics. In some, such as the Baltic states, the motive force came from widely supported nationalist separation movements, the representatives of which began to vie with the local Communist parties for the right to represent the people. Some of these movements even went so far as to co-opt the local

Communist parties to their cause, or at least the more progressive wings of such parties. Elsewhere, such as in Uzbekstan and Turkmenistan, existing Communist Party officials also took a more independent stance. But theirs was an effort to co-opt growing local nationalism and, in essence, to preserve their own ruling positions, which would be endangered if perestroika actually took root in their republics. These Party officials had few intentions of leaving the union but began to demand that the union treaty be amended so as to grant them more autonomy and thus more independent control over the natural resources and economic activity of their republics.

Unavoidably, issues as to the legality of the republics' initial entry into the Soviet Union and inevitably as to the jurisdiction of the USSR Constitution also began to be raised. The Baltic states grounded their right to leave the Soviet Union on the illegality of the infamous Molotov-Ribbentrop Pact by which they were originally ceded by Hitler's Germany to the Soviet Union. The Chechen argument was more direct: they simply held that they had never signed a union treaty or even a peace treaty with tsarist Russia.

Thus the legal concepts available for use in such negotiations were insufficient for the task. Even the term "federation" as used by Gorbachev was misleading. The federation scheme contained in the USSR Constitution involving a recognition of the sovereignty of the member states with a right to secede intimated, at best, a confederation rather than a federation. In a confederation, a state preserves its full sovereignty and thus its right to secede. In a federation, it necessarily cedes a part of its sovereignty to the center and thus gives up its right to secede.

The concept of "sovereignty" was also problematical. In a strictly legal sense, if the republics were already sovereign, what was there left then to negotiate with the center? For one, additional declarations of sovereignty would be redundant as this was already recognized in the USSR Constitution. Second, in order to change the existing union or to form a new union, the republics, in theory, only needed to decide among themselves (without the center) what kind of union, if any, they wanted. They then only had to impose their will on the center. In the alternative, they were also free to create a new center (without Gorbachev), or, using their constitutionally guaranteed rights to secede, opt to leave the union.

This was assuming that the center did not have any residual legal rights over the republics separate and apart from those "delegated" by the republics themselves to the center. But the center had, after all, inherited an empire and hegemony over the republics by right of "conquest." The unwillingness of the representatives of the center to abandon these residuary rights of empire was the crux of the problem between the center and the republics. Gorbachev's insistence that the center could impose onerous conditions for the secession of the republics clearly intimated such residuary rights. When political intimidation did not work, the forces of empire abandoned the veneer of negotiations altogether and attempted to preserve the empire by instigating the putsch.

The putsch was unsuccessful, and with its demise, the fifteen republics of the USSR quickly moved to effectuate their legal sovereignty, although a number of the republics still considered membership in some form of union to be to their advantage. Clipped of its former powers, the USSR lingered on, with the USSR's Supreme Soviet and the other institutions associated with the center still functioning for a lack of alternatives. The Declaration of Adherence to the Commonwealth of Independent States signed in Alma Ata on December 21, 1991, vacated its powers altogether. The Russian Federation thus finally became a truly sovereign state united in the Commonwealth of Independent States with eleven other former Soviet republics.

The USSR's demise as an entity, however, did not solve the legal problems associated with claims of sovereignty. The Russian Soviet Republic had originally been a patchwork of territories brought together by conquest under the hegemony of tsarist Russia. Many were inhabited by non-Russian ethnic populations living in their own historical territories. Their separate identities were reflected in the Soviet Russian Republic by their organization as autonomous republics, provinces, and regions.

Although independence for such nationalities was not a practical possibility during tsarist and then Soviet times because of the might of the central government, many of these nations did not fully assimilate into the predominant Russian culture and still harbored hopes of independence or at least some form of more independent national existence. As their legal status had previously been determined by the whim of the center and, with the demise of the center, there remained confusion as to their legal status, there seemed to be few legal or other impediments to the assumption of greater practical autonomy.

The separatist sentiment dominating the union republics quickly swept into the Russian Federation, and the leaders of the autonomous units in Russia also began to claim rights to sovereignty. Within weeks of the end of the putsch, at least ten Autonomous Socialist Soviet Republics (ASSRs), from Yakutia and Buratia in eastern Siberia to Udmurtia and Tatarstan in the Urals to the Karelian ASSR near Finland, declared their sovereignty and claimed the same rights as the union republics, often with the right to secede. This independence fever spread into ever smaller and smaller units, including autonomous provinces and districts.

Boris Yeltsin was thus suddenly put into an awkward position. Although the acknowledged leader of the separatist republics, he still had to be concerned with the territorial integrity of his own Russian Federation. With his own federation suddenly splitting at the seams, Yeltsin was forced to do a turnabout and act as guardian of the empire. Given the imperfections of his own federation's political and legal mechanisms and the apparent unacceptability of the self-determination of subject nations in the system, the lack of viable alternatives to force becomes apparent.

CHAPTER 13

The "Election" Campaign

After the assassination attempt on General Romanov, the situation in Chechnya became so tense that the Organization for Security and Cooperation in Europe (OSCE) mission, which had already spent an extended time in Grozni, was forced to make preparations to withdraw from Chechnya.[1] The mission had been asked by Sergei Kovaliov, the human rights defender, in November, 1994, to help regulate the Chechnya conflict and had arrived in Chechnya after the New Year's assault against Grozni. It succeeded in visiting Bamut in January, 1995, only to be shot up by Russian artillery. Understandably, it could go only where the Russians allowed it access. Russia refused to allow any real internationalization of the conflict and without a stronger mandate from the European Community, it was left with a severely limited observer role. The mission's main function was to host the Russian-Chechen talks which started in June, 1995, after Budionovsk.

The Chechens continued to intensify their attacks against the positions of the Russian Federal Forces. Just during the night of October 9, 30 attacks were committed, in which 2 Russian soldiers were killed and 7 wounded. Eight attacks were committed in Grozni itself. Two more soldiers were killed and three were wounded when an armored vehicle ran over a mine in the Zavodskaja region.

The Russian military forces reinforced the isolation of the Asinovskaja and Sernovodsk communities and other settlements, threatening ever more fiercely to destroy them if they did not lay down their arms. The situation became especially tense in the region of Asinovskaja where three Russian OMON detachments and a special-purpose detachment were deployed.

The bombing of the communities was again renewed. During the bombing on October 8 of Roshi Chu and Mesker Jurt, 28 inhabitants were killed. On October 14, when Russian military aircraft bombed the villages of Darga, Charsenoja, and Belgatoja, 17 more inhabitants were killed and 23 were injured. Eight attack aircraft and 6 helicopters participated in the air strikes.

The Russian High Command hurriedly denied that they had bombed the villages, contending that the provocation was organized by Dudajev. Allegedly Dudajev had 6 helicopters hidden in the mountains and a light aircraft base in Azerbaijan. But no one believed their denials. Not one of the earlier Russian allegations of provocations had ever been confirmed by facts. Instead, the attacks were always later confirmed to have been the work of Russian military aviation after all. By that time, it was hardly believable that Dudajev's forces would have had any aircraft left.[2]

In the middle of October, a group of Russian generals submitted a declaration concerning the situation in Chechnya to the Russian president, who was again on one of his vacations. In it, they offered two possible alternatives for getting out of the situation that had developed. One was to attack. Once it received the order to destroy the illegal armed formations, the army would win the war using all possible means, including aviation, artillery, and armor. The second choice was a withdrawal. If such a decision was made, the army would leave Chechnya and set up security zones around its territory. In both cases, actions were possible only until the middle of November. A decision had to be made quickly as the coming winter would make the use of military aviation much more difficult and the roads would become impassable for armored equipment and artillery. The army was simply not equipped to spend another winter under field conditions.

Ministers Grachev and Kulikov spoke out in favor of the immediate use of force, for harsher army actions against the Chechen formations, and for the declaration of martial law in Chechnya or at least in Grozni. Their reasoning was that in late fall the Chechens were expected to intensify the partisan war on Chechen territory and that there was no real possibility for successfully resolving the conflict through negotiations.[3]

Yeltsin was strongly affected by the generals' declaration and wavered between the two choices given him. But neither alternative totally satisfied him. He could not simply withdraw, and he could not agree with the suggestion made by the ministers controlling the Armed Forces to declare martial law. It was clear that such declaration of martial law was purposeless, as combat actions were continuing without it. There were also few doubts that martial law would be used only as a cover for "cleaning out" the villages. That would be useful only to the representatives of the pro-Moscow Chechen opposition government to strengthen their own position.

A decision was apparently postponed. No immediate steps were taken other than that a badly injured General Romanov was replaced as commander of the Combined Federal Battle Group in Chechnya by the Internal Affairs Army commander, General Lieutenant Anatoli Shkirko.[4]

On October 9, the Chechen government's Defense Committee reevaluated the increasingly tense political and military situation at a meeting held in one of the mountain communities. The actions of the Russian Federal Forces were viewed as intentional measures to preserve the sources of tension, especially in the communities of Asinovskaja and Sernovodsk, and as attempts to renew combat actions. They decided to suspend the peace negotiations and the execution of the military agreements until international observers and United Nations Peacekeeping Forces arrived.[5]

One more source of tension arose on October 16. The Russian Federal Forces surrounded Achchoj Martan where Dudajev's supporters had maintained positions since the end of August, and a fierce firefight ensued. The tension was caused by the fact that the Chechens took an Internal Affairs officer prisoner after he attempted to enter the community.[6]

Chechnya again neared the brink of war. Although the truce had been honored until then, it had been so conditional that during the two months of its existence, forty-five Russian soldiers were killed and more than two hundred were wounded. In the opinion of Russian military experts, by the end of October, the situation had changed to such a degree that the "right to administer the first blow" had passed back into Chechen hands. The Federal Army was slowly being shot apart. Dudajev had been able to rebuild his army's command and control system and had even supplemented his army's arsenal with some thirty to fifty units of new armored equipment. There were also some sixty to eighty thousand individual weapons still in Chechen hands. What was even more important, there were still more than enough people to shoot the weapons. Obviously, it was hard to find a family in Chechnya who had not lost close relatives to Russian war actions.

During the period of negotiations, the Federal Army had not only weakened but had been demoralized. One could count on one's fingers the forces left in its ranks that were still able to seriously fight. These were only the paratroopers and several infantry and Internal Affairs units. By autumn, the situation within the Federal Army units occupying positions in the mountains since May had become unenviable. Having been held almost under siege by the Chechens during this whole time, the troops had become so demoralized that it was only too clear that they would not be able to hold their positions much longer. It had been especially difficult to resupply them with stores and munitions. Columns traveling to Grozni and back could expect to run over mines, be shot at by the Chechens, or even be ambushed. Quite often, the supply people were also selling off a major share of the supplies allotted to the units along the way, leaving the soldiers in the forward units half-starved. Also, drunkenness in Russian military units had become rampant.

The 506th Motorized Rifle Regiment occupying positions near Vedeno found itself in an especially difficult state. On October 24 near Dyshne Vedeno, a column from the regiment, consisting of several trucks and fifteen armored vehicles, moving to the rescue of an armored vehicle encircled by local inhabitants was itself ambushed. During the attack against the column, eighteen Russian soldiers were killed, seventeen wounded, and five taken prisoner. Five armored vehicles were also destroyed. The ambush was carried out by orders from Basajev. After the attack, the Chechens issued an ultimatum to the regiment's command, demanding that the regiment be withdrawn from the mountains. The regiment's command gamely answered that revenge would be meted out for the dead soldiers and Vedeno would be attacked.[7]

On October 28, a column of the regiment's armored vehicles actually began to move toward Vedeno and succeeded in blocking off the Vedeno gorge in five places. But it could not bring itself to attack the city as it did not have sufficient strength to mount the attack or even to maintain its earlier positions. The Federal Battle Group's Command finally ordered the withdrawal of the regiment to Elisandzhi. To avoid further attacks against the regiment during its withdrawal, the assistant commander of the Combined Battle Group, V. Vlasenkov, was forced to enter into an agreement with Maschadov and the commandant of the Vedeno region, Shervani Basajev.[8]

The Russian soldiers had been so demoralized over such an extended period of time that when the regiment finally withdrew, many of its soldiers stayed on in the Vedeno area, some joining the ranks of the Chechen fighters, some opting to become "voluntary" prisoners, and others simply hiding out. A similar situation had developed with the Russian units occupying positions in the Shatoja region.

Khasbulatov's Plan to Normalize the Situation in Chechnya

The attempt on the life of General Romanov was only a pretext for terminating the negotiations. In fact, they already had been deadlocked because of disagreements arising from two months of trying to agree upon the terms of the self-defense formations question.

Just about that time, Ruslan Khasbulatov began once again to move actively onto the Chechen political scene after having almost disappeared from it following the opposition's unsuccessful assault of Grozni on November 26, 1994. This time Khasbulatov's position was much clearer: he began to lean to Dudajev's side, apparently having been much influenced by the war's results and its effects. Some time later, he even became the Chechen president's advisor.

According to Khasbulatov, the issue of the self-defense formations was of little actual importance and could be resolved by methods other than negotiations. Khasbulatov attributed the stalled negotiations to two problematic circumstances. The first was that there existed a dual government in Chechnya: Dudajev represented one government, and the Temporary Council, in effect appointed by Russia, represented the other. According to Khasbulatov, there in fact was no legal government in the republic, at least not one that was recognized by all parties.

Second, the objects of the negotiations and its purposes had not been sufficiently defined. Russia's official partner in the negotiations had been Dudajev's delegation, completely without the participation of the Temporary Council officially recognized by Russia. The negotiations delegation appointed by Dudajev represented the Chechen nation, but it was unable to use the radio, the television, or the press to communicate with the people directly. These were all under Russian control and unavailable to the Dudajev government. The Chechen people were thus insufficiently informed as to the progress of the negotiations, their results, the Chechen delegation's positions, and the tactics that it was using. The people could not form sufficiently clear opinions as to how much the successes of the negotiations corresponded to what was expected by them and how the objects of the negotiations were being sought.

The gaps in this information were being filled by rumors and self-serving commentaries. The public information media controlled by the Russians was attempting to convince the Chechen people that Dudajev's supporters were being too inflexible and were not making sufficient concessions and that they were holding on too strongly to the idea of the recognition of the complete independence of Chechnya. But obviously one could also agree with Khasbulatov's query: "How can Dudajev's side 'concede' anything, knowing full well that immediately after giving up their weapons, the conceding side to the negotiations would be subject to arrest, even execution without a trial. And the threats to renew combat actions that were being heard from time to time from Moscow could only be regarded as direct blackmail."[9]

But that was not the most important issue. A necessary precondition for successful negotiations also had to be the legalization of the Chechen side. This meant that the outstanding criminal charges issued against Dudajev needed to be dismissed. The legalization of Dudajev's status also had to be the subject of negotiations. Besides, the negotiations could not be successfully completed unless the tasks of the negotiations were formulated clearly, their time frames limited, and the ranks of the Russian negotiators raised.

Such measures would be of interest to all Chechens and would reduce the skepticism of the Chechen fighters and resistance leaders toward the negotiations and its results. They would show the Chechens that their fight had not been purposeless since they were achieving their original goals.

In analyzing the causes for the negotiations' lack of success, Khasbulatov came to the conclusion that the primary negotiation issues should be the status of Chechnya, the future agreements between the Russian Federation and the Republic of Chechnya, the formation of a coalition government, the republican and the federal government elections, and the withdrawal of the federal forces from Chechnya. He noted that, at the same time, the disarmament and dissolution of the resistance forces should also be discussed and that the soldiers of the resistance forces should be guaranteed that they would not be prosecuted and that their actions should be recognized as legally equivalent to the actions of the Russian soldiers.[10]

A way out of the deadlock could be the formulation and signing of the general principles of the treaty between the Russian Federation and the Republic of Chechnya. The principles should define the limits of the authority that Chechnya could delegate to the Russian Federation without doing harm to the issue of human rights and the rights of citizens, as much to Russia as to the people of Chechnya. Mentioned was the delegation of four authorizations by which the Republic of Chechnya would:

> Recognize the necessity that citizens of the Chechen Republic could at the same time be citizens of the Russian Federal Republic and that each citizen of the Russian Federation wanting to reside in the territory of the Chechen Republic could receive Chechen citizenship without any discrimination because of his sex, religion, race, or nationality;
>
> Recognize the necessity of open borders and the mutual defense of such joint borders on the basis of a special treaty;
>
> Recognize the necessity of a common Russian Federation monetary system;
>
> Agree to give up any rights to dislocate the Russian Federation army in the Republic of Chechnya and agree to the creation of a demilitarized Republic. [This was apparently intended for the Temporary Council.]
>
> Agree that there should not be any reference in the principles as to whether Chechnya was "in the Russian Federation" or "outside the Russian

Federation." All other questions should be within the republic's own competence or be decided by negotiations and special treaties.

This would still not be sufficient in Khasbulatov's opinion. The republic had to have international guarantees that the massacres would not reoccur. Such guarantees needed to be realized through international, political, diplomatic, and other relationships and links. These relationships should not be entered into against Russia's will but with its agreement and support.

In Khasbulatov's opinion, it was also unfortunate that Russia did not have anyone with whom it could sign a treaty regarding the political issues. Here Khasbulatov was at least partially correct: Russia was forced to negotiate with Dudajev but Dudajev himself had not able to participate in the negotiations, as Russia still had a warrant for his arrest. Khasbulatov was silent as to any possibilities that Russia should negotiate with its appointed Temporary Council. Khasbulatov's main concern revolved about the formation of a government in Chechnya, an issue that had become one of the major problems during the postconflict period.

It would be best, according to Khasbulatov, to resolve the issue of the formation of the government by means of democratic elections. He was greatly displeased that Moscow decided to postpone the previously agreed election date of November 5 for half a year. The first task should be the advancement of the date for the elections and the creation of conditions under which they could be held. This should be the Temporary Council's primary assignment. But elections would be the second step.

While the elections were still yet impossible, it would also be necessary, according to Khasbulatov, to form a coalition government and to include in it people who had not participated in the conflict. A possible alternative was to concentrate all government functions in the hands of a representative of the Russian government and its territorial administration. At least in this way all responsibility for the situation in the republic, including its positive and negative aspects, would be borne by the Russian federal government. This would legalize the occupation, but at least it would be equivalent to postwar conditions.

Khasbulatov's stance had that lingering sense that while everything he said was reasonable and commendable, still something was gravely wrong. Khasbulatov was still not ruling out the Temporary Council's participation even though it had been effectively isolated and pushed out of the negotiations. In fact, he was giving it the task of organizing the elections of the government that was to eventually take power. Also, he was suggesting that the Russian government continue to temporarily administer Chechnya, thus legalizing the status quo. It was a way out of the present predicament but hardly gave the Dudajev government much maneuvering room in which to attempt to realize its earlier goals.

In the Background of "Democratic" Elections

It is unclear how much of Khasbulatov's plan was acceptable to Dudajev, but in Russia interest in it was growing, at least on the issue of elections in Chechnya. Moscow's leaders debated on more than one occasion ways to push Dudajev from the political arena as a prime actor. Of the various alternatives, the organization of "democratic" elections in Chechnya seemed to be the most appropriate. To put the organization of the elections program into effect, pro-Moscow government leader Salambek Chadzhijev was replaced by the former leader of parliament, Doku Zavgajev, and Umar Avturchanov was replaced by L. Mahomed.

These changes only brought on a new wave of tension. Anti-Russian demonstrations were held in Grozni and in other communities. About 2,500 people participated in a demonstration held in Grozni on October 24.[11] They demanded that the Russian Army be withdrawn from Chechnya and protested the change of leaders in the pro-Moscow government. The meeting could not be complete without casualties. The militia under the control of the pro-Moscow mayor of the city began to shoot at the people. One person was killed and four were wounded. But even after this bloody occurrence in the square in front of the ruins of the presidential palace, the people refused to disperse, even when they were encircled by the militia.

On November 1, the pro-Moscow opposition Chechen parliament appointed Doku Zavgajev as the country's leader, giving him authorization to act as president. Thus formally a dual government in Chechnya was created. A great majority of Chechens, however, refused to recognize the new government created at the point of a bayonet.[12]

Some time later, on November 17, the presidium of the pro-Moscow Chechen Supreme Council passed a law declaring presidential elections in the Republic of Chechnya. December 17 was announced as the date of the new elections. Just how "democratic" these elections were going to be was fully understood by everyone, especially the organizers. There was also no doubt left that Dudajev's supporters and fighters would not participate in the elections, as to do so they would have to leave their defensive positions. And what about the more than 400,000 Chechens who had left their homes because of the war activity? The situation was agitated even more by Doku Zavgajev's announcement that Russian soldiers would be allowed to vote in the elections. This meant that whoever they were ordered to vote for would be elected, even more so as no one accurately knew just how many Russian soldiers were present in Chechnya. In effect, the task of electing the new Chechen government was left to the Russian troops.[13] Dudajev was left with only the option of publicly announcing that any new elections would be illegal until the Russian army was withdrawn from the republic's territory.

The attacks by the Chechen fighters increased once the elections were announced. During just four days, from November 17 through 20, the Federal Army suffered casualties of forty soldiers killed and wounded. On November 20, an attempt was made to assassinate Doku Zavgajev, but he was only slightly injured during the explosion.

As the relationship became even more tense, the command of the Federal Battle Group in Chechnya began to take measures to reinforce the blockade of the mountain regions, at least to close down in part the Chechen fighters' access to the flatlands. A blocking post was thus again established near Kurchaloja, and the bombardment of the community of Roshi Chu was intensified. But no one believed that this would bring any real results: these actions were intended simply to demonstrate that measures were being taken to ensure the normal course of the elections. According to the Federal Army's High Command, Dudajev's forces were yet sufficiently strong. The Chechens even had heavy weapons available: twelve tanks, almost twenty armored vehicles, and seventeen artillery systems. The Chechen formations reestablished their combat strength and were prepared for new battles. Thus the High Command's primary attention was directed to ensuring the security of the Federal Army's units as, on the eve of the elections, the Chechen forces became especially active: the number of blocking posts manned by the Chechen fighters increased along with the attacks against the Russian army unit columns. Because they were almost constantly under fire, the Russian forces in the communities began to feel very insecure. Most often, they were deployed in groups of one army battalion and about thirty fast-reaction special-purpose specialists.

The situation at that time was related quite graphically by the Russian troops themselves.[14] Aleksander Shevchenko, an intelligence specialist, said: "On December 12, our intelligence commander told us that a Chechen blocking post had been established in Novyje Atagi. We decided to attack it and to take the Chechens prisoner so that later we could exchange them for our own people. But when we arrived at the post, everything suddenly appeared differently. There were some 25 Chechens at the post with 'muchas' [grenade launchers]. We were only 12 troops. They began to shoot us up. Two of our group were killed immediately. Those that were up front were immediately cut off from the second armored vehicle. They had to defend themselves until the infantry could come to their rescue. I myself was prevented from help-ing by three bullet wounds. I was cursing and, admittedly, screaming."

Aleksej Chrolionk, a soldier, said: "I was wounded on December 14 near Shatoja. Our assault group as always was accompanying a column with mu-nitions and other stores. We were nearing Shatoja, and when I looked around, there was no one to be seen. All of this appeared to be suspicious. . . . Sud-denly, at a turn in the road, the last vehicle was shot at. The armored person-nel carrier was hit immediately. It flamed up, and one of the boys in it was burned alive. We then understood what to expect. Immediately there were wounded. Our communications were lost, and we began to pull back. Dur-ing that time, I was also wounded. At first in the chest, afterwards in the legs. For fifty minutes, I lay rolling on the ground until help arrived. Just within my sight, two people were killed and five wounded. What happened later, I do not know."

As election organizers believed that one day would not be sufficient to get the necessary number of voters to the polls so that the election could be de-clared to have taken place, they decided that the elections would be held on four consecutive days, December 14 through 17. The elections began on De-cember 14 without any voter lists. To vote, it was only necessary to show some sort of identification document. But almost no voters came to the polls, and even if they had come, they could not have voted. News correspondents re-ported that, even in Grozni itself, only one voting booth had been established.

On the eve of the elections, December 13, Dzhochar Dudajev announced that the war was entering a new stage: "The war is just beginning!" [15] With the elections began the Chechen operation in Gudermes. At the same time, Du-dajev's fighters intensified their attacks in the other communities, especially in the regions of Shali and Urus Martan. Fierce confrontations also began near Bamut, the Russian detachment on the northeast edge of Shatoja was block-aded, and several administration buildings in Urus Martan were taken. [16]

The "Elections" in Gudermes

The Gudermes takeover operation was planned under the command of Chech-nya's chief of staff, Aslan Maschadov, and operational command was assigned to the commander of the Aleroja fighter group. The operation itself was con-ducted by Salman Radujev's fighter group. The mission of the operation was to take up positions in Gudermes and hold them for three days, that is, until the end of the elections.

Before the operation, the Chechen fighter groups that were to participate in the operation were concentrated in the forested foothills communities to the south and east of Gudermes: in Aleroja, Centoroja, Bachi Jurt, Belorechje, Kurchatoja, Novaja Zhizna, and Oktiabrskoja. It had been taken into account while planning the operation that the 33rd Internal Affairs Army Brigade located on the outskirts of Gudermes had not established fortifications and blocking posts to the south of the city. From this direction, the road into the city was open to the Chechens, especially when the brigade's attention was directed to the approaches from the north. According to Russian intelligence information, the Chechen fighter force concentrated in the community of Komsomolskaja to the north was particularly dangerous. This fighter group, commanded by A. Bantajev, was considered to be the Chechen Southeastern Front's strike force.

Attempting to hinder the elections, a small Chechen fighter group entered Gudermes on December 12. Because of their presence, the commandant of the federal force in Gudermes anxiously decided to close all the roads out of the city. But the Russian forces group did not do so in time or, more accurately, did not have the ability to do so effectively. During the night of December 13, the Chechen forces already in the city were reinforced by a group of about forty Chechen fighters who, upon entering the city, fortified themselves in the city hospital. The local inhabitants and patients were all allowed to leave the hospital; only the chief doctor remained. Shortly thereafter, the railroad station was attacked and later the commandant's headquarters (Internal Affairs) was put under siege. By morning, the Chechens had succeeded in concentrating several hundred fighters within the city.

When the Chechens began to shoot up the commandant's headquarters and the railroad station, the commandant of the Russian force in the city called for reinforcements. But the Chechens were prepared for this, knowing from where and along what route the reinforcements would have to arrive. An ambush was set up for the reinforcing force at Tereshkov Street. After allowing the scout detachment through, the main reinforcement column was attacked.

The scouting party consisted of two armored vehicles, and the main column was made up of two armored vehicles, a tank, a heavy antitank grenade launcher team in a Ural truck, and antiaircraft artillery and mortar detachments. During the attack against the main column, the crew of one of the armored vehicles sustained losses of three killed and four wounded. The armored vehicle escaped being totally destroyed only because a tank came to its rescue. The armored vehicle was able to reach the bridge where only bullets could reach it and then forced its way to the commandant's headquarters. When the reinforcement force itself called for assistance, another group from the battalion was sent out, commanded by the battalion's commander, S. Karaulov.

That day the reinforcement force sustained eighteen killed and twenty-eight wounded. Three burned-up armored vehicles and the Ural truck were left at the scene of the ambush.[17]

In the city, the Chechens mounted their fiercest attack against the joint Russian force taking up positions in the railroad station. Apparently this was not by chance, as this force was made up of a combined Russian OMON group and supplemented by the opposition's Chechen militiamen. The OMON group consisted of troops from the Moscow, Mordovia, Marij Elo, Karachoi Cherkesia, Adygeja, Chiuvashija, Kabarda Balkaria, and Volgoviatsk regions. They had arrived in Gudermes on November 7 for their duty shift. In all, the group was made up of some 134 OMON soldiers, mostly officers.

Once the Chechens surrounded the railroad station, the commander of the combined force, who was also the commander of the Moscow OMON detachment, was forced to call for assistance. The city's commandant answered that help was already on its way in the form of four armored vehicles and the Volgograd Special Purpose Fast Reaction Detachment. Several hours later, however, when the commander of the combined Russian force again inquired about the reinforcements, he was told: "The Volgograd Special Purpose Fast Reaction Detachment is no more: thirty were killed and thirteen are missing in action together with their commander." It was becoming clear that the combined force would have to hold on and depend on its own resources.[18]

The people blockaded in the commandant's office were also uncertain as to when help would arrive and were forced to attempt to break through the encirclement. But the attempt did not succeed: a scout group of 8 sent to find a breakout route was quickly wiped out, with only 1 returning. Thus they were forced to remain within the encirclement until the commandant's headquarters was finally relieved after the Chechens left the city.

It should be noted that the Chechens did not attempt to take either the railroad station or the commandant's headquarters, though they did have the capability of doing so. Apparently attempting to conserve their own forces and to avoid large losses during the attacks, they were satisfied with intensively shooting them up.

Fierce battles were fought not only at the railroad station and in the vicinity of the commandant's headquarters but also throughout the city. Even the High Command of the Federal Forces in Chechnya were forced to admit that the situation of those encircled in the city was critical: during just the first day of the battle, 18 soldiers had been killed, 44 had been wounded, and 20 were

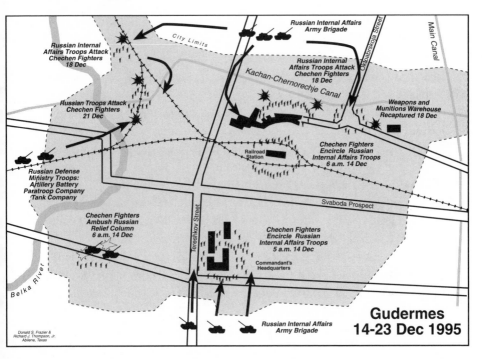

Russian Internal Affairs
Army Brigade

City Limits

Russian Internal
Affairs Troops Attack
Chechen Fighters
18 Dec

Russian Internal
Affairs Troops Attack
Chechen Fighters
18 Dec

Kachan-Chernorechje Canal

Oktabrskaja Street

Main Canal

Russian Troops Attack
Chechen Fighters
21 Dec

Weapons and
Munitions Warehouse
Recaptured 18 Dec

Chechen Fighters
Encircle Russian
Internal Affairs Troops
6 a.m. 14 Dec

Railroad
Station

Russian Defense
Ministry Troops:
Artillery Battery
Paratroop Company
Tank Company

Svaboda Prospect

Chechen Fighters
Ambush Russian
Relief Column
6 a.m. 14 Dec

Tereshkov Street

Chechen Fighters
Encircle Russian
Internal Affairs Troops
5 a.m. 14 Dec

Commandant's
Headquarters

Belka River

Russian Internal Affairs
Army Brigade

**Gudermes
14-23 Dec 1995**

Donald S. Frazier &
Richard J. Thompson, Jr.
Abilene, Texas

missing in action. However, these figures should not be given undue weight, as the Volgograd Special Fast-Reaction Detachment alone lost 30 killed.

The Federal Army High Command had to take quick measures to save its forces. One more Internal Affairs Brigade was sent in to help. Taking up positions around the city, it began to shoot up the city with barrages from Grad rocket salvo artillery systems, artillery, and mortars. Helicopters from the Kizliar Air Base in Dagestan were also used for the attacks. It was announced that the brigade had succeeded in blockading the city, but, in reality, this was done only for appearances. The units belonging to the Defense Ministry (the artillery battery, the paratroopers, and the tank company) in fact just affected the appearance of a blockade.

The Federal Army's most pressing task was to relieve the railroad station and the commandant's headquarters. But the Federal Army units did not take any further actions to effect this until the end of the elections and continued to demonstrate their diligence only by shooting up the city. During this whole time, they continued to make preparations for the assault, but knowing that the Chechen fighters, once they accomplished their mission, would leave the city after the elections without further resistance, they held off from attacking.

Nevertheless, on December 18, the bombardment of the city was intensi-

fied. It had become clear that the Federal Army units were about to begin their
assault. The Federal Army operated according to its already traditional procedures. Once the city was encircled, "corridors" were left open, enabling the
civilian inhabitants to leave the city. One of these corridors was the road to
Kurchaloja.

The assault of the city was finally begun on December 19. But instead of
retreating as expected, the Chechens decided to organize further resistance.
They divided their forces in the city into five primary groups and, on December 21, even attempted to reinforce their forces in the city by sending in a group
of fighters from Shali in six buses. This decision was prompted when their operation to take the city succeeded better than they expected.

The Federal Army did not conduct any special measures to assault the
city. Two Internal Affairs Army brigades began moving toward the city under
cover of intensive artillery and mortar fire barrages and rocket fire from helicopters. One approached from the north, the other from the south. Once the
Federal Army units entered the city, the usual "cleaning-out" procedures were
instigated.

After fully controlling Gudermes for four days (December 18–22), the
Chechens decided to leave, and on December 23, they began their retreat. On
orders from Maschadov, the main fighter groups withdrew from the city, leaving behind only small groups of fighters to cover their retreat. After ten days
of being under siege, the commandant's headquarters and the combined force
at the railroad station were finally "relieved."[19]

According to official Russian information, by December 23, 36 Russian
soldiers had been killed, 141 had been wounded, and 37 were missing in
action in Gudermes (32 bodies were later found). Later these figures were
corrected, and it was announced that 70 Russian soldiers had been killed and
150 wounded. It was also reported by the Russian High Command that the
Chechens had lost 300 fighters.[20]

According to Chechen sources, 107 Chechen fighters had been killed and
19 had been wounded during the Gudermes operation. About 700 of the opponent's soldiers had also been killed, more than 40 armored combat vehicles
had been destroyed, and 1 helicopter had been shot down.

The largest losses, however, were suffered by the inhabitants of the city.
Immediately after the operation, the commander of the Combined Federal
Group in Chechnya, General Shkirko, reported that 267 inhabitants of the
city had become casualties during the confrontations, but later he did not confirm these casualty figures and instead significantly decreased their numbers.
The Chechens reported that 1,271 civilian inhabitants had been killed, mostly
women and children who had been unable to leave the city before the artillery

barrages started. More than 50 percent of the city was reportedly destroyed. Although this percentage was questionable, the results of fourteen days of continuous bombardment of the city were readily obvious.[21] The first shipment of humanitarian aid was allowed into Gudermes only on December 27.

The operation conducted by the Chechens in Gudermes showed that the Federal Army was not prepared for unexpected attacks, particularly when they were conducted by large Chechen forces. The initiative had been passed completely into the hands of the Chechens. The Chechens, on their part, also were becoming convinced of the effectiveness of large operations that at the same time forced the federal forces groups to take additional measures against such attacks. The importance of the General Staff to the overall effort and the trust placed in it also increased once it was shown that it was possible to inflict the most painful blows to the Russian forces by painstakingly planning operations and concentrating forces into temporary combined groups for the execution of such operations. The results of the coordination of well-planned combat actions became obvious to the separate Chechen fighter groups. Also for the Chechens, a very important aspect of the Gudermes operation was that it again demonstrated that Dudajev's armed forces were not weakened but, to the contrary, had grown in strength and were capable of carrying out large-scale operations.

The operation conducted by the Chechens in Gudermes, however, did not have any great influence on the course of the political events. As expected, it was soon announced that Doku Zavgajev had won the elections.[22] But the Gudermes operation became the cornerstone on which the foundations of new large operations were constructed. Almost immediately after it, preparations began for the Kizliar operation. The Kizliar Military Airport became an object of revenge for the bombing of Gudermes, which had been executed by helicopters flying from this base.

Part 4

The Third Period
of the War in Chechnya

CHAPTER 14

The Second Terrorist Operation

During the war, lasting one and a half years, the Chechens executed two military terrorist actions outside the borders of Chechnya. The first one was on June 13–21, 1995, in the city of Budionovsk in the neighboring Russian province of Stavropol. The second was on January 9–18, 1996, in the city of Kizliar and the village of Pervomaiskoje on Dagestan territory. The purposes and specific events of these actions were different, but their general characteristics were similar: the sacrifice of civilian inhabitants, the taking of hostages, and the takeover of hospitals.[1]

The Kizliar incident began early the morning of January 9, 1996, when the inhabitants of the city were awakened by gunfire. Having forced its way into the Dagestan Republic's city, the Chechen fighter detachment acted according to a well-rehearsed scenario. They attacked the airport and the railroad station and blockaded the Internal Affairs battalion and the militia building. They then took the city hospital. The Chechen fighters took hostage 314 patients, 51 medical personnel, and numerous local inhabitants, in all about 2,000 people (some sources say 3,000).[2]

During the operation in Kizliar itself, 34 inhabitants of Dagestan were killed, among them 7 militiamen and 2 soldiers. Four Chechen fighters were also killed.[3]

The Chechen fighter detachment, consisting of almost 250 fighters, was commanded by the commander of the Northeast Group, Colonel Salman Radujev, and the commander of the Southeast Group, Colonel Ch. Israpilov.

According to Radujev, the purpose of the operation was not to take hostages but to attack the airport at which, according to their information, 8 helicopters were to be found that had flown in to deliver a cargo of munitions and antitank rockets. But only 3 helicopters and 2 armored vehicles were found at the airport. Once they were destroyed, the operations plan had to be corrected because of tactical circumstances that had developed.[4]

The fighter group had traveled to Kizliar in Kamaz (Russian-made cargo) trucks, which they had left some 7 or 8 kilometers from the city. They then proceeded the rest of the way on foot. As soon as the operation began, Russian government officials stated that they had known about preparations for the operation on December 23, but apparently the arrival of the Chechen group in Kizliar still was unexpected. In the opinion of journalists, it would not have been very hard for the Chechen fighter group to get to the city. There had been almost no control posts along the way, and with appropriate bribes, getting through without inspection would have been quite possible.[5]

According to Israpilov, however, the first stage of the operation was changed because all the posts through which the column traveled were passing along the column's movement toward Kizliar by radio and even knew his name and how many soldiers were in the group. They had even attempted to block the road at various places, but no serious barriers were set up. For this reason, the leaders of the Chechen group got the impression that they were being enticed into Dagestan, where the Russians would attempt to destroy the group or cut off its way back. They decided only then to take hostages as a guarantee for the group's safety.

The local forces in the city acted quickly. The Internal Affairs Army battalion succeeded in breaking out of Chechen encirclement and surrounded the hospital building. But they had assumed that Radujev's force consisted of about 400 fighters and that the local forces in the city (250 militia personnel, 300 Internal Affairs Army troops and officers, and 30 border policemen from the Kizliar Commandant's Headquarters) would be insufficient to destroy the terrorists. Thus, special Internal Affairs Ministry detachments and Defense Ministry units were called in to assist.

That evening, Dagestan Parliamentary Council leader M. Magamedov and Premier A. Mirzobekov met with Radujev and discussed the release of hostages. In exchange, Radujev demanded that 11 buses and 3 Kamaz trucks be provided by morning and that guarantees be given for his forces' safe passage back to Chechnya.[6]

The majority of the hostages were released during the night. Early the next morning the column carrying the Chechen fighters and the remaining 128 hostages began to move out in the direction of Chechnya. Among the hos-

tages were seven ministers of the government of Dagestan who had volunteered to accompany them. The column consisted of 11 buses that had been
provided according to the terrorists' demands and the 2 Kamaz trucks with
which the terrorists had come to Kizliar.

Why the Village of Pervomaiskoje?

During the deliberations with the leaders of Dagestan, Radujev stated that
their purpose was to return to Novogroznensk. Both sides agreed on the route
back, and the Chechens agreed that they would release the hostages in the village of Pervomaiskoje, located a little more than a kilometer from the border
of Chechnya.

The actual events did not unfold as agreed, however. As the Chechen column passed Pervomaiskoje, the hostages were not released, which saved the
fighter group from destruction. Colonel Radujev would not release the hostages as it was becoming quite clear from the developing situation that a
bloodbath was being prepared for the column across the river. While the column was still traveling towards the village, Russian authorities decided to destroy the column in the vicinity of Pervomaiskoje. The operation was to be
executed as soon as the column released the hostages, entered the territory of
Chechnya, and crossed the bridge across the Terek River. There, a 6-kilometer
section of road stretched from the river to Azamat Jurt, the nearest Chechen
village. This section of the road was deemed appropriate for such an operation, as north of it lay a sparse forest and the unfrozen Terek River and to the
south stretched a field crisscrossed by irrigation ditches.

The operation was to have been conducted as follows: two Su-25 attack
aircraft were to strike the column of buses on Chechen territory and stop its
forward movement. Then a flight of Mi-24 helicopters was to shoot up the
buses with rockets. Two companies of the 7th Paratroop Division, deployed
along both sides of the road, were then to capture the fighters running from
the buses, dead or alive. The troops executing the operation were not told that
the column would still be carrying hostages, apparently because the operation
planners believed they would have already been released.[7]

Just as the terrorist operation and the taking of hostages was beginning in
Kizliar, Moscow resolutely announced that, unlike what happened after the
incident in Budionovsk, this time the terrorists would be dealt with severely.
All means would be taken not to allow terrorism to expand beyond the borders of Chechnya.[8] Obviously such a categorical statement by the Russian
president had to be backed up, and therefore the response was, in fact, different. Unlike Budionovsk, the negotiations with the terrorists were not undertaken by the Russian central government but were delegated to the govern-

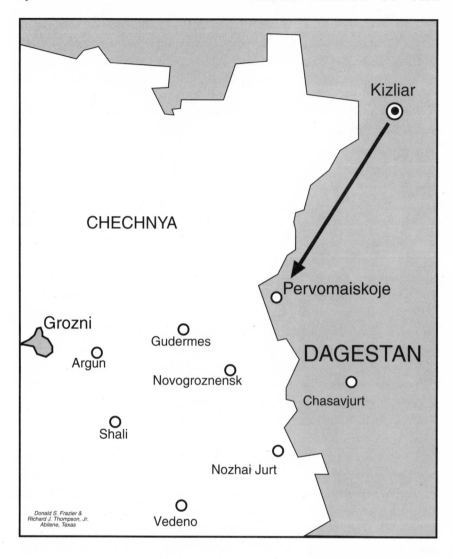

Kizliar

CHECHNYA

Pervomaiskoje

Grozni
Argun   Gudermes
         Novogroznensk

DAGESTAN

Chasavjurt

Shali

Nozhai Jurt

Vedeno

Donald S. Frazier &
Richard J. Thompson, Jr.
Abilene, Texas

ment of Dagestan. However, command of the operation to destroy the terrorists and to free the hostages remained under the central government's control.
As this operation was to be conducted while in Chechen territory, any guarantees or promises given to Radujev and his group by the Dagestan government would have no validity outside the borders of that republic. Furthermore, the armed forces commanded by the federal central government did
not have to answer to the government of Dagestan for its actions. The freeing
of the hostages appeared not to be their main concern.

As soon as it crossed the border separating Dagestan and Chechnya, the forward movement of the column with the hostages was stopped by helicopters that began to fire at it. The Russian operations headquarters, sensing that their plans for stopping the column were coming apart, became overly exited and began to hurry the course of events. Helicopters were ordered to attack the column without waiting for the Su-25 aircraft. The helicopters hit the Dagestan auto-inspection automobile leading the column, but the two militiamen escaped alive. Two buses were also slightly damaged.

Quickly appraising the developing situation and seeing that the column was in danger of being immediately surrounded and blockaded, the Chechens decided not to linger. They turned back, took the militia blocking post located in Pervomaiskoje, and quickly spread out through the village to make preparations for defense. The 150-man paratroop group flown in by helicopter to set up the ambush was set down along the road. Only the fact that they were set down at the wrong time and the wrong place saved them from immediate destruction. Apparently both companies were set down in an open field just fifty meters from the column just as it stopped. The Chechens were so surprised by such stupidity that they did not open fire.[9]

The local inhabitants hurried to flee the village, some jumping into their cars, some leaving on foot. Most of them fled to the neighboring village of Terechnoja. But not all succeeded in getting away before the village was blockaded by OMON, Specnaz, and Internal Affairs Army soldiers.

Further events perhaps would have evolved differently if the blocking post near Pervomaiskoje, manned by thirty-seven militiamen from Novosibirsk, had not surrendered without resistance. They were ordered not to shoot by the Russian Internal Affairs Ministry's chief of operational staff, as well as assistant chief of the Krasnodar Internal Affairs Council, militia colonel N. Gonchiarov. The militiamen thus became hostages, and the Chechen fighters succeeded in supplementing their arsenal with two armored vehicles, thirty-six automatic weapons, four portable grenade launchers, as well as ammunition and grenades.[10] When the militiamen were also added to the ranks of the hostages, the plans of the Russian strategists who had prepared the operation to destroy the hit men near Pervomaiskoje became hopelessly mixed up.

The village of Pervomaiskoje became the center of the tragedy only by a quirk of fate. This was in part because it had been agreed to release the hostages near the village and in part because the commanders of the operation decided to execute the operation not far from it.

Upon analyzing the course of events and the actions of both sides, unavoidably a conclusion must be drawn—that the Russian forces did not have sufficient time to prepare to stop the column with the hostages before they arrived in the village of Pervomaiskoje. This must have been caused by a woeful lack of organization and by gross inefficiency.

During the night of January 9, aircraft were flown into Machachkala Airport carrying troops of the Federal Counterintelligence Service and Internal Affairs Ministry special-purpose detachments. But buses were sent to the airport for only the Vitiaz group. Motor transport for the Alfa group and the others (8 buses and 1 Kamaz truck) were provided only after several hours of waiting. Several more hours were also spent waiting in Machachkala until the assignments were prepared, written up, and handed out. By the time these special troops arrived in Kizliar, it was learned that the column with the hostages was already on its way to Pervomaiskoje. They gave chase, but the Alfa special detachment troop contingent was being stopped at every militia blocking post along the way. While the situation and their group's authorizations were explained at every post, time ran by.

Russian president Yeltsin, the Federal Counterintelligence Service, and Internal Affairs Ministry commanders, Mikhail Barsukov and Anatoli Kulikov, contended afterwards that the village of Pervomaiskoje was picked by the Chechens and not by chance. They contended that Dudajev's forces established in advance a strong-point defense base in the village of Pervomaiskoje and that it contained underground defense fortifications, supplies of reserve weapons and ammunition, and all the things necessary to allow the Chechens to hold out in the village for a long time. This contention is not only groundless but also humorous in some respects. For one, Dudajev's fighters had never operated in this village until then, or even in its outlying regions. There were also no Chechen defense interests in it. Second, inhabitants, not only in this village but also in the villages nearby, never built any cellars for the simple reason that the area was marshy and wet and such structures would have been flooded by groundwater. Once the Chechens began constructing their defensive positions, they did, in fact, dig excavations. But man-height excavations were only possible to dig and to use because the ground was frozen.

After the operation was concluded, journalists scrupulously investigated the claims that a Chechen defense base existed. No fortifications prepared in advance were found, with the exception of one small cellar that was widely publicized on Moscow television as a defense position.[11]

Negotiations in the Village of Pervomaiskoje

Once Radujev's group took the village and fortified themselves in it, Dagestan's government became concerned once again. Immediately efforts were made to renew the negotiations for the freeing of hostages. Radujev agreed to renew the negotiations, as the circumstances had in fact changed. Upon flying into the village in two helicopters, the negotiators immediately issued a demand that the terrorists release all the hostages, as had been agreed previously. But this time Radujev agreed to release only the women and children, upon the additional condition that the Chechens be given safe passage back to Novogroznensk. The Dagestan negotiations delegation was not able to give such assurances, so, in addition to the other safe conduct terms, the Chechens added the demand that Russian premier Chernomyrdin participate in the negotiations. Problems also arose regarding the movement route. The Chechens were told that it was impossible to return to Chechnya along the route agreed upon earlier, as someone had blown up the bridge across the Terek River. Radujev and Israpilov then demanded that the route be changed and that they be allowed to go through Chasavjurt. Although the Dagestan leaders vacillated, they finally agreed to this change, but it was resisted by the commanders of the federal operation to free the hostages.

The negotiations with the Chechens were conducted for the most part by the Dagestan Internal Affairs minister, General Lieutenant Abdurazakov, and his chief of staff, General Major Bejev. Later the Chechens demanded that journalists participate in the negotiations as witnesses. Seven were chosen, among them the Lithuanian reporter S. Liutauras, a television journalist from the Reuters news agency.

As negotiations for the hostages' release continued, it became clearer by the minute that an assault by federal troops against the village was unavoidable. For this reason, Radujev and Israpilov decided to release a portion of the hostages, for the most part women with children, and began to prepare for defense. The remaining hostages were ordered to join in the digging of entrenchments and the construction of fortifications. The fact that the Chechens also released eight hostages who were members of the government and parliament of Dagestan and a Russian Duma deputy added to the certainty that the village would be stormed.

An ultimatum was issued to the terrorists that they release all the hostages by January 14, throw down their weapons, and proceed under a white flag to Chechnya. The ultimatum, as always, was not obeyed. The Chechens had earlier informed the Russian side that if one tank or armored vehicle came within one hundred meters of the village, they would begin to execute the hostages.

During this time, the Russians were making preparations to storm the village. Special units of the Federal Counterintelligence Service, Internal Affairs Ministry, and the Ministry of Defense took up positions around the village. It is not clear, however, why three antiaircraft guns were positioned to the north of the village.

For the assault of the terrorists fortified in Pervomaiskoje, the following forces were concentrated: in the first attack line were the Internal Affairs Ministry's Moscow City and District (130 people), Stavropol, Krasnodar, and Dagestan Special-Purpose Detachments, the Vitiaz Detachments, and the 8th Detachment of the Internal Affairs Army's Derzhinski Division. In the second attack line was the Alfa Group (250 people). To provide supporting fire were the 136th Brigade's artillery, the antitank guided missile detachment from the 166th Brigade, 3 Grad rocket salvo artillery systems, and a number of helicopters. In all, the following combat equipment were brought together for this operation: 54 armored personnel carriers, 22 armored vehicles, 4 armored intelligence vehicles, 1 tank, 12 artillery guns, 3 Grad rocket salvo artillery systems, 14 antiaircraft guns, 20 mortars, 15 antitank guided missile systems, 10 grenade launchers, and 16 flamethrowers.[12]

The group concentrated for the assault of the village and its blockade totaled 2,414 people. Of them 739 were Internal Affairs Army troops and 857 were militiamen. However, the blockade of the village was set up very strangely. The prime forces were positioned on the Dagestan side as if the Russians expected Radujev's group to attempt to break through to Kizliar and not toward Chechnya.

In positions to the west of the village were, for the most part, paratroopers from the 7th Division. In their center was the 22nd Company, consisting of 37 people. The 1st Paratroop Company was positioned on the right wing and a Special Purpose Detachment from the General Staff's Intelligence Command (GRU) was deployed on the left wing. This whole "western group" consisted of about a 100 people, In fact, these were all the forces protecting the administrative border with Chechnya and the bridge across the Terek River. For combat equipment, they had only one armored personnel carrier, which the commander of the 2nd Company "borrowed" from the motorized riflemen. This armored personnel carrier, however, was later knocked out and burned by the Chechens during the twentieth minute of their breakout operation and did not get a chance to fire a shot at them. Once the storming of Pervomaiskoje began, this "western group" was reinforced by the deployment at their rear of 86 people from the 21st Paratroop Brigade.

The plan for the assault of the village was prepared very intensively, but it had one big fault: the belief that it would be impossible to avoid large casualties among the hostages and the attacking forces. In judging the plan, one must consider that the unit commanders saw the map of the village with some of the elements of the Chechen defense system for the first time on January 13.[13]

On January 14, the director of the Federal Counterintelligence Service,

Mikhail Barsukov, and Internal Affairs Minister Anatoli Kulikov arrived near Pervomaiskoje. The ultimatum was extended for one more day.

The Storming of the Village

On January 15 at 9:10 A.M., the federal forces began the operation to "free the hostages." Twenty minutes before the operation's start, General Barsukov once more ordered the terrorists by radio and microphone to surrender and to come out in single file onto the road. There was no answer. After several minutes, at least ten helicopters appeared in the air above the village and struck the village with rockets. The first rockets were fired from the two helicopters that had appeared from the direction of Azamat Jurt. At the same time artillery fire was opened up. Immediately the armored vehicle previously captured by the Chechens was lit on fire; then a bus standing nearby with the hostages was destroyed. The Chechens answered the fire with antitank rockets and knocked out a Russian armored personnel carrier.[14]

Almost immediately after the start of the operation, the Federal Counterintelligence Service broadcast an official announcement by radio, stating that the military units were forced to attack after the Chechens began to shoot the hostages and even shot the vehicle of General Barsukov with grenade launcher fire. Hearing this on their radio receivers, the soldiers and officers participating in the operations were greatly astonished. No one had heard so much as a pistol shot coming from the direction of the village. The conclusion was drawn that "the Federal Counterintelligence Service was announcing the official version of the assault and at the same time preparing a basis for a decoration for their chief."[15]

One hostage actually was shot sometime earlier. An Avar, whose nerves were not holding out, grabbed an automatic weapon from one of the Chechen fighters and began firing. He killed two people and wounded several others before he himself was shot.

What took place next was nothing even remotely similar to an operation to free hostages. Journalists observing the operation from a distance reported that it was being conducted exactly like an assault on an enemy village, using all possible force and means. The hostages, positioned as a shield by the Chechens, received the brunt of it. In a January 18, 1996, report the *Izvestija* correspondent V. Jakov expressed this clearly: "The Special [Counterintelligence] Services, themselves not being capable of freeing the hostages, had somehow without being noticed passed on the responsibility for their actual destruction to the Federal Army."

After an hour of intensive bombardment by artillery, mortars, and air power, the Specnaz (special purpose group) soldiers began to move forward.

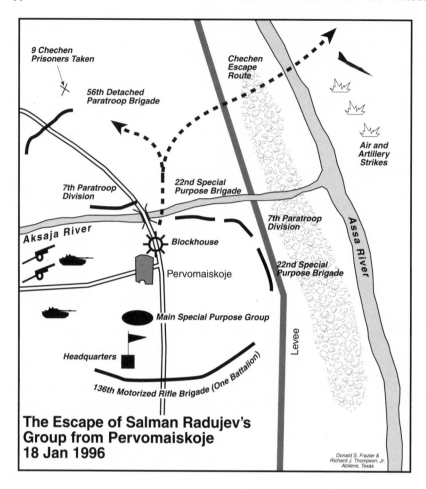

The Escape of Salman Radujev's Group from Pervomaiskoje 18 Jan 1996

Donald S. Frazier &
Richard J. Thompson, Jr.
Abilene, Texas

Under intensive Chechen fire, they succeeded in reaching the outskirts of the village. There they dug in and later were even able to reach almost the center of the village. At one point they were only about fifty meters from the mosque. But the armored equipment that was to support them somehow fell behind, and the generals commanding the operation decided to support their troops with artillery fire. The troops were struck by their own fire, and unable to withstand such "support," the special-purpose detachments began to withdraw. Chechen sniper bullets also took down some of the Specnaz troops. A portion of them did not return from the battle; others were carried out on the shoulders of their friends.

After a repeat artillery preparation of the village, the Russians attempted another attack, but this time the troops did not succeed in even nearing the village. The attackers took most of their losses not from Chechen fire but from their own artillery rounds and their helicopters' continuous fire of unguided rockets from the air.

The assaults of the village, interspersed with squalls of artillery and rocket fire, lasted three days. Later Ch. Israpilov reported that the village had been assaulted twenty-two times. The firefights had lasted for eighty-two hours without a break.

But the fiercest attack came the next day. On January 17, the Russians decided that most likely there were no more hostages left alive and so authorized use of the Grad rocket artillery systems.[16] The Chechens were left with no alternative but to try to break out at any cost, particularly since only positions in the area of the mosque and the school had been left under Chechen control. They were saved from destruction only by their covered entrenchments. The success of the breakout operation was enhanced by actions coordinated with the Chechen General Staff. Chechen reinforcement detachments arrived to help those besieged in the village of Pervomaiskoje to break out.[17]

During the night of January 17, one of these Chechen detachments struck the federal forces from the rear in the region of Sovietskoja village, some three kilometers from Pervomaiskoje. During the attack, the blocking post located there was destroyed. Attempts to break the siege were also made in other places. Using these, Radujev and Israpilov's group were able to break through not in the direction of Sovietskoja but toward the Terek River where a it was apparently least expected. At that time, thirty-seven Russian soldiers were positioned in this part of the encirclement ring. One small Chechen group also broke through in the direction of Bulat Jurt. The inhabitants of this village assisted the Chechens in crossing the Terek by boat to get to Chechnya.

Although the Chechens prepared and executed the breakout operation faultlessly from a military standpoint, it still resulted in large losses for them. The breakout had to be made through not only the encirclement ring but also three mine fields. The first fighters opened up the way for the others but at the price of their lives. While breaking through, the Chechens counted that they lost sixty-two fighters. Also, almost without a doubt, a Chechen kamikaze fighter group (a black-band formation dedicated to sacrifice their lives for their country) remained behind with the intention of drawing enemy fire to themselves. Some of the other Chechen fighters apparently were also unable to join up with the primary group in time.

The day after the breakout, shooting was still being heard in the village, and artillery and mortars continued to thunder. After that, the "cleansing" part of the operation began. "Cleansing" had become a slang term by then;

the process involved checking the cellars of houses, other structures, and supporting buildings and immediately opening fire at the slightest movement or sound.

How to Evaluate the Results

According to General Barsukov, 2,414 people participated in the operation against the terrorists fortified in the village of Pervomaiskoje. During the operation, 26 soldiers were killed and 95 were wounded. Again, the figures raise some doubts, as 106 wounded from the Pervomaiskoje battlefield were brought to the military hospital in the region of the Northern Airport in Grozni alone. The wounded were most likely taken to other hospitals as well. On January 23, 1996, the Russian daily newspaper *Sovietskaja Rosija* corrected these figures, stating that they only included the losses suffered by the Internal Affairs Ministry forces. The corrected figure was larger: 37 killed and 148 wounded. In the estimate of the Chechens, the number of Russian soldiers and militiamen killed and wounded should have been about 800. Four armored vehicles were also destroyed. Additionally, seven helicopters were mentioned as destroyed.[18]

The Russian High Command also reported that during the operation 153 Chechen hit men were killed and 30 captured (later this was lowered to 16). Apparently these casualty figures also included the hostages that were killed. It was later confirmed that the Chechens left behind the bodies of 38 fighters. The Chechens estimated their own losses as not more than 80 fighters killed. As to those taken prisoner, hostage witness reports indicate that not all the hostages were able to prove that they were not Chechen fighters. Almost all were immediately taken to the filtration camps and interrogated. Many of the freed hostages later contended that they were treated very harshly at these camps.

In all, according to information submitted by the Russians, 82 hostages were "freed." The actual number of hostages killed is not known, nor is the number of hostages taken along by the Radujev group to carry out the wounded and dead Chechen fighters during their breakout through the encirclement. (It obviously was necessary for the fighters to keep their hands free.) A portion of the hostages also voluntarily joined those attempting to break out through the encirclement, some even with weapons in hand. In their opinion, there had been no other alternative: if they had chosen to remain in the village, undoubtedly they would have been killed, as the village was going to be swept from the surface of the earth by artillery and mortar fire. Besides, they had already seen for themselves that the force attacking the village was not making any distinction between the Chechen fighters and the hostages: every movement was shot at. After the operation, 16 bodies of hostages were found.[19]

Once the attack began, the Chechens stopped guarding the hostages and allowed them to act according to their own judgment. To keep them prisoner while the Federal forces shot at the hostages was purposeless.

Upon arrival in Novogroznensk, some of the hostages were released, mostly those who had come out carrying weapons in their hands. Clearly, these people would never wish to admit that they had been hostages. The militiamen from Novosibirsk were declared prisoners. The Chechens decided to exchange them for the fighters who had been taken prisoner and for the bodies of those killed.[20]

After the operation finally concluded, 8 bodies were found in the village itself. Four were thought to be Chechen fighters. The local inhabitants found several more dead in the village and its surroundings after the Russian forces left.

The village of Pervomaiskoje, which had consisted of about 300 courtyards (houses and supporting structures were built around courtyards), was almost completely demolished. There was not one courtyard in which there were not dead animals. Upon their return, the inhabitants decided that it was not worthwhile to rebuild the village and that it would be better to reconstruct it somewhere else.[21]

Who Won in the Village of Pervomaiskoje?

On January 19, Yeltsin's interview given to the American television company ABC was broadcast on Russian television channel ORT (Russian community television). The Russian president, in evaluating the results of the Pervomaiskoje operation, remarked that he would categorically deny any allegation "that [Russian] soldiers were incapable, that they could not do anything right." In Moscow's official opinion, the operation had been executed and concluded successfully.

Was this in fact true?

The Pervomaiskoje operation executed by the federal forces has to be considered a complex undertaking made up of several disparate parts. All at one time, a special operation to free the hostages, a militia operation to detain and liquidate a terrorist group, and a purely military operation to assault a village that was occupied by the enemy were conducted.

A. Konovalov, director of Russia's Military Politics and Systematic Analysis Center, was correct in evaluating the special operation to free the hostages as a completely failure. No special measures, technical means, or methodology were used to free the hostages. The 82 "freed" hostages mentioned in official reports can hardly be considered to have been freed by the Russian forces. They were left alive more by chance than because of Russian efforts. A portion of them were released by the Chechens themselves and, once the assault began, another portion succeeded in hiding when the Chechens stopped guarding them.[22]

Also very curious is the fact that there is no official information as to the hostages that were killed. Reported were only the hostages that were released and those missing without a trace. Although the Russians counted the bodies of 153 Chechen fighters after the operation, they claimed to have found not even one hostage among them!

The results of the militia operation are also well known. In spite of Yeltsin's pronouncement that the terrorists under no circumstances would be allowed to break out of the encirclement and avoid responsibility for their terrorist acts, they did in fact break through and were able to return to Chechnya, even bringing with them some of the hostages. The operation to detain the terrorist group and to liquidate its core was thus less than a complete success.[23]

The scale of the Russian military operation was described by its commanders as an attack against a "battalion-strength defense position." But to equate Radujev's group by its number of people, weapons, equipment, and firepower to a battalion is possible only with a large dose of fantasy. Its defensive positions were only quickly dug entrenchments. Besides, a military operation must be seen as strangely conducted when the opponent is given ample time to dig in and five days to prepare to resist an attack and when one's own helicopters and artillery keep blowing up one's own troops, not to mention the poorly organized and executed coordination of one's own forces.[24] It should also be noted that the Russian force concentrated in the region of Pervomaiskoje was, by sheer numbers of troops, some twenty times larger than Radujev's fighter group.

Furthermore, the Russian force had not even been supplied with food, appropriate clothing for winter conditions, or shelters to get warm. The Russian soldiers were forced to feed off the animals they were able to kill. Some of the Specnaz groups even had to purchase fuel for their transport vehicles with their own money. The wounded soldiers at the medical field facility suffered more from the cold than from their wounds. Very telling are the casualties of the Internal Affairs Ministry's Moscow Special Purpose Detachment. Of its 50 soldiers, 4 were killed and 13 were wounded. Another 20, along with the commander, were hospitalized with a diagnosis of "frostbite of the hands and feet" and "pneumonia."

The Chechen defense of the village of Pervomaiskoje also demonstrated that it was possible to successfully resist a far superior force in even a small flatlands community that had not been prepared for defense in advance and that had become a defense position only by chance. Thus, how many forces and time would be required to take all of Chechnya's communities, especially in the mountains? Obviously, the prognosis of Dudajev and the Chechen High Command that the Federal Army could be resisted as much as was required was not without a firm basis in fact.

When the two Chechen military terrorist actions executed outside the borders of Chechnya are compared, it is apparent that in Budionovsk, the action was been conducted much more resolutely, much more ruthlessly. But in Budionovsk, the hostages were taken in an attempt to force the termination of the war in Chechnya. In Kizliar, the operation's purposes were cloudy. According to Dudajev, this was supposed to have been a purely military operation. However, even at its very start, it was clear that the operation could not be successfully completed, as the helicopters with the awaited cargo had not arrived. But perhaps this was only a justification of the operation in the eyes of the general population.

The Budionovsk incident was re-created in Kizliar only to the point that hostages were taken and a hospital was captured. But the purpose for the taking of hostages was different than in Budionovsk. In Pervomaiskoje, they were only taken in order to use them as a shield to secure passage back to Chechnya. These were two quite different actions.

Would terrorist actions outside of Chechnya's borders be repeated? Dudajev officially stated that such terrorist acts with the taking of hostages would be discontinued. Basajev also was reported as saying that there were sufficient matters in Chechnya itself.[25]

The Wave of Hostage Taking

Radujev's and Israpilov's force encircled in Pervomaiskoje was assisted not only by the rescue group sent by Maschadov. As soon as the assault of Pervomaiskoje began, the activity of the Chechen fighters also intensified on Chechen territory. Not only did the attacks and the shooting up of Russian positions become more frequent but the taking of hostages also began.[26]

On the morning of January 16, the Chechens took 38 Russian workers from Volgadonsk and Rostov by the Don and 2 Chechens hostage in the Kirov community electric power station on the outskirts of Grozni. The 2 Chechens were working for the Russians. They were taken in an unknown direction.[27] The next day, 37 Russian construction workers were taken hostage in the region of Achchoj Martan.

The Federal Army units in Chechnya were forced to show at least some activity. Their response was bombardment of the Centoroja community in the Nozhai Jurt region on January 17; about 70 people were killed in its marketplace. Preparations also began for the "cleansing" of Sernovodsk.

The Chechen group blockaded in Pervomaiskoje also received support from Turkey. On the evening of January 16, the ferry *Avrazija,* which was to sail to Sochi, was taken over by terrorists in Turkey's Trabzon Harbor. There were 255 people aboard, mostly Russian citizens. The 9-person terrorist group taking it over demanded that Chechnya be granted independence. They also threatened to shoot the passengers if the ferry did not put out to sea. They contacted Turkish television by telephone and stated that they would blow up the ferry in the Bay of Bosnia if the Chechen fighters held in encirclement in Dagestan were not freed. The ferry sailed out to sea but was continuously kept under surveillance and followed. When Radujev's group broke through the encirclement, the terrorists holding the ferry decided on January 19 to surrender to the Turkish government. On January 23, the ferry returned to Sochi.[28]

Upon Radujev's group's return to Novogroznensk, the government of Dagestan began negotiations for the freeing of hostages and succeeded in freeing some of them. The Chechens also agreed to free the militiamen who were taken hostage, first declaring them to be prisoners of war and then exchanging them for the Chechen fighters who were captured in the region of the village of Pervomaiskoje. This, however, could not be done until February 19, when the Russian Duma declared an amnesty for those Chechens who had participated in the Kizliar action.

According to Basajev, Radujev's operation had cost the Chechens 20,000 U.S. dollars. A part of this sum was used to bribe the militia posts along the way. There was also a widely publicized report in the press that Dudajev rewarded Radujev's group with 1.5 million U.S. dollars for their successfully executed operation.

On March 3, Radujev was seriously injured and, as was announced publicly, died three days later in the Urus Martan hospital. One of the field commanders, U. Chaschanov, who had been with him during the firefight was also killed.[29] Two different versions of Radujev's death surfaced.[30] One was that Radujev was attacked by the other Chechens who had participated with him in the action in Pervomaiskoje. This version contends that Radujev hid the reward paid out by Dudajev from his fellow terrorists, attempting to keep it for himself, and was killed out of revenge.[31]

The other version was that the operation to liquidate Radujev was planned and executed by soldiers of the Russian General Staff's Intelligence Command's (formerly GRU) Special Purpose Brigade. Reportedly, they pledged to seek revenge for the deaths of the 58th Army's intelligence commander, the commanders of two of its groups, and several of its soldiers near the village of Pervomaiskoje. Intelligence agents learned where Radujev's father lived, and one of the intelligence groups incited the attack of Radujev's father's home by people from an opposing teip. During the attack, Radujev's father was killed. It was expected that Radujev, upon learning of his father's death, would arrive at the funeral to meet out "blood vengeance." It was here that an ambush awaited him.[32] Later, this story goes, it became clear that Radujev had been only severely wounded. His recuperation lasted for a long time and, because of injuries, his face was reconstructed by plastic surgery. But upon recovery, he once again returned to Chechnya to carry on the battle.[33]

As sometimes happens, with time yet a new, even more surprising version was widely publicized in the Russian press.[34]

In the spring of 1997, the Russian daily *Komsomolskaja pravda* reported that the wounded Rudajev had been evacuated first to Dagestan, then via Azerbaijan to Turkey. He was then taken to Germany where he was "looked after" by the German Intelligence Service and treated at an American hospital near Munich. There he recovered. Then apparently on July 7, 1996, a Russian general and an accompanying colonel arrived in Berlin via a regular Aeroflot flight from Moscow and met there with a former Stasi operative. Together they traveled to Munich and met with Radujev and German intelligence personnel at a bar. An apparently voluntary turnover was completed. With passports provided by the Russians, Rudajev traveled in the company of the Russian general and colonel via automobile to Barcelona, where a new switch of passports was made. On July 9, 1996, the three allegedly flew back to Moscow. According to this version, Rudajev's unexpected reappearance in Chechnya was then organized, and he was reinserted the next day into Chechnya.

The unavoidable conclusion offered by the latter version is that Rudajev is now a secret agent of the Russian intelligence services and just perhaps had always been an Russian agent who was infiltrated into the Chechen armed forces from the very beginning of the conflict. But this could also be "disinformation" put out by the Russian security services.

On October 1, 1997, Radujev was again seriously injured when a bomb tore apart his car as it was pulling away from a hospital. He again recovered and continues to play an active role in Chechen affairs.

CHAPTER 15

The "Peace Protocols"

The sufficiently successfully completed Kizliar-Pervomaiskoje operation, once Radujev's group was able to break out of the encirclement, again strengthened the Chechens' will to resist.

At the end of January, 1996, a wave of protest demonstrations swept through almost all the Chechen communities. The participants demanded that the war actions be stopped and that the Russian Army be withdrawn from the republic. On February 4, all these protest demonstrations came together in Grozni. This was by far the largest demonstration since 1994, and about 35,000 to 50,000 people were reportedly gathered there. According to official Russian information, there were about 2,500 to 3,000 people. Martial law had been declared in the city but, nevertheless, about a thousand people remained in the Freedom Square even at night. Later, several thousand people also gathered in the square each day, determined to continue the demonstrations until the Russian army left Chechnya.[1]

Freedom Square was surrounded by OMON troops and armored vehicles, but no other control measures were taken, other than the surveillance of these events. Blocking posts were set up on the roads to Grozni and the guards were ordered to let through only people with special passes, but this did not cause much of a problem. For the soldiers, bottles of alcohol could be substituted for the passes.

On the fifth day of the protest, the Chechens began to construct barricades by collecting and piling stones, rebar construction steel, and other rubble. There was certainly no shortage of rubble from the many demolished buildings. But gradually the numbers of people at the meetings began to decrease. The demonstrations had lasted a week. On February 10, the demonstrators were driven back in buses to their homes in the outlying districts.[2] During the whole demonstration period, only a woman and her child were killed by an accidental explosion.

The demonstrations induced the Russian Military Command in Chechnya to respond, and on February 15, the pro-Moscow Chechen government decided to demolish the presidential palace, issuing an announcement that it was being torn down for safety reasons as the ruin posed a danger to passersby. But it was clear that they were seeking to destroy the symbol of Chechen resistance to the Russian Army. The Russian Army's demolition experts brought up several tons of trotyl explosive, but the Russian soldiers could not complete even this operation successfully. After a powerful explosion, only a third of the building fell. Even the ruins of the destroyed presidential palace were resisting the Russian soldiers.[3]

The echoes of the demonstrations also reached Moscow. On February 7 during the height of the demonstrations, a group led by Chernomyrdin was formed at a meeting of the Russian Security Council and assigned to investigate how to regulate the situation in Chechnya by peaceful means. The group was to prepare a plan in two weeks.[4]

Novogroznensk

While Moscow was deliberating the regulation of the situation in Chechnya by peaceful means, the federal army was increasing its pressure against the communities. It demanded that they give up their weapons and threatened that if they did not, force would be used. The manner by which force would be applied was by then well-known: continuous and long-term bombardment of the communities by artillery and from the air and, after that, a "cleansing" operation. However, not all the communities were being threatened, only those that had not yet signed the "peace protocols." This was a new method of putting pressure on the Chechen fighters.

The pro-Moscow Doku Zavgajev government began negotiating with the regional administrations for the signing of "peace protocols." Once such protocols were signed, the region was proclaimed a peace zone and given a guarantee that the Federal Army would not shoot up or bombard the communities within the zone. This was obviously conditioned in each case upon the hit men leaving them. The communities who signed the protocols were also obligated to allow Internal Affairs detachments to "convince" themselves of the absence of the hit men by checking the documents of all the inhabitants in the communities and to search their homes for weapons caches. In this way, the Russians attempted to push the Chechen fighters out of the communities and force them to return to the mountains, isolating them from the flatlands and foothills regions.

Attempting to effectuate such a plan to "peacefully regulate the situation," Doku Zavgajev's government signed a "peace protocol" on February 12 with the regional administration of Gudermes. The negotiations had lasted all week. Once the protocols were signed, units of the Federal Army began to check the region's communities and search for weapons caches. They succeeded in checking this region's Gerzen Jurt, Koshkeldy, Kadi Jurt, and Engel Jurt villages, but the community administrations of Novogroznensk, Centoroja, Aleroja, and others refused to allow the Russians to do the same in their settlements.

Attempting to check Novogroznensk on February 16 by force, the Federal Army was met with fire, even mortar and artillery fire. Ten Russian soldiers were killed, 8 were wounded, and several of their armored vehicles were burned up. Confrontations began when the Russian Army units surrounded not only Novogroznensk but also the nearby villages of Suvorov Jurt, Bachi Jurt, and Centoroja, leaving only corridors by which peaceful inhabitants could leave.

The assault of Novogroznensk was begun the next day, but after meeting strong Chechen resistance, it was called off. After that began the daily bombardment of the city by Grad rocket artillery and by air strikes in preparation for a new assault.[5] It was important for the Federal Army to take the city— but not only because the Chechens had refused to lay down their arms there and because there was a sizable group of Chechen fighters in the city, about 300. After breaking through the encirclement in Pervomaiskoje, Radujev's group had come straight to Novogroznensk with their hostages. Also both Basajev and Maschadov often and openly visited the town. It was thought that Maschadov's temporary headquarters was in this town. Besides, the Federal Army had to take blood revenge for its shame at Pervomaiskoje.[6]

The operation against the city was planned at the Russian High Command and the headquarters of the Northern Caucasus Military Region. Because of its connection with Radujev, the operation against Novogroznensk became a continuation of the Gudermes-Kizliar-Pervomaiskoje chain. Without a doubt, this was not being announced publicly. Officially, the reason for the operation was announced by the commander of the Federal Forces Group, General Viacheslav Tichomirov. He accused the Chechens of violating the peace protocols.[7]

Novogroznensk, in which about 10,000 people had lived until the war, was exceptional in that throughout the war, it had stayed opposed to both the Federal Army and the pro-Moscow Chechen opposition government. After the takeover of Gudermes in the spring of 1995, this small city remained the only community along the Rostov-Baku highway still controlled by the supporters of Dudajev. The Chechen fighters in Novogroznensk openly went around armed.

According to the Chechen field commander N. Edilchadzhijev, the city was not very well adapted for defense as it did not have cellars in its houses or serious defense fortifications, even entrenchments. For this reason no preparations were made to defend it, and by agreement with the inhabitants, the Chechen fighters left the city the night before the assault. Only about 60 fighters remained behind.

The assault began on February 20, and by the next day, the operation was concluded.[8] The cleansing of the city then began. But neither Maschadov, Basajev, nor Radujev was found in the city as had been expected. The Internal Affairs Ministry soldiers then took 38 local inhabitants who looked suspicious into custody. Sometime later, after a request from the inhabitants, 18 people were released. The Russian soldiers kept the others in custody in the buildings of the wine factory.

There was no information reported as to how many Russian soldiers were killed. Only the Defense Ministry announced that during the Novogroznensk operation conducted February 17–21, 4 of its soldiers were killed and 19 wounded. The Internal Affairs Ministry did not report any losses, but according to the Defense Ministry, they were much larger than those suffered by its units. It is only known that the Federal Army Command admitted that from February 16 until the beginning of the attack, it lost 30 killed during the operation. It also reported that Chechen losses were 200 fighters killed.

The Chechens themselves reported that 6 of their fighters were killed and that Russian losses were 300 soldiers, The local inhabitants confirmed that 20 Chechen fighters were killed.[9] Nothing is mentioned about the casualties of the local inhabitants.

However, contrary to what was contended by the Russians, a corridor had not been opened up prior to the assault to enable the local inhabitants to leave the city. Instead, trying to force the inhabitants to turn against the fighters, the Russians told them that this would be done only after the inhabitants disarmed the hit men. But when a flood of women and children began to flow from the city, they were not fired upon.[10]

For several days after the operation ended, no one was allowed into the city, not even journalists. The cleansing of Novogroznensk had turned into a plunder and pillage operation.[11] After Novogroznensk began the bombardment of Centoroja and Aleroja.[12] The "signing of peace protocols" process was continued.

Sernovodsk

At the end of February, the Federal Army also intensified its activity in the western part of Chechnya, where its most important objectives became Sernovodsk and Bamut, both of which had managed to hold out since the very beginning of the war. The Federal Army's Southwest group was commanded by General Artiomov.

At the same time that the Bamut operation began, the Federal Army once again encircled Sernovodsk. The Russians contended that concentrated in this city was one of the strongest Chechen fighter groups, about 250 to 300 (other sources say 660) fighters, although local inhabitants contended that only a 50–60-man self-defense group was present in it.

Sernovodsk was a resort city with little strategic value. It was also unclear to which administration it rightly belonged. It was right on the Chechen and Ingushian border, which had not yet been clearly delineated, and some considered it to be part of Chechnya, others Ingushia. Since the start of the war, Russian soldiers had not set foot in the city, as the Elders' Council had entered into peace agreements with all sides. The city had thus become a center for refugees. Before the war, some 15,000 people had lived in Sernovodsk, but with the influx of refugees, this number grew to some 30,000.[13]

The Russians first encircled the city and afterwards repeated the Novogroznensk tactic. First, an ultimatum was issued, and then the Russian troops began to bombard and shoot up the city. These preparations lasted for three days. Some of the inhabitants were allowed to leave the city through a corridor. In all, about 15,000 people succeeded in leaving the city before and during the encirclement.[14]

On the morning of March 5, it was announced that the operation in Sernovodsk was almost completed, that active combat was no longer taking place, and that only the cleansing of the city was continuing.[15] Cleansing operations in Chechnya had already become a daily occurrence. They were usually conducted by OMON units and the special fast-reaction groups. To "clean out" a community, street, or neighborhood meant to conduct a search for weapons and fighters. Without a doubt this was a very complex undertaking, especially in districts containing multistory buildings and where there were many cellars or complex underground utility and other communications networks. The cleansing was done under the cover of armored vehicles, the Russian troops being divided into teams. As the armored vehicles crawled along the street in a wedge, soldiers in threes quickly moved forward from one cover to another while the others kept watch of the surroundings through their gun sights. After that, the next team of three followed, and so on. Most of their attention was focused on the openings in the walls, on windows, and on the cellars. The Chechens most often fired from there, and the Russians needed no further convincing that their shots were very accurate. For this reason, fire was opened up almost immediately at the slightest suspicion. During such cleansing operations, most of the attention was placed on the men, as all of them were suspected of being Chechen fighters. Once they were taken into custody, they were carefully searched for telltale marks—calluses on their fingers and bruises on their shoulders—indicating the frequent use of firearms. In each cleansing unit were assigned operational specialists called "owls," whose function was to work with the local inhabitants and the prisoners. These were human intelligence specialists running informer nets.

But before the Russians could finish with Sernovodsk, the Chechens began their operation in Grozni. The Chechens had also intensified their activity in the communities of Urechov, Komsomolskoja, Alchazurov, Urus Martan, Goichi, and Gajskoja. Thus the Russians were forced to cut short the cleansing part of their operation in Sernovodsk. The Chechen fighters also decided to withdraw their remaining forces from the city. Once it became convinced that the Chechen fighters had actually left, the Federal Military Command, on March 11, allowed the local inhabitants to reenter Sernovodsk.

The nature of the cleansing operation conducted in Sernovodsk is indicated by the fact that, after its conclusion, 140 men from Sernovodsk who earlier had no intentions of fighting the Russian Army took up weapons and joined the ranks of the fighters.[16]

Grozni

A special role in the Chechen spring of 1996 campaign was assigned to the Chechen operation conducted March 6–10 in Grozni.[17] The scrupulously planned and executed Grozni operation was intended to show that such continuous and intensive shooting up and bombardment of Chechen villages as had been done in Novogroznensk and was being continued in Sernovodsk would not go unanswered. Also, it was to be a response to the pro-Moscow opposition government and the Federal Army Command for their year of using force to make the regional and village administrations sign "peace protocols." Third, the taking of Grozni was to demonstrate once again that Dudajev's forces were not beaten down and were able to conduct large-scale operations at any time and in any location, even in Grozni itself, and that the initiative remained in the hands of the Chechens. The choice of the time when the operation was to be conducted was decided in part by Russian defense minister Grachev's visit to Grozni. It was announced during the visit that Grachev was prepared to meet with Dudajev at any time and at any place. The Chechen fighters' entry into Grozni immediately after Grachev's departure from Grozni was to be understood as a positive answer to his invitation to meet.

Maschadov planned the operation not only scrupulously but also secretly. The preparations were made in advance, and some even began immediately after war activity stopped and while the negotiations were taking place. Chechen fighters began to concentrate in Grozni, returning as peaceful inhabitants. They then went about building up weapons caches in hideouts prepared in advance. A large number of the Chechen fighters also obtained employment in the Republican Internal Affairs Ministry system then being formed by the pro-Moscow Chechen government.[18]

Only several of the high-level Chechen field commanders knew about the upcoming operation. Command of the operation was assigned to Basajev. Entry into the capital was to be forced from three directions. Ruslan Gelajev was given command of the group operating from the direction of Chernorechje as Radujev, who had been previously assigned to command this group, had been seriously injured. Vacha Arsanov was assigned to command the breakthrough from the direction of the community of Berdakela, and his forces were to take positions in the Oktiabrsk district. The group commanded by Achmed Zakajev was to force its way through the Sunzha ridge into the district of Staropromyslovsk and to take it. The Chechens concentrated some 350 to 600 fighters in these assault groups.

Formally, the Federal Army Group in Grozni had been preparing for a possible Chechen attack. It was provided in the Grozni Defense Plan, confirmed December 26, 1995, that the Internal Affairs Army's 4th Tactical Group under the command of the commandant of the Chechen Republic, Colonel Protogen Andrejevski, would have to cut off the entry of the Chechen forces groups into the city. The Internal Affairs Force consisted of about 5,000 troops, but, given the need, it was to be reinforced by a Defense Ministry brigade and regiment.[19]

In planning the operation, the Chechen General Staff took into consideration the specific weaknesses of the Grozni Defense Plan. It was possible to enter Grozni along almost 100 streets, but in the defense plan, measures were taken to control only 22 primary exit points, at which blocking posts were set up. The approaches to the control posts were not mined, and barriers were not set up that could not be blown up. The units dislocated in the city also lacked sufficient armored equipment.

The operation began the morning of March 6. At 5:25 A.M., the defense positions of the detachment dislocated at Minutka Square were shot up. From 6 to 10 A.M., seven control posts were put under fire and the military base in the city was harshly shot up.

Having forced their way into the city from three directions, the Chechen groups in a short space of time took over three of the four districts of Grozni: Staropromyslovsk, Zavodskaja, and Oktiabrsk. By 9 A.M., the Zavodskaja and Oktiabrsk district militia offices were also taken over. Within several hours after the start of the attack, the Chechens had taken control of about 80 percent of the territory of the city, destroyed some 20 armored vehicles, and taken all the bridges across the Sunzha River. Almost all the blocking posts were surrounded.

The Chechen execution of the operation was made markedly less difficult by the fact that the designated federal reinforcement units were not in Grozni at that time. The brigade and regiment assigned to this task by the defense plan were conducting assignments in other areas: near Novogroznensk, Chasavjurt, and Vladikaukaz. Once the attack began, the command of the Defense Ministry Forces could assist the troops in the city with only two reinforced battalions and with helicopters and mortar fire.

Having blockaded the Federal Army units in their deployment areas and at their posts, the Chechen fighters were able to move about freely in the city and organize ambushes without hindrance for Russian columns moving to assist those under siege. The ambushed columns lost several armored vehicles and armored personnel carriers. The Russians were especially hurt by the Chechen ambush in the region of the Kredit bank, where one armored vehicle was knocked out and two motor vehicles destroyed.

By noon, several government buildings were taken, as well as the Chechen Republic's television station. At 2 P.M., Dudajev went on the air and announced that the attack was being conducted by his order. Speaking on television after Dudajev, the Chief of Staff Maschadov stated that the Russians had lost about 500 troops while the Chechens had lost 1 killed and 4 wounded. He added that as all the planned assignments had been accomplished ahead of schedule, it was possible even then for the Chechen forces to leave the city.[20]

Toward evening, the Chechens cut off Grozni's telephone and radio communications with the outside world. Events in the city sank into the unknown. That evening, fighting took place some 300 meters from the presidential palace. The harshest fighting during daylight hours took place in Minutka Square and in the region of the blocking post near which the attempt on General Romanov had taken place.

As was reported in the press, during the first day of confrontations, 26 Internal Affairs Army troops were killed and 50 wounded; later this was corrected to 107 wounded. Also 82 construction workers were taken hostage in the very center of the city. The Grozni defense contingent, which up to the attack had consisted of more than 3,500 Internal Affairs army soldiers, militiamen, and members of the OMON, was rendered powerless. In the district of Zavodsk, the Chechen fighters even besieged an entire special-purpose battalion.

The Chechen militiamen hired by the opposition government, however, did not even attempt to fight. For example, on March 6, the local OMON group drove out with 4 militia vehicles to the Staropromyslovsk district and, upon meeting there with the Chechen fighters, fired their weapons for show and then gave over to the fighters their brand new Uazik vehicles. Together with the fighters, they then robbed a bank.

On March 7, the shooting up of the control posts continued. At 11:30 A.M., the 7th Post was completely destroyed. At 12:40, the soldiers manning the 13th Post were forced to withdraw to the Zavodskaja District Commandant's Headquarters. At 2 P.M., the troops of the 6th Post were also forced to withdraw.[21]

The commandant, Colonel Protogen Andrejevski, was forced to call for assistance. On March 7 at 11 A.M., he reported to the commander of the Internal Affairs Army Group in Chechnya, General Major Pankov, that the Defense Ministry units were not rendering assistance and that it had been impossible to reach the commander of the Defense Ministry Group, General Tichomirov, or the commander of the 205th Brigade, Colonel Nazarov.

Having accomplished that which had been planned, on March 7 the Chechen fighters began to withdraw from the center of the city, and on March 10, the primary Chechen forces left the city itself. The Federal Forces Command in Chechnya announced that the city had been liberated from the Chechen groups thanks to the resolute efforts of the Federal Forces and that on March 8, a reinforced battalion had been inserted into the city and had joined the combat action. However, this was not very believable, as the Chechens had not attempted to hold the city and risk losing their best forces during protracted battles. They had only attempted to demonstrate their might.

In order to minimize the importance of the Chechen victory, the Russians reported that during the Grozni assault operation, Federal Forces suffered 14 dead and 22 wounded while the Chechens took ten times that number of casualties. But these figures were negated by the Russian daily *Komsomolskaja pravda* (March 12, 1996), which reported that the real losses were more than 100 Russian soldiers killed, more than 220 wounded, and 47 still missing in action. The Chechens had taken about the same losses. As had become the practice, no one even bothered to count how many civilians were killed.[22]

The Russians' announced casualty figures were also negated by other sources. Just at the blocking post at the edge of Katajama, 24 soldiers were killed and 25 wounded from the Nizhnegorodsk District's Special Purpose

Fast Reaction Detachment. On March 13, the unit from Jekaterinburg buried 10 OMON soldiers who were killed during the assault. They had been ambushed while accompanying a column with munitions, but the bodies were not retrieved until March 9. After the operation conducted by the Chechens in Grozni, Days of Mourning were proclaimed in three districts of Russia.[23]

When the Russia's Military Prosecutor's Office began its investigation of the causes for the Federal Group's failures, it became clear that during March 6–11, 97 Russian soldiers were killed and 331 wounded; of these, the Internal Affairs Army lost 48 soldiers killed and 230 wounded. During the operation, the Chechens destroyed 21 combat vehicles. Twenty Chechen militiamen and 250 peaceful civilians also died.

Ambushes of Russian Columns

Because of the forced signing of the peace protocols, the Chechen military commanders were forced to seek new and more effective combat tactics. The tactic of ambushing large enemy columns was chosen.[24] The successfully executed earlier operations in Gudermes, Pervomaiskoje, Novogroznensk, and Grozni, where the enemy had sustained large losses, raised the Chechens' confidence in their own might. They had already gained sufficient experience in conducting ambushes. The basic requirements for success and effectiveness in conducting ambushes were well-organized intelligence, scrupulous operational planning and preparation, surprise, and camouflage. Two locations for ambushes were used: in the communities and along the columns' movement routes.

The blackest day for the Federal Army after the New Year Grozni assault was March 16, 1996, when ambushes were executed in Staryj Achkhoj and Samashk. During that single day, 55 Russian soldiers were killed and about 200 were wounded.[25] The casualties in Staryj Achkhoj were suffered by units of the 19th Motorized Rifle Division after they entered the city in one column and stopped near the school. The Chechen attack was not expected, and, having opened up fire from ambush, the Chechen grenade launcher marksmen kept firing without opposition. The remnants of the column barely managed to break out of the town, leaving 15 knocked-out armored vehicles, 27 dead soldiers and officers, and 76 wounded behind. An Internal Affairs Ministry column was similarly shot up in Samashk, with 28 soldier killed and 118 wounded.

Another reason for attacks from ambushes of columns along the movement routes was to create such conditions that the Federal Army units could not hold out for long in the mountains because of the problem of resupply. Basajev stated openly that all means would be taken to cut the supply lines bringing stores, munitions, and fuel into the mountains. This threat began to be put into effect with the destruction of a Federal Army column in the region of Vedeno on the night of March 30.

Even larger losses were suffered on April 16 when the Chechens executed an ambush of a column of the 245th Motorized Rifle Brigade in the region of Shatoja about 15 kilometers to the south of Jarysh Mardy.[26] Russian defense minister Grachev was forced to admit that large losses had been suffered: 53 Russian soldiers were killed and 52 wounded. However, after a criminal action was filed, the Military Prosecutor's Office set the losses at 95 soldiers killed, of which 26 had been officers. The press reported approximately the same figures.[27]

Because of such large losses, a furor broke out even in Russia's Duma, to which the defense minister was called on April 19. After Grachev's report, the Duma appointed a commission to investigate the circumstances of the destruction of the column. For this reason, more complete information as to this combat episode is available.

Upon arriving at Chankala Airport on April 15, the column was issued supplies for the supplementation of the reserves of the 245th Regiment. They were issued 6 motor vehicles with munitions, 4 gasoline trucks loaded with fuel, 4 motor vehicles with supplies for the armored equipment, and 2 motor vehicles with clothing and ammunition. The next day the column began its journey back to its dislocation area.

All told, the column consisted of 30 combat and other vehicles. Besides the previously mentioned vehicles, the column included 3 tanks, 4 armored vehicles, 1 infantry combat command vehicle, 1 combat intelligence vehicle, 1 paratroop armored vehicle, and several other special-purpose vehicles. Traveling with the column were 199 soldiers: 29 officers, 17 warrant officers, and 153 soldiers and sergeants, for the most part "contractors." Security along the return route was to be provided by two permanent blocking posts to the north of the village of Chishkj and to the south of the village of Zona. The column's senior officer was the regiment commander's assistant for weaponry, Major Terzovec.

By 1:30 P.M., the column successfully arrived at the central base of the 324th Regiment, where one more motorized rifle company from this regiment, coming back from their combat shift in the region of the community of Gojskoja, attached itself to the column.

After an hour, just having passed through the village of Jarysh Mardy, the column's forward movement was stopped when the first armored vehicle was knocked out. Immediately thereafter, the command vehicle was also hit and set on fire, killing the column's commander and his staff. Communications with the regiment were broken off.

Upon hearing the sound of explosions, the commander of the 245th Regiment, Colonel Lieutenant Romanichin, ordered the commander of an intelligence company at a temporary blocking post in the Argun gorge to move in the direction of the column to investigate the situation and, if need be, assist the column. However, the company commander soon reported that at 3:30 P.M. on the southern outskirts of Jarysh Mardy, the company was stopped by Chechen fire. One soldier was injured and the company was forced to take up defensive positions while surrounded. At 4 P.M., to rescue the column, the commander of the regiment sent out an armored column consisting of 2 tanks and 6 armored vehicles with the 2nd Battalion commander and his forces up in front. At 4:50, the battalion commander reported that two Chechen machine guns were destroyed by tank fire on the southern outskirts of Jarysh Mardy and that at 5:30, they came out by the column. At about the same time, the column was reached by another column of 2 tanks and 4 armored vehicles from the neighboring 324th Motorized Rifle Regiment. One Mi-8 helicopter and 2 Mi-24s were also sent to assist the ambushed column. At 6 P.M., the Chechens withdrew.

Officially, it was announced that the Chechens burned 1 tank, 6 armored vehicles, an armored intelligence vehicle, and 13 motor vehicles. Correspondents later visiting the scene of the tragedy counted 37 still burning vehicles. These numbers were, in fact, slightly exaggerated, as another column had been burned in the same place and under much the same circumstances the year before, also in April, during the beginning of the assault on Shatoja. Apparently some of the vehicles destroyed the year before had once again caught fire.

The results of this battle were impressive: 70 percent of all the motorized equipment was destroyed. About 50 percent of all the troops in the column were killed. There is other information that after April 16, the remains of 163 soldiers were taken to various districts of Russia. A commission formed in the Russian Duma accused not only the commands of the regiment and the military group in Chechnya but also the Defense Ministry of being responsible for these casualties. The commission's report noted that negligence and tactical incompetence was rampant in the Federal Army Group and the regiment itself, that there had been no coordination between the units, and that vigilance had been absent.

The report also noted that from the time the regiment was sent to Chechnya it lost 220 soldiers. This had been the third severe blow the regiment sustained just during the past four months. The first had been when, after attacking the 24th Blocking Post and killing 12 regiment troops and wounding 8, the Chechens disarmed the other guards and took 31 soldiers prisoner. The second was when 24 soldiers were killed, 41 were wounded, and 3 became missing in action during the battle for the village of Gojskoja.

One more painful attack against a column was executed the morning of May 5. The Chechen force attacking a column on the road from Gudermes to Argun destroyed 15 armored vehicles and captured a large number of weapons.

The "Effectuation" of Yeltsin's Peace Plan

As the election campaign for the Russian presidency began, the most important "wild card" affecting Yeltsin's candidacy was the problem of the war in Chechnya. There were few grounds to believe that he could be reelected without solving this problem. Thus on March 31, Yeltsin announced on television his plan to regulate the crisis in Chechnya as he had promised to do earlier.[28] The next day, he signed a decree legalizing the announced program.

Seven basic means were provided in Yeltsin's plan to regulate the crisis in Chechnya:

1. To terminate military operations by March 31 at midnight.
2. To gradually withdraw the Federal Army from the "peaceful" regions to areas outside the administrative borders of Chechnya.
3. After preparations, to elect the parliament of the Chechen Republic.
4. To recommend that the country's Duma declare an amnesty for the participants in the armed actions who had not committed serious crimes.
5. To give financial and material support only to those regions where stabilization of the situation was achieved.
6. To prepare and sign a agreement granting Chechnya exceptional status in its relationships between the federal government and the authorized representatives of the Chechen Republic.
7. To create a government commission led by Premier Chernomyrdin that would be given the control of the regulation of the situation in Chechnya.[29]

During the signing of the decree, a provision for negotiations with Dudajev through intermediaries was added. The decree contained not one word, however, about the recognition of the independence of Chechnya or the unconditional and immediate withdrawal of the Federal Army. There was, in fact, nothing new in it, except, perhaps, that it finally agreed to negotiate with Dudajev. Such a plan was obviously unacceptable to the Chechens. That same night, it was answered with attacks against the Russian military units.[30]

Russia's Military Command did not even attempt to execute the president's decree or to stop military activity. To the contrary, the confrontations only intensified. Already the next day, fierce battles began near Vedeno, where, during the day's fighting, more than 30 Russian soldiers were killed and 75 were wounded.

On April 2, the Federal Army began an operation in southeastern Chechnya.[31] The Federal Army's assault was conducted in three primary directions: in the southwest, against Bamut; in the south, against Vedeno; in the southeast, against Dargo.

The Federal Army Group commanded by General Major Vladimir Shamanov attacked in the southwest. This group consisted of about 5,000 Russian soldiers and officers. According to Russian intelligence information, about 4,000 hit men were concentrated in this part of Chechnya, and the group still had 2 tanks, several armored vehicles, antiaircraft guns, and other equipment.

As usual, the Russian Army, after approaching a village, would concentrate all its available firepower (artillery guns, self-propelled artillery, tanks, mortars, salvos from Grad and Uragan artillery systems, air strikes by close air support aircraft) onto the Chechen positions. Afterwards, the village would be blockaded by the Motorized Rifle Brigade Assault Groups with support from tanks. After destroying the Chechen fighters on the outskirts of the village and after taking the surrounding heights, Internal Affairs detachments would be sent into the village to conduct a cleansing operation. But as usual, even in the larger villages, almost no inhabitants were ever found except for the elderly.

The Chechen tactics in the mountains were to operate in small groups of some 20 people and included attacks of Russian unit columns and positions, the execution of ambushes on mountain roads, and the blowing up of roads in hard-to-approach places. The fighters operated on foot and with light weaponry (sniper rifles, grenade launchers, and mortars).

Already, the first day of the planned assault, units of the Federal Army's Southwest Group, supported by artillery and fire from aircraft, moved 10 kilometers into the mountains and took over the communities of Sajasano, Centoroja, and Belgatoja.

During the Belgatoja assault operation, the 136th Motorized Rifle Brigade lost 10 soldiers killed and about 15 wounded. The Chechens also knocked out 3 tanks and an armored vehicle. A bit earlier in the same place, 3 armored vehicles from the 135th Motorized Rifle Brigade were ambushed by the Chechens and burned up, together with their crews. The cleansing of the villages was conducted by the Internal Affairs Ministry's 8th Special Purpose Detachment, also named the Rusj. The 131st Maikop Brigade, which had been almost destroyed during the New Year's assault of Grozni, also participated along this attack direction. After a year, it had again been sent to Chechnya.

On April 4, the Federal Forces had already neared the villages of Dargo, Benoja, and Tavzen Kala. The assault of the regions of Ca Vedeno and Elistanzhi was stopped, but the Chechen positions began to be fiercely bombed from the air. During the bombings, the villages of Machet, Salazha, and Kadyr Jurt were almost completely destroyed. Refugees began to stream from Dargo, Belgatoja, Ca Vedeno, and Vedeno into the flatlands.[32]

Shamil Basajev explained quite simply and clearly the intensification of the Federal Army's activity after Yeltsin's order to terminate them: "Russia is a land of miracles. There, if they say one thing, they will necessarily do otherwise."

What was being sought by this operation was also not fully understood by Chechnya's chief of staff, General Maschadov. In his opinion, it was hard to explain the logic of this military operation, particularly when Chechen detachments were being forced to defend in the mountains while the largest portion of the Chechen fighters were in the flatlands. The Russian units were forcing their way forward, taking large casualties, while the Chechen groups were moving in the opposite direction and into their rear areas. While descending from the mountains, the Russian units would again have to fight for every community and mount assaults against them. This was clearly a purposeless massacre of Russian soldiers. This was equally mystifying to the Chechen fighters. Some of them even began to suspect that the Federal Army, after breaking though the Chechen defenses, was preparing to exit through the gorges into Dagestan.

Apparently, even after a year and a half of war, the Russians still did not understand that they could not destroy the Chechen fighters without destroying the whole Chechen nation.

Only on April 6 did Russia's defense minister Grachev sign the order to terminate combat activity. The order had been delayed for almost a week after the president's decree to terminate war activity. This was how much time was needed to execute the planned and prepared operation in the mountains.

CHAPTER 16

War during Negotiations

Although by decree of Russian president Boris Yeltsin, combat actions were officially terminated as of April 1, skirmishes and confrontations continued in Chechnya. The towns and villages that in the opinion of the Russian federal High Command were sheltering groups of Chechen fighters continued to be put under siege. This situation, however, was eased somewhat by Russian defense minister Pavel Grachev's order of April 6 to terminate combat actions.

The termination of combat actions should have meant that negotiations to regulate the situation by peaceful means would begin, as had been announced in Yeltsin's plan. But they did not take place. Neither were any concrete measures taken to begin them, although there was much discussion about the fact that they would start. The intensity of the skirmishes and confrontations decreased somewhat, but the situation in Chechnya remained tense and unclear. What would happen with the negotiations became even more unclear when, on April 21, the president of the Chechen Republic of Ichkerija, Dzhochar Dudajev, was killed.[1] Vice President Zelimchan Jandarbijev, officially took over the duties of president, as specified in the Chechen Constitution. Much depended on what position the new leader would take.

Dzhochar Dudajev's death brought a wave of confusion. Before it could settle, another wave of confusion swept up: on April 29, the pro-Moscow Chechen opposition government announced that Dudajev's successor, Jandarbijev, had also been killed. Only after several days did it become clear that it had been Jandarbijev's nephew who had been shot to death.

This confusion stalled the beginning of negotiations, but it was becoming obvious that Russia was in no hurry to begin them. The command of the Combined Federal Forces in Chechnya was strongly disposed against them and was basing its opposition on two basic arguments. According to the command, a complete cease-fire and the withdrawal of its units from Chechnya at this time would, in effect, nullify all the successes the Federal Army had achieved. The Chechen fighters would then be given the opportunity to regroup once more and prepare for new battles. Additionally, an even larger barrier, in its opinion, to the start of any negotiations was the fact that it was practically impossible to completely terminate combat actions immediately.

A number of the Chechen field commanders also did not expect much from negotiations, having been disappointed by the results of the negotiations that began after the Budionovsk operation. Shamil Basajev had best expressed their opinion: "I am for the continuation of combat operations without interruption. I was against the negotiations from the very start as they only interrupted our fighters' tempo. . . . They [the Russians] only use the negotiation to catch their breath. This helps them but not us." [2] He, like most of the commanders, was convinced that the war would end only then when the last Russian soldier was driven from Chechnya. In other words, neither side believed in the possibility of terminating combat actions by means of negotiations.

In reality, the Federal Forces Command was not ready to heed the instructions of either the Russian president or the defense minister, arguing that the Russian forces were being forced to ignore these instruction because of the continuing attacks by the Chechens. At least this was what the Russian people were being told. The Chechens, it was suggested, were themselves to blame for the continuation of combat actions.

Battles continued in the Vedeno region and in Bamut. For more than two weeks from the end of April into early May, Shali was blockaded—and obviously not without the efforts of Doku Zavgajev. On April 16, Shali became the center of efforts to unify the Chechens, although Zavgajev was excluded from the talks. For the first time, the various Chechen political forces united and signed a document outlining a program in which provision was made for a moratorium of further combat actions, for bilateral negotiations between Russia and Chechnya at the highest levels, for the withdrawal of the Russian Army, and for Chechen parliamentary elections. The document was signed by representatives of all the political forces, from the field commanders to the supporters of Ruslan Khasbulatov.[3]

The signing of this document did not help the city of Shali to avoid the threat of an assault. But an assault was nevertheless avoided when the Chechen fighters decided to voluntarily leave the city and the city administration agreed to give up its weapons. Once 80 firearms were collected, an agreement was reached allowing the Russian forces to check the identity papers of the inhabitants. Urus Martan, which had stayed neutral during all the war actions but which had twice been bombed intensively, followed suit.

Not only in Shali but in the other communities as well, the weapons that were being turned in were only those that were bought for this purpose from the Russian soldiers. The weapons surrender process was only a formality. Its most important aspect was to document the fact of the surrender of the weapons, allowing the Federal Army Command to report back that, after all, it was successfully executing its mission of "disarming the illegal armed formations." The commanders of Russian units often agreed to accept money instead of weapons from some of the communities, including Kurchaloja, Geldygen, Mairtup, and Bachi Jurt. The Chechens often surrendered brand-new weapons that had never been fired. Later, these same weapons invariably found their way back into the hands of the Chechens and were once again surrendered. This was, after all, a good business for the commands of the Russian Internal Affairs Ministry units.[4]

The attempt to disarm the Chechens was used to justify the continuation of the use of force, which for the Chechens also meant new civilian casualties, an increase in the stream of refugees, and the further destruction of its communities. On March 28, 1996, the commander of the Northern Caucasus Military Region, General Colonel Anatoli Kvashnin, in an interview with the Russian daily *Izvestija,* attempted to minimize the effects of the Russian actions by saying that force had been used only against 15 communities. But if the use of force is to be understood as only the assault of cities and villages defended by Chechen fighters, not counting the communities that were bombed from the air or bombarded by artillery, even then armed force was used against no fewer than 50 Chechen settlements. In these communities, about 70 percent of all that was necessary in order to live in them (dwellings, personal property, and so forth) was destroyed.

With the presidential elections drawing near, continuing the use of force was not very convenient, especially as these actions were not inflicting any definable damage to the Chechen fighters. As the war in Chechnya could also become a very real barrier to Yeltsin's victory in the polls, the Russian leadership found it worthwhile to take some real measures to stabilize the situation. Thus three divisions were withdrawn from the Vedeno region in early May, leaving only one in the region. This meant that large battles would no longer take place in this region. But it actually did not make much of a difference whether one or four divisions were deployed in this region as, in either case, they were not able to destroy the Chechen formations commanded by Basajev that were operating there.

In the background of skirmishes and almost daily casualties, the Kremlin's actions were awaited with impatience. The question of whether the end of combat actions would be neared was discussed even more after Yeltsin's announcement that he would personally go to Grozni in May in order to sit the warring sides down at a negotiating table.

The possible date and circumstances of Yeltsin's trip to Grozni were kept secret. Basajev publicly remarked that the president of Russia would not return from Chechnya. But on May 14, at a meeting of the Ichkerija Defense Committee in the mountains, it was decided that no steps would be taken to hinder Yeltsin's visit and that all possible security measures would be taken to guarantee his safety. The Chechen government announced that Jandarbijev would be ready to sit down at the negotiations table. On May 23, it was announced by the Chechen information office that President Zelimchan Jandarbijev had accepted the invitation of the Russian president to come to Moscow to negotiate the end of the war that had gone on for seventeen months.

But the negotiations had to be prepared for. Obviously the advice of Russia's high-ranking commanders to begin the negotiations only after the strongest Chechen armed groups had been destroyed or scattered was taken into consideration. Then it would be easier to dictate terms to the Chechens and to force them to make concessions during the negotiations. Again the Russians took the mistaken view that it would only be necessary to blow a little harder and the Chechen armed resistance would collapse. For this reason, in the first part of May, the activities of the Russian Federal Battle Group in Chechnya were again intensified.

Headlines soon began to appear in newspapers about the victorious actions of the Russian units and the cleansing of Chechen fighters from the communities. In the second part of May, the Russian Army began an especially fierce attack on Bamut, as its takeover had become a matter of honor. On May 24, the Russians announced that the Federal Army had taken Bamut. General Kvashnin evaluated the taking of Bamut as the end of the war, from a political standpoint.

After the taking of Bamut, the confrontations again quieted down. In the opinion of the Kremlin, it was now possible to negotiate, as the enemy was nearly defeated and peaceful means would be sufficient to regulate the situation in Chechnya.

On May 27, 1996, the Chechen negotiations delegation led by President Jandarbijev flew out from Ingushia's Slepcovsk Airport to Moscow. Joining the president were one of the most notable field commanders, Achmed Zakajev, as well as Said Chasan Abubuslinov, Ch. Jerichanov, and the foreign diplomats from the Organization for Security and Cooperation in Europe (OSCE) who had helped prepare the negotiations. In all, about 10 people were in the party. Forty Chechen soldiers also accompanied Jandarbijev to the airport.[5]

During Yeltsin's meeting with Jandarbijev, the issues related to the termination of war activity were settled quite quickly. Chernomyrdin and Jandarbijev signed the agreement. Again, there was nothing new in the agreement. A similar agreement had been reached a year prior. The only difference was that Jandarbijev had succeeded in reaching a compromise for the participation of the official leader of the pro-Moscow Chechen Republic, Doku Zavgajev, this time only as a member of the Russian delegation.[6]

What is much more interesting is that Boris Yeltsin also kept his promise to go to Grozni. After signing the agreement for the complete cessation of war activity from June 1 at midnight, Yeltsin flew to Chechnya—secretly and in an unusual fashion. He left Zelimchan Jandarbijev in Moscow where the negotiations delegation was still continuing to discuss issues regarding the termination of war activity and the exchange of prisoners. Jandarbijev was not even told of Yeltsin's departure and thus effectively became the guarantee for Yeltsin's safety in Grozni.

Upon his arrival in Chechnya, Yeltsin quickly proclaimed the victory of the Russian forces. According to him, there were several small Chechen armed formations left in Chechnya that still needed to be destroyed, but this would not require major efforts.[7]

The war in Chechnya was almost over. According to the information available to the commander of the Northern Caucasus Military Region, General Colonel Kvashnin, during the war activity the Ministry of Defense Forces lost 1,947 killed, 3,175 wounded, and 376 missing in action and the Internal Affairs Ministry lost 678 killed and 3,065 wounded. Judging from even officially published reports, this "victory" cost Russia very dearly: 2,805 soldiers had been killed, 10,319 had been wounded, 393 were missing in action, and 133 had been taken prisoner by the Chechens.

On June 2, the Chechen government's Defense Committee confirmed the peace agreement signed in Moscow and the continuation of talks for its effectuation.[8] It had been agreed in Moscow that the talks would continue in Machachkala on Dagestan territory, but later a different negotiations site was picked: Nazran, the capital of Ingushia. But the negotiations again had to be put off for a while because of renewed combat activity. The day that the talks were to be continued, the situation near Shali flared up again. The Chechens had again taken 26 Russian soldiers prisoner, and the Russian military units were again encircling the city. General Vladimir Shamanov, commanding the Shali operation, was demanding that the Chechens lay down their arms and give back the prisoners. As usual, the ultimatum was ignored. When the Russian forces entered the city, the 166th Internal Affairs Brigade did not find any fighters there. As a matter of course, they then took 10 suspicious-looking Chechens prisoner. The situation from a year ago was repeating itself. Both sides began to blame each other for not keeping the truce.

Bamut: The Most Tenacious Chechen Fortress

The takeover of Bamut was for Boris Yeltsin a very important argument for proclaiming a final victory in Chechnya. It was also a severe blow for the Chechens, as Bamut had become the symbol of their tenacity. It had been said with pride that the Russian jackboot had never yet stepped in Bamut.

The name of Bamut was first mentioned in the press on January 12, 1995, a month after the beginning of the war. Grozni at that time had been the focus of all attention. In the effort to take it, Russia had concentrated all the primary might of its Combined Federal Battle Group in Chechnya. At the same time, news agency correspondents reported that the Chechen armed forces were concentrating in the region of Bamut.

An integral part of the plan for the defense of Chechnya had been preparations for a partisan war and the establishment of bases where weapons, munitions, stores, and medical supplies could be stored. Sooner or later, Grozni would have to be abandoned and a withdrawal would have to be conducted from the flatlands to the mountains. It was thus not surprising that great importance had been given to Bamut in the plan, as the abandoned facilities of a strategic rocket battery previously existing there greatly enhanced this village's defenses. The Chechens decided to establish a strong-point defense position in this area and to fortify themselves in the previously existing military base and strategic rocket silos located some two kilometers from the village.

The rocket silos had been built at the beginning of the 1950s. They were made up of four 6-meter-diameter shafts for the rockets, whose depth reached six stories. In the center of the shafts, an underground control facility had been constructed for the watch teams, and each shaft had been connected with the control facility by an underground tunnel. Besides these, emergency underground exits had been built that led out beyond the perimeter of the rocket base. The control facility was well camouflaged, and its surface was level with the ground. The thick concrete slabs covering its surface gave ample protection from artillery rounds and bombs. The internal facility was sufficiently spacious and could house a company of soldiers. Previously, the command facility had been able to function completely autonomously and to protect the people inside it from harmful external agents such as poison gas and radio-active dust. But in the early eighties when this battery was relocated, part of this equipment was removed. For the defense of Bamut and the military base from the flatlands side, the Chechens constructed blocking posts built out of concrete slabs taken from the road to the rocket silos.

Without a doubt, Bamut, with such defense positions, was a hard nut for the Russians to crack. Bamut's location in a forested area added to its de-fense capabilities. The village was also surrounded by mountains from whose heights the surrounding areas could be controlled. The mountains were im-passable for any armored equipment from the south and southeast, and even on foot they could be transversed only if one knew the mountain goats' trails. According to the Chechens, even during the war for the Caucasus, fought in the last century, not one Russian soldier ever set foot into the village.[9]

That the Chechens had set up a strong-point defense base in Bamut was known to the Federal Army Command. However, while its forces were con-centrated for the takeover of Grozni, special actions against Bamut were not taken.

Combat actions near Bamut began on January 15, 1995, after three Rus-sian soldiers in the vicinity of the village were killed and their heads cut off. Local inhabitants reported that this was done not by the local fighters but by an armed group that had come from elsewhere. This apparently was a provo-cation, perhaps committed by Beslan Gantemirov's people.

The bombing of Bamut began on February 21, 1995, almost immediately after the takeover of the presidential palace in Grozni. Later the bombings be-came a daily occurrence. In the opinion of the Russian Military Command, one of Dudajev's strongest armed formations, organized as the Southeastern Front, was located in the western part of Chechnya. It was commanded by Colonel Ruslan Gelajev. Its chief of staff was Captain Shirmani Albakov, but later Albakov was killed and was replaced by R. Charcharojev. The comman-dant of Bamut was Major Batajev. The Chechen fighters were concentrated mostly in the communities of Samashk, Davydenko, Novi Sharoj, Achchoj Martan, and Bamut and their surrounding regions. As the Federal Army units operating in this region were incapable of taking and holding these commu-nities, the Russian High Command decided after taking Grozni to strengthen the Federal Army Group in western Chechnya by augmenting it with units withdrawn from Grozni. The plan for the operation provided that the strong-est forces would be concentrated in the direction of Bamut, as this was the most important Chechen defense base, not only in the western part of Chech-nya but also in the whole country.

After March 6, 1995, when the Federal Army succeeded in cutting what

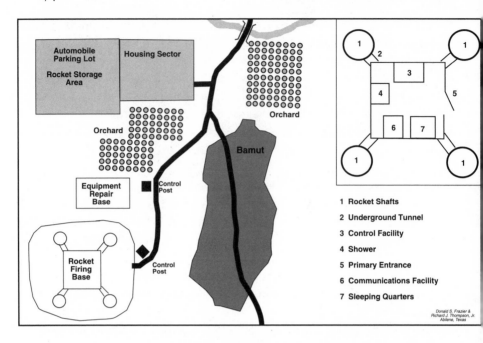

Donald S. Frazier &
Richard J. Thompson, Jr.
Abilene, Texas

had become the strategic highway between Novi Sharoj and Achchoj Martan, the Western Chechen Group was conditionally cut into two parts. The Samashk, Davydenko, and Novi Sharoj formations found themselves separated from the Achchoj Martan and Bamut forces by the positions of the federal forces wedged in between them. This eased the preparations for the assault operation, as heavy artillery could then be concentrated near Bamut. Thus constant barrages of the village and the former rocket base by Grad rocket salvo systems and artillery were begun from this time by the federal forces.

The first large-scale assault of Bamut was conducted on March 15. The first attack did not succeed, although the Russians fought their way up to the outskirts of the village. The federal forces were able to enter the village only after three more days of intense fighting, but they were not able to hold on to it. After taking significant losses from the fire of Chechens fortified on the heights surrounding the village, they were forced to leave the village. Clearly, in order to take the village, it would be first necessary to knock out the Chechen fighters from the surrounding heights. Most of the artillery fire thus began to be concentrated against these heights.

The second assault of the village was conducted at the end of May, 1995. But again it was unsuccessful. After that the village was only bombarded by artillery and air strikes, leaving it in ruins. Of the village that remained, only the surviving cellars, about one on each street, were left usable as defense positions.

One more assault of Bamut was conducted at the end of November. According to the Russian Military Command's official reports, about 50 Russian soldiers died during this unsuccessful operation. But the Chechen fighters reported that the exact count of the Russian dead was 238. This was the number of the bodies of soldiers that were given over during the exchanges of prisoners and the dead.

Yet another operation to assault Bamut, conducted by the Federal Forces' Southwestern Group, ended in failure before it could even begin.[10] The Russians planned to attack the village, with the then existing Federal Army forces being augmented by a combined battalion made up of units from the 693rd and the 503rd Motorized Rifle Regiments. These regiments were part of the 19th Motorized Rifle Division, itself attached to the 58th Army. The combined battalion, formed up in Vladikaukaz, began to move toward Bamut on February 22, 1996. After traveling along the Rostov-Baku highway, this battalion then turned right onto the Galashka-Arshty road and, after passing through the hamlet of Nesterovsk, broke up into four columns. One column moved on toward the village of Data in order to go around Bamut from the southern flank. The second column moved forward but then dug in near the village of Arshty, mistakenly thinking that it was the village of Bamut. The third column was to move through the village of Alchast and go around Bamut to its other flank. The fourth column was assigned to establish a cross fire from the direction of the hamlet of Nesterovsk.

But the column moving toward the village of Data along an almost impassable road got stuck in the mud. The third column, upon meeting Chechen fire, began to withdraw toward Arshty, where it collided with its own already dug-in forces. This possibility had not been foreseen in the operations plan, and both opened fire, convinced that the other side was the enemy. The skirmish lasted about an hour before the mistake was noticed. During the firefight, the Russian forces were also shot up by helicopters that arrived to support them. Once the situation was clarified, both columns joined together and, upon nearing the outskirts of Arshty, began to bombard the village with artillery fire, believing that they were firing at Bamut. The mistake was corrected only sometime later, but the engagement had already lasted for about two days.

When the bombardment of Arshty began, some of its inhabitants fled to the surrounding regions while the majority withdrew to the hamlet of Slepcovskaja in Ingushia. During the confrontations, 4 civilian inhabitants were killed, 10 were wounded, and 5 disappeared without a trace. The two-day operation also cost the combined battalion 14 killed and 20 wounded. One armored vehicle was burned up. The commander of the battalion, Major E. Tenitashvili, was also killed.

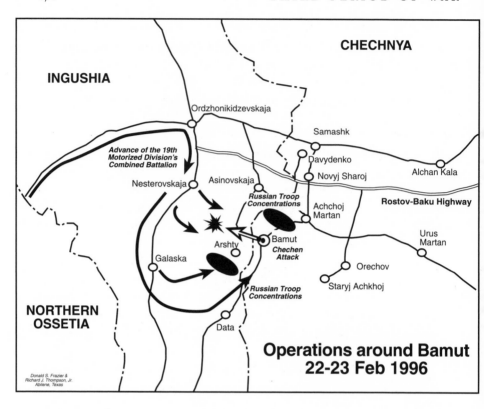

Operations around Bamut
22-23 Feb 1996

The Command of the Federal Forces in Chechnya blamed the losses that it sustained on Ingushia, supposedly for not taking proper measures to ensure the safety of the columns during the march and because it had allowed the Chechen fighters to operate on its territory. For military specialists this was a strange conclusion as it was obvious that once the commander of the Bamut force received information about the movement of a column towards his positions he could not do anything other than send his fighters out to stop it. Anything else would have been not only illogical but also disastrous for the defenders of the village. War is, after all, war. Once the president of Ingushia issued a protest because of the Federal Army's illegal actions in the region of the villages of Galashka and Arshty, the Russian units were forced to leave this republic's territory.

The battalion's operation obviously can be evaluated as a failure. But beneath this failure may have also been hidden a specially organized operation. The assault of the Ingushian villages could have drawn the Ingushians into the war, particularly as it took place during the celebration of the Muslim feast of Uramz.

After this operation, the villages and their surrounding areas continued to be bombarded by artillery and air strikes. In other parts of Chechnya, the campaign continued to force the signing of the three-party peace protocols between the Federal Army Command, the pro-Moscow Chechen opposition government, and the regional, city, and village administrations. By the end of May, 1996, almost all the regional administrations had been forced to sign. Bamut was the last community in which there were no peaceful inhabitants, the village being inhabited only by Chechen fighters. During more than a year and a half of continuous fighting, Bamut had become an undefeatable Chechen fortress. The Federal Army Command then decided to take it, regardless of the price. The command of the operation was assigned to the commander of the Defense Ministry's forces in Chechnya, General Lieutenant Vladimir Shamanov.

Before attacking Bamut, the Russians first attempted to blockade it from the west, south, and east. The primary direction of the attack was from the north, the best approach for armored equipment. The Federal Forces Attack Group was made up of Defense Ministry and Internal Affairs Ministry units.

The last and decisive assault of Bamut began on May 21, 1996. The village was attacked by four battalions and a combined paratroop brigade, all belonging to the Defense Ministry. Troops of the Internal Affairs Ministry's 94th Brigade and the 66th Special Purpose Regiment conducted the blockade of Bamut, setting up blocking posts and pickets in its surrounding area. During the first day of the attack, the attacking force lost 14 killed. Only the next day did it succeed in taking the dominant heights to the south and east of Bamut. This eased the course of the attack as it was now possible to bombard the Chechen positions by direct fire from tanks and armored vehicles.

The Chechens attempted to break the blockade of the village by attacking the paratroop battalion from the direction of the villages of Arshty and Chemulga but were unable to accomplish this because of attacks from close air support aircraft and fire from artillery set up in positions to the east of the village of Asinovskaja. The Russian troops were able to take up positions in the northern part of the village after losing 40 soldiers. The comparatively small losses were explained by the fact that this time a new tactic was used to take the village. All week before the assault, the village was intensively bombarded by artillery and bombed from the air. More than 1,000 rockets were shot into Bamut and 500 bombs were dropped. Mi-24 helicopters helped to level what was left of the village by shooting 5,000 unguided rockets into it.

During the night of May 22, about 40 Chechen fighters attacked the positions of the Federal Forces several times in an attempt to push the Russian troops out of Bamut. During these fierce engagements, which even included

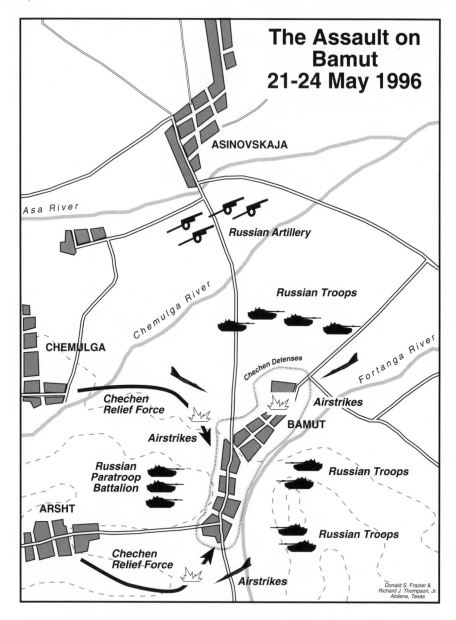

The Assault on Bamut 21-24 May 1996

fights with bayonets, 22 Russian soldiers were killed and 57 were wounded. Representatives of the Russian Army contended that the Chechens lost about 120 fighters during this part of the battle.

On May 24, Defense Minister Grachev announced that Bamut and all four shafts of the rocket installation had been taken, that the cleansing of the surrounding territory of Chechen fighters had begun, and that mine-clearing work was being conducted. He reported that during five days of fighting, about 400 Chechens and 30 Russian soldiers were killed.

But according to the government of Ichkerija, the battles for Bamut were continuing. According to its spokesmen, the Russians had attempted to break the Chechen defensive line five times, but the majority of the positions had held. During this operation, the Russians sustained 400 troops killed and 200 wounded. Also destroyed were 6 tanks, 19 armored vehicles, and 2 helicopters. Even Russian Duma deputy V. Iliuchin confirmed that during the attack of this village the Federal Army lost 700 soldiers killed.[11]

Until that point, in the estimation of the Federal Army Command, Bamut had been defended by about 100 fighters; after the Chechen attack, it was being announced that a Chechen force of some 800 people was concentrated there.[12] Thus it may be worthwhile to give some attention to reports of witnesses. One of the 29 Stavropol construction workers who had been taken hostage on December 16 in Achchoj Martan and held in Chechen captivity for half a year, Anatoli Voitenko, reported that "if one was to talk about our [Russia's] victory, then we will have to wait for yet a long time. I base my opinion on Bamut where I was. It was defended by several small groups who could not have totaled more than about 80 people. But the Russian generals were telling stories about how they were fighting thousands of bandits."[13]

Some of the Bamut defenders withdrew to the surrounding communities. Russia's military intelligence fixed the appearance of small Chechen fighter groups in at least ten of the neighboring communities. About 80 Chechen fighters withdrew to Ersenoja and about 50 to Nozhai Jurt. But the largest number forced their way to the region of Vedeno. After 17 fierce confrontations and many months of being held under siege, Bamut had become a fortress of legend.

Negotiations for the Peace Agreement

On June 3, the Russian negotiations delegation announced that the withdrawal of the Federal Army was temporarily being suspended because of the unstable situation in Chechnya. The Chechen work group was accused of inactivity.[14]

But in essence, this was the Russian negotiators' reaction to the Chechen delegation's negotiating position. In the agreement project prepared and submitted by the Chechen delegation, provision was made for the Russian Army to be withdrawn from Chechnya by July 1, for the Republican Parliamentary elections set for June 16 to be canceled and rescheduled for two months after the withdrawal of the Russian Army, and for the decision as to Chechnya's status to be left to the Chechen people. It was also stressed that if the elections were not called off, the war would be greatly intensified by June 12. The leader of the Russian delegation contended that the Chechen delegation's insistence that the Russian Army be withdrawn before the Chechens disarmed their own formations was the most important disagreement between the parties.

The negotiations edged a bit forward when the commander of Russia's Combined Forces in Chechnya, General Major Vechiaslav Tichomirov and the Chechen chief of staff, General Aslan Maschadov, met in Nazran on June 10 to discuss the effectuation of the military agreement. In five days, they succeeded in agreeing and signing two protocols.[15]

One of these was for the regulation of the military situation in Chechnya. This was to be executed in two stages. During the first stage, from June 11 to July 7, Russia was to withdraw its army from the Chechen villages being held under siege. During the second stage, from July 7 until August 7, provision was made for the disarmament of the Chechen fighters.

Besides this, the time limits, from June 11 until July 7, for the liquidation of the Federal Army's outposts near the communities were agreed upon. It was also agreed that all the Combined Federal Forces temporarily in the country would be withdrawn by August 31. Work groups led by Tichomirov and Maschadov were created to work out the time schedules for the withdrawal of Russian forces in stages. The territories out of which the Russian units were to be withdrawn were to be demilitarized.

The other protocol was for the freeing of individuals who had been detained by force. It was agreed that the Chechens would immediately release 14 of the 26 Russian soldiers captured at the end of May. Lists of captured Chechen fighters were also exchanged, although the numbers in these lists differed: the Russians listed 1,089 people, the Chechens 1,322.

After the signing of the protocols, the Russian High Command announced that the withdrawal of the Federal Forces would begin June 11. The first unit, the 245th Motorized Rifle Regiment, was to be withdrawn from the Shatoja region.

But execution of the agreements was soon threatened by the emotions brought on by the elections in Chechnya, which Doku Zavgajev had decided to connect with the Russian presidential elections scheduled for June 16. The Chechen delegation categorically protested the holding of any elections before the Russian Army was withdrawn from the Republic's territory since only then could the elections be considered democratic and free. For this reason, they decided to boycott the elections.[16]

President Yeltsin held to the opinion that the elections were an internal Chechen matter and that the Chechens should themselves decide when they should be held. The same position was held by the Russian negotiations delegation. But disregarding the protests of the Chechens, Doku Zavgajev's announced elections were nevertheless held. Naturally, these elections were "won" by Doku Zavgajev and his supporters.

After the elections, Doku Zavgajev proclaimed that the elections gave him and the newly elected Chechen Parliament the authority to govern the region during the period of the changeover from war to peace. However, since the elections took place under conditions of military control and without the participation of foreign observers, the election results were not considered valid by most. Even the representative of the Russian General Staff, General Lieutenant Andrei Ivanov was forced to admit indirectly that to consider the elections as having taken place was only possible with a large amount of fantasy. The elections did not take place at all in Krachaloja and the region surrounding it or in the regions of Bachi Jurt, Aleroja, Centoroja, Gudermes, Vedeno, Shchelkovsk, and Shali; they took place only partially in the regions of Kali and Sovietskoja, and almost not at all in the communities of the Nozhai Jurt and Achchoj Martan regions.[17]

That the Chechen parliamentary elections did not meet the Organization for Security and Cooperation of Europe (OSCE) standards was also noted in the report of the chairman of the Permanent OSCE Council in Vienna, Swiss diplomat Benedikt von Tscharner, published in Austria. The elections also conflicted with the agreement signed by Russia and Chechnya, as they had to take place only after the Russian Army was withdrawn from Chechnya and the republic was demilitarized.[18]

As one might expect, the situation in Chechnya after the elections again became tense, especially after June 22 when the Chechens knocked down a Russian helicopter in the region of the community of Centoroja. One Russian soldier was killed and 7 wounded in this incident. At about the same time, two armored vehicles were blown apart in Grozni after they ran over mines. Again there were casualties: 5 Russian soldiers were killed and 5 were wounded. No one even attempted to determine who had mined the road or when. The Chechens were accused of organizing a "war of mines."

Both sides continued to blame each other for not following the terms of the agreement and accuse each other of violating it. The Chechen High Command contended that the Russians had not withdrawn even one unit from the communities, except for the 245th Regiment from the vicinity of Vedeno, and were continuing the bombardment of Chechen positions. Just in the first three weeks of June, Chechen positions were shot up 400 times, resulting in 25 Chechen fighters being killed and 72 wounded. The Federal Forces Command contended that during the same time, the Chechens shot up Russian positions 350 times, resulting in 30 Russian soldiers being killed and more than 100 wounded.[19]

Still, the negotiations continued. The Chechen delegation held strictly to the tactic that during each step, they had to force Russia to concede at least a little bit, that the successes of each meeting had to be larger than those won at the prior meeting, and that they could not withdraw even one step from the purposes that they were seeking. After the elections, they sought to discredit the elections results during the negotiations, to gradually isolate Doku Zavgajev from the negotiations, and to continue the negotiations only between the Russians and the government of the Chechen Republic of Ichkerija.

Although the skirmishes became more frequent, the situation began to stabilize. In part this was because of the results of the first round of presidential elections in Russia and the nearness of the second round. The front-runners in the first round were Boris Yeltsin, the Communist Party leader Genadi Ziuganov, and, unexpectedly, Aleksander Lebed, a fierce supporter of the termination of the war in Chechnya. Attempting to win the elections, Boris Yeltsin was forced to find ways of drawing Aleksander Lebed's supporters to his side. Aleksander Lebed agreed to withdraw his candidacy on the condition that he be appointed to a high Russian Security Council post, preferably as secretary, that he be given wide authority, and that a number of undesirable individuals be removed from their positions—first of all, Russia's defense minister Pavel Grachev; the president's personal security chief, Aleksander Korzhakov; and the head of the Security Council, Mikhail Barsukov. The president was forced to agree. Appointed as the new defense minister was the commander of the General Staff Academy, General Colonel Juri Rodionov.

Aleksander Lebed also firmly spoke out in favor of ending the war in Chechnya, saying that Chechnya had a right to independence if this demand was confirmed by a referendum. On June 25, Yeltsin signed a decree for the withdrawal of the Russian Army from Chechnya.[20]

As had been foreseen, the 245th Motorized Rifle Regiment was the first to move out. On July 1–3, the regiment went back in three trains to the Moscow Military Region and their permanent deployment base in the city of Mulin in the district of Nizhnigorod. During a year and a half of combat, the regiment, having attempted during almost that whole time to take control of the Vedeno region, lost 231 soldiers (12 officers, 12 warrant officers, and 206 sergeants and soldiers), and 186 were soldiers wounded.[21]

The Russian Military High Command contended that the return of the regiment to Russia was the start of the withdrawal, but the Chechens continued to view it as simply a normal rotation of units. Obviously, the Chechens were right. The situation immediately began to change once Boris Yeltsin won the Russian presidential elections.

Combat actions were renewed because of a sudden change in General Lieutenant Tichomirov's views, a change that was obviously inspired by Moscow. On July 7, rumors began to fly that the Russian president was about to remove the commander of the Federal Forces Group in Chechnya, General Viacheslav Tichomirov, from his post because of his "inactivity." Whether this was so or not is hard to determine. However, when Tichomirov returned from Moscow where he had been recalled to account for the nineteen-month-long war, he firmed up his positions. The Chechens were first given an ultimatum to release the prisoners. If they were not released by noon, July 9, the most rigorous actions would be taken.[22]

The Chechen answer was an attack of Russian positions near the village of Gechi in the Urus Martan region. During the attack, 3 Russian soldiers were killed. When the Federal Army units, together with the opposition Chechen militia, surrounded the village, the largest battle since the start of the cease-fire broke out. A corridor was formed for women, children, and old people to leave, and it had been announced that only men were left in the village. But about 8,000 people had not had sufficient time to make their escape. About 70 fighters were present in the village at that time. During two assaults, both of which were repulsed, the Russians lost 100–150 soldiers. On the third day of the engagement, the assistant commander of the Northern Caucasus Military Region, General Major N. Skripnik, was killed when his armored vehicle ran over a mine. During the operation against this village, 15–30 civilian inhabitants of this village were killed and 42 of the wounded were hospitalized at the Urus Martan hospital.[23]

When General Lieutenant Tichomirov did not receive an answer to his ultimatum from Zelimchan Jandarbijev, he threatened to institute martial law from July 10. The Chechens were accused of not abiding by the terms of the cease-fire agreement signed in Moscow and of violating it 580 times from that date, May 27, killing 27 Russian soldiers and wounding 200.[24]

Much more important, however, was Tichomirov's signed order to arrest President Zelimchan Jandarbijev. On July 10, Federal Army units surrounded the village of Machet where it was thought Jandarbijev and his headquarters were located. His headquarters was bombarded by artillery and air strikes. During the first day of the assault on the village, 20 peaceful inhabitants of the village were killed, 8 Russian soldiers were killed, and 20 Russian soldiers were wounded. The Russians were able to take the village on July 15 but found neither Jandarbijev nor Maschadov nor Basajev. The commander of the Defense Ministry's forces, General Lieutenant Vladimir Samanov, who had also commanded the operation, announced that the Chechen fighter group in the village had been liquidated, that 300 Chechen fighters had been killed, and that the headquarters, with its 14-meter radio tower, 40 automobiles, and 2 munitions depots, was destroyed. But about 300 "separatists" were able to escape. The village was taken with minimal losses: 2 Russian soldiers were killed and 5 wounded.

Unavoidably there were also civilian casualties: 25 civilians were killed. That same day that the village of Machet was taken, 7 Russian helicopters attacked the village of Staryje Atagi. Six of their rockets destroyed the same number of houses. This attack apparently was not without purpose, as Jandarbijev's mother's house was in this village.[25]

The Russians attempted to institute martial law in Grozni from July 10. It was forbidden to enter or exit the city by motor transport, and all earlier permits were voided. The opposition's Chechen militia was put on alert. The Federal Army units also intensified their activity in the Vedeno and Shatoja regions. At least 30 people were killed when Dargo, Belgatoja, Vedeno, and other villages in the Vedeno region were shot up.

In the Shatoja region, the most important assault objective was the community of Agishbat, where it was thought that a Chechen fighter group of some 300 people were concentrated. Fierce battles also began in the region of the village of Bamut. According to the Chechen information minister Movlad Udugov, during three days, 370 Chechen inhabitants were killed and 170 wounded because of unexpected attacks by Russian aircraft, helicopters, and artillery against the southern Chechen communities. Russia had once again commenced total war against the Chechens.

In spite of his efforts, Tichomirov was nevertheless recalled to Moscow and replaced by the assistant commander of the Northern Caucasus Military Region, General Lieutenant Konstantin Pulikovski. Pulikovski had his own account to settle with the Chechens: his own son had been killed in the war.

As had become customary, after the taking and cleansing of each village, the Russian High Command announced large Chechen casualties together with insignificant losses suffered by its own forces. In the village of Agishty, the Chechens also supposedly "lost" 60 of their fighters.[26]

The Russian Military Command was firmly convinced of its own supremacy over the Chechen fighters and did not believe that the Chechens had preserved any potential to strike serious blows against the Federal Army units. But again they were mistaken. Only a small portion of the Chechen forces had in fact been fighting the Federal Army. The Chechens had succeeded in preserving their fighter forces and had been making preparations for new, large-scale operations and for new battles.

The Chechens had plans to conduct their most important operations in Grozni and the other large cities. And this they succeeded in doing.

CHAPTER 17

The End of the War in Chechnya

I t proved to be impossible to reach a complete termination of war actions in Chechnya even after a year of continuing negotiations, which Russia had been forced to enter into after the Chechen operation in Budionovsk. After each new round of negotiations began, a new wave of confrontations commenced and combat actions flared up with renewed force. Neither the cease-fire announcements nor the president's decrees officially terminating war activity helped very much. Not only were both sides determined to hold firmly to their positions but also Moscow held too strong a belief in its own military power.

The Chechens believed that there was no way of terminating war actions but to stop force with force. Only equals could negotiate on an equal footing. Thus to demonstrate that they were equal in force to the Russians, the Chechens needed to mount an operation that could prove that the resistance forces were not only not exhausted but, to the contrary, had regrouped and become even stronger. It thus was necessary to strike at the very heart of the Combined Federal Army Group and to strike in such a way that Russia would finally begin to understand the futility of continuing the war. Russia's hopes of a quick victory in this war had to be shown to be only an illusion. The purpose of the operation was to force the acceptance of a complete termination of war actions since neither side could defeat the other side, at least not within the foreseeable future. Both sides had to be left with a "zero" option, or no option other than to negotiate a termination of the war. The operation had to begin simultaneously in Grozni and in the other largest cities of Chechnya and then expand by degrees to cover the whole territory of the republic.

The operation to take Grozni was planned under the overall command of Chechen chief of staff, General Aslan Maschadov. Painstaking planning went into the operation's preparation. Each fighter group was assigned to a sector where it was to operate and was tasked with specific missions during each stage of the operation. Exact attention was also given to the security of all information regarding the operation; thus the general order with the actual specification of assault objectives was given out only to the commanders of the military formations, and even then, only on the eve of the operation.

The operational plan was prepared based on a concept developed by Maschadov. It set the following as the primary missions:

To blockade the Federal Army units and subunits in their deployment areas and at their control posts so that they could not take part in the defense of objectives that the Chechens were planning to take over;

To concentrate forces in Grozni for the assault of the most important objectives (the government buildings and the most significant Defense Ministry and Internal Affairs positions);

To establish defense lines along the Federal Army's most probable movement routes to Grozni from the other regions of Chechnya, also to organize ambushes and attacks from such positions using grenade launchers in order to stop the enemy's columns from moving to the assistance of the forces blockaded in the city;

To force the Federal Army to expend its material, technical means and munitions to the maximum;

To pin down the Federal Army Forces dislocated in the other areas of Chechnya by striking all the units simultaneously and by intensifying combat activity in the areas where the largest Russian formations were located.[1]

The planners of the operation took into consideration that under city conditions and in street battles the Federal Army lost the advantage of its heavy weapons, combat equipment, and close air support. Calculated into the plan was also the fact that the Russian soldiers were unfamiliar with the city and did not know the weaknesses of the Russian control posts as well as did the Chechen fighters.

In preparing for the takeover of Grozni, the Chechens made good use of the experience gained during their earlier assault operation conducted on March 6–10. Especially helpful was the fact that even after this successful Chechen operation, the command of the Combined Federal Forces Group in Chechnya had not taken any additional measures to improve the defenses of

Grozni. Even the number of blocking posts along the roads entering Grozni had not been increased, and thus only 22 blocking posts remained, even though the city could be entered along more than a hundred roads and streets. Command of the operation in Grozni was assigned to Shamil Basajev.

To ensure the success of the operation, strike forces were inserted into the city in advance with the assignment that once the operation was begun, they were to pin down the Russian units in their dislocation areas or control posts by means of intensive fire so that the other Chechen fighter groups could move about in the city without hindrance. The appearance of these strike forces in the city did not go unnoticed. But by that time it was already too late. Russian military intelligence spotted the concentration of large Chechen fighter groups of up to 500 people in the communities of Shchelkovskaja, Kargalinskaja, Staroshchedrinskaja, and Novoshchedrinskaja.[2]

The Chechen operation, code-named "Zero Option," commenced early on the morning of August 6. And not only in Grozni. At the same time, Chechnya's two other largest cities, Gudermes and Argun, were also attacked, although it would be more accurate to say that the Chechen fighter groups simply entered them. The Russian newspapers soon began to shimmer with headlines: "The hit men are storming all the Chechen cities at once!"

By noon of the same day, the Chechens succeeded in taking the militia building in Argun without a battle and disarming the militiamen in it. They also were able to shut up the military command section that had been deployed in the city by forcing them to withdraw into the school building. The city was quickly taken over by the Chechens, and the Federal Army units were forced to dig in a kilometer and a half outside the city. The fighting in Argun was intense, with the Russian forces supported by rocket fire from helicopters. The Federal Army, however, lost 15 armored vehicles during the fighting. Apparently, the commander of the Argun operation, Salman Radujev, was telling the truth when, after unexpectedly "rising from the dead" and again finding his way back to Chechnya, he boasted that he brought back with him ten shoulder-fired antiaircraft rocket units. This time, the fire from helicopters was answered with antiaircraft rockets.

The Chechens also announced that they had taken a greater part of Gudermes. But no special efforts of any kind were needed for this, as practically no resistance of any kind was met there: the local Internal Affairs forces laid down their weapons without firing a shot and a majority of the militia went over to the side of the Chechen fighters. The Chechens fortified themselves in the railroad station, took control of part of the strategic Rostov-Baku highway, and then began to negotiate with the Federal Army units that the Russian units leave the city without a fight.

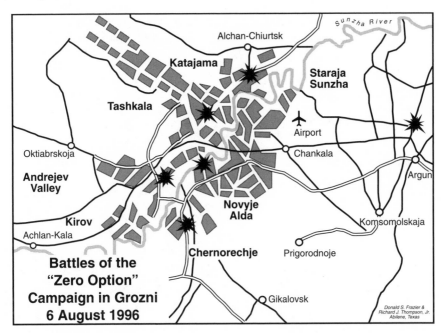

Battles of the "Zero Option" Campaign in Grozni 6 August 1996

But the most important events took place in Grozni. At 6:55 A.M., fighter groups of 30 – 40 people began to attack in the direction of the city's central market and the railroad station. In the skirmishes near the railroad station, even mortars were used.

Fierce fighting also took place along the borders of the Staropromyslovsk and Zavodskaja districts and near the building complex housing the pro-Moscow Zavgajev government. But the government buildings themselves were not assaulted. Instead, in order to avoid purposeless casualties, the commander of the Chechen group, Ruslan Gelajev, ordered his fighters to take up positions around the government building complex in the ruins of the central post office, the 41st School, and the first aid hospital. Once the complex was blockaded, snipers took positions and began to shoot up the government buildings.[3]

Helicopters and artillery were sent in against the Chechen fighters forcing their way into the city. Attempts were also made to assist the besieged Federal Army units by sending in reinforcements from the Northern Airport and from Chankala. The Chechens, however, were ready for this. During the confrontations that ensued, several Mi-24 helicopters were destroyed and 4 armored vehicles were burned up on the road connecting the capital of Chechnya with the Northern Airport. The 166th Motorized Brigade moving in column formation to reinforce the other federal units was forced to turn back.

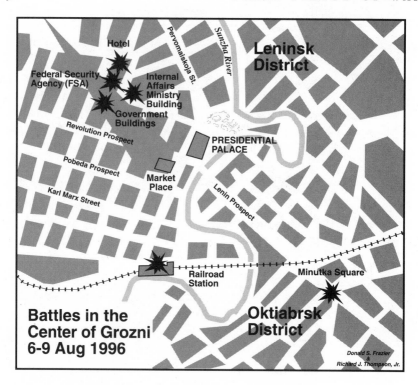

By noon, 13 Russian troops had been killed and 53 wounded, and by the morning of the next day, the Russian casualties had grown to 29 killed and about 100 wounded.[4] The Russian units at the blocking posts, the commandant's offices, and other locations where as yet no fighting was taking place were warned not to go out of their deployment areas because of security considerations.

During the night of August 6, the battles calmed down somewhat, but they erupted again in the morning with new force. During the second day of the assault, the situation of the Federal Army units in the city was becoming critical. The pro-Moscow opposition government together with Doku Zavgajev had been forced to leave the capital and to withdraw to the Chankala Military Base. But even there they did not feel safe. The base had been under constant fire from the beginning of the operation and its commander, Colonel Ashlapov, had been killed.[5]

Reinforcements were sent to help the forces in the besieged government building complex. A column from the Chankala Military Base was able to force its way into the center of the city, but about 500 meters from the government complex it was stopped and surrounded. Reinforcements from the military base at the Northern Airport also were unable to break through. The Chechen assault was so fierce that even the Federal Forces Command was forced to admit that it lost 8 helicopters and 15 armored vehicles during this early part of the assault.

Once the operation in Grozni began, the Chechen Forces Group that had forced its way into the city was constantly being strengthened. After three days of confrontations, the Chechen forces in the city had grown to 3,000 troops.[6] The Chechens succeeded in taking and holding the center of the city and about 80 percent of the city's territory. According to a report released by Chechnya's information minister, Movladi Udugov, almost 1,000 Russian soldiers were killed during the first three days of the operation, 44 armored vehicles and 9 helicopters were destroyed, 8 armored vehicles were taken as trophies, and 300 firearms and much ammunition were captured. The first stage of the operation to end the war in Chechnya had been concluded successfully. Preparations were being made for the second.[7]

At the same time, the Chechens expanded the combat zone and commenced active battles in the republic's southwest in the Bamut, Orechov, and Staryj Achkhoj regions. They also reinforced the blockade of the Federal Army units in the mountains of southern Chechnya.

The Federal Army Command showed itself to be unprepared for a Chechen attack on this scale. Even though almost all the reserve forces, the 7th and 104th Paratroops Divisions, the 166th and 205th Motorized Rifle Brigade, the 34th Internal Affairs Army Brigade, and other units, had been sent in against the Chechen fighters in Grozni, they were unable to change the operational situation in the Federal Forces' favor. On the contrary, the Chechens were able to take up even stronger positions after blockading several thousand Russian troops in the various commandant headquarters and blocking posts and after taking the railroad station and Minutka Square. The Federal Army found it impossible to make effective use of its aviation and artillery superiority as the probability of hitting their own troops had become about equal. In the opinion of the commander, General Colonel Kvashnin, the correct course at that time would have been to send mobile antidiversion groups into the city with armored equipment support to provide cover. But to reestablish positions in the city without huge casualties, the tactic of block-by-block street battles would have had to be used.

Such block-by-block tactics would have meant the prolongation of the battles. But to wait until the Chechens left the city by themselves as they had in March or until their ammunition ran out would have also been an error. For one, the Chechens brought along sufficient ammunition with them and built up some amount of reserves in the city in advance. Second, all the roads from Grozni to the west, south, and northeast were in Chechen hands and available for the resupply of munitions. Only a narrow corridor to the southeast toward the Chankala Military Base was still being controlled by the Federal Army. Besides, an additional source of munitions resupply had become the Federal Army units themselves. For example, when after several days of fighting, a column consisting of two tanks and an Ural truck loaded with ammunition was sent from the Northern Airport to resupply the Russian troops blockaded at the Staropromyslovsk commandant's headquarters, one of the tanks was knocked out and the other, together with the ammunition truck, wound up in Chechen hands.

The Chechens apparently had more than sufficient weapons as they did not even try very hard to take weapons away from the Russian soldiers. Later when an agreement was reached for a cease-fire and the 34th Internal Affairs Army Brigade was allowed to return to the Northern Airport base from Minutka Square where it had been blockaded, the Chechens took only the SVD (Dragunov) sniper rifles and the Mucha grenade launchers away from the Russian soldiers. In exchange, they allowed the Russian soldiers to keep their automatic weapons so that they would be able to account for their weapons. When the surprised soldiers asked why they were not taking away the automatics, the Chechens answered that they had them in abundance.[8]

After a week of confrontations, the situation of the Federal Army units in the city became unenviable. Russian television reported that 221 Russian soldiers had been killed, 766 wounded, and an unknown number missing in action. Among those listed killed were 109 Internal Affairs Army troops and 3 OMON Special-Purpose Militia soldiers. Chechnya's information minister, Movladi Udugov, announced instead that 1,230 Russians had been killed and that Chechen losses had been 37 fighters killed. The losses were so unexpectedly high that Russia proclaimed August 10 as a Day of Mourning.

But it had been even more disastrous for the civilian inhabitants of the city, namely, the old people, women, and children, among whom there were also many wounded. Again, no one even bothered to count how many had died, and indeed, doing so was hardly possible. Thousands of refugees had been concentrated in the communities not far from Grozni, especially in the villages of Staraja Sunzha and Kalinin and in the community of Mikrorajon. For several days, efforts were made to create a corridor allowing the refugees to leave the city and to take their wounded toward the village of Petropavlovskaja to the north of Grozni. Humanitarian aid and medical assistance awaited them in the village of Tolstoi Jurt. The Chechen fighters agreed to the creation of a corridor, but for several days no answer was received from the Federal Army Command. In spite of this, a corridor was opened up at the initiative of the Chechen forces as, apparently, the Federal Army were not capable of participating.

The situation in Chechnya and especially Grozni raised serious concerns in the Kremlin. There apparently being no other way out, on August 9, Yeltsin appointed the secretary of the Security Council, Aleksander Lebed, as his representative in Chechnya. The Chechens evaluated this appointment very favorably. Hope finally appeared that the war could be terminated.

Having received with his assignment supplemental authorizations from the Russian president for the stopping of war actions in Chechnya, Lebed unexpectedly flew to Chechnya on August 11 and met with its leaders. During Lebed's visit, both sides agreed upon the necessity of stopping war actions. They also agreed to continue negotiations for the terms of a cease-fire in Grozni, for the creation of a corridor for the refugees, and of the corridor's untouchability by both sides. The commander of the Combined Federal Forces Group, General Lieutenant Konstantin Pulikovski, was assigned to work out the details of the cease-fire with the Chechen chief of staff, General Aslan Maschadov.

The day after returning to Moscow, Aleksander Lebed held a press conference. What he said indicated an important and unexpected change in Russian and Chechen relations. It appeared that, after all, the Chechens were not intending to separate completely from Russia and would be satisfied with a status for Chechnya similar to what had been granted to Tatarstan. The Tatarstan Constitution provided that Tatarstan was a part of the Russian Federation but was also a sovereign country and recognized as a subject of international law. Its relationship with Russia was regulated by a bilateral treaty.

Lebed acted decisively. After several days in Moscow, he returned to Chechnya, where he met with Zelimchan Jandarbijev and Aslan Maschadov in the village of Novyje Agati. The president of Ingushia, Ruslan Aushev, also participated in the meeting. During this second meeting, both parties agreed to a cease-fire and arranged for a special Observers' Commission to be created to decide all the military questions and to regulate the cease-fire. They also agreed that the other members of the Observer Commission could be the secretaries of the Northern Caucasus Republics' Security Council and that this commission was to evaluate objectively violations of the cease-fire.

Although battles continued not only in Grozni but elsewhere, and the Russian units were still being attacked near Bamut, Shatoja, Argun, Dzhalka, and Shali, the engagements began to quiet down after the agreement was reached. By August 16, only solitary shots were being heard in Grozni.

During 11 days of battle, 265 Russian soldiers were killed and more than

1,000 were wounded. The Russian forces also lost more than 100 tanks and armored vehicles in the fighting. These figures about the Federal Army's losses were announced in the Russian press. Later the Federal Army Group's Military Prosecutor, Igor Shevchenko, corrected these figures, stating that during this Chechen operation, 1,800 Russian soldiers were either killed, wounded, or missing in action. Of this number, 1,264 soldiers had been wounded, and 130 were missing in action.[9] The number of soldiers killed was confirmed by the fact that by the announcement, 376 bodies had been shipped through the morgue at the Northern Airport and 30 more were still left in it. The Chechens contended that at least 2,500 Russian soldiers had died in Grozni during this operation.

On August 18, an agreement was signed for a cease-fire. Both sides exchanged orders for the termination of combat actions and the determination of zones of responsibility in Grozni. The purpose of the first stage of the operation "Zero Option" had been accomplished by the Chechens.

The Efforts of Lebed and Maschadov to Terminate War Activity

Although cease-fires had been agreed to on a number of other occasions, this time the Chechens began to believe that its terms would be held to. They saw Aleksander Lebed, a longtime supporter of the termination of the war in Chechnya, as their guarantor.

The Chechens also sensed their upcoming victory. But the passions had still not died down, and to ensure their victory the Chechens continued to make efforts to liquidate the Russian points of resistance in Grozni. Thus they held direct talks with the 140 members of the Krasnodar and Karelia OMON, who had spent 13 days blockaded without food and water in the Staropromyslovsk commandant's headquarters, and convinced them to return to their base at the Northern Airport. On their part, the Chechens agreed not to hinder the move. The commander of the Chechen group, Vacha Arsanov, even agreed to allow the Russian troops to take their weapons with them. He also released with them 100 Internal Affairs Ministry troops who had been taken prisoner at Minutka Square.

Still, isolated confrontations and Chechen attacks continued. On the night of August 19, the Chechens attacked the Chankala Military Base, killing 5 Russian soldiers and wounding 5. Skirmishes also continued in Bamut, Argun, Urus Martan, and in other regions.

The Federal Army Command reverted to old tactics. Disregarding the agreement, General Pulikovski quickly accused the Chechens of violating the terms of the cease-fire and on August 20 issued an ultimatum. He gave both the Chechen fighters and the inhabitants of the city 48 hours to leave the capital through a corridor route passing through Staraja Sunzha, Petropavlovsk, and Argun. After the passage of the 48-hour time period, he threatened to attack the city using aviation and heavy artillery. He issued the ultimatum after the Chechens attacked an intelligence battalion on the northern outskirts of Grozni.

The ultimatum not only increased already high tensions but also raised the threat that war actions would be renewed. Thousands of refugees began to stream from the capital toward Staraja Sunzha. Aslan Maschadov issued orders to the Chechen fighters to prepare for the second stage of operation "Zero Option," which would be executed if the Russians began to carry out their threats.

On the surface, it was not readily apparent how Moscow was reacting to the threat of the renewal of war actions raised by the issuance of General Lieutenant Pulikovski's ultimatum. There were clear indications of dissatisfaction, as during a meeting of the executive government the decision was made to reappoint General Lieutenant Viacheslav Tichomirov as commander of the Combined Federal Forces Group in Chechnya in place of General Pulikovski. Quickly flying into Chechnya to replace Pulikovski, Tichomirov, although he did not take any steps to void the proclaimed ultimatum, also did not take any measures to execute it.

Concerned with the developing situation, Aleksander Lebed also flew into Chechnya on August 21. He quickly characterized General Pulikovski's ultimatum as an unsuccessful prank and announced that it was withdrawn. But prank or not, 60 Grad rockets were fired by the Russian forces into the city on the day that the ultimatum was announced. The next day, 30 more Grad cassettes were released while bombarding Minutka Square. These 30 rockets were sufficient to "plow" an area of 12 hectares.[10]

The same day, Aleksander Lebed also met with Aslan Maschadov in the village of Novyje Atagi, some 25 kilometers from Grozni. The evening of the next day, Lebed and Maschadov signed an agreement for the institution of quick measures to normalize the situation in Grozni and in the Chechen Republic.

Both sides agreed to a cease-fire in Grozni and in the territory of the whole republic to commence at noon on August 23. Also, prisoners and the bodies of those killed were to be quickly exchanged on an all-for-all basis without preconditions. According to the agreement, the Federal Army Command had to withdraw all its units from Grozni and from the southern regions of Chechnya—Shatoja, Vedeno, and Nozhai Jurt—by August 26. The units from Grozni were to proceed to their nearest bases. The Russian units in the mountains of southern Chechnya, where the Chechens had encircled them and were holding them under siege, were to proceed to Staryje Atagi, Chankala, and Kurchaloja and to the village of Gamijacha in Dagestan some 7 kilometers to the west of Chasavjurt. Later, a withdrawal of all the Federal Army units from the territory of Chechnya was to be conducted in stages. The Chechens, on their part, were to withdraw their armed formations from Grozni.

In order to keep order in the city, to guard the abandoned houses against looting, and to prevent possible provocations that could impede the peace process, it was agreed by both sides to create five jointly staffed commandant's headquarters in Grozni, one central and four regional. The central headquarters would be manned by 30 people from each side and the regional headquarters by 60 people from each side. The formation of the enumerated commandants' headquarters was to begin immediately and be completed by the evening of August 24. The Russian commandant's headquarters detachment was to be formed in the 429th Motorized Rifle Regiment's 2nd Battalion's base from soldiers who had not participated in combat.[11] The guiding principle of the agreement was that not one more soldier should be killed. This was also the primary assignment given to the commandants' headquarters.

The Chechen fighters viewed the signed agreement very favorably. Their opinion was best expressed by Chechen president Zelimchan Jandarbijev: "For the Russian and Chechen people, a real possibility has now been created to stop the sacrifice of their best sons in this purposeless war."[12]

That same evening when the agreement was signed, combat activity in Grozni quieted down, although the Oktiabrsk and Zavodskaja regional commandant's headquarters manned in the city by the Russians remained blockaded. The battles in Minutka Square also stopped.

After his meeting with Lebed, Chief of Staff Maschadov also gave orders that a Federal Army motor transport column be allowed to enter the center of Grozni with food, water, and other humanitarian supplies for the blockaded Russian soldiers. He also ordered that the blockade of Russian units surrounded in the mountains to the south of Grozni be lifted and that columns carrying food and medicine be allowed to reach them.

The signed agreement helped a brittle peace to take hold in Chechnya, but, by itself, it was not sufficient to normalize the situation in the country or to regulate Russia's and Chechnya's relations. For this reason, on August 25, Aleksander Lebed once again flew into Chechnya to discuss with Aslan Maschadov a plan to reestablish peace in Chechnya. Returning to Moscow after his meeting with Maschadov, Lebed submitted his proposals for the regulation of the conflict in Chechnya to Yeltsin on August 27, informing him that the situation in Chechnya continued to be unstable and that this was so connected with "certain circumstances" that they could force the Russian government to change its tactics in the negotiations. This latter phrase was interpreted by many as Lebed's personal recognition that the war had been lost militarily. Thus due to the changed circumstances, the earlier negotiation tactics had to be changed. During this period, however, and based on Lebed's earlier efforts to remove from their posts those in charge of running the war, there was a growing expectation that Lebed was getting ready to disclose the corruption and illegal money dealings that had led to the war in the first place. Many interpreted Lebed's statement as a threat to begin naming the people responsible for the war, starting with those still attempting to continue the war at any cost. As these had been Yeltsin's closest advisors, it was also interpreted as a veiled threat against Yeltsin himself.

Tichomirov and Maschadov signed a protocol on August 25 for joint measures to effectuate the normalization of the situation in Grozni and the Chechen Republic during the first stage. As the withdrawal of the Russian units was stopped because of the increased tension in Grozni, by means of this protocol both sides obligated themselves to withdraw their units from the city during the period of August 28 to September 1.[13]

In Grozni at that time, the Chechen fighters were concentrated into two large groups, each numbering about 1,200 people, and several smaller formations that were operating in their assigned regions. One of the strongest groups was deployed in the region of Minutka Square, with its reinforcement reserve concentrated in Chernorechje. This group was equipped with 2 tanks, 4 armored vehicles, 2 armored personnel carriers, and 8 mortars. The other formation, equipped with 2 tanks, 2 armored vehicles, and 2 self-propelled artillery guns, was concentrated in the eastern part of Staropromyslovsk region with a 500-fighter reserve deployed in the communities of Pervomaisk and Dolinsk. In all, more than 4,500 Chechen fighters were concentrated in Grozni and equipped with 6 tanks, 25 armored vehicles and armored personnel carriers, and 3 self-propelled artillery guns. Additionally, almost all of the larger Chechen communities had passed into the hands of the Chechen fighters.[14]

As had been provided in the protocol, both sides began the withdrawal of their units from Grozni on August 28, and their movements were almost fully completed in three days. The Russian units were simultaneously withdrawn from the mountain regions, and their move was also almost completed in the allotted time: 2,000 Russian troops were withdrawn from Kurchaloja, 1,500 from Vedeno, and 1,000 from Shatoja. A bit earlier, the withdrawal of Russian units from the region of Nozhai Jurt was also completed. The Chechen opposition government's Internal Affairs Ministry's troops also left the government building complex in Grozni and redeployed to the Northern Airport

Military Base. In the demilitarized regions of Grozni, the joint commandant's headquarters began to function. They first began to operate in the Leninsk and Oktiabrsk regions.

Misunderstandings during the withdrawal of units from Grozni could not be avoided. However by August 2, the representatives of the Federal Army and the Chechen Armed Forces Command were able to sign a final protocol, agreeing that the armed forces of both sides had been withdrawn from Grozni to their earlier deployment bases or had moved to the new agreed-upon deployment areas. By August 1, the Federal Army had withdrawn 5,124 soldiers from Grozni: 3,313 Internal Affairs Ministry troops and 1,811 Defense Ministry soldiers. The Chechens had also withdrawn 4,349 of their fighters.

It was noted in the final document that "the interested parties have no further pretenses toward each other," although according to the commander of Russia's Internal Affairs Ministry Army Group in Chechnya, General Lieutenant Anatoli Shkirko, the Chechens had not been inclined by any means to withdraw their fighters from Grozni. He contended that they left not less than 2,000 fighters in the city, as well as 2 tanks, 7 armored vehicles, 3 armored troop carriers, 3 self-propelled artillery guns, and 5 large-caliber mortars. At the same time, of the Federal Forces only the 105th Militia Regiment and the 101st Internal Affairs Army Brigade's detachments remained in Grozni. The Chechens were also allowing movement for communications between these two units along only one street.

The plan prepared by Aleksander Lebed to regulate the situation in Chechnya was discussed in a meeting on August 29 at Premier Victor Chernomyrdin's office. It was attended by the heads of the armed services and the chairmen of the parliamentary sections. The plan was in essence approved but with the condition that it be corrected. The next day, Aleksander Lebed flew to Chasavjurt with the intention of signing a joint proclamation with the Chechen leaders as to the principles for determining the status of the Chechen Republic.

On August 31, 1996, the secretary of the Russian Security Council, Aleksander Lebed, and his assistant Sergei Charlamov, together with Chechnya's chief of staff, Aslan Maschadov, and Chechnya's vice president, Said Chasan Abubuslimov, signed two documents that later became known as the Chasavjurt Treaty. One was a general proclamation; the other contained the "General principles for the establishment of the relationship between the Russian Federation and the Chechen Republic."

What was new in these documents was that it was agreed to put off the determination of the question of Chechnya's political status for five years, that is, until 2001. This meant that the Chechens won the right to decide for themselves whether or not to remain in the Russian Federation.

Another principal condition contained in the signed documents was that, on the basis of Yeltsin's decree No. 985, signed May 25, 1996, Moscow obligated itself to withdraw its army from Chechnya. Of course, not all of it: the withdrawal of the 205th Motorized Rifle Brigade and the 101st Internal Affairs Army Brigade would require a separate decision from the president of the Russian Federation.

An important aspect of these documents was also the agreement to form, not later than October 1, 1996, a joint commission consisting of representatives of the Russian Federation and the Chechen Republic to carry out the temporary coalition government's functions during the transition period from war to peacetime conditions. This in essence recognized the fact that the Doku Zavgajev government represented Russia.

Premier Victor Chernomyrdin viewed the Chasavjurt treaty favorably, emphasizing that it sufficiently corresponded with the terms approved by his government earlier and that the several changes made during the negotiations were not in themselves significant. In a speech given in Nalchik on the occasion of the seventy-fifth anniversary of Kabarda Balkaria, he defined a program for the further regulation of the situation in Chechnya: Before any kinds of political decisions were to be made concerning Chechnya, it was first necessary to normalize the situation in Chechnya and in the whole Northern Caucasus region; categorically, combat actions could not be allowed to be renewed, and, in all cases, a takeover by emotions had to be avoided. This had to be done by involving all the significant community and political forces in the region into the peace process. The question of the exchange of prisoners and others being held by force had to be solved immediately; the representatives of one and the other side who had participated in the negotiations could not be allowed to be charged with blame; general elections would have to be held and a legal system would have to be created. Only after that could the status of Chechnya be decided. After the signing of the Chasavjurt treaty, war actions in Chechnya were terminated.

Aleksander Lebed, evaluating the situation in Chechnya, expressed the opinion that the peace process was developing in a favorable direction. In Chechnya itself, the process of demilitarization and liquidation of the effects of the results of the war was continuing, although the issue of the exchange of prisoners was being unduly prolonged. According to him, his negotiation partner, Aslan Maschadov, was in full control of about 60 percent of the Chechen hit men, in partial control of another 30 percent, and not in control of the last 10 percent. Maschadov himself was referring to the latter group as "Indians," that is, people who were fanatics and common bandits, people who had psychiatric problems and were provocateurs.

Lebed also disclosed some figures as to the results of the war. According to Lebed, the civilian war casualties were 80,000 people killed and 24,000 wounded.

At about this time, Russia's Internal Affairs Ministry also released figures as to casualties suffered by its troops during the war: 921 Internal Affairs Army soldiers had been killed, 4,500 had been wounded, 279 were missing in action, and 50 still remained prisoners of the Chechens. As to the Internal Affairs Ministry's militia forces, 280 had died, 2,013 had been wounded, 7 militiamen were missing in action, and 1 militiaman was still a prisoner of the Chechens.

The Russian Defense Ministry was still not releasing comprehensive figures as to its losses. General Tichomirov, however, stated about this time that the Russian soldiers had "honorably carried out their soldierly duties" and that 14,000 commemorative medals would be made to be worn on their chests and would be given out to soldiers and officers who participated in combat. This perhaps gives some indication as to how many Defense Ministry troops participated in combat during the war in Chechnya but may also be grossly misleading.

The only other figure announced that sheds some light is that the Internal Affairs Ministry until July 1, 1996, had held 1,743 people in the filtration camps established in Grozni and Mozdok.

The End of War Actions, the Withdrawal of the Federal Army

After the signing of the Chasavjurt treaty, the situation in Chechnya was as yet not stable enough to guarantee the nonrenewal of combat actions. The source of instability was the Federal Army's continuing presence in Chechnya, since its units had been withdrawn only from Grozni and southern Chechnya. It was thus still necessary to effectuate the remaining portion of the agreements, and on September 5, Lebed met with Maschadov for the sixth time to discuss the issues remaining unsettled in the military block.

The most important issue was, of course, the withdrawal of the Federal Army. Lebed and Maschadov quickly agreed to begin a new stage of the Federal Army's withdrawal on September 8. Although there were no discussions as to a complete withdrawal of the army, they succeeded in coming to an agreement that, during the first stage, units and detachments not part of the Northern Caucasus Military Region, about 4,500 troops, would be withdrawn next. Success was also reached on most of the political issues once it was agreed to include three representatives of Doku Zavgajev in the formation of a coalition government.

The withdrawal of the Federal Army began on September 8 as had been agreed. That day, the 133rd Battalion withdrew from Chankala, Russia's most important military base in Chechnya. Three hundred soldiers of this battalion, together with 24 T-80 tanks, were sent back to the St. Petersburg Military Region. The Russian Internal Affairs Ministry also announced that it was considering relocating the headquarters of the Internal Affairs Ministry Forces Group from Chankala to Mozdok. The leaders of the Chechen Armed Forces also announced their intention of dissolving a portion of their fighter detachments after the Federal Army units were withdrawn.

But just as it began, the withdrawal of the Federal Forces began to bog down once again. From the very start of the cease-fire, the hardest question to solve had been the all-for-all exchange of prisoners and the release of the people being held by force. On September 12, the commander of the Federal Army, General Tichomirov, announced that the withdrawal of the Federal Army was being stopped until a solution to this block of questions was found. The underlying problem was the fact that neither side had any accurate information as to how many prisoners were being kept by the other side and how many people were actually being held by force (hostages, criminals, etc.). According to the news agency Interfax, the Chechens had taken some 1,500 Russian soldiers prisoner and about 130 civilians. The Russians had taken about 1,250 Chechens into custody. Aleksander Lebed promised to clarify the reasons why this part of the agreement was not being executed and on September 17, flew back to Chechnya for the seventh time, intending to resolve the issues regarding the formation of the coalition government and the joint commission.

The results of his meetings with General Lieutenant Tichomirov and General Kvashnin, as well as with President Jandarbijev and Chief of Staff Maschadov, were positive. It was confirmed to Aslan Maschadov that the withdrawal of the Federal Army would continue and that the second unit would leave Chechnya in three days. It was also agreed that the exchange of prisoners would begin. With the intention of demilitarizing Grozni, the 101st Internal Affairs Army Brigade was to be withdrawn from the city in early October. The Internal Affairs Army Brigade from Nalchik, dislocated to the area of Bamut, would also leave Chechnya after clearing the mine fields near Bamut, Staryj Achkhoj, and Orechov. This brigade was ordered to begin the mine-clearing work in the upcoming days.

Toward the end of September, the tempo of the withdrawal of the Federal Army was increased. On September 21, the withdrawal of the 276th Regiment to its permanent base in the Ural Military Region was begun. On September 25, the 627th Internal Affairs Regiment's Special Purpose Battalion was returned to Komsomolskaja by the Amur. On September 27, the 506th Motorized Rifle Regiment also was pulled back to the Pavolga Military Region. During these same days, the 633rd Internal Affairs Detached Battalion from Pskov, the commandant's headquarters unit, and the Militia Battalion from Saint Petersburg were redeployed from Shali to Mozdok. In the beginning of October, the withdrawal of the 136th Motorized Rifle Brigade to Buinaksk was also completed. The withdrawal of the 166th Motorized Rifle Brigade back to Tver was also begun, and the first units of the 7th Paratroop Division began to leave Chechnya. By the end of October, the whole Defense Ministry Forces Group, numbering about 11,000 people, was to be withdrawn from Chechnya.

At last Chechnya was able to take a breath and begin the task of liquidating the results of the war. As a tactical step in this regard, Zelimchan Jandarbijev's visit to Moscow became very important. After relatively short negotiations, Chernomyrdin and Jandarbijev signed a joint resolution on October 3 in which the joint commission's tasks were defined. One of the most important was to prepare and submit to the Russian government for its consideration a program for 1997 for the reconstruction of Chechnya's economy and social institutions. It was emphasized in the joint resolution that during the first stage, the most important tasks would be to look after those who had suffered from the armed conflict and to prepare for the coming winter.

In Chechnya, the formation of the structures of government was also actively begun. Jandarbijev appointed Aslan Maschadov as the prime minister. Maschadov agreed to accept this post only after the Chechen field commanders seconded his appointment. The Chechen Parliament decreed that presidential elections and the elections for the new parliament would be held on January 27, 1997.

The peace process had already gone so far that it could not be stopped by a change of personnel in Moscow. The president of Russia decided to remove Aleksander Lebed from the post of secretary of the Security Council and assigned Ivan Rybkin in his place. By that time, however, almost 70 percent of the Defense Ministry's units and 40 percent of the Internal Affairs Army units had been already withdrawn from Chechnya. According to Movladi Udugov, the Chechens did not have any special grievances as to the Federal Army's performance of its obligations under the Chasavjurt treaty.

The peace process was finalized by an agreement signed on November 23, 1996, in Moscow by Russian premier Victor Chernomyrdin and the premier of the Chechen Coalition Government, Aslan Maschadov, delineating the principles of cooperation to be abided by Chechnya and the Russian government until the Chechen presidential and parliamentary elections. Russia's president Boris Yeltsin at the same time signed a decree ordering the withdrawal of the last Russian units, the 105th Motorized Rifle Brigade and the 101st Internal Affairs Army Brigade, from Chechnya.

Many political figures considered the agreement signed by the premiers of Russia and Chechnya to be a peace treaty and an unequivocal recognition of the independence of Chechnya. Both sides, however, announced that Chechnya would remain a part of the Russian Federation at least for the next three months. It was envisioned in this agreement that during this three-month period, further agreements would be concluded as to the principles of a special economic relationship between the two countries. This would include the reestablishment of the operation of the civilian airport in Grozni; the preparation and confirmation through a joint effort of a customs system for the declaration of goods crossing borders; the preparation of an agreement concerning the pumping, refining, and transportation of oil, oil products, and natural gas on the territory of Chechnya; the effectuation of measures to rebuild installations considered to be most crucial for the communities; the effectuation of measures to ensure the payment of pensions and wages; the establishment of compensations for individuals who had suffered from war activity and the establishment of a means of payment.

Specialists calculated that the effort to "reestablish constitutional order on the territory of Chechnya," which had lasted 1 year, 11 months, and 12 days, cost 150–200 billion U.S. dollars. Eighty percent of all Chechen industry had been destroyed. As always, there were no accurate figures available as to the sacrifices made by individual people, both military and civilian.

The final information published in the press was the following:

The Defense Ministry Forces Group losses were 2,837 killed, 13,270 wounded, 337 missing in action, and 432 taken prisoner. Two trillion rubles worth of combat equipment had been destroyed (a sum that would have been sufficient to support the whole Russian Army for half a year). One trillion rubles had been spent to keep the Federal Army in Chechnya. Thirteen thousand people were given combat decorations (800 posthumously). Five hundred and forty generals, officers, and warrant officers had refused to participate in the war activities in Chechnya. They had all been released from further service in the Armed Forces. According to the information of the Federal Forces Command, the Chechen fighter losses had been 15,000 people killed.

On October 12, 1996, the Russian daily *Krasnaja zvezda* published a list of 2,941 names of soldiers who had been killed. However, it was noted that this included only Defense Ministry soldiers and did not include soldiers from the Internal Affairs Army or the Border Army Forces who had been killed. The Internal Affairs Ministry losses were about the same as those of the Defense Ministry.[15]

In an article published in the Lithuanian daily *Kauno Diena* on April 9, 1997, Algirdas Endriukaitis, chairman of the executive committee of the

22-nation International Parliamentary Commission formed to investigate the problems of Chechnya, reported the following losses suffered by Chechnya:

According to information submitted by the Chechens, 62,400 houses and 59,360 apartments had been totally destroyed during the war and the personal property of 486,000 civilians had been either completely burned up or stolen; 87,500 noncombatant civilians had been killed, and 9,250 civilians had been seriously injured and left invalids; 38,000 more had been injured less seriously. The homes, apartments, supporting buildings, and personal property of 96,000 other civilians had been partially destroyed by fire or otherwise. The total losses, including damages to the country's infrastructure, agricultural sector, and ecology, were 104 billion U.S. dollars.

CHAPTER 18

Dudajev as a Symbol of the Fight for Freedom

O n April 22, 1996, news that Dzhochar Dudajev, president of the Chechen Republic of Ichkerija had been killed was heard around the world. For many, this came as no surprise. The first Chechen president had sufficient enemies among both the Russians and the Chechens.

Dzhochar Dudajev's life had been closely connected with the fate of the Chechen nation. He was born in January, 1944, in the village of Alcheroja in the region of Achchoj Martan in the former Chechen-Ingushian Autonomous Republic. That same year, his family was forced to leave Chechnya during the massive deportations ordered by Stalin. They then lived in the district of Pavlodar and in Kazakstan until 1957. When the Chechens were finally granted amnesty after Stalin's death and allowed to come back to Chechnya, Dzhochar and his family returned from exile and settled in Grozni. Here, he completed high school during evening sessions and later studied physics and mathematics in Vladikaukaz. But after the first university course, Dzhochar left Vladikaukaz and entered the Tambov Advanced Aviation School, from which he graduated in 1966. He then continued to serve in the Soviet military forces in various assignments.

Dzhochar Dudajev received his combat experience in 1986–87 while serving in Turkmenia and participated in the intensive air strikes conducted from there against the positions of the Modzhachedin in the western regions of Afghanistan.

From 1987 until the summer of 1990, Dudajev, now an Air Force general major, served in Estonia as commander of a bomber division. At the same time, he was commander of the Russian garrison in Tartu, Estonia. In 1990, he was reassigned to Grozni and, some time later, released at his own request to the reserve. In Grozni, he quickly established close ties with the Chechen Peoples' National Congress leaders Zelimchan Jandarbijev and Jaragi Mamodajev. During the first assembly of the Chechen National Congress in November, 1990, he was elected with their support to the executive committee of the congress.

Dzhochar Dudajev's wife, Ala, was Russian and originated from the city of Pushkin in the district of Moscow. Dudajev first met his future wife in Kaluga while he was still a senior lieutenant, and they were married three years later after he graduated from the institute. They had two sons and a daughter.

It would appear that Dudajev's biography contains little that is very exceptional, except for the fact that he had chosen the military profession, rose to a high post, and then had become the president of the Chechen Republic. After his death, however, a great deal of disinformation about him was released.

In one of the versions, doubts were even raised as to his nationality, with the contention that he was not even a Chechen but an Ingushian. According to the authors of this version, the information as to his date and place of birth had been falsified in his identity documents, and, in reality, Dudajev was born in April, 1943, in the village of Galashka in Ingushian territory. Since Chechens had never lived in this village, this had to mean that he also could not be a Chechen. The Ingushian nationality was written into his brothers' passports and therefore, they concluded, Dzhochar Dudajev, born into a family of seven children, also had to be an Ingushian.[1]

In another version, it was contended that Dudajev became president of Chechnya only as the result of a special operation conducted by the Russian KGB.[2] According to the Russian daily *Moscovskij komsomolec* (April 1, 1995), in 1989, when nationalistic tendencies began to appear in Chechnya, Moscow came to the conclusion that unless appropriate measures were taken immediately, the situation in the Northern Caucasus region would become very complicated and uncontrollable. The largest threat to Moscow was the possible appearance of a new source of armed conflict under the cloak of a fight for national independence. Thus Moscow was left with no other option but to attempt to influence the development of events in Chechnya. A special KGB group was created, which, after analyzing the situation in Chechnya, decided that an appropriate action would be to organize the overthrow of the existing government of Chechnya. The game plan called for a person subservient to Russia to take power in Chechnya.

But a change of government openly inspired by Moscow would not have been very convincing and could have brought negative results. Thus the most appropriate method of reaching the required results was through the infiltration of the national movement itself while supporting its leaders. The problem facing Moscow, however, was that not one of the leaders in the national movement at that time was considered suitable for this purpose. A neutral person who had as yet not gotten involved in the political intrigue in Chechnya was needed. Such a person was found, according to this version, in Dudajev. His candidacy for a leadership role was first confirmed by Ruslan Khasbulatov and Doku Zavgajev. General Major Dzhochar Dudajev was released to the reserve and, with KGB guidance, became involved in political activity.

As is also quite often the case in such tales, this version is not without the sudden appearance of a double, or stand-in. Everything proceeded according to plan until, in the spring of 1992, exactly when the division and parceling out of leadership positions was taking place in Chechnya, Dzhochar Dudajev suddenly took ill with yellow jaundice. His sudden disappearance for two months would have wrecked Moscow's efforts. But again in the best tradition of the Secret Services, a way out was found in three days. A vegetable warehouse driver, Albert Petrovich Zaicev, was found living in the city of Serpuchov in the district of Moscow. Born in 1948, he was identical in every way to Dudajev. The version dutifully notes that it was impossible to determine whether Zaicev also originated from the Caucasus as there was no notation on his birth certificate as to his father.

Zaicev was then taught the rudiments of the Chechen language for a week and at the same time was familiarized with the political situation in the Chechen Republic. Then, accompanied by two bodyguards from the KGB, he went to Chechnya. The week of instruction was apparently sufficient, as Zaicev showed himself to be very talented. It was not necessary for him to learn the Chechen language well as Dzhochar Dudajev himself had not spoken it very well. The secret of the substitution was disclosed to only a selected few, including Dudajev's wife, Ada, as it had been impossible to also find a double for her on such short notice.

But after a while, as is always the case in these scenarios, Zaicev got so used to his new role that he did not want to return to his previous identity and allow the real Dudajev to return. Allegedly, those in Chechnya who knew his secret also did not want him to give up his role, as Zaicev did not interfere with their machinations with oil dealings, contraband, and other illegal undertakings. Supposedly when the KGB agents finally arrived to take him back, the commander of his personal guard, Ruslan Labazanov, politely showed them the door. As it happened, the real Dudajev also did not want to return to Chechnya. Not wanting to accept the responsibility for what had already been done, he decided to remain in the Podmoskovski district.

To Locate and Destroy!

On February 1, 1995, in the aftermath of the failed Grozni assault, the Russian Prosecutor General's Office filed criminal charges against Dzhochar Dudajev and issued an order for his arrest. Dudajev was charged under four sections of the Russian Criminal Code, all of which carried the death penalty.

The charges against him consisted of attempting by intentional means to usurp the government of the Chechen-Ingushian Autonomous Republic, interfering with the lawful activities of the constitutionally elected government, publicly inciting the perpetration of terrorist acts, and instigating national, social, and religious antagonisms on the republic's territory. Especially accented in the legal documents were the large casualties suffered by the Russians in December, 1994, and in January, 1995, when, "in an attempt to hold on to power," Dzhochar Dudajev, together with his illegal armed formations, organized armed resistance to the Federal Army and to the forces of the Internal Affairs Ministry and the Federal Counterintelligence Service (former KGB) while they were carrying out their duties of "reestablishing constitutional order on Chechen territory."

Dzhochar Dudajev's reaction to the announcement that criminal charges had been filed against him was quite swift and uncompromising. During a press conference held on the night of February 7, he had warned the Russian government that it should not attempt to arrest him, Shamil Basajev, or the other Chechen military commanders and threatened: "If I should die, the war will take on such a character that even your hair will stand up."

Toward the middle of March, the pro-Moscow, temporarily appointed Chechen prosecutor general, B. Baschanov, announced that he had filed additional criminal charges and issued warrants of arrest for seven of Dudajev's most important supporters: Vice President Zelimchan Jandarbijev; chief of the Military Staff Aslan Maschadov; the director of the Chechen government's Security Service, Sultan Gelischanov; the former Internal Affairs minister, Kazbek Machashev; minister of Economics and Finances, T. Abubakirov; and field commanders Ruslan Gelajev and Shamil Basajev. All were charged with treason and banditry except Abubakirov, who was charged with exceeding the authority granted him by his government and the scope of his duties.

Once the criminal action was filed, Russia's Internal Affairs Ministry issued orders to locate and arrest Dudajev. Apparently at the very beginning, this task was assigned to the Russian General Staff's Intelligence Command (formerly GRU), but by spring, the task of effectuating Dudajev's arrest passed on to the Justice Department.

Nothing was being mentioned about the Federal Counterintelligence Service's participation in the announced manhunt. In the middle of March, the commander of the Federal Counterintelligence Service for the territory of Chechnya promised to catch Dzhochar Dudajev within several days. But that remained only a boastful promise.

Toward the end of April, however, a special group from the central apparatus of the Federal Counterintelligence Service was deployed to Chechnya. This group included counterintelligence operations specialists and specialists from the military counterintelligence services. In May, they returned to Moscow and reported that the seizure of Dudajev was impossible, mostly because the director of the Federal Counterintelligence Service, Sergei Stepashin, had not yet signed an order for the execution of the special operation.

Apparently not one of the service commanders dared to sign such an order, purportedly because Dzhochar Dudajev's capture operation would have resulted in significant losses to both sides and large civilian casualties. During the operation, Special Purpose troops were to have effected the actual capture operation while Internal Affairs Ministry and Defense Ministry forces would have supported them by providing internal and external encirclement ring security. But according to the calculations of these specialists, during the execution of a special operation for the capture of each of the persons charged, losses would have been sustained by the Internal Affairs Specnaz soldiers of up to 10 killed and 20 wounded and by the Federal Army troops of up to 20 killed and 30 wounded. Dudajev's capture operation would also have cost the Special Services up to 35 of its troops killed and 60 wounded. It was impossible to estimate how many civilian casualties would have been sustained, but most likely this figure would also have been high.

Considering the continuous high losses sustained by the Federal Forces in the subsequent war, such uncharacteristic concern for casualties has to be looked upon with a certain amount of skepticism. But the operative fact was that in spite of the existence of an arrest order issued by the prosecutor general, no one was prepared to execute it.

As Dudajev's capture was judged to be difficult, if not almost impossible, there was only one option—to kill him.[3] This had been attempted in various ways, and the attempts had been numerous.

Specially prepared teams had made attempts on the life of Dudajev, but on all four occasions, the Chechen Security Service had been able to identify and liquidate them. Several attempts had also been made to blow him up by mining the roads along which he was expected to travel. One of these attempts almost succeeded, and Dudajev escaped death only by chance. A mine was set off under a car he was expected to get into. But at the last moment, Dudajev got into column's third car instead of the second car, which he customarily rode in. His wife, Ala, was sitting in the fifth car, and their twelve-year-old daughter was in the first car. They all escaped injury.

Special efforts were also made to kill Dudajev by sudden and unexpected attacks from the air. A special squadron was formed for this mission in one of the air bases near the Chechen administrative border. As soon as the squadron received information as to where Dudajev had been seen, that community was immediately bombed and shot up by rockets. At times, these air strikes were so accurate that the Chechens began to accuse journalists of leaking information. Journalists who were suspected of cooperating with the Russian Security Services were not allowed by the Chechens to enter areas under their control.

Most of these air strikes, however, were executed too late, only after Dudajev had already left the area. But there were several instances when Dudajev escaped death only by chance. For this reason, Dudajev was forced constantly to change his location, not staying in any one place longer than two hours.

That Dzhochar Dudajev was being massively hunted did not go unnoticed. There had even been quite a few open discussions printed in the newspapers as to why the Russian Armed Forces could not find snipers or other specialists who would be able to find him and kill him. The conclusion often drawn in these discussions was that although Dudajev's death was highly desirable, it may also have been very much feared by certain people in high office. Could there not be a packet lying in the safe of the *New York Times* or the *Washington Post* with a notation "To be opened in case of my death"? And perhaps the packet contains something the disclosure of which may not be very much liked by Pavel Grachev or Sergei Stepashin and the others who for several years were involved with Dudajev in matters involving large sums of money.[4]

Perhaps only one thing concerning the manhunt for Dzhochar Dudajev has drawn little comment: Why was the Russian president and his closest circle proclaiming Dudajev a criminal, who had to be found and executed without any investigation or trial?

Versions of the Circumstances of Dudajev's Death

"I am prepared to meet with Allah," Dzhochar Dudajev said after one of the many unsuccessful attempts on his life.[5] This meeting apparently took place late on the evening of April 21, 1996.

The vice president of the Chechen Republic of Ichkerija, Zelimchan Jandarbijev, reporting about the death of Dudajev, stated that it took place near the village of Gechi Chu in the region of Urus Martan. He and Shamil Basajev confirmed Dudajev's death. According to them, Dudajev and his escort were traveling that fateful evening in several automobiles from Gechi Chu to a nearby mountain clearing where they intended to converse with several people by satellite telephone. With Dudajev were his assistant, Vacha Ibrahimov; military prosecutor Mahomed Dzhakijev; and his former assistant in Moscow, Chamid Kurbanov. His wife, Ala, and several other people were in another car. While Dudajev was talking on the telephone, military aircraft appeared and fired air-to-ground rockets at them with amazing accuracy. The first rocket struck the Niva automobile in which Dudajev was seated, the second two rockets turned it to rubble.[6]

This version of Dudajev's death is based on the fact that, already for three months, attempts had been made to triangulate by radio location techniques the places from which Dudajev had been conversing by satellite telephone. During that period, military aircraft took to the air immediately upon any indication that a transmission was being made. The aircraft were armed with rockets that were able to home in on a source radiating radio signals, in this case the satellite telephone antenna.[7]

Technically this would not have been very hard to do with radio intelligence satellites that can determine within several minutes the exact location of a source of radio signals. This would have been even less difficult since the Russians knew exactly what type of telephone was being used; Radujev had left behind a telephone of the same type in Pervomaiskoje during his breakout from that village. An automobile battery provided a source of power. The greatest problem with the tracking process was only that the radio pulse beam was very narrow.

The Russians had already made four attempts to shoot air-to-ground rockets at locations from which Dudajev was talking by telephone. But the conversations were so short that by the time the aircraft rose into the air, conducted search operations to pinpoint the target, and executed the procedures necessary to set the rockets' homing systems, the rockets did not have sufficient time to complete their flight to the target while being guided by the signal along their full trajectory. Once the telephone and therefore the radio signal was shut off, guidance was interrupted and the rockets were flown their final course without guidance, falling sufficiently far from the locations at which they were aimed and causing no damage to the target.

However, even if the conversations by satellite telephone had been of sufficient length, the probability of the rockets destroying the person talking by telephone would not have been very high. The rockets could only home in on the antenna itself, and this could be separated from the telephone and the person talking by a sufficient length of cable. The rocket guidance systems also produced a certain degree of error.

It is obvious that Dzhochar Dudajev knew the capabilities of such rockets quite well, having himself previously been a military pilot. For this reason, security measures were instituted. His personal guard had been instructed to control the length of the telephone conversations, and if the conversation lasted longer than what was allowed by security considerations, he was to shut off the telephone even against Dudajev's will.

Dudajev was fully aware that Russian aircraft had been attempting to home rockets in on his satellite telephone radio signals. He even attempted to calculate the time needed from the initiation of the telephone for the rockets to strike the source of the signals.

On this occasion, however, two telephone conversations were planned. Four people were seated in Dudajev's Niva automobile; Dudajev sat to the right of the driver. The back seat was occupied by military prosecutor Mahomed Dzhanijev and Chamid Kurbanov, who had been appointed two days previously minister of Foreign Affairs. The prophet of the coming disaster was an apparently broken telephone antenna cable. In spite of the lack of an appropriate cable, it was decided not to put off the planned telephone conversations. Thus the normal procedures to offset the antenna at a distance was skipped, and the antenna was placed on top of the occupied automobile and connected directly to the telephone.[8]

Kurbanov was the first one to use the telephone, using it to read a proclamation to Svododa Radio (Radio Free Europe). After that, Dudajev used the telephone to get in touch with journalist Konstantin Borovoj. They had been talking for about 3–4 minutes when Dudajev remarked that he was hearing the sound of approaching aircraft and broke off the conversation. The transcript of this final conversation was later published in the Russian daily newspaper *Moscovskij komsomolec* (April 25, 1996). They were perhaps Dudajev's last words.

During this fateful last conversation, the possibilities of beginning peace negotiations was discussed. Dudajev informed Borovoj about the Chechen Peoples' National Congress, which had taken place the prior day, and its decision that negotiations were impossible with those who were committing crimes against humanity in the territory of the Chechen Republic of Ichkerija. During the conversation, Dudajev threatened retribution to these criminals.

Dudajev's wife was positioned with a personal guard further away from the Niva. Witnesses heard a whistle and then a not especially loud explosion.

Ala was knocked back by the shock wave but, after gathering herself, ran to the remains of the Niva and discovered the automobile covered over with earth. When the vehicle was dug out, all those inside were already dead.

Vacha Ibrahimov, who had been at that moment kneeling by the front wheel, was blown by the shock wave to the side and, although seriously injured, survived.

According to Ala, Dzhochar Dudajev appeared to be still alive but unconscious. His sleeves had been ripped off, and his arms were covered with many small wounds from the shattered window glass. His hair and mustache were singed. When Ala lifted Dzhochar's head, she felt a large wound in the back of his head the size of three fingers. Only when he was brought back to the village nearby did she realize that Dzhochar was dead:

> "In the home where Dudajev was brought, the nurse told me that he was still alive. But when they started to bomb the house and we hid in the cellar, I began to think: If Dzhochar is still alive, then why did they leave him upstairs? Then when we went upstairs, I finally realized that he had been killed immediately but had been slowly cooling down.
>
> "Dudajev was washed and dressed in white clothes. He lay on the floor, but his face had remained tense as if he was still sensing danger. I prayed all night by his side and in the morning, I noticed that his face had released its tension and had become calm and blessed.
>
> "After that there came one more night. The owner of the house and the other men had gone out to search for four horses so that they could take Dzhochar into the mountains to the elder Amaci where he had wished to be buried. But later they began to talk us out of this, saying that the aircraft would bomb the cemetery and the gravesite. And, in fact, the next day, they bombed that place so intensively that we would hardly have come back alive. We finally buried him nearby." [9]

Another version of Dudajev's death was published in the press.[10] This version contended that Dudajev could not have died from a rocket homing in on his radio telephone signal. The probability of a rocket striking so accurately was very small. According to this version, Dudajev's death was organized by the Russian special security services, but this time they made use of the need for the representatives of both the Chechen and Russian governments to have a confidential direct communication link. Since a regular satellite communications telephone could not ensure the confidentiality of telephone conversations with Dudajev, as had been attested to by the publication of recordings of his conversations from time to time, the Russians gave Dudajev a satellite telephone equipped with a secret "black box" that could encode the conversations. Together with the black box, a specialist was sent to Chechnya from the Federal Government's Communications and Information Agency. A bomb was placed into the black box, but the specialist was not informed of this fact. He was responsible for looking after the black box and was obligated to ensure that its seals not be violated, unaware that he had been picked to die along with Dudajev.

According to this version, Dudajev's death was the result of an explosion of a plastic explosive. This aspect of the operation was then masked by the publication of the version about an attack by air-to-ground rockets. The baselessness of the rocket version was allegedly confirmed by the Federal Military Command itself. Not knowing about the special security services operation, the command inadvertently admitted that there had not been any flights over the village of Gechi Chu at that time and that no rocket artillery salvos were fired.

The real cause of Dudajev's death, whether it had been from aviation rockets or from a plastic bomb, could have been easily determined by specialists. But neither the body itself nor photographs of the body were shown anywhere. According to the authors of the second version, this fact was an indication of the intention to hide the real cause of death. It also had to mean that the plan could not have been carried out without the assistance of those closest to Dudajev. Proponents of this version pointed out that none of the best-known field commanders or even his usual bodyguards, the Arsanukajev brothers who were constantly at his side, were with Dudajev during this final excursion. This was indeed a very strange and telling circumstance. Purportedly, their absence was a precondition insisted upon for the use of the secret telephone communications link so that the secrecy of the negotiations with the representatives of the Russian government would be assured.

However, the people close to Dudajev apparently remain convinced that the cause of his death was rocket fire from an aircraft overhead. According to them, the hunt for Dudajev had been continuously intensified. A week before his death, the electricity in that whole region was shut off and all radio stations shut down to make it easier to perform radio location of Dudajev's whereabouts.[11]

Very few people actually know where Dzhochar Dudajev is buried. It was announced in the beginning that the Chechens had buried him near the village of Salazha. This is not quite believable, as according to Chechen tradition, the dead are buried in the place where they were born and Dudajev was born in the village of Alcheroja.

As far as is known, he was buried with rites prescribed by Islamic tradition somewhere high up in the mountains not far from the village of his birth.

The Muslim ceremony was supplemented only by a salute from automatic weapons. Only his wife, brother, and several close friends participated in the burial ceremony. Even his children were not present. Purportedly, the complete ceremony was recorded on video and put in a safe place. For security reasons, the secret of where Dudajev is buried was to be made public only after the war. According to witnesses who were present, the following words are written on a gravestone set on his grave:

> Oh, son! If you shall live to the next century
> And standing on the high Caucasus
> will gaze about you,
> Think that here too were men
> who had raised up the nation
> And had gone out to defend freedom and
> the most holy ideals!

But did Dudajev in fact die? There can be no satisfactory answer since Dudajev's death was confirmed by only a few people and no one else saw his body. Even his wife, Ala, spoke very circumspectly during an interview with journalists concerning the circumstances of his death and funeral.

At the end of May, Ala Dudajev was taken into custody at the Nalchik Airport while attempting to fly to Turkey with a forged passport. She may have wanted to fly to her youngest son, Dega, who had been settled in one of the Muslim countries while his father was still alive. After Dudajev's death, his oldest son, Alvur, was also sent there. But then again, some suggested, perhaps Ala was attempting to get to her seriously wounded husband, Dzhochar Dudajev.

Ala Dudajev was released by instruction from Boris Yeltsin. After expressing a wish to live at the home of her father, she was escorted by agents of the Russian special security services to the town of Pushkin in the Podmoskovski district. She stayed there for only two weeks, however, and then disappeared. According to her father, Fiodor Kulikov, several men of Russian nationality came to visit her on July 12, accompanied by a woman Ala had apparently known from before. After their meeting, Ala packed her things, climbed into their automobile, and drove away without saying where she was going. From Ala's father's and Dudajev's nephew's hints, one could gather that she was in some foreign country.

The biggest doubts as to Dudajev's death, however, were raised by the unexpected "resurrection from the dead" of field commander Salman Radujev. After several months of being listed among the dead, Salman Radujev suddenly reappeared on July 18, 1996, at a press conference held at a secret location in Chechnya. But an even larger sensation was created by Radujev's announcement that Dzhochar Dudajev was still alive but in critical condition.

Although the belief that Dzhochar Dudajev was still alive was already widely held by a number of Chechens, this belief only grew stronger after Radujev's unexpected confirmation. That Dudajev was still alive was also hinted at by his brother Bekmurz. Thus, during the assault of Grozni in August, 1996, the Chechen fighters were convinced that Dudajev would reappear in Chechnya within a short period of time.

The question as to whether Dzhochar Dudajev was actually killed has still not yet been answered with any degree of certitude.

Once the war ended, the Chechens decided to rename Grozni after Dzhochar Dudajev. Grozni is now called Dzhochargala.

Evaluations of Dudajev in the West

The treatment of Dzhochar Dudajev in this book may be seen in some quarters as too kind. Dudajev was undeniably a highly controversial personality, inciting at the same time great loyalty and immense personal animosity. His enemies have repeatedly accused him of being a military dictator without the least interest in sharing power and the perpetrator of countless atrocities. He has also been accused, rightly or wrongly, of illegal arms dealing, of making personal use of Chechen oil revenues, and of other illegal financial activities.

This book, however, is the story of an emerging nation fighting a war against a vastly superior attacking force, and it attempts to outline the actions, tactics, and thinking of both sides. We have limited descriptions to only those actions of Dzhochar Dudajev that were found to have a significant effect on the course and outcome of this war. Admittedly, value judgments were made. But every effort was also made to attempt to preserve objectivity and to ground opinion on sound evidence.

In writing about a controversial event, a historian invariably is faced with the problem of how to avoid undue bias without, at the same time, tying himself into the straightjacket of an overly "neutral" stance, which, by its own internal workings, necessarily negates all further possibilities of making value judgments, even where they would be otherwise appropriate. While it is not valid for a historian to moralize or to polemicize, it is equally not valid for him to attempt to avoid issues of value or to operate on the basis of only fashionable myth. The historian's duty is to constitute factually what is and then to attempt to decipher why things are as they are. Where facts are uncontroverted, this, of course, is easier to do. But when there is the danger that conclusions will also flow from one's own stance, then some explanation is necessary as to the parameters of the stance taken.

Events are unavoidably seen through one's own cultural and experiential prism. Thus the view from Eastern Europe may understandably be somewhat different from that seen from the shores of the Potomac or, for that matter, of the Thames or even the Seine. In Eastern European countries such as Lithuania, Soviet efforts to "preserve territorial integrity" are still alive in everyone's memory. As late as 1991, Soviet tanks were still maneuvering on the streets of Vilnius, and Soviet military forces and Internal Affairs units were storming its parliament and ransacking its television tower.

Moreover, the "truth" of events as seen in Eastern Europe and in many of the countries previously occupied by the Soviet Union is not judged merely from what is reported in the press but also invariably from what is written between the lines. That is the legacy of the peoples' experience with a press that has been controlled by the Communist State. To the betterment or, some would even say, to the detriment of the "truth," anything that is perceived as propaganda, especially Russian propaganda, is often discarded immediately. Such propaganda still has a sour taste, and aversion to it has been bred into the people almost to the point of its being genetic. After all, during half a century of Soviet occupation in Lithuania, all resistance to Soviet rule has also been cast as banditry.

Although the Soviet Union is now referred to in the past tense, the actions of its successor state, the Russian Federation, are still looked upon with some anxiety by its geographical neighbors. The great hope is that the Russian Federation is different from its predecessor. But when the Russian Federation periodically allows itself to speak in strident tones of "zones of influence" outside its own borders and of the preservation and even the reconstitution of its "territorial integrity," this time in the form of a "Great Russia" with obvious imperial pretensions, Eastern Europeans cannot but help wonder who are the targets referred to in such formulations.

Solidarity with other small nations now undergoing a similar trial by fire is thus not only grounded on an elementary sense of justice or support for what is seen as a noble cause but also on a sense of déjà vu. But for the fortuitousness of history and the grace of God, Chechnya's fate could very well have been the fate of the Baltic countries and others that are now free and independent and anxiously working to secure Western assurances that the events of the past shall not reoccur. Undeniably, at least through Eastern European eyes, Russia's recent actions in Chechnya have an uncanny resemblance to the colonial practices of the Soviet Union.

There is little equivalent in the Western sensibility for the experiences preserved in the psyche of those many small nations that underwent Soviet occupation: Memories of devastation, of foreign rapacious armies, of brutal, unending occupation by a foreign totalitarian regime, of mass arrests and periodic mass deportations to the barren wastes of Siberia or other parts of the Asian land mass are still alive among the people and have an immediacy and realism not sensed elsewhere. The people also remember great personal loss, of futures unrealized and, perhaps what is worse, of the dangers of an imperceptible growth of a belief that nothing will change, that one's fate is inevitable and that acceptance is preferable to the unending frustration. Unavoidably, these feelings also include an unspoken sense of abandonment by the civilized world.

It is thus understandably hard for a reader from "another world" to fathom this sensibility. It is equally hard for him to understand the motivations behind an independence movement of a nation whose existence was not even known to him until this war began to appear in the world's headlines.

The problem for the Westerner is the real lack of objective information as to what is really going on outside his own geopolitical and experiential framework. Commonplace notions in the West say that the world is, after all, going through an integration rather than a separation process. Rule from Moscow is even considered in some circles as perhaps the equivalent of rule from Brussels. Often heard is the geopolitical postulate that since a small nation is geographically located at Russia's back door, it is rightfully within Russia's "zone of influence." Chechnya is Russia's problem and not a place where the West should meddle. The Chechen people should accommodate and learn to live with their neighbors.

But the view from the other end of the telescope is different. Commonplace notions here are that while young democracies are usually full of wide-eyed notions that the right of nations to be free is God-given, that human rights, regardless of where they are, are worthy of protection, that all peoples, however unpretentious in their wealth and numbers, still have a rightful place in the World Community of Nations, something drastic happens to democracies when they become middle-aged. Then their own dreams and hard-won democratic heritages are somehow forgotten and their present "national interests," that is, their access to resources, their comparative advantage to trade, their international relations with other, even totalitarian regimes, begin to displace these earlier values. Somehow, mature democracies begin to draw the conclusion that their now "more refined" views of where their real national interests lie require that they forgo their own democratic traditions, at least as far as external relations are concerned. This realpolitik view convinces them that their own positions in the world will be hurt by any further championing of the values of democracy, even when these values are based on their own earlier principles. Not without reason, all this results in a naked "power politics" view of events. But when these policies are viewed by other, still emerging, still yearning-to-be-free nations, they appear, at best, to be myopic and, at worst, an outright betrayal of the West's own democratic heritage.

Both are biases. Understandably, such views necessarily also color judgments of events. In the West, the situation in Chechnya is mostly seen from a position of neutrality, often through European Community "observers" or through the eyes of western diplomats who themselves are outside the fray. But to get a true sense of the hunt, one must also spend some time among the hunted. Thus in the formerly occupied countries, the tendency is still to "root for the underdog," especially if he is taking on your former antagonist and tormentor.

In evaluating the place of Dzhochar Dudajev in this war, albeit from a Eastern European vantage point, several preliminary conclusions as to Chechnya as a nation state and Chechens as a people have to be drawn:

Based on three hundred years and more of history, it is almost inconceivable that Chechens will ever voluntarily accommodate and become Russians. Thus, regardless of the outcome of their present campaign to gain international recognition or of what stance the West takes, there is little likelihood that their fight for freedom will cease. They will remain a thorn in Russia's side until factual independence is achieved and their nation state is free of external interference. The problem of Chechnya will not go away and will continue to plague the international conscience. The Chechens see their own place under the sun, and that is in their own traditional homeland, under their own laws and as a free and sovereign nation. The view in Eastern Europe is not only that this is their right under international law and under the United Nations Charter but that, if all else fails, they have also earned it by force of arms. After all, they won the war.

The contentions of Dudajev's "criminal regime" also have to be addressed honestly and directly. On one hand, the press, including the Western press, have made repeated references to the "Chechen mafia," to "narco-business," to "international terrorism," namely all those things that, if true, civilized nations should be the first to condemn. One can argue on good grounds that these were but oversized fictions developed by the Russian government's disinformation machine. But there is also ample internal evidence that belies this point.

When the actual events of this war are examined, one cannot but sense that something crucial is missing in such accusations, that such press reports are not reflecting a much greater reality. The essence of any organized crime syndicate is the quest for personal profit regardless of the consequences to others. The glue holding any such criminal syndicate together is this striving for personal profit. Loyalty, courage, and especially self-sacrifice simply do not enter the equation. But as can be seen from every aspect of this conflict, the driving force for the Chechen forces was self-sacrifice for the national good. This massive outpouring of valor, duty, courage, and perseverance in the face of almost insurmountable odds on the part of literally tens of thousands of Chechens has rarely been seen in any conflict. The basis of all Chechen tactics, even those minutely formulated by the Chechen General Staff, was also individual initiative. It should be obvious that these attributes cannot be bought for money or instilled at the point of a gun. It should thus also be obvious to everyone still having an open mind that these are not the indications of a "criminal syndicate" but the classic signs of a close-knit people having a keen sense of national purpose who are fighting for their nation's survival and freedom.

The war in Chechnya was also fought in the background of countless, massive atrocities. Without chronicling once more the events in Samashk, Pervomaisk, or the myriad other Chechen communities that were mercilessly destroyed, it should suffice to say that some of the worst wartime atrocities inflicted in the last half century occurred in Chechnya.

Westerners, for some reason, find it easier to speak of war crimes in Bosnia but cannot bring themselves to confront the same issue in Chechnya. The Western press and international institutions have all been somehow strangely reticent, even meek, when it comes to the apportionment of blame. Some apportionment of blame, however, has to be made, regardless of present relationships with Russia. Even if one were to rest one's case only on the prosecution's evidence, Dudajev's own "sins" and those of his followers pale in comparison with what was perpetrated by the Russian side. Selection among events with the intent of finding not what is objective but only what is "usable" or what is simply more advantageous to perceive is simply not acceptable. Although one cannot justify any crime or atrocity, one also cannot put some under a magnifying glass while disregarding countless others.

The problem of Russia's colonial empire also has to be seen for what it is, not what the West would like it to be. The hope that Russia will eventually develop into a democratic state, will begin to serve all its people equally and equitably, and will no longer be a threat to her neighbors is upheld by all, including the countries formerly occupied by the Soviet Union. The West should take all steps to further such cause.

But the process begun in Chechnya is but the obvious symptom of centrifugal forces that most likely will continue to tear at the Russian Federation, at least in the foreseeable future. The harsh fact of life is that there is as yet insufficient available glue to hold the Russian Federation together, and this insufficiency will remain until the people inhabiting the territories of the Russian Federation either separate into their own states or create some form of real voluntary union through the growth of truly democratic processes. Force as a method of preserving the Union is not going to be enough, and after the war in Chechnya, it is even highly doubtful that it is any longer available.

The West thus cannot continue to pick and chose what facts it wants to hear that will allow them to push off the burden of dealing with this continuing problem of Russian colonialism and thus of Chechnya. A prime example of this is the still fashionable view in some quarters that the Chechen people were somehow talked into "acting against their natural interests" and "hoodwinked into forgoing their 'rightful' place in the Russian Federation." If true, this state of affairs, of course, would be to the West's advantage, as the West could continue its present policies without having to delve into the harsher realities. But, in reality, doing so would only prolong the problem and serve the Russian position.

There is a final aspect to these preliminary conclusions. For a people fighting for their independence, the apparent successes of such propaganda has the effect of negating any lingering hope that help or even sympathy for their cause will come from the West. This often results in an underlying anger, even rage, for the fact that the West's views are often so short-sighted, that it only conveniently sees what it wants to see. The danger is that such newly emerging nations will turn away from the West to the detriment of the formation of a unified, well-regulated, and civilized world community.

This having been said, some answer still has to be given to those Western observers who argue that the war had personally "gotten to Dudajev" and that, by the end, he had deteriorated psychologically. They often bring up various "crimes" allegedly committed under his direction by his followers as a prime reason for condemning him.

The first accusation, that the war "had gotten" to Dudajev, can perhaps be addressed most easily, again if only from a personal point of view. Dzhochar Dudajev was the leader of a nation at war, a nation that was being methodically exterminated. He himself was constantly hunted by all the means available to a major military power, and his chances of surviving the duration of the war, even by his own estimation, were slim. The survival of his people and their centuries-old quest for independence was at stake, and this indeed must have been a very heavy burden for him to carry.

It would have been highly abnormal and even the sign of a pathological personality had Dzhochar Dudajev *not* been deeply effected by the events around him. The more precise question should instead be whether Dudajev continued functioning effectively during the whole duration of the war. Did he continue to perform at the level of effectiveness that it was his obligation to his people to be at? By all indications, this has to be answered affirmatively, even that he acted brilliantly as both a political and military leader. Was he indulging in any actions that either harmed the cause of his people or could be termed pathological or aberrational? Again, all indications show that this was not the case.

But what of the accusations of "atrocities" as reported by the press? It must also be said that these all occurred in the background of a merciless war during which multiple senseless deaths were occurring daily. If Dudajev was at fault for any of them, then history should record this fact. But the fact of the matter is that he may not have been to blame for many of them even though the responsibility had been laid at his doorstep.

Events obscured by the fog of war are never clear-cut and often leave few surviving witnesses. This is even more so in the special operations war where the effect sought is to disinform and mislead. Russian propoganda was based on the allegation that the Dudajev government was a "criminal regime" committing crimes, even atrocities, against the people of Chechnya, a province of the Russian Federation. Thus crimes were needed. If Dudajev's people were not committing crimes, then appropriate crimes had to be committed in his name.

That this was being done by the Russian special operations people was pointed out by Algirdas Endriukaitis, Lithuanian parliamentarian and Chairman of the International Parliamentary Commission to investigate the problem of Chechnya. In an article published October 23, 1997, in the Lithuanian daily *Lietuvos Aidas,* he stated that Russian-organized diversion teams were very much at work in Chechnya during much of the war:

> During the war, two thousand Chechen criminal offenders had been released from Russian and Chechen jails. In 1994, Russian Secret Services [intelligence, security agencies] established a base in the Prudboja community in the Volgagrad district where they selected from among these offenders and prepared them for "diversion" work in Chechnya. ["Diversion" actions included abductions, robberies, and killings per order.] After the war,

the Russians did not need to organized new "diversion" groups but only to pick from the existing groups which were the most appropriate. Some of these groups were primitive and were useful only for medium and small-sized jobs. Others which were better organized, better armed, and trained were given special tasks such as the abduction of specific people. The abductors sell their victims to the ordering party who either take them out of Chechnya or keep them within the country. When the victims are taken out of Chechnya, a mandatory rule is that the negotiations for their release be held on Chechen soil. The organizational structure for the abduction of "political" victims is as follows: The abductors (a well organized "diversion" group), the local ordering party (the local "resident" in intelligence terms), and the agency ordering party (the security agency executing the political requests and plans). With such an organizational structure, only the criminal aspects ever appear and the probability of finding evidence of the agency order party are very slight. At this time, a special GRU (Russian Federation Defense Ministry Intelligence Command) Center is operating in Northern Ossetia and is tasked with "diversion-disruption" operations.

In Chechnya to the present, the idea is being created that Chechnya has become the gathering place for criminals and that it is impossible for people to live there peacefully. The inability to get wages and pensions, the blockage of the airport, the unavailability of reparations for war damage, all these are intended to instill in the minds of the people that they will not be able to survive without Russia.

Given this "active" formation of the "truth" during the whole course of the war, it is hard to get definitive evidence of any single event or to evaluate any specific atrocity.

In spite of views elsewhere, Dzhochar Dudajev is undeniably a hero to his people. There is a Caucasus expression: "It is in God's hands that we live and die and that God often takes the dearest and the best. When men die here, we clean our minds of bad thoughts about them."

Perhaps the best advice would be for us to do the same.

CHAPTER 19

Closing Words

Much attention has been devoted to the military action in Chechnya, especially in the Russian press. Still, politicians, military specialists, experts, and analysts continue to hold markedly different views as to the nature of this action. Some continue to characterize it as simply a "special operation to reestablish constitutional order and the rule of law," others tend to view it as an "armed conflict," yet others call it a "war" or some other form of armed confrontation.

In Russia, there continues to be a studied avoidance of the term "war" to characterize this recent combat event. Instead, use for the most part is made of the term "special operation to reestablish constitutional order and the rule of law," as was contained in the Russian president's decree. According to General Colonel Leontijev Shevcov, commander of the Russian General Staff's High Operational Command, the participation of the Russian Armed Forces in the events in Chechnya cannot be characterized as military combat actions in the classical sense. The operation was conducted because a dictatorial regime established itself in one of the regions of the Russian Federation, namely the Chechen Republic, by means of an armed insurrection and its illegal armed formations then began to threaten not only the neighboring subjects of the Russian Federation but the integrity and stability of the whole of Russia.

According to the military terminology in use in Russia, an armed confrontation participated in by armed forces such as occurred in Chechnya is classified as a "military conflict." Russian military theorists use the term "military conflict" to describe a confrontation and battle between sovereign countries or internally between social or ethnic groups or other community groups using military force. According to Professor A. Beliajev of the Russian General Staff Academy, the concept of a military conflict is markedly wider than that of a war. A military conflict can be a war as well as an "armed conflict." It is thus necessary to distinguish the concept of a military conflict from that of an armed conflict. Any war is an armed conflict, but not all armed conflicts can be categorized as wars.

An armed conflict, according to such definition, differs from a war in that it is much smaller in scale and the purposes that are being sought by the parties to the conflict are also much more limited. Weak parties can participate in an armed conflict just as much as states having significant economic and military potentials.

In a war, according to this definition, a state is transformed into an exceptional state of existence that effects all its people and pervades all spheres of its functional activity. During the time that a war is being fought, all the state's efforts are directed towards the achievement of the war's purposes, and although a war necessarily includes political, ideological, diplomatic, psychological, economic, and other efforts, the primary and decisive means by which the war effort is conducted is by force of arms.

In an armed conflict, such large changes in the activities of a government and its subject people do not occur, and for this reason, each of the sides to the armed conflict can view the conflict quite differently: One side can consider it to be an all-out war while the other side can still view it as only an armed conflict. But an armed conflict cannot be strictly distinguished from a war in either a theoretical or a practical sense. The experience of the twentieth century has shown that even small-intensity armed conflicts can quickly transform themselves into large wars.

For Chechnya, the influence of this military action was so pervasive that the republic's armed conflict with Russia became a war. Because of such war activity, all government and community institutions in fact stopped functioning in the manner they had functioned in peacetime. The war for the Chechens became a part of their daily existence, and hardly a family was left within its territory that did not suffer losses because of it or was not affected by it in some other way.

Contrary to what was happening in Chechnya, this war remained only an armed conflict for Russia since only a small part of its government and community structures, mostly the armed forces, were directly or indirectly affected by it.

Other criteria can be used in characterizing this military conflict, such as scale and duration. But there are no hard-and-fast rules that can be used to determine when an armed conflict becomes a war. Another way of evaluating a military conflict is to consider the issue of whether this was an internal matter, that is, whether it was an "internal federal issue" or, in fact, "aggression." The United Nations General Assembly in a plenary session held on December 14, 1974, confirmed a definition of "aggression" (Article I) as follows: "Aggression is the use of armed force by a State against the sovereignty, territorial integrity or political independence of another State, or in any other manner inconsistent with the Charter of the United Nations, as set out in this Definition." The explanatory note in Article I states that in this definition, the term "State" is used without prejudice to questions of recognition or to whether a State is a member of the United Nations.

The resolution in Article 3 enumerates the types of actions that shall be considered to be acts of "aggression":

> Any of the following acts, regardless of a declaration of war, shall, subject to and in accordance with the provisions of Article 2 (Rules of Evidence), qualify as an act of "aggression":
>
> (a) An invasion or attack by the armed forces of a State of the territory of another State, or any military occupation, however temporary, resulting from such invasion or attack, or any annexation by the use of force of the territory of another State or part thereof;
>
> (b) Bombardment by the armed forces of a State against the territory of another State or the use of any weapons by a State against the territory of another State;
>
> (c) The blockade of the ports or coasts of a State by the armed forces of another State;
>
> (d) An attack by the armed forces of a State on the land, sea or air forces, or marine and air fleets of another State;
>
> (e) The use of armed forces of one State with the agreement of the receiving State, in contravention of the conditions provided for in the agreement or any extension of their presence in such territory beyond the termination of the agreement;
>
> (f) The action of a State in allowing its territory, which it has placed at the disposal of another State for perpetrating an act of aggression against a third State;
>
> (g) The sending by or on behalf of a State of armed bands, groups, irregulars or mercenaries, which carry out acts of armed force against another State of such gravity as to amount to the acts listed above, or its substantial involvement therein.

These enumerated conditions would have been fully sufficient to charge Russia with "aggression" against Chechnya, especially if one bases one's case on the terms of the preamble defining "aggression" in which the General Assembly confirmed the obligation of states not to use armed force to take away from nationalities their right of self-determination, their freedom or independence, or to violate their territorial integrity. However, not one country in the world has been prepared to recognize Chechnya's right to independence. Russia's actions in Chechnya have been tactfully held to be an "internal matter" for the Russian Federation. Politicians and military experts, both from Russia and from foreign countries, have avoided calling the Federal Army's incursion into Chechnya's territory an act of aggression. Most often, Moscow's actions in Chechnya have been characterized as an attempt to suppress a disobedient federal subject, although, of course, the means used have not always been approved.

The armed conflict in Chechnya was Russia's first serious attempt to preserve its territorial integrity as a federal state. It remains obvious that for a long time to come similar conditions will continue to exist in Russia allowing situations to develop where the use of only political means to regulate such situations will not be enough and, therefore, the necessity of using military force will inevitably arise.

A possible theoretical basis and justification for the use of armed forces in Chechnya was found by experts at the Russian Strategic Research Institute once their attention was drawn to the "small intensity conflicts" doctrine developed in the United States. This doctrine was developed toward the end of the 1970s and has been integrated into long-term American political and military strategy.

Why did the Russian Strategic Research Institute become so interested in the "small-intensity conflicts" doctrine? It appears that in essence, since many states in the world are organized as federal structures and as their federal governments' meddling in their federal subjects' affairs using even repressive means is widely accepted as one of the lawful means of ensuring the functioning of the central government's legal system and the preservation of its territorial integrity, the use of this aura of legality was of great interest to Russia. The small-intensity conflict doctrine outlines the methods for the use of force against insurrectionists and for the reestablishment of order in the rebellious territories. For this reason, it was thought that it could be adapted to conditions in Russia, not only regarding Chechnya but also to any future "internal" conflict.

The small-intensity conflict doctrine was based on a consensus among

American specialists that, with the end of the cold war, a "limited political-military effort" might suffice to achieve America's intended political, economic, social, and psychological purposes during a confrontation. Although the legal basis of the "small-intensity conflict" doctrine assumes that it is to be used by a central government to establish order within its own territories, extraterritorial applications were obviously contemplated. These involve instances when a foreign government requests that another government help it establish order within the first government's territories. Such requests are assumed and do not change the practical workings of the doctrine, although, of course, such requests can come from any of the parties to the internal conflict. The extraterritoriality issue raises the most legal problems because, with the fall of the Soviet Union, a new western-oriented hegemony is being established in many parts of the world. Thus, requests to intervene have been coming not only from the governments or parties involved in the conflicts, but also from external sources such as the United Nations or other territorial defense organizations such as NATO. Thus, the traditional limits of sovereignty are gradually being redefined and the prohibition against involvement in another state's "internal matters" is being watered down. By providing an aura of legality to extraterritorial applications of force, this doctrine was seen in Russia as a ready-made solution to its problems of preserving territorial integrity.

It should not be mistakenly understood, however, that, in terms of organization and conceptualization, small-intensity conflicts are only smaller copies of large wars. There are several essential differences. First, the primary accent in a small-intensity conflict is given over to nonmilitary means, as repressive measures do not always help to achieve the sought-after purposes where there is a confrontation between the central government and illegal armed insurrectionary formations.

Second, unlike in a regular war, victory in a small-intensity conflict means not the physical destruction of the adversary but the creation of such new conditions in the country or territory that it becomes impossible for the insurrectionists to achieve their political goals.

Third, the units executing the military actions against the illegal armed formations have to be prepared to carry out specific military, intelligence, police, administrative, social, diplomatic, and other tasks, the majority of which under normal circumstances would be performed by the civilian government.

Fourth, during suppression operations within the framework of the small-intensity conflict doctrine against regions or territories in which various organized insurrectionist movements are active, the actions of security services, police, and armed forces must be concentrated with equal vigor, as much on work with the local inhabitants as on the battle against the insurrectionists themselves. There are basic principles of actions against insurrectionists. The system of measures against insurrectionist forces has to be put into effect as a preventive measure and not as a reaction against the attacks of extremists. Only realistically achievable steps can be publicized. The use of force must be limited to the most minimal effective level, and its execution has to be done by specially trained and highly disciplined units. Priority also has to be given not to the destruction of the armed formations of the extremist movements but to the liquidation of their sources of supply of material and equipment and the removal of the political, economic, social, and other factors that gave rise to the existence of the extremist movements. During the period of the reestablishment of order, the battles with the insurrectionist forces must be limited in scope and directed to their complete destruction at one time or to the infliction of maximum losses to their operational personnel. The most important purpose must be the neutralization and curbing of insurrectionist activity to a level that does not allow the expansion of their activity throughout the whole region and does not require the further repositioning of forces or measures for the purpose of opposing them.

Fifth, armed forces participating in small-intensity conflicts have to be ready to execute political and military functions such as the assurance of the country's "internal defense," the fight against terrorism, peacekeeping, and peacetime operations.

In the view of military theorists, the concept of internal defense involves the suppression of highly developed, large-scale, antigovernment secession movements using repressive measures. The basic elements of "internal defense" are operations by civilian armed forces whose purpose is to mobilize the local inhabitants to support the government's battle against the insurrectionists. This work with the civilian population has to be an integral and prioritized part of the stabilization strategy. The local inhabitants have to sense that the armed forces in executing their functions against the illegal armed formations are only temporarily executing the functions of the civilian government and are not opposing the people.

Once the illegal armed formations are liquidated or disarmed, demilitarized zones have to be formed in the "cleaned-out" territories in which no military contingent remains stationed and no "militarized" civilians are left behind, not even "volunteer" formations. The local civilian administration has to retake power. The stimulus for the cooperation between the local and the central governments has to be that territory's security, conducted by the regular army along the perimeters of the "cleaned-out" territories. With the help of the army, obstacles have to be set up to block destabilization influences from coming in from neighboring territories. Besides this, efforts have to be made to solve the problem of refugees wanting to return to their homes or to resettle elsewhere, convoy guards have to be provided for transport carrying humanitarian aid to the "demilitarized zones," mine fields have to be cleared, unexploded bombs and shells have to be defused, and assistance has to be provided to rebuild and reestablish the functioning of vitally important community services.

It is all too clear that Russia failed to adapt the American small-intensity conflict doctrine to its efforts in Chechnya. Its armed forces were not trained to execute such measures, and, most important, the primary accent continued to be given over to military measures that just increased the population's resistance. Also, the Chechen "illegal armed formations" were neither liquidated nor disarmed. The federal army also never gained the support of the local populace and neither did Moscow's politics regarding Chechnya.

For the first time in Russian armed forces' practice, a Combined Federal Forces Group was formed to execute its armed activity in Chechnya. Its structure was finalized in early 1995 and remained substantially unchanged until the conclusion of the military action.

The Combined Federal Forces Group, sometimes called the Federal Army, consisted of forces from the Defense Ministry and the Ministry of Internal Affairs, units of the Border Army, and detachments of the Federal Security Service, later renamed the Federal Counterintelligence Service. Besides these, the Combined Federal Forces Group's commander's and staff's interests were served by the Federal Government Communications Agency attached to the Office of the Russian President, by the units of the Special Situations Ministry, and even by the president's protection service. The nucleus of the Combined Forces was made up of groups formed from the forces of the Defense Ministry and the Ministry of Internal Affairs.

Units of the Land Army, the Paratroop Forces, and the Military Air Forces continuously remained a part of the Defense Ministry Group. During the period of active warfare, this group was reinforced by Combined Marine Infantry units formed from the Baltic, Northern, and Pacific Fleets' Marine Infantry organizations. The Internal Affairs Ministry Group was formed from Internal Affairs Army units, combined OMON, and other special-purpose detachments. The Defense Ministry and the Internal Affairs Ministry Groups were led by commanders appointed by these services who at the same time were subordinated to the commander of the Combined Federal Group. Each group had its own headquarters.

For the execution of operations, other separate groups were formed and named according to the part of Chechnya—western, northern, or southeast-

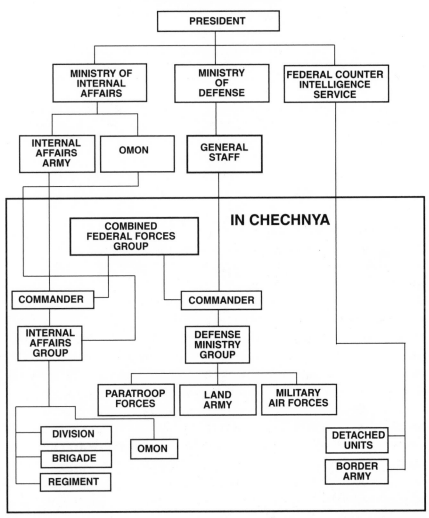

COMBINED FEDERAL FORCES
COMMAND STRUCTURE

Donald S. Frazier &
Richard J. Thompson, Jr.
Abilene, Texas

ern—that they were to operate in. These groups were mixed, formed from units and detachments subordinate to the Defense and Internal Affairs Ministries. The primary Combined Federal Forces Group operating bases in Chechnya were the Chankala and Northern Airports.

If evaluation by the customary criteria was made of the Combined Federal Forces Group's combat potential, one would have to say that it had sufficient forces available to successfully do battle with the Chechen armed formations. Reality, however, shows that there was a gross failure to make effective use of such potential. As is contended by a majority of military experts, some of the most important reasons for this were the strong service rivalry, the lack of coordination of actions among the services, and even the opposition of each service against the others.

Another very strong factor was the fact that Dzhochar Dudajev succeeded in creating an effective system to resist the Federal Army. This was done on the basis of three basic principles: volunteerism, decentralized supply of weapons and equipment, and wide authority of field commanders to take independent actions. The choice of these principles was decided as much by the mentality of the Chechen nation with its dislike for any domination as by the realities of the developing operational situation.

The results of the war actions showed that, under the circumstances, the right decision was made. Although not once during the duration of the war was a general mobilization ordered, a shortage of fighters never developed, and the fighters invariably located and supplied themselves with weapons and equipment. Centralized supply of Chechen formations was organized only in those specific instances when large operations were being prepared and conducted.

The grant of full authority to field commanders and primarily to Aslan Maschadov to take independent actions was forced upon Dudajev by developments in the operational situation during the spring of 1995 when centralized command of the highly dispersed Chechen armed formations became impossible. From that time on, the actual military structures began to take final form. The president remained the supreme commander while decision making as to military issues was left to the Chechen chief of staff, Aslan Maschadov. The latter proceeded to divide up the Chechen armed formations into six objective-orientated parts according to their deployment areas. These parts were then subdivided into sectors. He kept the little artillery he had left directly subordinate to himself. Shamil Basajev was ordered to look after the Chechen specnaz.

The war in Chechnya also brought to the fore several new conditions that will have some bearing on warfare in the future. First of all, the war in Chechnya was only the second instance (after the Finnish resistance in 1940 against the Soviet Union's armed forces) when on the continent of Europe a small country dared to resist the armed onslaught of a much more powerful country. In both instances, armed forces having great advantages in numbers of troops, armament, and equipment were unable to defeat their much weaker adversaries, even when the weaker countries lacked the assistance and support of other nations. Thus the question necessarily arises as to whether a powerful country, after attacking such a smaller country, can actually win a war against it, particularly if that nation is bent on resisting to the end and has resolved to use all possible means. That question becomes even more relevant when the other nations of the world also begin to hold a distinctly negative view of the conflict.

Second, in the Chechen resistance against the Russian Federal Forces, military terrorist operations had an important effect on the further course of the war. Such operations were not a Chechen invention, although perhaps their scale and the determination of the participants to achieve their intended purposes regardless of the amount of blood spilt has been previously unseen. These operations showed themselves to be one of the most effective means available to a small nation to stop a large aggressor's war against it. It thus becomes apparent that military terrorism is not only an abstract concept found in military theory but inevitably a realistic part in any small country's arsenal against a large aggressor.

During the war in Chechnya, the command of the Russian Federal Army was also forced to pay ever greater attention to operations in which the primary role was to be played by special-purpose units and detachments.

The war in Chechnya has ended. The howl of bullets has died down, bombs have stopped falling, and blood is no longer flowing. But it will take many years, perhaps even centuries, to heal the wounds of this war.

Notes

Series Editor's Statement

1. See, for example, Chris Hables Gray, *Postmodern War: The New Politics of Conflict* (New York: Guilford Press, 1997).

2. See, for example, Carlotta Gaall and Thomas de Waal, *Chechnya: Calamity in the Caucasus* (New York: New York University Press, 1998).

3. See Anatol Lieven, *Chechnya: Tombstone of Russian Power* (New Haven, Conn.: Yale University Press, 1998).

4. Norman Cigar, *Genocide in Bosnia* (College Station: Texas A&M University Press, 1995).

5. Robert Kaplan, *Balkan Ghosts* (New York: Simon & Schuster, 1993).

6. Chuck Sudetic, *Blood and Vengeance* (New York: W. W. Norton, 1998).

7. Stjepan G. Meštrović, *Habits of the Balkan Heart* (College Station: Texas A&M University Press, 1993).

Chapter 1

1. *Chechenskiy krizis: Ispytanie na gosudarstvennost'* (Moscow: Izd. "Kodeks," Obyedinennaya redaktsiya MVD RF, 1995).

2. Obrashchenie Prezidenta Rossiyskoy Federatsii B. N. Yel'tsina k grazhdanam Rosii, Dec. 11, 1994.

3. "Shamil'." *Nauka i religiya* 6 (1996).

4. I. L. Bunich, "Khronika chechenskoy boyni i shest' dney v Budennovske," *Oblik* (1995): 11.

5. *Chechenskaya tragediya: Kto vinovat?* (Moscow: RIA *Novosti,* 1995), 14–15.

6. E. Pain and A. Popov, "Chechenskaya politika Rossii s 1991 po 1994 g.g.," *Mirovaya ekonomika i mezhdunarodnye otnosheniya* 5 (1995).

7. "Problemy Rossii v Chechne," *Informatsionnyy sbornik Viniti,* series "Vooruzhennye sily i voenno-promyshlennyy kompleks," 2 (1996).

8. *Chechenskiy krizis,* 11.

9. *Chechenskaya tragediya,* 16.

10. Ibid., 17.

11. J. Glinskis, "Čečėnija: Įvykiai ir datos" (Chechnya: Events and Dates), *Lietuvos aidas,* Jan. 5, 1995.

12. Bunich, "Khronika chechenskoy boyni," 36–37.

13. Pain and Popov, "Chechenskaya politika."

14. Ibid.

15. D. Bal'burov, "Mir Ob'yavlen: Labazanov ubit," *Moskovskie novosti* 22 (1996).

16. S. Knezys, *Karas Čečénijoje* (The War in Chechnya) (Vilnius: Lithuanian Ministry of Defense Publishing Center, 1996), 19.

17. Glinskis, "Čečénija: Įvykiai ir datos."

18. T. Dudnikova, "Chechnya, Rossiya i Evropa," *Mirovaya ekonomika i mezhdunarodnye otnosheniya* 8 (1995).

19. Glinskis, "Čečénija: Įvykiai ir datos."

20. D. Ukhlin, "Raskol i vseobshchaya mobilizatsiya," *Moskoviskie novosti* 33 (1994).

21. G. Visockas, "Čečénijoje įvedama karo padėtis" (Martial law is declared in Chechnya), *Lietuvos aidas,* Sept. 16, 1994.

22. A. Mayami, "Opozitsiya," *Soldier of Fortune* 6 (1996).

23. Pain and Popov, "Chechenskaya politika"; A. Zhilin, "Boris Gromov: 'Operatsiya gotovilas' v glubovskoy tayne," *Moskovskie novosti* 1 (1995).

24. Bunich, "Khronika chechenskoy boyni," 39–40.

Chapter 2

1. A. Kapkin, "Nezakonnye vooruzhennye formirovaniya Chechenskoy Respubliki, ili Protiv kogo i s kem sobiralsya voevat' Dudaev," *Voyskovoy vestnik* 4 (1995).

2. Ibid.

3. A. Kapkin, "'Udaril-ubezhal,' ili nekotorye voprosy taktiki deystviy nezakonnykh vooruzhennykh formirovaniy v Chechenskoy Respublike," *Voskovoy vestnik* 3 (1995).

4. Kapkin, "Nezakonnye vooruzhennye."

5. A. Chelnokov, "Chem sil'na chechenskaya spetssluzhba?" *Izvestiya,* July 7, 1995.

6. Yu. Bespalov and V. Yakov, "Kto vooruzhal Dzhokhara Dudaeva?" *Izvestiya,* Jan. 10, 1995.

7. "Otkrytoe pis'mo marshala aviatsii E. I. Shaposhnikova Ministerstvu oborony Rossiyskoy Federatsii i nekotorym deputatam Gosudarstvennoy dumy Rossii (v svyazi s ikh zayavleniyami i vystupleniyami)— 'Kakoy vzdor!'" *Moskovskiy komsomolets,* Feb. 5, 1995.

8. A. Portyanskiy, "Dzhokhar Dudaev: Uregulirovanie konflikta vozmozhno, esli prekratit' agresiyu," *Izvestiya,* Dec. 10, 1994; S. Yastrebov, "Kupets i diplomat Pavel Grachev," *Moskovskiy komsomolets,* Jan. 18, 1995.

9. The Russian rank "proporshchik" is translated as "warrant officer," although it is not identical to the Western warrant officer rank. Persons having previously served in the enlisted ranks who come back into the armed forces under contract to perform certain specific functions are issued this rank. For the most part, they service the rear areas, depots, and supply warehouses and function in the same role that career "lifer" sergeants perform in the West. Their rank in the command pyramid is lower than that of a junior officer but higher than a senior sergeant.

10. Bespalov and Yakov, "Kto vooruzhal Dudaeva?"

11. V. Belykh and N. Burbyga, "Odna iz versiy: Oruzhie v Chechne bylo pazgrableno," *Izvestiya,* Jan. 12, 1995.

12. Kapkin, "Nezakonnye vooruzhennye."

13. "Oruzhie Dudaevu prodolzhayut postupat' iz Rossii," *Izvestiya,* Jan. 25, 1995.

14. Bunich, "Khronika chechenskoy boyni," 146.

Chapter 3

1. Bunich. "Khronika chechenskoy boyni," 65–66.

2. I. Korotchenko, "Operatsiya v Chechne: Uspekh ili porazhenie rossiyskoy armii?" *Nezavisimoe voennoe obozrenie,* prilozhenie k (supplement to) *Nezavisimoy gazete* 1 (Feb. 1995).

3. Ibid.; V. Yakov, "S provokatsii rossiyskikh spetssluzhb god nazad nachinalas' voyna v Chechne," *Izvestiya,* November 24, 1995.

4. R. Zaripov, "General Grachev predal svoikh leytenantov," *Komsomol'skaya pravda*, Dec. 3, 1994.

5. "S chego nachinalas' voyna v Chechne: Strana dolzhna znat' svoikh geroev," *Izvestiya*, November 25, 1995.

6. Ibid.

7. V. Litovkin, "General Polyakov sdelal vybor," *Ekho Litvy*, Dec. 13, 1994.

8. N. Pachegina, "Popytka svergnut' pezhim Dudaeva provalilas'," *Nezavisimaya gazeta*, November 29, 1994.

9. "S chego nachinalas' voyna v Chechne," *Izvestiya*, November 25, 1995.

10. G. Mikšiūnas, "Mūšį nulėmė generolo Dudajevo manevras" (The battle was decided by General Dudajev's maneuver), *Lietuvos aidas*, November 29, 1994.

11. Pachegina, "Popytka svergnut'."

12. Mikšiūnas, "Mūšį nulėmė."

13. Pachegina, "Popytka svergnut'."

14. Knezys, *Karas Čečenijoje,* 28.

15. A. Zheludkov and A. Chelnokov, "Oppozitsiya do sikh por zhdet rossiyskie voyska," *Izvestiya*, Dec. 10, 1994.

Chapter 4

1. Bunich, "Khronika chechenskoy boyni," 77.

2. N. Pachegina, "Kreml' gotovitsya k vedeniyu chrezvychaynogo polozheniya v Chechne," *Nezavisimaya gazeta*, November 30, 1994.

3. Bunich, "Khronika chechenskoy boyni," 86–90.

4. "Pavel Grachev vysoko otsenil deystviya armii v Chechne: Osnovnye tezisy vystupleniya ministra oborony RF generala armii Pavla Gracheva na sbore rukovodyashchego sostava Vooryzhennykh Sil 28 fevralya," *Nezavisimaya gazeta*, Mar. 1, 1995.

5. Ibid.

6. Korotchenko, "Operatsiya v Chechne."

7. Bunich, "Khronika chechenskoy boyni," 18–21.

8. N. D., "Kak vse nachinalos?" *Soldier of Fortune* 1 (1996).

9. A. Kuz'minov, "Shtyrm," *Soldier of Fortune* (1996).

10. V. Egorov, "Ofitsery Genshtaba na Severnom Kavkaze," *Nezavisimaya gazeta*, Dec. 3, 1994.

11. Korotchenko, "Operatsiya v Chechne."

12. Zaripov, "General Grachev."

13. J. Glinskis, "Čečėnija su nerimu laukia savaitgalio" (Chechnya awaits the weekend with anxiety), *Lietuvos aidas*, Dec. 6, 1994.

14. "Pavel Grachev," *Nezavisimaya gazeta*, Mar. 1, 1995.

15. Glinskis, "Čečėnija: Įvykiai ir datos"; Portyanskiy, "Dzhokar Dudaev."

16. V. Kononenko, "Voyna v Chechne—voyna protiv Rossii," *Izvestiya*, Dec. 9, 1994; "Pavel Grachev," *Nezavisimaya gazeta*, Mar. 1, 1995.

17. Knezys, *Karas Čečenijoje,* 34.

18. S. Knezys, "Keturi karo Čečénijoje etapai" (The four stages of the war in Chechnya), *Karys* 4 (1995).

19. Yu. Kalinina, "Operatsiya 'Novy god': Groznyy bombili dizelisty po navodke pontonerov," *Komsomol'skaya pravda*, Jan. 6, 1995.

20. Knezys, "Keturi karo," *Karys* 4 (1995).

21. The Russian term for hit man is "bojavik." The term had already been used in the tsarist army to describe a soldier who went deep into enemy territory and struck suddenly and hard. It had also been used to describe Bolshevik fighters from the underground who had fought the tsarist army. The word has a sense of the commando but without the rigorous organization of modern soldiering. It also has a connotation of an irregular force structure, and thus a bojavik did not have to be a permanent soldier but could revert to

civilian life after an operation. In modern usage, it also has a criminal connotation since terrorists are also sometimes called "bojaviki" or hit men. The term "hit man" is used throughout this book with the understanding that it only reflects the term actually used in Russian newspapers to describe the Chechen fighters. In no sense is there any intention to label the Chechen fighters as anything other than armed fighters fighting for their country.

22. N. N. Novichkov, V. Ya. Snegovskiy, A. G. Sokolov, and V. Yu Shvarev, *Rossiyskiye vooruzhennye sily v chechenskom konflikte: Analiz, itogi, byvody* (Paris and Moscow: Kholveg-Inglob-Trivola, 1995), 36, 37.

23. Knezys, *Karas Čečénijoje*, 37.

24. A. Frolov, "Soldaty na peredovoy i polkovodtsy v Mozdoke," *Izvestiya*, Jan. 11, 1995.

25. Yu. Kalinina, "BMP uezzhali na front bez pulemetov," *Moskovskiy komsomolets*, Mar. 4, 1995.

26. S. Leonenko, "Ovladenie gorodom," *Armeyskiy sbornik* 3 (1995).

27. N. D., "Kak vse nachinalos?"

28. "Kto razvyazal krovavyy konflikt v Chechne: Materialy komissii S. Govorukhina," *Pravda*, Feb. 27– Mar. 6, 1996.

29. J. Glinskis, "Peržengtas Kaukazo karo slenkstis" (The threshold of the war in Chechnya is crossed), *Lietuvos aidas*, Dec. 13, 1994.

Chapter 5

1. Obrashchenie Prezidenta Rossiyskoy Federatsii B. N. Yel'tsina k grazhdanam Rosii, Dec. 11, 1994.

2. "Pavel Grachev vysoko otsenil deystviya armii v Chechne," *Nezavisimaya gazeta*, Mar. 1, 1995; "Vystuplenie general-polkovnika A. Kvashina na sbore rukovodyashchego sostava Vooruzhennykh sil 28 fevralya: 'Voyska obretali boevuyu zrelost' v tyazhelykh ispytaniyakh,'" *Kraznaya zvezda*, Mar. 2, 1995.

3. Knezys, "Keturi karo," *Karys* 5 (1995).

4. "Vystuplenie general-polkovnika A. Kvashina na sbore rukovodyashchego sostava Vooruzhennykh sil 28 fevralya," *Kraznaya zvezda*, Mar. 2, 1995.

5. Obrashchenie Prezidenta Rossiyskoy Federatsii B. N. Yel'tsina k zhitelyam Chechenskoy Respubliki, Dec. 15, 1994.

6. "O rossiysko-chechenskom konflikte," *Informatsionnyy sbornik Viniti*, series "Vooruzhennye sily i voenno-promyshlennyy kompleks" 12 (1995).

7. "Vystuplenie general-polkovnika A. Kvashina na sbore rukovodyashchego sostava Vooruzhennykh sil 28 fevralya," *Krasnaya zvezda*, Mar. 2, 1995.

8. "Pavel Grachev vysoko otsenil deystviya armii v Chechne," *Nezavisimaya gazeta*, Mar. 1, 1995.

9. Kapkin, "'Udaril-ubezhal.'"

10. "Khronika chechenskikh sobytiy s 16 po 31 dekabrya 1994 goda," *Nezavisimaya gazeta*, Dec. 26, 1995.

11. I. Kotenev, "Takaya neobychnaya voyna, ili Nekotorye voprosy neklassicheskoy taktiki deystviy chastey i podrazdeleniy vnutrennikh voysk operativnogo naznacheniya v rayone rezhima chrezvychaynogo polozheniya," *Voyskovoy vestnik* 2 (1995); Kapkin, "'Udaril-Ubezhal.'"

12. Kapkin, "'Udaril-Ubezhal.'"

13. Ibid.

14. Frolov, "Soldaty."

15. Novichkov et al., *Rossiyskiye vooruzhennye sily*, 31–36.

16. Bunich, "Khronika chechenskoy boyni," 96, 97.

17. "O rossiysko-chechenskom konflikte," *Informatsionnyy sbornik Viniti* 12 (1995).

18. Frolov, "Soldaty."

Chapter 6

1. "Pavel Grachev vysoko otsenil deystviya armii v Chechne," *Nezavisimaya gazeta*, Mar. 1, 1995; "Vystuplenie general-polkovnika A. Kvashina," *Krasnaya zvezda*, Mar. 2, 1995; S. Knezys, "Čečěnijos gynyba"

(Chechnya's defense), *Lietuvos aidas,* Dec. 14, 15, 16, 1995.

2. IMA-press, Sergey Yushenkov, "Reshenie o novogodnem shturme Groznogo bylo prinyato na dne rozhdeniya Gracheva," *Izvestiya,* Jan. 18, 1995.

3. Kapkin, "'Udaril-ubezhal.'"

4. Yu. Zaynashev, "Chernaya rosa," *Moskovskiy komsomolets,* Jan. 11, 1995.

5. "Vystuplenie general-polkovnika A. Kvashina," *Krasnaya zvezda,* Mar. 2, 1995.

6. Korotchenko, "Operatsiya v Chechne."

7. Novichkov et al., *Rossiyskiye vooruzhennye sily,* 45.

8. V. Litovkin, "Rasstrel 131-y Maykopskoy brigady," *Izvestiya,* Jan. 11, 1995.

9. Ibid.

10. I. Dement'eva, "Novy god v Groznom," *Izvestiya,* Jan. 5, 1995.

11. Kalinina, "Operatsiya 'Novy god.'"

12. S. Overchuk, "Razgrom," *Moskovskiy komsomolets,* Jan. 28, 1995.

13. S. Krylov, "Zabytye uroki," *Soldier of Fortune* 4 (1995).

14. Novichkov et al., *Rossiyskiye vooruzhennye sily,* 68–70.

15. Kalinina, "Operatsiya 'Novy god.'"

16. Novichkov et al., *Rossiyskiye vooruzhennye sily,* 43–44.

17. E. Abdulaev, "Nad Groznym gorodom zakaty," *Soldier of Fortune* 4 (1995).

18. Ibid.

19. N. Gritchin, "Gorod osveshchayut pozhary I rakety," *Izvestiya,* Jan. 6, 1995.

20. "Pavel Grachev vysoko otsenil deystviya armii v Chechne," *Nezavisimaya gazeta,* Mar. 1, 1995.

21. Yu. Khaytina, "Chasti morskoy pekhoty uzhe v Groznom," *Moskovskiy komsomolets,* Jan. 11, 1995.

22. "Pavel Grachev vysoko otsenil deystviya armii v Chechne," *Nezavisimaya gazeta,* Mar. 1, 1995.

23. Yu. Zaynashev, "Morskaya pekhota na skovorodke: Za peryvuyu nedeliu pogiblo uzhe 17 morskikh pekhotintsev," *Moskovskiy komsomolets,* Jan. 19, 1995.

24. S. Konovalov and M. Serdyukov, "Partizanskaya voyna ne za gorami," *Izvestiya,* Jan. 19, 1995.

25. "Nad rossiyskim gorodom Groznyy otnyne—vnov' rossiyskiy flag," *Krasnaya zvezda,* Jan. 21, 1995.

26. A. Plutnik, "Egorov est,' ostalos' nayti Kantariya," *Izvestiya,* Jan. 19, 1995.

Chapter 7

1. B. Vinogradov, "Moskva zayavila: Voennyy etap zavershen; Boi v Groznom prodolzhayutsya," *Izvestiya,* Jan. 21, 1995; A. Minkin, "Bomby, rakety, tanki i grad: Podlost', trusost', glupost' i lozh'," *Moskovskiy komsomolets,* Feb. 3, 1995.

2. Vinogradov, "Moskva zayavila."

3. B. Vinogradov, "Zdes' soldaty umirayut ne s ulybkoy, a s proklyatiem na ustakh," *Izvestiya,* Jan. 24, 1995.

4. Kapkin, "'Udaril-ubezhal.'"

5. "Pamyatka lichnomu sostavu chastey i podrazdeleniy po vedeniyu boevykh deystviy v Chechenskoy Respublike," *Armeyskiy sbornik* 1 (1996).

6. Kapkin, "'Udaril-ubezhal.'"

7. "Pavel Grachev," *Nezavisimaya gazeta,* Mar. 1, 1995.

8. Novichkov et al., *Rossiyskiye vooruzhennye sily,* 139, 43.

9. Pain and Popov, "Chechenskaya politika."

Chapter 8

1. Yu. Zaynashev, "Argunskaya vesna," *Moskovskiy komsomolets,* Mar. 18, 1995.

2. A. Gusev and S. Knyaz'kov, "104-ya iz boya ne vykhodit," *Krasnaya zvezda,* Mar. 4, 1995.

3. M. Bagdonavičius, "Mirties ir vilties žemė," *Respublika,* Mar. 14, 15, 16, 17, 18, 1995.

4. V. Ermolin and P. Karapetyan, "Vysoty Arguna, Shali, Gudermesa," *Krasnaya zvezda,* Apr. 5, 1995.

5. I. Vishnevskiy, "Ot Arguna k Gudermesu," *Nezavisimaya gazeta,* Mar. 25, 1995.

6. V. Ermolin and P. Karapetyan, "Argun vzyat," *Krasnaya zvezda,* Mar. 25, 1995; A. Kolpakov and M. Kustov, "Polevye komandiry: 'My zhivem po bozh'im zakonam,'" *Moskovskiy komsomolets,* Mar. 28, 1995; A. Stasovskiy, "Okruzheny Gudermes i Shali," *Krasnaya zvezda,* Mar. 31, 1995.

7. Yu. Kalinina, "'Argunskiy variant' po-chechenski," *Moskovskiy komsomolets,* Mar. 30, 1995.

8. Yu. Gavrilov, "Obryv u Chechen-Aula," *Krasnaya zvezda,* Mar. 24, 1995.

9. N. Starodymov, "Vzyatie Gudermesa i Shali—povorotnyy moment razvitiya situatsii v Chechne," *Krasnaya zvezda,* Apr. 1, 1995.

10. N. Starodymov, Gudermes "Dvoynoy blok," *Krasnaya zvezda,* July 8, 1995.

11. Starodymov, "Vzyatie Gudermesa."

12. V. Ermolin and P. Karapetyan, "Shali: 506-y zadachy vypolnil," *Krasnaya zvezda,* Apr. 1, 1995; V. Ermolin and P. Karapetyan, "Eto bylo pod Shali," *Krasnaya zvezda,* Apr. 4, 1995.

13. N. Gorodetskaya, "Chechenskie opolchentsy ostavi i Shali: Federal'nye voyska ego vzyali," *Segodnya,* Apr. 1, 1995.

14. ITAR-TASS, "Chechnya: Nashi voyska uspeshno zavershili operatsiyu v rayone Samashek," *Krasnaya zvezda,* Apr. 11, 1995.

15. S. Knezys, "Samašků kaimo tragedija," *Lietuvos aidas,* Apr. 12, 13, 1996.

16. Razdel 2 iz doklada komisii po pravam cheloveka pri Prezidente Rossiyskoy Federatsii: Narusheniya prav cheloveka i mezhdunarodnogo gumanitarnogo prava v khode vooruzhennogo konflikta na territorii Chechenskoi Respubliki, Feb. 5, 1996.

17. *Vsemi imeyushchimisya sredstvami: Operatsiya MVD RF v sele Samashki 7–8 Aprelya 1995 g.* (Moscow: Pravozashchitnyy tsentr "Memorial." 1995).

18. Ibid.

19. "Raketno-bombovye udary ne nanosilis'," *Krasnaya zvezda,* Apr. 12, 1995.

20. Knezys, "Samašků kaimo tragedija."

21. "O rossiysko-chechenskom konflikte," *Informatsionnyy sbornik Viniti* 1 (1996).

22. Knezys, "Samašků kaimo tragedija."

23. I. Rotar', "Selo Samashki unichtozhaetsya: Rossiyskie generaly sleduyut primeru Ermolova," *Izvestiya,* Mar. 21, 1996.

24. J. Glinskis, "FSK: izoliuoti ir sunaikinti!" (Federal counterintelligence service: to isolate and destroy!), *Lietuvos aidas,* Apr. 20, 1995.

25. Bagdonavicius, "Mirties ir vilties."

26. J. Glinskis, "Jelcinas paskelbė moratoriumą karo veiksmams Čečénijoje" (Yeltsin proclaims a moratorium for war actions in Chechnya), *Lietuvos aidas,* Apr. 12, 1995.

Chapter 9

1. Glinskis, "Jelcinas paskelbė moratoriumą."

2. Glinskis, "Dudajevo kariai sugrįžo į Grozną" (Dudajev's soldiers return to Grozni), *Lietuvos aidas,* May 3, 1995.

3. S. Knyaz'kov, "Nesmotrya na ob'yavlennyy moratoriy, v Chechne gremyat vystrely," *Krasnaya zvezda,* May 4, 1995.

4. J. Glinskis, "Čečénija naujų mūšių išvakarėse" (Chechnya on the eve of new battles), *Lietuvos aidas,* May 6, 1995.

5. D. Varnavin, "Rossiyskie voyska v Groznom: Smert' zhivet po sosedstvu," *Komsomol'skaya pravda,* May 13, 1995.

6. A. Dudajeva, "Nepaklupdoma tauta" (The nation that could not be forced to its knees), *Lietuvos aidas,* May 3, 10, 19, 1995.

7. Varnavin, "Rossiyskie voyska."

8. E. Suponina, "Voyna prodolzhaetsya, chechentsy nastroeny reshitel'no: Polevye komandiry utverzh-

dayut, chto rossiyskie soldaty prodayut im oruzhie i tekhniku," *Segodnya,* May 11, 1995.

9. A. Zhilin, "Pobeda otkladyvaetsya," *Moskovskie novosti* 22 (1995).

10. "Rusai puola pietuose, čečėnai—Grozne" (Russians attack in the south, the Chechens in Grozni), *Lietuvos rytas,* May 16, 1995.

11. Novichkov et al, *Rossiyskiye vooruzhennye sily.*

12. N. Gritchin, "Federal'nye voyska shturmuyut gory," *Izvestiya,* Jan. 6, 1995.

13. "Specialiai žudyti sukurtas dalinys" (A special killing detachment is formed), *Lietuvos aidas,* June 6, 1995; Yu. Golotyuk, "Federal'nye voyska schitayut vzyatie Vedeno strategicheskim uspekhom," *Segodnya,* Sept. 22, 1995.

14. "Specialiai žudyti," *Lietuvos aidas,* June 6, 1995.

15. N. Gorodetskaya, "Federal'noe komandovanie razrabatyvaet plan prodvizheniya v gory," *Segodnya,* June 8, 1995.

16. J. Glinskis, "Džocharas Dudajevas: 'Kova dar nebaigta, ji tik įgyja kitas formas'" (Dzhochar Duda-jev: "The battle is not ended, it has only taken on other forms"), *Lietuvos aidas,* June 15, 1995.

17. A. Andryushkov, "Doroga na Shatoy," *Krasnaya zvezda,* July 5, 1995; N. Starodymov, "Tak brali Shatoy," *Krasnaya zvezda,* July 8, 1995.

18. P. Karapetyan and V. Strugovets. "Vzyatie Shatoya i Nozhay-Yurta nashimi voyskami pokazyvaet: Dudaevskie boeviki obrecheny." *Krasnaya zvezda,* June 15, 1995.

Chapter 10

1. Karapetyan and Strugovets, "Vzyatie Shatoya."

2. Glinskis, "Džocharas Dudajevas."

3. A. Procenka, "Budionovsko tragedija: Karas iš Čečėnijos jau persikelia į Rusiją?" (The Budionovsk tragedy: Is the war being transferred from Chechnya into Russia?), *Lietuvos rytas,* June 16, 1995; Yu. Kali-nina and S. Teterin, "Nachalas' boynya v Rossii," *Nezavisimaya gazeta,* June 16, 1995.

4. G. Sanin, "'Marsh smerti' Shamilya Basaeva," *Segodnya,* June 16, 1995.

5. Kalinina and Teterin, "Nachalas' boynya."

6. Ibid.

7. Sanin, "'Marsh smerti.'"

8. M. Chudakova, "Kak chuzhaya voyna stala svoey," *Izvestiya,* June 20, 1995.

9. *Budennovsk: Sem' dney ada* (Moscow: Izd. "Kodeks," Obyedinennaya redaktsiya MVD RF), 1995.

10. N. Gritchin, "Shamil' Basaev utverzhdaet, chto shel brat' Kreml'," *Izvestiya,* June 17, 1995.

11. A. Zheludkov, "Operativniki gotovyatsya k sakhvatu terroristov," *Izvestiya,* June 21, 1995; A. Chel-nokov, "MVD i 'Al'fa schitayut nepravil'nym reshenie Chernomyrdina," *Izvestiya,* June 28, 1995.

12. S. Knezys, "Čečėnija: karas, terorizmas ir politika" (Chechnya: war, terrorism and politics), *Lietu-vos aidas,* June 11, 12, 13, 1996.

13. Chelnokov, "MVD i 'Al' fa' schitayut"; V. Strugovets, "'Al' fa' shla na vernuyu gibel'," *Krasnaya zvezda,* July 8, 1995.

14. Knezys, "Čečėnija: karas."

15. Ibid.

16. A. Minkin, "Boevik i prem'er ostanovili voynu: No nenadolgo," *Moskovskiy komsomolets,* June 20, 1995.

17. G. Sanin, "Konvoy ukhodit v neizvestnost'," *Segodnya,* June 21, 1995.

18. V. Yakov, "Kak eto bylo," *Izvestiya,* June 23, 1995.

19. Sanin, "Konvoy ukhodit."

20. Yu. Kalinina, "Karavan bedy," *Moskovskiy komsomolets,* June 22, 1995.

21. N. Gritchin, "Budennovsk posle tragedii," *Izvestiya,* June 21, 1995.

22. V. Ladnyy, "Chechnya vstrechala terroristov kak geroev," *Komsomol'skaya pravda,* June 22, 1995.

23. O. Latsis, "Zhestokost' porozhdaet tol'ko zhestokost'," *Izvestiya,* June 20, 1995.

Chapter 11

1. Razdel 2 iz doklada komisii; *Chechenskoe gore Rossii (o bezhentsakh, no ne tol'ko . . .)* (Moscow: Koordinatsionnyy sovet pomoshchi bezhentsam i vynuzdennym pereselentsam, 1995).

2. "Zhurnal boevykh doneseniy kombata Maksimova, Groznyy, Yanvar' 1995 goda: 'Po nam nanosit udary artilleriya svoya i protivnika; Obstrel vedetsya s trekh storon.'" *Komsomol'skaya pravda,* Jan. 16, 1996.

3. V. Shurygin, "Sorok chetvertoe dekabrya: Federal'nye voyska shturmuyut Groznyy," *Soldier of Fortune,* 10 (1995).

4. Novichkov et al., *Rossiyskiye vooruzhennye sily.*

5. S. Roshchin, "Proverka na deesposobnost': Iz opyta tekhnisheskogo obespecheniya boysk v Chechne," *Armeyskiy sbornik* 10 (1995).

6. R. Sodraitas, "Karas" (War), *Respublika,* Apr. 7, 10, 11, 12, 13, 1996.

7. J. Glinskis, "Ligi ko prisigyveno vyreliai . . . " (To what levels have the boys descended . . .), *Lietuvos aidas,* May 10, 1995.

Chapter 12

1. "Budionovsko teroristų odisėja" (The odyssey of the Budionovsk terrorists), *Respublika,* June 21, 1995.

2. A. Gasiūnienė, "Čečėnai sutiko padėti surasti Šamilį Basajevą" (Chechens agree to help find Shamil Basajev), *Vakarinės naujienos,* June 22, 1995.

3. N. Gorodetskaya, "Rossiya trebuet vydachi Shamilya Basaeva," *Moskovskiy komsomolets,* June 22, 1995; V. Litovkin, "Generaly ne veryat v uspekh peregovorov," *Izvestiya,* Jan. 11, 1995.

4. J. Glinskis, "Rusų ir Čečėnų derybos: Politiniai susitarimai gali užtrukti" (Negotiations between the Russians and Chechens: Political agreements can be delayed), *Lietuvos aidas,* June 24, 1995.

5. V. Kononenko and V. Yakov, "Mir v Chechne nuzhen narodu, a ne terroristam," *Izvestiya,* June 28, 1995.

6. I. Rotar', "Dudaev otvergaet nulevoy variant: Poiski kompromissa prodolzhayutsya," *Izvestiya,* July 4, 1995.

7. J. Glinskis, "Susitarimo protokole trūksta tik 4 eilučių" (The agreement lacks only four lines), *Lietuvos aidas,* July 20, 1995.

8. "Čečėnijos derybininkai pasirašė karinę sutartį su Maskva" (Chechen negotiators sign a military treaty with Moscow), *Lietuvos aidas,* Aug. 1, 1995; M. Eysmont, "V Groznom podpisano soglashenie po bloku voennykh voprosov," *Segodnya,* Aug. 8, 1995; T. Mamaladze, "Soglashenie v Groznom otkryvaet put' k miru: Ugroza prodolzheniya voyny ostaetsya," *Izvestiya,* Aug. 1, 1995.

9. "Rusijos pajėgos Čečėnijoje įsikurs ilgam" (Russian forces in Chechnya will stay a long time), *Lietuvos rytas,* July 5, 1995; "Ukaz o dislokatsii armii v Chechne," *Izvestiya,* July 5, 1995.

10. M. Eysmont and Yu. Golotyuk, "Peregovory v Groznom okazalis' na grani sryva," *Segodnya,* July 8, 1995; "Vozle Groznogo ybili 7 mirnykh zhiteley," *Izvestiya,* July 8, 1995; I. Rotar', "Krovavaya provokatsiya oslozhnila peregovory," *Izvestiya,* July 11, 1995.

11. A. Andryushkov and S. Prokopenko, "Mir ob'yavlen, no do mira, pokhozhe eshche daleko," *Krasnaya zvezda,* Aug. 1, 1995; Mamaladze, "Soglashenie v Groznom"; "Rusija per 10 dienų pradės išvesti armiją iš Čečėnijos" (Russia will begin to withdraw its army from Chechnya in 10 days), *Lietuvos rytas,* Aug. 2, 1995.

12. M. Eysmont, "Aslan Maskhadov prikazal prekratit' ogon'," *Segodnya,* Aug. 2, 1995.

13. M. Eysmont, "Vypolnenie voennogo soglasheniya deystvitel'no nachalos'," *Segodnya,* Aug. 8, 1995.

14. Yu. Kalinina, "Dudaevtsam mogut ponadobit'sya novye plennye," *Moskovskiy komsomolets,* Apr. 5, 1995.

15. Ibid.

16. "Čečėnijos kovotojai nuginkluojami" (Chechen fighters are being disarmed), *Lietuvos aidas,* Aug. 9, 1995.

17. A. Mnatsakanyan, "V Groznom teper' uzhe strelyayut ot radosti," *Izvestiya,* Aug. 18, 1995.

18. M. Eysmont, "General Kvashnin predlozhil vyvesti voyska I likvidirovat' blok-posty federal'nykh voysk," *Segodnya,* Aug., 11, 1995.

19. "Rusija pateikė ultimatumą čečėnams" (Russia issues an ultimatum to the Chechens), *Lietuvos rytas,* Aug. 15, 1995; "Rusijos ultimatumas Čečėnijai" (Russia's ultimatum to the Chechens), *Lietuvos aidas,* Aug. 15, 1995; M. Eysmont, "Chechenskaya storona otvergaet rossiyskiy ul'timatum," *Segodnya,* Aug. 15, 1995.

20. "Čečėnija vėl ant karo slenksčio, bet ginklai dar tyli" (Chechnya is again on the threshold of war, but the guns are as yet silent), *Lietuvos rytas,* Aug. 16, 1995; A. Stasovskiy, "Federal'noe pravitel'stvo trebuet ot Chechni vypolneniya podpisannogo soglasheniya," *Krasnaya zvezda,* Aug. 16, 1995; M. Eysmont, "Boris El'tsin prodlil srok ul'timatuma," *Segodnya,* Aug. 16, 1995; T. Zamyatina, "Anatoliy Romanov i Aslan Maskhadov: My bol'she ne smozhem strelyat' v drug druga," *Izvestiya,* Aug. 18, 1995.

21. Mnatsakanyan, "V Groznom teper'."

22. S. Galkina, "Argun: Psikhologicheskiy udar po Dzhokharu Dudaevu," *Izvestiya,* Aug. 23, 1995.

23. A. Budberg, "Razvedka boem," *Moskovskiy komsomolets,* Aug. 23, 1995.

24. "Čečėnija: slaptųjų rusų tarnybų ranka Arguno įvykiuose" (Chechnya: The hand of the Russian secret services in the events in Argun), *Lietuvos aidas,* Aug. 24, 1995.

25. V. Gavrilenko and A. Stasovskiy, "Pokushenie na Olega Lobova, zakhvat zalozhnikov, vzryv na zavode—i vse za odni sutki," *Krasnaya zvezda,* Sept. 22, 1995.

26. Yu. Golotyuk, "V Groznom prodolzhayutsya terakty," *Segodnya,* Sept. 22, 1995.

27. J. Glinskis, "Smurtas—kaip derybų 'argumentas'" (Violence—an "argument" in the negotiations), *Lietuvos aidas,* Sept. 26, 1995.

28. L. Dapkus, "Čečėnijos konfliktas—didžiojo Kaukazo karo preliudija" (The Chechen conflict—prelude to the great war of the Caucasus), *Lietuvos rytas,* Oct. 7, 1995.

29. J. Glinskis, "Sunkiai sužeistas Rusijos ginkluotųjų pajėgų vadas Čečėnijoje" (Leader of the Russian forces in Chechnya is seriously injured), *Lietuvos aidas,* Oct. 7, 1995; M. Semenova, "Sledovalo ozhidat'," *Nezavisimaya gazeta,* Oct. 7, 1995; K. Svetitskiy and A. Mnatsakanyan, "Bor'ba za zhizn' generala Romanova prodolzhaetsya: Kto pokushalsya na nego?" *Izvestiya,* Oct. 10, 1995.

30. J. Glinskis, "Nafta, kraujas ir 'trečioji jėga'" (Oil, blood, and the "third" force), *Lietuvos aidas,* Oct. 11, 1995.

31. E. Krytikov, "Nachalo kontsa chankhoyskoy grupirovki," *Novoe vremya* 20 (1996).

32. V. Marsov, "Ob uregulirovanii chechenskogo krizisa: Analiticheskiy doklad," *Nezavisimaya gazeta,* November 29, 1994.

33. N. Ul'yanov, "Chechenskiy krizis vnov' stanovitsya obshchenatsional'nym: Pokushenie na generala Romanova opyat' prevratilo Moskvu v politicheskiy progorod Groznogo—Khronika," *Nezavisimaya gazeta,* Oct. 10, 1995; I. Rotar', "Teper' voynu v Chechne mozhet raskachat' 'tret'ya sila,'" *Izvestiya,* Oct. 18, 1995.

Chapter 13

1. A. Kasaev, "U OBSE problemy: Dudaev prekrashchaet vypolnenie soglasheniya po voennym voprosam," *Nezavisimaya gazeta,* Oct. 12, 1995; B. Vinogradov, "Diplomaty iz OBSE pokidayut Groznyy, opasayas' za svoyu bezopasnost'," *Izvestiya,* Oct. 12, 1995.

2. J. Glinskis, "Subombarduotos dar dvi čečėnų gyvenvietės" (Two more Chechen communities are bombed), *Lietuvos aidas,* Oct. 17, 1995; P. Pliev, "'Neizvestnye' samolety bombyat sela," *Nezavisimaya gazeta,* Oct. 17, 1995; V. Litovkin, "V Chechne snova bombyat sela: Armiya i spetssluzhby snova snimayut s sebya otvetstvnnost'," *Izvestiya,* Oct. 17, 1995.

3. N. Gorodetskaya, "Prezident i prem'er protiv chrezvychaynykh mer v Chechne: Ministr oborony prizyvaet k 'samym zhestokim deystviyam,'" *Segodnya,* Oct. 17, 1995.

4. "Naujas Rusijos armijos Čečénijoje vadas" (The new commander of the Russian army in Chechnya), *Lietuvos rytas,* Oct. 13, 1995.

5. M. Eysmont, "Dzhokar Dudaev zayavil o priostanovke peregovorov: Chechenskaya storona ugrozhaet povtoreniem Budennovska," *Segodnya,* Oct. 12, 1995.

6. "Rusų pajėgos puola čečėnų kaimą" (Russian forces attack a Chechen village), *Lietuvos aidas,* Oct. 20, 1995.

7. J. Glinskis, "Čečėnija: kraujuose įklimpusi taika" (Chechnya: The peace stuck in blood), *Lietuvos aidas,* Oct. 27, 1995.

8. M. Eysmont, "Rossiyskie voyska ukhodyat iz chechenskikh gor," *Segodnya,* Oct. 31, 1995.

9. I. Vladimirov and P. Konstantinov, "Vykhod iz chechenskogo krizisa vozmozhen: Ruslan Khasbulatov delaet konkretnye predlozheniya po mirnomu uregulirovaniyu," *Nezavisimaya gazeta,* Oct. 25, 1995.

10. Ibid.

11. "Čečėnija: per demonstracijã žuvo žmonių" (Chechnya: people were killed during demonstrations), *Lietuvos aidas,* Oct. 25, 1995.

12. N. Gorodetskaya, "Verkhovnyy sovet Chechni naznachil Doku Zavgaeva glavoy respubliki," *Segodnya,* Nov. 2, 1995; "Rusai paskyre Čečėnijos vadovą," *Lietuvos aidas,* Nov. 3, 1995.

13. A. Budberg, "Bitva gigantov: Mnogie v Cjecjne ne perezhivut 17 dekabrya," *Moskovskiy komsomolets,* Dec. 8, 1995.

14. A. Babitsky and A. Evtushenko, "100 rossiyskikh boytsov ne sdayutsya v gudermesskom 'kotle,'" *Komsomol'skaya pravda,* Dec. 23, 1995.

15. "Dž. Dudajevas sako, kad karas Čečénijoje tik prasideda" (D. Dudayev says that the war in Chechnya has only begun), *Lietuvos rytas,* Dec. 14, 1995.

16. I. Maksakov, "Dudaev pytaetsya sorvat' vybory: Tyazhelye boi idut v Gudermese—vtorom po velichine gorode Chechni," *Nezavisimaya gazeta,* Dec. 15, 1995.

17. A. Stasovskiy, "Sobytiya v Chechne yasno pokazali, chto dudaevtsam mir v Chechne ne nuzhen," *Krasnaya zvezda,* Dec. 26, 1995.

18. Babitsky and Evtushenko, "100 rossiyskikh boytsov."

19. B. Karpov, "Budennovsk—Gudermes—Kizlyar—Pervomayskaya," *Sluzhba,* Jan. 23, 1996.

20. M. Eysmont, "Gudermes vnov' kontroliruetsya federal'nymi voyskami: V gorode naydeny tela propavshikh bez vesti rossiyskikh soldat," *Segodnya,* Dec. 26, 1995.

21. Ibid.

22. M. Gafarly, "Dudaevtsy ne priznayut itogi vyborov," *Nezavisimaya gazeta,* Dec. 23, 1995; V. Strugovets, "Dudaev dolzhen uyti: Glavoy respubliki izbran Doku Zavgaev," *Krasnaya zvezda,* Dec. 29, 1995.

Chapter 14

1. S. Knezys, *Kizliaro-Budionovsko variantas* (The Kizliar-Budionovsk variant), *Karys* 7 (1996).

2. J. Glinskis, "Čečėnai kartoja 'Budionovsko' variantą" (The Chechens repeat the 'Budionovsk' variant), *Lietuvos aidas,* Jan. 10, 1996; A. Kolpakov and M. Kustov, "Krovavyy vtornik v Dagestane," *Moskovskiy komsomolets,* Jan. 10, 1996.

3. N. Gritchin, "Kizlyar khoronit pogibshikh," *Izvestiya,* Jan. 11, 1996.

4. I. Maksakov, "Budennovsk—Gudermes—Kizlyar. Stanet li posledniy prelyudiey k okonchatel'nomu silovomu usmireniyu Chechni?" *Moskovskiy komsomolets,* Jan. 10, 1996.

5. A. Budberg and I. Zhuravlev, "Korrespondenty 'MK' peredayut s mesta sobytiy," *Moskovskiy komsomolets,* Jan. 11, 1996.

6. A. Evtushenko, "Kak eto bylo v Kizlyare," *Komsomol'skaya pravda,* Jan. 13, 1996.

7. G. Sanin, I. Dvinskiy, and V. Akopov, "Okhota na 'odinokikh volkov,'" *Segodnya,* Jan. 24, 1996.

8. Maksakov, "Budennovsk—Gudermes—Kizlyar."

9. Sanin et al., "Okhota na 'odinokikh volkov.'"

10. *U nas tam ne okazalos' podvodnoy lodki, Khronika zadymleniya* (Moscow: Pravozashchitnyy tsentr "Memorial," 1996).

11. Yu. Kalinina, "Sily net, uma tem bolee ne nado," *Moskovkskiy komsomlets,* Mar. 30, 1995.

12. Article in *Sovietskaya Rosija,* Jan. 23, 1996.

13. Sanin et al., "Okhota na 'odinokikh volkov.'"

14. V. Sokirko, "Plennykh ne brat'! Zalozhnikov osvobozhdat' po mere vozmozhnosti," *Komsomol'skaya pravda,* Jan. 16, 1996.

15. V. Yakov in article in *Izvestiya,* Jan. 18, 1996.

16. J. Glinskis, "Rusai vaduoja įkaitus koncentruota artilerijos ir raketų ugnimi" (Russians attempt to free the hostages by concentrating artillery and rocket fire), *Lietuvos aidas,* Jan. 17, 1996.

17. V. Yakov, "Duel' Raduev-Barsukov: Pobedil professional," *Izvestiya,* Jan. 24, 1996.

18. Zh. Kas'yanina, "Strannaya pobeda na Tereke," *Sovetskaya Rossiya,* Jan. 23, 1996.

19. V. Yakov, "Operatsiya v Pervomayskom zavershena: Lzhi ne men'she, chem pravdy," *Izvestiya,* Jan. 20, 1996.

20. J. Glinskis, "Čečėnų štabas paleidžia įkaitus, Maskva laidoja žuvusius" (Chechen headquarters frees the hostages, Moscow buries their dead), *Lietuvos aidas,* Jan. 23, 1996.

21. I. Rotar', "Zhiteli Pervomayskogo, vernuvshis' na pepelishcha, nedoumevayut i vozmushchayutsya," *Izvestiya,* Jan. 23, 1996.

22. A. Konovalov, "Voyna kak predvybornyy manevr: Razmyshleniya posle zaversheniya operatsii federal'nykh sil v Pervomayskoy," *Nezavisimaya gazeta,* Jan. 24, 1996.

23. A. Fomin, "V osade," *Moskovskiy komsomolets,* Jan. 26, 1996; E. Loriya, "Besstrashnyy Raduev udral, brosiv svoikh," *Komsomol'skaya pravda,* Jan. 27, 1996.

24. Sanin et al., "Okhota na 'odinokikh volkov.'"

25. "Džocharas Dudajevas: aš visada smerkiau visus smurto ir teroro veiksmus" (Dzhochar Dudajev: I always condemned all violent and terrorist actions), *Lietuvos aidas,* Jan. 24, 1996.

26. "Poka v Pervomayskom idet boy, v Groznom vzyaty novye zalozhniki," *Izvestiya,* Jan. 17, 1996.

27. A. Evtushenko, "A v eto vremya v Groznom," *Komsomol'skaya pravda,* Jan. 17, 1996.

28. I. Maksakov, "Obmen plennymi vse-taki sostoyalsya: V to zhe samoe vremya u Novogroznenskogo idut tyazhelye boi," *Nezavisimaya gazeta,* Feb. 21, 1996.

29. "Sunkiai sužeistas čečėnų lauko vadas" (Chechen field commander is seriously injured), *Kauno diena,* Mar. 6, 1996.

30. V. Yakov, "Kto ubil Salmana Radueva?" *Izvestiya,* Mar. 7, 1996.

31. A. Belonovskiy, "Groznyy v ogne: A Salman Raduev otpravilsya k Allakhu," *Moskovskiy komsomolets,* Mar. 7, 1996.

32. V. Shurygin, "Spetsnaz ne znaet zhalosti, no i poshchady ne prosit," *Zavtra* 13 (1996).

33. "Sklinda gandai, kad Dudajevas gyvas" (Rumors spread that Dudajev is still alive), *Lietuvos aidas,* Aug. 3, 1996.

34. These reports were summarized in the Lithuanian daily *Lietuvos Rytas,* May 10, 1997.

Chapter 15

1. J. Glinskis, "Masinė demonstracija Grozne" (Massive demonstrations in Grozni), *Lietuvos aidas,* Feb. 6, 1996.

2. V. Strugovets and A. Stasovskiy, "Chechnya: Miting kak sposob prodolzheniya voyny?" *Krasnaya zvezda,* Feb. 10, 1996.

3. "Čečėnija: Rusijos kariai bijo net Dž. Dudajevo rūmų griuvėsių" (Chechnya: Russian soldiers fear even the ruins of D. Dudajev's presidential palace), *Lietuvos rytas,* Feb. 17, 1996.

4. "Mitingas Grozne ir neaiški Kremliaus pozicija" (Mass meeting in Grozni and the unclear position of the Kremlin), *Kauno diena,* Feb. 8, 1996.

5. A. Stasovskiy, "Chechnya: Novyy ochag napryazhennosti—Novogroznenskiy," *Krasnaya zvezda,* Feb. 20, 1996.

6. Yu. Snegirev and A. Kakotkin, "Tyazhelye boi v Novogroznenskom," *Izvestiya,* Feb. 21, 1996.

7. "Zayavlenie komanduyushchego Vremennyi obyedinennymi silami RF v Chechne general-leytenanta Tikhomirova V. ot 18 fevralya 1996 goda: 'Kem narushen Protokol o mire i soglasii,'" *Krasnaya zvezda,* Feb. 20, 1996.

8. Stasovskiy, "Chechnya."

9. A. Evtushenko, "Zachem sterli s litsa zemli Novogroznenskiy?" *Komsomol'skaya pravda,* Feb. 22, 1996.

10. A. Kasaev, "Boeviki vybity iz Novogroznenskogo," *Nezavisimaya gazeta,* Feb. 22, 1996.

11. I. Rotar', "Zachistka Novogroznenskogo prevratilas' v maroderstvo," *Izvestiya,* Feb. 23, 1996.

12. I. Rotar', "Chechenskie sela Alleroy i Tsentoroy unichtozheny," *Izvestiya,* Feb. 24, 1996.

13. J. Glinskis, "Sernovodskas: iki rusų atakos čia buvo 30 tūkst. žmonių" (Sernovodsk: until the Russian attack, there were 30 thousand people here), *Lietuvos aidas,* Mar. 5, 1996.

14. "Prodolzhaetsya voennaya operaciya v Sernovodske," *Izvestiya,* Mar. 6, 1996.

15. I. Vladimirov, "Operatsiya v Sernovodske ne zavershena," *Nezavisimaya gazeta,* Mar. 6, 1996.

16. J. Glinskis, "Sernovodskas sugriautas, nužudyta keli šimtai žmonių" (Sernovodsk is in ruins, several hundred people killed), *Lietuvos aidas,* Mar. 6, 1996.

17. J. Glinskis, "Čečėnų pajėgos iš Grozno pasitraukė, Rusijos problemos liko" (Chechen forces have withdrawn from Grozni, Russia's problems remain), *Lietuvos aidas,* Mar. 12, 1996.

18. L. Turpalov, "Zavershiv operatsiyu v Groznom, dudaevtsy dobili' postavlennykh tseley," *Nezavisimaya gazeta,* Mar. 13, 1996.

19. O. Blotskiy, "Zapadnya sredi razvalin: V nee ugodili federal'nye voyska, zakhvativshie Groznyy," *Nezavisimaya gazeta,* Mar. 28, 1996.

20. I. Maksakov, "Boi v Groznom: Mnozhatsya bessmyslennye zhertvy," *Nezavisimaya gazeta,* Mar. 12, 1996.

21. Blotskiy, "Zapadnya sredi razvalin."

22. A. Evtushenko and A. Khokhlov, "Ch'ya ochered' shturmovat' Groznyy zavtra?" *Komsomol'skaya pravda,* Mar. 12, 1996.

23. J. Glinskis, "Rusija laidoja savo vaikus, karo vadai ruošiasi naujiems mūšiams" (Russia buries its children, military commanders prepare for new battles), *Lietuvos aidas,* Mar. 13, 1996; "Interfaks: Sverdlovsk prostilsya s pogibshimi militsionerami," *Nezavisimaya gazeta,* Mar. 14, 1996.

24. Yu. Golotyuk, "Dudaevtsy perekhodyat k taktike 'krupnykh diversiy,'" *Segodnya,* Apr. 18, 1996.

25. V. Litovkin, "Tragediya u Yarysh-Mardy: Prezident potryasen, generaly vinovny, deputaty shumyat," *Izvestiya,* Apr. 20, 1996; Yu. Kalinina, "Grachev priumen'shil nashi poteri: Rossiyskie voyska uzhe gibli na doroge v Shatoy," *Moskovskiy komsomolets,* Apr. 23, 1996.

26. N. Musienko, "Ognem po avtokolone," *Pravda,* Apr. 20, 1996.

27. Kalinina, "Grachev priumen'shil nashi poteri."

28. "Zayavlenie Prezidenta Rossiyskoy Federatsii Borisa Yel'tsina," *Krasnaya zvezda,* Apr. 2, 1996.

29. "Ukaz Prezidenta Rossiyskoy Federatsii: 'O programe uregulirovaniya krizisa v Chechenskoy Respublike,'" *Krasnaya zvezda,* Apr. 2, 1996.

30. E. Yakovleva, "Dudaevskie boeviki vosprinimayut mirnuyu programmu Kremlya kak 'vtoruyu peredyshku' v voyne," *Izvestiya,* Apr. 3, 1996; A. Mikhaylov, "Chechnya: Na yugo-zapade po-prezhnemu idut perestrelki," *Krasnaya zvezda,* Apr. 3, 1996.

31. "Rusai šturmuoja kalnų gyvenvietes," *Lietuvos aidas,* Apr. 3, 1996.

32. M. Eysmont, "Chechnya posle ukaza," *Segodnya,* Apr. 12, 1996.

Chapter 16

1. J. Glinskis, "Ičkerijos viceprezidentas patvirtina Dudajevo mirtį, Rusijos pareigūnai tuo netiki" (Ichkeria's vice president confirms Dudaev's death, Russian officials do not believe it), *Lietuvos aidas,* Apr. 25, 1996.

2. "Š. Basajevas: netrukus įsiliepsnos naujas karas su Rusija" (Sh. Basajev: Shortly, a new war will break out in Russia), *Lietuvos rytas,* July 2, 1996.

3. S. Maigov, "V chem vina Shali?" *Moskovskie novosti* 18 (1996).

4. M. Eysmont, "Boeviki sbili ocherednoy rossiyskiy shturmovik," *Segodnya,* May 6, 1996.

5. "Rusijos ir Čečėnijos derybos prasidėjo Kremliuje" (Russia's and Chechnya's negotiations begin in the Kremlin), *Lietuvos aidas,* May 28, 1996.

6. A. Procenka, "Ar bus laikomasi susitarimo dėl taikos Čečėnijoje?" (Will the agreement for peace in Chechnya be honored?), *Lietuvos rytas,* May 29, 1996.

7. "B. Jelcinas Čečėnijoje paskelbė Rusijos karių pergalę" (B. Yeltsin while in Chechnya declares victory of Russian forces), *Lietuvos rytas,* May 29, 1996.

8. "Taikos susitarimo nesilaiko nei rusai, nei čečėnai" (Neither Russians nor Chechens honor the peace agreement), *Lietuvos rytas,* June 3, 1996.

9. S. Knezys, "Bamutas—atkakliausia čečėnų tvirtovė" (Bamut: Most resilient Chechen fortress), *Lietuvos aidas,* June 27, 1996.

10. A. Iskandaryan, "Bitva pri Arshty," *Novoe vremya* 12 (1996).

11. "Rusijos vadovai kviečia čečėnus į Maskvą derėtis" (Russian leaders invite Chechens to Moscow to negotiate), *Lietuvos rytas,* May 24, 1996.

12. V. Litovkin, "Genshtab preduprezhdaet: S padeniem Bamuta voyna v Chechne ne zakonchitsya," *Izvestiya,* May 25, 1996.

13. N. Gritchin, "Polgoda mezhdu zhizn'yu i smert'yu: Rasskaz stroitelei, otpushchennykh iz chechenskogo plena posle vstrechi El'tsina i Yandarbieva v Kremle," *Izvestiya,* June 6, 1996.

14. "Atnaujintos Rusijos ir Čečėnų derybos" (Negotiations between Russia and Chechnya are renewed), *Lietuvos aidas,* June 5, 1996.

15. "Čečėnija: susitarimai pasirašyti, bet sprogimai ir toliau griaudėja" (Chechnya: Agreements are signed, but explosions continue to be heard), *Lietuvos aidas,* June 12, 1996; A. Mikhaylov, "Chechnya: Separatisty ne speshat vypolnyat' dogovorennosti," *Krasnaya zvezda,* June 13, 1996.

16. "Čečėnija: susitarimai pasirašyti," *Lietuvos aidas,* June 12, 1996.

17. E. Krutikov, "Kadrovyy nokdaun," *Novoe vremya* 26 (1996).

18. "Čečėnijos Įvykiai" (Events in Chechnya), *Lietuvos aidas,* June 19, 1996.

19. I. Maksakov, "Protivostoyanie prodolzhaetsya," *Nezavisimaya gazeta,* June 22, 1996.

20. "B. Jelcinas įsakė pradėti išvesti karius iš Čečėnijos," *Lietuvos rytas,* June 26, 1996.

21. A. Oleynik, "Pervyy eshelon 245-ogo motostrelkovogo polka pribyl v Munino," *Krasnaya zvezda,* July 2, 1996.

22. "Rusijos generolas vėl grasina čečėnams" (A Russian general once again threatens the Chechens), *Lietuvos rytas,* July 9, 1996.

23. "Kremlius vėl pamiršo pažadus dėl taikos Čečėnijoje" (The Kremlin once again forgets its promises for peace in Chechnya), *Lietuvos rytas,* July 11, 1996; "Rusijos kariškiai medžioja buvusį derybų partnerį" (Russian forces hunt for their previous negotiation partner), *Lietuvos rytas,* July 12, 1996.

24. "Rusai teigia likvidavę čečėnų kovotojus Machkety gyvenvietėje" (The Russians contend that they have liquidated the Chechen fighters in the Machet community), *Lietuvos aidas,* July 17, 1996.

25. Ibid.

26. "Per specialią operaciją Čečėnijoje Šatojaus rajone žuvo du rusų kareiviai, septyni buvo sužeisti" (During a special operation in the Shajoja region of Chechnya, two Russian soldiers are killed and seven are injured), *Lietuvos aidas,* July 24, 1996.

Chapter 17

1. "Kremlius vėl pamiršo," *Lietuvos rytas,* July 11, 1996.

2. A. Levin, "Komu sdali Groznyy," *Novosti razvedki i kontrrazvedki* 18 (1996).

3. "Maskvos kalobarantai traukiasi" (Moscow's collaborators retreat), *Lietuvos aidas,* Aug. 8, 1996.

4. "Grozno šturmas—akibrokštas inauguracijos išvakarėse (The storming of Grozni: An impolite act on the eve of the inauguration), *Lietuvos rytas,* Aug. 7, 1996.

5. M. Kustov and A. Belonivskiy, "Zavgaev bezhal iz Groznogo," *Moskovskiy komsomolets,* Aug. 8, 1996.

6. M. Eysmont, "Boeviki pytayutsya zakrepit'sya v Groznom," *Segodnya,* Aug. 9, 1996.

7. "Čečėnai atrėmė rusų ataką" (Chechens repulse Russian attack), *Lietuvos aidas,* Aug. 9, 1996.

8. Yu. Kalinina, "Otkuda boeviki berut boepripasy?" *Moskovskiy komsomolets,* Aug. 23, 1996.

9. I. Maksakov, "V eti dni v Chechne reshaetsya, kto upravlyaet Rossiey," *Nezavisimaya gazeta,* Aug. 23, 1996.

10. V. Litovkin and B. Urigashvili, "Kogda Lebed' v Groznom—voyna ostanavlivaetsaya," *Izvestiya,* Aug. 23, 1996.

11. V. Litovkin, "Lebed' privez Kremlyu shans na mir v Chechne," *Izvestiya,* Aug. 24, 1996.

12. I. Maksakov, "Krovopolitie v Chechne priostanovleno," *Nezavisimaya gazeta,* Aug. 24, 1996.

13. P. Pliev, "Segodnya dolzhen nachat'sya vyvod rossiyskikh voysk i otryadov opozitsii iz Groznogo," *Nezavisimaya gazeta,* Aug. 28, 1996.

14. M. Gafarly, "Aleksandr Lebed' predstavil Borisu El'tsinu svoi predlozheniya po uregulirovaniyu konflikta v Chechne," *Nezavisimaya gazeta,* Aug. 29, 1996.

15. A. Grishin, "Bukhgalteriya voyny," *Itogi,* Sept. 24, 1996.

Chapter 18

1. B. Glebov, "Ustranenie Dudaeva," *Nezavisimaya gazeta,* June 5, 1996.

2. Yu. Kalinina, "Podmoskovnyy sled Dzhokhara Dudaeva," *Moskovskiy komsomolets,* Apr. 1, 1995.

3. I. Dement'eva and V. Yakov, "Alla Dudaeva: 'Dzhokhar ochen' khotel mira,'" *Izvestiya,* June 8, 1996.

4. Bunich, "Khronika chechenskoy boyni."

5. A. Iskandaryan, "Ya gotov k vsreche s Allakhom," *Novoe vremya* 18, 19 (1996).

6. R. Guseynov, "Bomba dlya general-prezidenta," *Komsomol'skaya pravda,* May 7, 1996.

7. Dement'eva and Yakov, "Alla Dudaeva."

8. Yu. Kalinina, "Poslednie slova Dudaeva," *Moskovskiy komsomolets,* May 4, 1996.

9. Dement'eva and Yakov, "Alla Dudaeva."

10. Glebov, "Ustranenie Dudaeva."

11. *Kauno Diena,* Apr. 8, 1997.

Index

8th Army Corps (Volgograd), 61, 91, 98; 33rd Motorized Rifle Regiment, 115; 255th Motorized Rifle Regiment, 115

34th Motorized Division (Ural Military Region): 276th Motorized Rifle Regiment, 75, 115, 131, 133, 301; 324th Motorized Rifle Regiment, 132, 134, 157, 262, 263

45th Motorized Rifle Division (St. Petersburg Military Region): 129th Motorized Rifle Regiment, 75, 91, 92, 101, 102, 109, 133; 133rd Battalion, 300

58th Army: 19th Motorized Rifle Division (Vladikaukaz), 71, 87, 91, 100, 102, 109, 143, 197, 261; 503rd Motorized Rifle Regiment, 110, 134, 275; 693rd Motorized Rifle Regiment, 275. *See also* negotiations, military issues

Abdurazakov, General, 241
Abchaz battalion, 35, 95
Abrekians, 13
Abubakirov, T., 308
Abubuslinov, Said Chasan, 271, 298
Achchoj Martan, 114, 128, 135, 140, 144, 201, 203, 219, 249, 273, 274, 281, 305
Achialov, General Vladislav, 168
Achikulak, 171
Achtiubinsk Flight Center, 96
Adygians, 13
Afghanistan, 305

Agapov, Boris, 118
Agishbat, 284
Agishta, 154, 155, 156
aggression, 326
Akacija artillery, 115
Akajev, V., 25
Albakov, Captain Shirmani, 273
Alchan Jurt, 117, 149
Alchan Kala, 93, 117, 127,
Alchast, 275
Alchazurov, 257
Alcheroja, 305, 314
Aldi, 116
Aleroja, 150, 154, 205, 226, 227, 254, 255, 281
Alistan, 153
Alma Ata, 96
Alpakov, Captain, 135, 174
Amin, Hafizullah, 44
amnesty, 222, 250
Andrejevski, Colonel Protogen, 258, 260
Andrijevski, Colonel, 99
annihilation battalions, 65
Antiaircraft Defense Communications and Information Processing Center (Grozni), 36
Antonov, Anatoli, 136
Argun, 22, 47, 75, 92, 93, 113, 117, 127, 128, 130–32, 202, 203, 288, 293, 294, 295
Argun gorge, 155, 263
Argun-Gudermes highway, 133

Argun militia building, 288
Argun railroad station, 132
Argun River, 131
Armivir Aviation School, 36, 39; commandeered
    aircraft, 39
Arsanov, Vacha, 258, 294
Arsanukajev brothers, 314
Arshty, 143, 201, 275, 276, 277
Artiomov, General, 256
Ashlapov, Colonel, 290
Asinovskaja, 117, 127, 128, 135, 140, 202, 217, 219,
    277
Aslanbekov, S., 131
Astrakhan, 74
attitudes toward the war: officers, 87
Aushev, Ruslan, 293
autonomous republics, 16
autonomy, 195, 213. *See also* negotiations, Chech-
    nya's political status
Avars, 12
Avrazija ferry, 250
Avturchanov, Umar, 21, 22, 24, 31, 32, 47, 51, 195,
    201, 224
Azamat Jurt, 205, 237
Azarychev, Sergeant G., 111
Azerbaijan, 27, 74, 131
Azov Sea, 74

Babichev, General Major Ivan, 109, 114, 129
Bachi Jurt, 154, 202, 227, 254, 269, 281
Baku, 59
Baku-Rostov highway, 128, 131, 133, 141, 254, 275,
    288
Baltic states, 213, 214, 317
Bamut, 114, 117, 128, 134, 140, 144, 149, 150, 153,
    156, 157, 198, 217, 256, 265, 268, 270, 272–79,
    284, 291, 293, 294, 301
Bantajev, A., 227
Baratynski, Count Aleksander, 14
Barsuk, 72
Barsukov, Mikhail, 240, 243, 246, 282
Basajev, Shamil, 40, 98, 114, 128, 147, 152, 157, 162,
    164, 165, 168, 169, 170, 172, 193, 194, 207, 208,
    220, 250, 254, 255, 258, 262, 265, 268, 270, 284,
    288, 308, 311
Basajev, Shervani, 161, 220
Baschanov, B., 308
Baskajev, General Lieutenant A., 205
Batajev, Major, 273

Bejev, General Major, 241
Belgatoja, 218, 265, 266, 284
Beliajev, A., 325
Beliajev, General Colonel Vladimir, 59
Belorechje, 227
Beni Kotar, 155
Benoja, 266
Benoja teip, 11
Berdakela, 258
Berlin, 123
Beslan, 58, 60
black headband formations, 65, 245
Black Sea, 74
bombing of cities, 62–63, 85, 91, 92, 117, 218, 266
Borovoj, Konstantin, 312
Borz special purpose battalion, 35, 94
Brezhnev, Leonid, 16
Briansk, 209
Budionovsk, 158–70, 174, 207; airport, 96, 160;
    hospital, 158, 161
Bulat Jurt, 245
Bumin, Colonel S., 111
Buratia, 215
Burdas, 25
Burdiajev, D., 168

"Cargo 200," 159
Caspian Sea, 74
casualties: calculation methodology, 86; civilian,
    88, 138, 139, 143, 179, 218, 230, 235, 261, 284,
    292; Chechen military, 49, 136–43, 147, 154,
    157, 179, 230, 255, 259, 260, 261, 281, 284; Rus-
    sian military, 49, 101, 103, 115, 131, 132, 135, 136,
    144, 146, 150, 154, 156, 157, 179, 180, 181, 205,
    219, 220, 225, 228, 230, 246, 254, 255, 259, 260,
    261, 262, 263, 265, 271, 275, 277, 278, 279, 281,
    282, 283, 284, 290, 291, 292, 294, 300, 303
Caucasus Nations Federation, 35
Ca Vedeno, 266
Cchinvali, 59
Centoroja, 227, 250, 254, 255, 265, 281
Centoroja teip, 11
Chabarovsk Airport, 110
Chadzhijev, Salambek, 24, 50, 151, 195, 224
Chamzadov, Alandi, 203, 204
Chankala Airport, 35, 39, 64, 92, 93, 102, 116, 129,
    149, 262, 289, 290, 292, 294, 296, 300
Chankala district, 95
Chankala gorge, 13

Charachoja, 156

Charachoja teip, 11

Charlamov, Sergei, 298

Charsenoja, 218

Chasavjurt, 171, 241, 259, 296, 298

Chasavjurt Assault Group, 60, 61

Chasavjurt region, 73

Chasavjurt Treaty, 298, 299, 300, 302

Chaschanov, U., 250

Chasimikov, S., 35

Chatumia, 155

Chechen Armed Forces, 20, 73, 332; Air Force 34, 63–64; annihilation battalions, 65; Command Headquarters, 134, 156; defense committee, 34, 116, 219, 270, 271; Internal Affairs Ministry formations, 33; Military High Command (General Staff), 36, 48, 66, 93, 116, 132, 133, 231, 245, 258; National Guard, 20, 22, 33, 34; National Security Service, 33, 309; organization, 33–35; Presidential Guard, 94; Regular Army, 33, 66, 75, 93, 95; Regular Army Abchaz battalion, 35, 95; Regular Army Borz special purpose battalion, 35, 94; self-defense formations, 34, 66; Supreme General Headquarters, 33; volunteers 49, 66, 94

Chechen Aula, 9, 117, 132, 133, 185

Chechen Autonomous Republic, 9

Chechen government, 64

Chechen imamate, 13, 15

Chechen-Ingushian Autonomous Republic, 15, 18, 305, 307; Supreme Council, 18, 19

Chechen language, 10

Chechen mafia, 27–30, 319

Chechen national anthem, xv

Chechen National Assembly (Congress), 18, 24, 31, 118, 306, 312

Chechen National Rebirth Government, 195

Chechen opposition, 21–24, 26, 30, 44, 46, 47, 51, 73, 207, 208, 219, 267; armed formations, 32, 46, 49, 201; militia, 151, 258, 260, 284; parliament, 281; Supreme Council, 224; Zavgajev government, 253, 254, 257, 277, 290, 297

Chechen Republic of Nochchi-Cho, 18

Chechens: flatlanders, 11, 25; mountain, 11, 25; name, 9; religion, 12, 25

Chemugla, 144, 277

Cherkassians, 11, 13

Chernomyrdin, Viktor, 162, 164, 168, 169, 170, 174, 208, 241, 253, 264, 271, 298, 299, 302

Chernorechje, 95, 114, 116, 117, 128, 258, 297

Chernov, Colonel A., 111

Chervlenaja, 73, 76

Chidi Chutor, 202

Chindarov, General Lieutenant, 59

Chiri Jurt, 153

Chirindin, V., 74

Chishkj, 262

Chkalov Airport, 45, 46

Chramchenkov, Colonel A., 58

Chrolionk, Aleksej, 226

Coalition National Council, 195

combat equipment losses: Chechen, 63, 64, 156, 180; Russian, 49, 103, 109, 123, 131, 133, 135, 184, 230, 263, 288, 291, 294, 303; Russian calculation methodology, 86, 87

combined regiments, other formations, 59–60, 330

command and control: Chechen, 94, 107, 156, 198, 299, 332; Russian, 69–70, 80, 81, 182, 331

commandant's headquarters, jointly staffed, 296, 298. *See also* Internal Affairs Army

command structure, 331

Constitution, Chechen, 194. *See also* negotiations, Chechnya's political status

Constitution, Russian Federation, 194, 195. *See also* negotiations, Chechnya's political status

Constitution, Soviet Union, 212, 214

contractors (soldiers), 143

coordination between units: Chechen, 81; Russian, 182

Cossaks, 30

criminality, 197

criminal regime, 208, 209, 319, 320, 322

Dagestan, 9, 71, 73, 74, 131, 238, 250

Daimohk movement, 22

Dapkus, Liudas, 206

Darga, 218, 265, 266, 284

Darga gorge, 158

data, 275

Davydenko, 135, 273, 274

Days of Mourning, 261, 292

defense lines (Grozni), 95

Deinekin, General Colonel Piotr, 96

demonstrations (Grozni), 224, 252

Denijev, commander, 34

deportations, 14, 15, 85, 318

Dermachiuk, 134

disarmament of Chechen units. *See* negotiations, military issues
disclosure of classified information, 189
diversion actions, 322
Dolinsk, 32, 73, 297
dual government, 223, 224
Duba Jurt, 153, 155
Dudajev, Ala, 306, 307, 311, 313, 315
Dudajev, Alvur, 315
Dudajev, Bakmiraz, 26, 316
Dudajev, Dega, 315
Dudajev, Dzochar, 15, 18, 21, 23, 25, 26, 30, 31, 37, 40, 48, 51, 53, 55, 61, 95, 105, 107, 116, 117, 141, 158, 162, 164, 165, 169, 188, 195, 199, 200, 203, 207, 208, 209, 210, 211, 218, 219, 221, 224, 226, 250, 257, 259, 264, 267, 305–23
Dyshne Vedeno, 220
Dzhakijev, Mohamed, 311, 312
Dzhalka, 293
Dzhochargala, 316
Dzumsoja teip, 11

Eastern Battle Group (Russian), 90, 111
Eastern Group (Chechen), 128, 129, 130
economic losses, 180, 303, 304
Edilchadzhijev, N., 255
elections, 223, 224, 226, 231, 280, 281, 302. *See also* negotiations, Chechnya's political status
Elistanzhi, 156, 220, 266
Endriukaitis, Algirdas, 303, 322
Engel Jurt, 254
Ersenoja, 279
Estonia, 15, 306
ethics of war, 185–87
European Community, 209

federal armed forces (Russian), 68; federal High Command, 38, 67, 68, 69, 75, 82, 86, 104, 131, 132, 141, 142, 144; Internal Affairs Army, 55, 56, 113, 140; Ministry of Internal Affairs, 20, 55. *See also* federal High Command; Internal Affairs Army; Land Army; Marine Infantry; military aviation; Paratroop Forces Headquarters
Federal Counterintelligence Service, 43, 44, 45, 55, 58, 83, 123, 309, 313; Alpha Special Purpose Unit, 163, 166, 169, 240, 242; Border Army, 44, 55, 197; detached units, 90, 309; Vega Special Purpose Unit, 163, 166
federal High Command, 38, 67, 68, 69, 75, 82, 86,

104, 131, 132, 141, 142, 144; General Staff, 43, 55; Intelligence Command, 43, 83, 308, 323; Operations Command, 4, 81; Operations Group (Chechnya), 59; Special Purpose Brigade, 250. *See also* Land Army; Marine Infantry; military aviation; Paratroop Forces Headquarters
federation, 214
Fergena, 59
Filatov, chief of administration, 44
filtration camps, 88, 151, 164, 199, 300
fire, rules for opening, 80, 81
Freedom Square, 252
Frolov, Colonel Lieutenant Aleksander, 78
fuga, 108

Gaidar, Yegor (Premier), 21
Gajskoja, 257
Galashka, 276, 306
Galashka-Arshty road, 275
Galgalians, 10
Galinganovsk, 30
Galkin, General Colonel A., 123
Gamijacha, 296
Gantemirov, Beslan, 22, 32, 44, 47, 51, 52, 187, 207, 273
gar, 11
Gazavat (holy war) fighters, 50, 65
Gazijurt, 72
Gechi, 283
Gechi Chu, 311
Gelajev, A., 135
Gelajev, Ruslan, 258, 273, 289, 308
Geldygen, 269
Gelischanov, Sultan, 35, 308
general principles, 222, 298
Georgia, 9, 39, 74
Georgians, 11
Georgijevsk, 163
German Army, 15, 51
Gerzen Jurt, 254
Gikala, 127
Giliana, 148
Goichi, 127, 257
Gojskoja, 262, 264
Gojten Kort heights, 132, 133
Gonchiarov, Colonel N., 239
Gorbachev, Mikhail, 18, 27, 209, 211, 212, 214
Govoruchin, Stanislav, 69
Grachev, General Pavel, 37, 38, 44, 46, 50, 54, 55,

56, 59, 60, 61, 62, 74, 75, 81, 87, 91, 93, 96, 108, 113, 122, 123, 146, 218, 257, 262, 266, 267, 282, 310

Grad rocket systems, 77, 80, 295

Great Russia, 209, 210, 317

Grebenskaja, 114

Gromov, General Boris, 88

Grozni, 9, 13, 20, 46–51, 55, 59, 71, 75, 90, 93, 114, 116, 127, 128, 151, 197, 202, 217, 257–61, 270, 271, 284, 286–300, 305, 306

Grozni airport field hospital, 157

Grozni Defense Plan (Russian), 258

Grozni television tower, 64, 259

Grozni-Vedeno highway, 132

Gudermes, 63, 93, 113, 117, 127, 128, 130, 131, 132–33, 144, 202, 203, 226–31, 254, 261, 281, 288

Gudermes-Chasavjurt highway, 150, 154

Guni, 202

Guniba Aula, 14

Gunoja teip, 11

Halifax, 165

hit man (bojavik), 337

hospital (Grozni), 114

hostages, 161, 162, 165, 206, 235, 236, 241, 245, 248, 249, 250, 323

Hurihulan River, 155

Ibrahimov, Vaca, 163, 311, 313

Ichkerija, 9, 25

Ichkerija bridge, 92

Ichkhoj Jurt, 150, 154

Igla-1 antiaircraft weapons, 35

Iliuchin, V., 279

illegal armed formations, 54, 200, 201

Imajev, Usman, 169, 193, 194, 199

Imran, 152

Ingushia, 9, 18, 19, 71, 72, 74, 276

Ingushians, 10

insurrections, 12–16,

intelligence (Chechen), 35; communication, 121–22; nets, 48, 78, 121, 205

intelligence (Russian), 123, 257; area reconnaissance, 79; detailed reconnaissance, 79, 83; reconnaissance, 83

Internal Affairs Army, 55, 56, 113, 140; 3rd headquarters (Grozni), 149, 151; 4th Tactical Group, 258; 8th Special Purpose Detachment (Rusj), 265; 33rd Internal Affairs Army Brigade, 227;

34th Internal Affairs Army Brigade, 291, 292; 66th Special Purpose Regiment, 277; 94th Brigade, 277; 100th Internal Affairs Army Division, 129, 135, 140; 101st Internal Affairs Army Brigade, 298, 299, 301, 302; 105th Militia Regiment, 298; 133rd Brigade, 242; 166th Brigade, 242, 272; 205th Brigade, 260; 556th Convoy Regiment, 36; 627th Internal Affairs Regiment, Special Purpose Battalion, 301; 633rd Internal Affairs Detached Battalion (Pskov), 301; 659th Motorized Rifle Regiment, 136; brigades, 131; commandant's headquarters (Gudermes), 227; commandant's headquarters (Kizliar), 236; commandant's headquarters (Oktiabrsk), 296; commandant's headquarters (Staropromyslovsk), 294; commandant's headquarters (Zavodsk), 260, 296; Don Division, 60; Dzerzinski Division, 129, 164; Dzerzinski Division, 8th Detachment, 242; Internal Affairs Command, 72, 83; Militia Battalion (St. Petersburg), 302; OMON, 36, 60, 92, 129, 132, 136, 151, 165, 171, 182, 187, 218, 228, 252, 256, 261, 294; Sofrin Brigade, 136; Special Detachments, Dagestan, 242; Special Detachments, Stavropol, 161, 162; Special Quick Reaction Detachments, 166, 228, 242, 248, 260; Specnaz, 136, 166, 243; Vitiaz, 58, 90, 93, 136, 240, 242

Internal Affairs Ministry Building (Grozni), 47, 50

Internal Affairs Ministry (Chechnya). *See* Chechen Armed Forces

Internal Affairs Ministry (Russia). *See* federal armed forces; Internal Affairs Army

internal matter, 326

International Parliamentary Commission on Chechnya, 304

Islam, 12, 25

Ismailov, Aslambek, 163, 164, 172

Israpilov, Colonel Ch., 235, 236, 241, 245

ITAR-TASS News Agency, 164

Ivanov, General Lieutenant Andrei, 281

Izvestija, 143, 189, 243, 269

Jakov, V., 243

Jakovlev, N., 10

Jandarbijev, Zelimchan, 17, 18, 267, 270, 271, 283, 284, 293, 296, 301, 302, 306, 308, 311

Jandy Chutor, 144

Jarysh Mardy, 156, 262, 263

Jegorov, General Colonel, 150, 151, 154, 166
Jegorov, Nikolai, 32, 54, 61, 92, 162, 163, 166
Jerevan, 59
Jerichanov, Ch., 199, 271
Jerin, General Victor, 54, 60, 93, 163
Jermolov, General, 13
Jiesk Airport, 96
joint commission, 299, 302
journals, military, 189
Jurchenko, Lieutenant A., 111
Jushenkov, S., 55

Kabardia Balkaria, 74, 131, 171, 299
Kadaria tarikat, 25
Kadi Jurt, 205, 254
Kadyr Jurt, 266
Kalinin, 292
Kalinovsk Airport, 35, 63
Kalinovsk Aviation School, 34, 39
Kaluga Air Base, 45, 306
Kandalin, Colonel G., 102
Kantemirov 4th Tank Division, 45
Karelian ASSR, 215
Kargalinskaja, 288
Karpinski hills, 77, 93
Katajama district, 90, 91, 92, 260
Kauno Diena, 303
Kazakstan, 305
KGB, 306, 307
Khasbulatov, Ruslan, 17, 18, 21, 24, 32, 43, 50, 51,
    220, 221, 222, 223, 224, 268, 307
killing fields, 77
Kiri, 156
Kirov Jurt, 155
Kirovsk, 92
Kizliar, 55, 59, 71, 171, 235, 236; hospital, 235, 236
Kizliar Air Base, 229, 231
Kizliar Assault Group, 72, 73
Kocheshkov, Colonel J., 110
Kolesnikov, General Colonel Mikhail, 44, 47
Komsomolskaja pravda, 151, 180, 189, 251, 260
Komsomolskaja, 131, 227, 257
Kondratjev, G., 74
Konovalov, A., 247
Korobeinikov, A., 169
Korzhakov, Aleksander, 44, 282
Koshkeldy, 150, 254
Kotenkov, A., 46, 47
Kovaliov, Colonel J., 160

Kovaliov, Sergei, 166, 169, 217
Krachaloja, 281
Krasnaja zvezda, 134, 139, 144, 188, 189, 303
Krasnodar, 74
Krivolapov, Major A., 151
Kruglov, A., 54
Krushchev, Nikita, 15
Krymsk Airport, 96
Kubinka Military Complex, 123
Kulikov, Fiodor, 315
Kulikov, General Anatoli, 54, 56, 113, 118, 132, 144,
    147, 156, 169, 171, 193, 206, 218, 240, 243
Kurbanov, Chamid, 311, 312
Kurchaloja, 202, 203, 225, 227, 269, 296, 297
Kurchaloja teip, 11
Kurskaja, 171
Kvashnin, General Lieutenant Anatoli, 44, 74, 92,
    118, 158, 201, 269, 270, 271, 291, 301

Labazanov, Ruslan, 22, 44, 51, 208, 307
Land Army, 56, 57, 113; 2nd Motorized Rifle Divi-
    sion (Tuman), 45; 4th Tank Division (Kan-
    temirov), 45; 8th Army Corps (Volgograd) 61,
    91, 98; 12th Motorized Rifle Training Division,
    36; 18th Motorized Rifle Brigade, 46; 20th Mo-
    torized Rifle Division (Samara), 81st Motorized
    Rifle Regiment, 91, 92, 96, 98, 103; 58th Army,
    see negotiations, military issues; 68th Army
    Corps, 164; 74th Motorized Rifle Brigade (Si-
    berian Military Region), 75, 133; 105th Motor-
    ized Rifle Brigade, 302; 131st Motorized Rifle
    Brigade (Maikop), 75, 96, 97, 98, 101, 105, 133,
    265; 136th Motorized Rifle Brigade, 265, 302;
    166th Motorized Rifle Brigade (Tver), 134,
    289, 291, 302; 173rd Regional Training Center,
    36; 205th Motorized Rifle Brigade, 291, 299;
    245th Motorized Rifle Regiment, 156, 157, 197,
    262, 263, 280, 281, 282; 429th Motorized Rifle
    Regiment, 2nd Battalion, 296; 506th Motor-
    ized Rifle Regiment (Pavolga), 131, 133, 134,
    220, 301; 905th Tank Division (Pavolga Mili-
    tary Region), 81st Motorized Regiment, 75, 79;
    Commissariat (Grozni), 206; Headquarters
    (Grozni, Lenininsk), 149, 150. *See also* 8th
    Army Corps; 34th Motorized Division; 45th
    Motorized Rifle Division; 58th Army
Latvia, 15, 39
Lebed, General Aleksander, 88, 282, 293, 294, 295,
    296, 297, 298, 299, 300, 301, 302

legal concepts, 211–16
Lenin, 15, 16
Lenin Park (Grozni), 100, 102
Lenin-Seripov Refinery, 95
Lietuvos Aidas, 322
Lietuvos Rytas, 206
Lithuania, 15, 17, 38, 39, 317
Liutauras, S., 241
Lobov, Oleg, 205, 206

Machachkala, 59, 240, 271
Machashev, Kazbek, 308
Machet, 155, 266, 283, 284
Madajev, I., 197
Magamedov, M., 236
Mahomed, L., 224
Mairtup, 202, 269
Majev, General Colonel S., 184
Malgobek district, 18, 21
Mamodajev, Jaragi, 17, 18, 21, 306
marine infantry: Baltic fleet, 75; Baltic fleet, marine brigade's paratroop battalion, 110; Northern fleet, 75; Northern fleet, marine battalion, 110; Pacific fleet, 75; Pacific fleet, 165th Marine Infantry Regiment, 110, 114, 131, 132, 133, 156
martial law, 54, 61, 210, 218, 284
Maschadov, General Aslan, 52, 71, 94, 105, 107, 116, 118, 150, 152, 164, 193, 196, 200, 201, 204, 220, 226, 230, 249, 254, 255, 258, 259, 266, 280, 284, 287, 293, 294, 295, 296, 297, 298, 299, 300, 301, 302, 308
Medvedickov, General Viktor, 170
Melchi Jurt, 140
Memorial Civil Rights Defense Center, 138, 179
mercenaries, 129
Meskerjurt, 117, 218
Mesket, 154, 155
Michailov, Viacheslav, 193
Mikrorajon, 292
military aviation, 46, 55
military courts, 66
Mineralnyje Vodi, 30, 161
Minutka square, 95, 116, 207, 258, 259, 292, 295, 296, 297
Mironov, A., 143
Mirzobekov, A., 236
Mitiuchin, General Aleksander, 74, 81
Molotov-Ribbentrop Pact, 214
Monsur, Shiek, 13

Moscow Military Region, 45
Moskovskij komsomolec, 105, 188, 306, 312
Mountain Republic, 15
Movsajev, Abu, 202
Mozdok, 46, 55, 58, 59, 60, 63, 71, 73, 74, 79, 90, 93, 171
Mozdok Airport, 96, 110
Mozdok Assault Group, 60, 61, 73
Mozdok field hospital, 86
Mozdok filtration camp, 137
Muchamed, Imam Gazi, 13
Muslim "annihilation" brigade, 35

Nachicevani, 59
Nadterechno region, 19, 21, 22, 24, 31, 52
nakji, 10–11
Nakshbandia tarikat, 25
Nalchik, 59, 299, 315
NATO, 209, 328
Nazarov, Colonel, 260
Nazran, 59, 72, 271, 280
Nazran district, 18
Neftekumsk, 171
Neftianka River, 206
Neftkiansk, 95
negotiations, 69, 92, 108; Chechnya's political status, 194, 264, 279, 298, 300; Commission, Special Observer's, 196, 199, 293; Commission for Exchange of Prisoners, 199; Commission for Resolution of Political Issues, 199; military issues, 193, 196; for peace, 193, 267; prisoner issues, 193, 199, 200, 280, 295. *See also* negotiations, Chechnya's political status; negotiations, military issues
negotiations, Chechnya's political status, 194, 264, 279, 298, 300; autonomy, 195; Constitution, Chechen, 195, 196; Constitution, Russian Federation, 195, 196; Dudajev's participation, 194; economic issues, 194, 264; elections, 194, 195, 264, 279
negotiations, military issues, 193, 196: amnesty for rebels, 196, 264; cessation of war actions, 194, 198, 264, 294, 295; disarmament of Chechen units, 193, 194, 200, 201, 280; Russian forces to remain (58th Army), 194, 197; self-defense forces, 194, 201, 206; withdrawal of Federal Forces, 193, 264, 279, 280, 295, 296, 297, 298, 300
Nesterovsk, 275

Newly Independent States, 209, 215

New York Times, 310

Nezavisimaja gazeta, 188

Nikolajev, A., 54

Nikolajev, Colonel M., 152

Nochchi, 9

Northeastern Battle Group, 90, 91, 130, 131

Northern Airport, 63, 205, 289, 291, 292, 294, 297; hospital, 246

Northern Battle Group, 90, 91, 109, 115, 129

Northern Caucasus Military Region, 37, 44, 46, 55, 56, 57–58, 61, 62, 67, 74, 81, 87, 96

Novaja Ezhednevnaja Gazeta, 80

Novaja Zhizna, 227

Novi Sharoj, 72, 114, 135, 140, 273, 274

Novi Uzenii, 59

Novogroznensk, 143, 150, 237, 241, 247, 250, 253–55, 259

Novoshchedrinskaja region, 288

Novyje Atagi, 225, 293, 295

Nozhai Jurt, 153, 154, 156, 157, 158, 200, 202, 279, 281, 295, 297

oil, 14, 27, 30, 173, 206

Oktiabrsk district, 47, 116, 258, 259

Oktiabrskoja, 227

Olenegorsk Airport, 110

OMON, 36

opposition (Chechen). *See* Chechen opposition

ordinance, defectiveness, 183

Ordzhonikidzevskaja railroad station, 118

Orechov, 144, 149, 150, 153, 156, 291, 301

Organization for Security and Cooperation in Europe (OSCE), 217, 271, 281

Orlov, O., 169

Orlovsk, 161

Ossetia, 74, 171, 323

Ossetian-Ingushian conflict, 59

Ossetians, 12

Panichev, V., 54

Pankov, General Major, 260

Papov, General, 205

Paratroop Forces Headquarters, 59; 21st Assault Paratroop Brigade (Stavropol), 164, 242; 21st Detached Paratroop Brigade, 71; 56th Detached Paratroop Brigade, 73; 76th Paratroop Division (Pskov), 71, 87, 91, 101, 102, 133; 104th Paratrooper Division's (Uljanovsk) Combined

Regiment, 75, 91, 101, 102, 130, 291; 106th Paratroop Division (Tula), 45, 60, 73, 91, 101, 102; 106th Paratroop Division Combined Regiment, 131, 132. *See also* Paratroop Forces Operations Group

Paratroop Forces Operations Group, 60; 7th Paratroop Division, 157, 237, 291, 302; 7th Paratroop Division 1st Company, 242; 7th Paratroop Division 22nd Company, 242

Pastuchov, B., 54

Patackas, Algirdas, 50

Pavlodar, 305

peace protocols, 253–57, 261, 277

Pervomaisk, 73, 74, 76, 92, 143, 297

Pervomaiskoje, 235, 237–50

Petropavlovskaja, 74, 76, 86, 92, 131, 292, 295

Petruk, General Major V., 90, 102, 109

Piatigorsk, 163

Pokojnoja, 162

Poliakov, General Major Boris, 46

Popov, General Lieutenant, 111

Potapov, V., 74

Praskovjev, 159

Pravda, 189

presidential palace, 49, 56, 63, 90, 91, 102, 108, 111, 253, 259

press, 187–90

Prigorodnoje district, 93, 197

prisoners, 49, 52, 54, 68, 72, 110, 111, 118, 146, 182, 183, 193, 271, 301. *See also* negotiations

Prizemlin, Colonel V., 109

Promyslovsk region, 127

Prosecutor's Office, military, 261, 262, 294. *See also* Russian Federation

Prudboja, 322

Pulikovski, General Major Konstantin, 90, 284, 293, 294, 295

punative actions, 139, 142, 143, 152

Pushkin, 306, 315

putsch (1991), 21

Radujev, Colonel Salman, 226, 235, 236, 237, 238, 240, 248, 250, 251, 254, 255, 258, 288, 311, 315, 316

Raff, Colonel Lieutenant L., 86

railroad station (Grozni), 90, 91, 97, 98, 113

readiness, combat, 80, 82, 103–105, 181, 183, 219

reconnaissance. *See* intelligence (Russian)

reconstruction, economic, 302

refugees, 65, 88, 146, 179, 256
repair of damaged vehicles, 84
Resht, 202
Riabkin, R., 168
Rochlin, General Leonid, 62, 79, 90, 109, 113, 114
Rodionov, General Colonel Juri, 282
Romanichin, Colonel Lieutenant, 263
Romanov, General Lieutenant Anatoli, 136, 138, 200, 206, 207, 217, 219, 220
Roshni Chu, 202, 203, 205, 218, 225
Rostov, 74
Rotar, I, 143
Rusakov, Lieutenant Maxim, 114
Ruskoj, Aleksander, 21
Russian armed forces, 36
Russian Army, 13, 21
Russian Duma (Parliament), 20, 21
Russian Federation, 9, 15, 317; Duma (Parliament), 20, 21, 61, 165, 250, 262; Duma Commission, 69; Duma deputies, 136, 139, 168, 169, 170, 171; executive government, 55; Federal Communications and Information Agency, 314; Federation Council, 61; Justice Department, 309; National Security Command, 55; National Security Council, 32, 53–54, 61, 92, 113, 253, 282, 302; Prosecutor General's Office, 62, 308 (*see also* Prosecutor's Office, military)
Russian population in Grozni, 65
Russian Strategic Research Institute, 327
Rybkin, Ivan, 302

Sadovija district, 101
Sajasano, 265
Salazha, 266, 314
Samanov, General Lieutenant Vladimir, 284
Samashk, 114, 117, 127, 128, 129, 134, 136, 261, 273, 274
Savin, Colonel Ivan, 99, 100
Savostjanov, General Major J., 45
secret war, 43–46
self-defense forces. *See* negotiations, military issues
Semionov, General Lieutenant A., 45
Semionov, Nikolai, 169, 193
Semovodsk, 206
Sernovodsk, 114, 127, 202, 203, 217, 219, 250, 256–57
Serpuchov, 307

Serzhen Jurt, 146, 149, 150, 153, 156, 185
Shabad, Anatoli, 139
Shakrai, Sergei, 32
Shali, 63, 114, 117, 127, 131, 132–33, 130, 134, 149, 202, 203, 226, 230, 269, 271, 281, 293
Shamanov, General Major Vladimir, 265, 272, 277
Shami Jurt, 74, 117, 140
Shamil, Imam, 13, 25
Shaposhnikov, Marshal Yevgeny, 37
Shariat, 31; courts, 152
Shatoja, 9, 155, 156, 157, 158, 197, 202, 205, 220, 226, 280, 284, 293, 295, 297
Shchelkovskaja, 114, 281, 288
Shevchenko, Aleksander, 225
Shevcov, General Lieutenant L., 59, 81, 324
Shilka antiaircraft guns, 97
Shirokin, General A., 196
Shirshov, P., 55
Shkirko, General Lieutenant Anatoli, 219, 230, 298
Sigutin, General, 60
Skripnik, General Major N., 283
Slepcovsk (Ingushia), 61, 202, 275
Slepcovskaja Airport, 118, 270
Smirnov, Sergeant I., 111
Solovov, V., 168
Soskevec, Oleg, 162
Southeastern Battle Group, 111
Southeastern Front, 273
Southern Battle Group, 129, 133
Southwest Battle Group, 256, 275
sovereignty, 213, 214, 328
sovereignty, Chechnya. *See* negotiations, Chechnya's political status
Sovietskaja Rosija, 189, 246
Sovietskoja, 245
Soviet Union, 15, 21, 209, 317
Specnaz. *See* Internal Affairs Army
Stalin, 15, 16, 305
Staraja Sunzha, 95, 292, 295
Staropromyslovski region, 151, 258, 259, 260, 289, 297
Staroshchedrinskaja region, 288
Starovoitov, A., 54
Staryj Achchoja, 156, 261, 291, 301
Staryje Agati, 284, 296
Staskov, General Major N., 90, 101
Stavropol, 74, 157

Stavropolimer Chemical Plant, 164
Stavropol province, 9, 30, 73
Stepanakert, 59
Stepashin, Sergei, 54, 61, 92, 123, 163, 309, 310
Stepnoja, 171
Strela-10 missile systems, 35
Strogov, General Igor, 37
Suchumi, 59
Sufi brotherhoods, 25
Sumgaiti, 59
Sunzha district, 18, 21, 201
Sunzha ridge, 140, 258
Sunzha river, 48
supply: Chechen, 36–40, 144, 152, 183, 219, 269, 292; opposition, 32; Russian, 60, 67, 79, 123, 220
Suvorov Jurt, 150, 254
Svaboda Radio, 312

tactics: Chechen, 48, 50, 77–78, 95, 105–108, 119–21, 129–30, 145, 152, 153, 156, 265; Russian 47, 50, 55, 68, 90–91, 103, 108, 109, 117, 120, 124–26, 129, 142, 145, 152, 256, 265
Tambov Advanced Aviation School, 305
Targo, 203
Tarikats, 25
Tartu (Estonia), 306
Tatarstan, 27, 215, 293
Tavzen Kala, 266
Tbilisi, 59
teip, 10–12, 25
Temporary Council (Opposition), 24, 46, 50, 221, 223
Temporary Information Center, 61
Terechnoja, 239
Terek Chechen Republic, 22
Terek Cossaks, 11
Terek hills, 75, 132
Terek River, 26, 237
terrorism, 118, 158, 163, 173–78, 193, 206, 208, 235, 237, 333
Terzovec, Major, 262
Third Force, 207–11
Tichomirov, General Viacheslav, 143, 254, 260, 280, 283, 284, 295, 297, 300, 301
Todorov, General Lieutenant S., 102
Tolstoi Jurt, 26, 32, 47, 73, 133, 208, 292
Trabzon harbor (Turkey), 250

Troshev, General Major Genadi, 129
Tsarist period, 12–14
Tscharner, Benedikt von, 281
Tugunska anti-aircraft guns, 96, 101
Turkey, 315
Turkmenistan, 214, 305

Udmurtia, 215
Udugov, Molvadi, 150, 188, 284, 291, 292, 302
United Nations Assembly, 326, 328
United Nations Charter, 176
United Nations Peacekeeping Forces, 219
Uramz, feast of, 276
Urechov, 257
Urus Martan, 22, 26, 32, 47, 52, 144, 203, 207, 226, 250, 257, 268, 283, 294, 311
Uzbekistan, 214

Vainach, 10
Valerik, 149
Vedeno, 9, 134, 153, 155, 156, 172, 202, 220, 262, 265, 266, 268, 279, 281, 284, 295, 297
Vedeno Aula, 14
Vedeno gorge, 220
Verchnye Ashaluk, 71
Verchotoja, 156
Victory Day celebrations, 146, 148–51
Vilnius, 67, 317
Vitiaz. *See* Internal Affairs Army
Viz-Chadzhi burda, 26
Vladikaukaz, 54, 55, 71, 259, 305
Vladikaukaz Assault Group, 60, 61, 72, 76
Vladikaukaz railroad line, 14
Vlasenkov, V., 220
Voitenko, Anatoli, 279
Volgograd, 50, 322
Volski, Arkadi, 169, 193
Vorobjov, General Major Edvard, 60, 75, 81, 87

warrant officer, 336
Washington Post, 310
Western Battle Group (Russian), 90, 91, 109
Western Group (Chechen), 128, 129
withdrawal of military forces. *See* negotiations, military issues

Yakutia, 215
Yeltsin, Boris, 15, 20, 21, 24, 27, 44, 51, 52, 54, 61–62, 74, 113, 116, 122, 146, 150, 165, 168, 195, 196,

209, 216, 218, 240, 247, 264, 267, 269, 271, 272, 280, 282, 283, 293, 296, 297, 299, 302, 315

Zaftra, 189
Zaicev, Albert Petrovich, 307
Zakajev, Achmed, 258, 271
Zakan Jurt, 117, 136, 140
Zakirov, A., 111
Zandak, 171, 172, 200
Zavgajev, Doku, 19, 224, 225, 231, 268, 271, 280, 281, 282, 290, 299, 300, 307

Zavodskaja district, 90, 91, 217, 259, 260, 289
Zelenokomsk, 163
zero option, operation, 286, 288
zero variant, elections, 195
Zhukov, General V., 47
Zimin, General, 60
Ziuganov, Genadi, 282
Ziurikov, General, 92
Znamenskoja, 46, 51, 52
Zolotov, L., 45
Zona, 262

Eastern European Studies

Stjepan G. Meštrović, Series Editor

Cigar, Norman. *Genocide in Bosnia: The Policy of "Ethnic Cleansing."* 1995.

Cohen, Philip J. *Serbia's Secret War: Propaganda and the Deceit of History.* 1996.

Gachechiladze, Revaz. *The New Georgia: Space, Society, Politics.* 1996.

Meštrović, Stjepan G., ed. *The Conceit of Innocence: Losing the Conscience of the West in the War against Bosnia.* 1997.

Polokhalo, Volodymyr, ed. *The Political Analysis of Postcommunism: Understanding Postcommunist Ukraine.* 1997.

Quinn, Frederick. *Democracy at Dawn: Notes from Poland and Points East.* 1997.

Teglas, Csaba. *Budapest Exit: A Memoir of Fascism, Communism, and Freedom.* 1998.